APPETITE FOR CHANGE

PANTHEON BOOKS
NEW YORK

APPETITE

WARREN J. BELASCO

FOR CHANGE

HOW THE COUNTERCULTURE TOOK ON THE FOOD INDUSTRY, 1966–1988

LIBRARY OF CONGRESS CATALOGING-IN-PUBLICATION DATA
BELASCO, WARREN J.
APPETITE FOR CHANGE: HOW THE COUNTERCULTURE TOOK ON THE
FOOD INDUSTRY, 1966–1988.
P.   CM.
INCLUDES INDEX.
1. NATURAL FOODS INDUSTRY—UNITED STATES.   2. FOOD INDUSTRY AND TRADE—UNITED STATES.   3. CONSUMERS—UNITED STATES.
I. TITLE.
HD9055.B44   1990   338.4'7641302'0973—DC20   89-42644
ISBN 0-394-54399-8

ILLUSTRATIONS BY JENNY VANDEVENTER
DESIGNED BY DIANE STEVENSON/SNAP-HAUS GRAPHICS

MANUFACTURED IN THE UNITED STATES OF AMERICA
FIRST EDITION

CONTENTS

CONTENTS

For Sonia, Nathaniel, and Amy

PREFACE

I t's early 1989 and the televised battle of the cold cereal nuggets is heating up. In one corner is the defending champion, Grape-Nuts, first developed back in 1898 by health food enthusiast Charles William Post. Since 1986 Post's commercials have featured an apparently married couple trading insults, feigning surprise about the crunch, and otherwise personifying the cereal archetypes of snap, crackle, and pop. In the other corner is the fibrous upstart, Kellogg's Nutri-Grain Nuggets. In its televised pitches we see two well-dressed young professionals who, as eager contenders, have no time for a proper home breakfast. Arriving early at the office, they are grabbing quick calories before getting a head start on an important case. While not as seasoned as Post's screwballs, they too banter and gibe. Reflecting her taste for heavy red lipstick, the bobbed brunette eyes an overglazed confection. When her nerdy colleague shows concern for her long-term health, she wonders, what *should* she be eating, "nuts and twigs?" Seeing a chance to move their professional relationship to a more physical level, he offers a spoonful of Nutri-Grain Nuggets. Hmmm, she allows, they're better than she'd expected. Shrewdly pursuing the analogy, he asks if the same might not be said about himself—to which she replies with a playful punch that is only half sisterly. Stay tuned, the ad implies; someday these incipient lawyers-in-love may be exchanging one-liners at home too.

Beyond exploiting the battle of the sexes, these commercials hint at the outcome of the recent food wars. After years of skirmishes between industry critics and defenders, it's now clear, as adpeople might say, that health is "hot." For a lexicon of current nutritional concerns, read a box of Grape-Nuts: "natural wheat and barley cereal," "no sugar added," "no preservatives," "provides 9 vitamins and minerals." The side panel lists a dizzying array of essential nutrients and reassures us that "all sugars . . . occur naturally." The back suggests we "top off" our salad or yogurt with the crunchy nuggets and even offers to pay for these wholesome companions—upon receipt of two proofs of purchase. Extending the synergistic possibilities, a new TV spot urges us to add Grape-Nuts (and "oooomph") to the hot oatmeal that, we're told, cuts cholesterol. All of this concern from a General Foods division (Post) whose siblings include Jell-O and Maxwell House, and that through the Philip Morris kinship network is first cousin to the Marlboro Man, Miller High Life, and, as of November 1988, Velveeta (Kraft)!

Kellogg too has stepped up the "good for you" appeals. Although descended from the nineteenth-century vegetarian healer —and inventor of granola—John Harvey Kellogg, the modern company generally followed food industry conventions that "nutrition doesn't sell"—until 1981, when it introduced Nutri-Grain vitamin-fortified, sugar-and-preservative-free flakes. Now, eight years later, Nutri-Grain serves as what marketers call an "umbrella," covering a variety of flakes, biscuits (the answer to Nabisco's Shredded Wheat), nuggets, and frozen waffles—with Nutri-Grain Bars and frozen microwaveable bread dough in the works. In addition, Kellogg makes bold health claims for All-Bran and boasts new cereals called Nutrific, Pro Grain, Common Sense, and Mueslix—the last a European-style mix of whole grains, fruits, and nuts previously found mainly in health food stores and countercultural co-ops.[1]

Despite these incursions, however, the food giants clearly do *not* want to be associated with health foods, which are still considered dreary, if not also dangerous. Thus, a commercial for one vitamin-fortified cereal shows a large guard dog barking rather fiercely when the announcer offers a wary little girl a bowl of something "good for you." Keeping a safe distance, the ads use irony and lighthearted banter to elicit surprise: gee, something can be good for you *and* taste good. Hmmm, better than I'd expected! Explaining the new "Grape-Nuts tops 'em off" campaign, one advertising executive observes, "People eat oatmeal because they know it's good for them. But most people say it's dull and boring or that it tastes like wallpaper paste."[2] Like yogurt and salad, the healthy mush apparently needs crunch to bridge the health vs. taste gap. Exploiting the same dichotomy, Kellogg emphasizes how surprisingly good its healthful cereals can taste. (The amazement works both ways, of course: can such a crispy, flavorful processed food also be wholesome?) Even more clever, the Nutri-Grain Nuggets commercial associates the competition with fringy health foods. The scarlet-lipped Danish maven's scorn for "nuts and twigs" is a not-so-subtle allusion to Euell Gibbons, the weed-eating wilderness-survival expert who, trading on his countercultural popularity, pitched Grape-Nuts back in the mid-seventies. Make no mistake, the ad tells us: *these* nuggets are for well-trimmed yuppies, not scruffy, back-to-nature yippies.

In drawing such contrasts, these campaigns reflect strong social ambivalence about food and health. We've changed, but the old conflicts persist. We seem to have come far from the days when fitness was just for faddists. Words like "natural," "whole grain," and "healthy" can now be voiced by respectable Reaganites, not just radical vegetarians—but the preferred context is ironic, light, self-deprecating. Health may be hot, but we need to stay cool about it. We're concerned about nutrition, but we don't want to seem too worried. And yet—and yet—we still wonder whether processed foods can really be good for us, hence again the ads' need to feign surprise. But joking aside, can we believe the claims of companies that, along with their "healthy" lines, market many other dubious—if not downright dangerous—products? We don't know how to live without or with the food industry.

3

Our current confusion has historical roots. One source, I believe, is a fundamental and long-standing misunderstanding of radical food reformers—the "nuts" and "flakes" of conventional stereotyping. Although historians have examined the food fights of the nineteenth and early twentieth centuries, little has been written about the latest flare-up, which started in the late 1960s, when young cultural rebels began to turn against mainstream foodways. Rather than meriting scorn, their rebellion deserves careful reconsideration, for it raised important questions about our food system and also suggested serious alternatives, a countercuisine. A coherent set of dietary beliefs and practices, the countercuisine had three major elements. A consumerist component offered survivalist advice and suggested what to avoid, especially processed "plastic" food. While radical consumerism was largely negative, the second, therapeutic component suggested ways to make food more fun— e.g., through a delight in improvisation, craftsmanship, ethnic and regional cooking. Addressing issues of food production and distribution, the third element was the organic paradigm, which posited a radically decentralized infrastructure consisting of communal farms, cooperative groceries, and hip restaurants. In Part 1, for the sake of analysis, I will treat these parts separately, but in practice they were inseparable, fused by a shared context—the ecology movement—and by a shared faith in the power of personal decisions to spawn political transformations.

In Part 2, I show what happened in the 1970s, when the arbiters of mainstream cuisine—a loose network of respected scientists, government officials, journalists, and marketers—confronted the countercuisine. While this food establishment unanimously opposed the most radical element, organic agriculture, it split over other questions of food safety, especially additives, cholesterol, and calories. The resultant public squabble was another source of our current confusion, as once-trusted authorities raised concerns without offering comprehensive solutions. Part 3 examines how food marketers have addressed—and reinforced— our dietary uncertainties.

The story has several dimensions. First, it examines recent trends in the way we produce, sell, buy, and, most of all, think about food. As a history of ideas, it shows how highly charged notions of "healthy," "natural," "fitness," "faddism," and "common sense" reflect social conflict and economic interest. As a generational study it traces the eating habits of certain "baby boomers" as we evolved from political and cultural alienation during the Vietnam War to professional-managerial success a decade later. It is thus a food history, a cultural commentary, and a personal memoir.

Since I am writing about the counterculture and food, it seems quite appropriate for me to start out autobiographically. For one thing, it seems that just about every book touching on the sixties offers a personal accounting, if not confession. Moreover, as a subject, food virtually demands self-disclosure. Knowing that eating is intensely personal and memorable, writers have long used food as a medium for self-reflection. It is impossible to read M. F. K. Fisher, Gael Greene, or Calvin Trillin without learning a lot about both the author and food. Or, at quite another level, think of the six volumes of remembrances spawned when Marcel Proust chanced to dip a favorite childhood snack—a madeleine—into a cup of tea! As one of my own hip sources observed, food is a strong "edible dynamic" binding present and past, individual and society, private household and world economy, palate and power. It is in this spirit, though certainly not with Proust's thoroughness or skill, that I open with a few personal madeleines.

Three of my grandparents were immigrants whose main ties to eastern Europe were their accents and their food. I don't hear the accents anymore, but I still taste the well-simmered *flanken*, potato kugel, onion rye smeared with chicken fat, and solid, buttery cookies. My father's mother made a chopped eggplant hors d'oeuvre that I hated as a five-year-old (1952), but twenty years later a vegetarian cookbook recipe for baba ghanouj zapped me back not just to my grandparents' dark Bronx apartment, but also to our Near Eastern roots two thousand years before. Before the Second World War my other grandparents ran Mama-Papa groceries in non-Jewish neighborhoods of Queens. From their stories about living over the store, I learned that selling food is hard work, and also full of contradictions: how else could my kosher grandfather sell ham? An excellent cook, my mother's mother suffered from arthritis that slowed her down just as I began, in the late 1960s, to appreciate her skills, but even so, on one of her increasingly scarce good days she pulled herself into the kitchen to teach me how to make potato knishes: a little of this, a little of that . . . Now I am the sole keeper of the recipe, for—in second-generation fashion—her daughters never learned, or maybe just forgot, what would later be called ethnic cooking.

Like most affluent suburbanites in the fifties and early sixties, we ate American at home. I remember especially the red meat: lamb chops, prime rib, London broil, steaks, premium franks, thick burgers, bacon, kosher bologna and salami—all delivered to our Long Island doorstep by a much-valued city butcher and, for the most part, requiring just a quick flaming. We must have lived half the year on our patio, for we replaced the portable grill and

5

aluminum furniture almost every year. We also enjoyed the latest convenience foods: individually wrapped slices of American cheese, fried onions in a pop-top can, toaster waffles, Rice-a-Roni, Mallomars encased in clear plastic bubbles. Although we grew tomatoes, I remember few fresh vegetables. A salad consisted of a solid wedge of iceberg lettuce covered with hard cherry tomatoes, peeled cucumber slices, and bottled Russian dressing. We ate lots of potatoes: baked (in foil), mashed (peeled), chipped (in bags), or french fried (defrosted). I remember canned and frozen peas, carrots, corn, and string beans, but I don't think I encountered zucchini, okra, or eggplant in any form—fresh or processed—until adulthood. Perhaps we had cabbage (with corned beef), but I doubt broccoli and cauliflower. My mother liked vegetables but catered to my father, who rejected "rabbit food." My father, in turn, claimed he became addicted to meat when he was served it three times a day during the war. Whatever the cause, no one felt the need to defend such a diet. When my father suffered a fatal heart attack in 1967, at age forty-seven, his doctor saw no significance in the fact that he had been overweight. Cholesterol was not yet a household word.

For reasons that had more to do with undergraduate life at Michigan than with my father's death, my tastes began to change at about that time. Like a million other potheads with the midnight munchies, I scarfed anything: M&Ms and FiddleFaddles, cinnamon bagels and baklava, pizza and felafel, champagne and Ripple. I learned to cook in one of Ann Arbor's New Deal–era co-op houses, where I made dinner once a week for forty hungry males. The menu was pretty much greasy meat and potatoes, with premixed white cake and margarine-sugar icing for dessert, but there were moments of stoned whimsy, as when my friend Hal and I injected the baked potatoes with green dye or, in a plea for "natural" honesty, ate the overdone beef slabs with our fingers. Why not, we proposed, ditch the boring menu and messy chores altogether and eat just millet? No one laughed. Once I innocently forgot to add the customary ten-pound hunk of ground beef to my lasagna, thereby inviting a violent protest that clearly underscored, in my moralistic mind, the fetishistic power of meat. Hal later provoked a similar reaction when, for reasons of economy and curiosity, he served up octopus salad instead of the scheduled tuna fish. Food, we discovered, had considerable shock value.

Graduating in 1969, I married Hal's sister, Amy, and we

moved to Manhattan. On our own for the first time, we ate anything as long as it was cheap. Already stereotyped by hair, music,
fashion, and politics, we felt exposed enough without the "health
food nut" label, which was beginning to be applied to some of the
freaks around us. But we evolved anyway. We got three fondue
pots as wedding gifts. In the Cuban-Chinese restaurants of our
Upper West Side neighborhood we discovered fried bananas, espresso, and flan. Returning from a tour as a VISTA volunteer in
the Southwest, Hal introduced us to oxtail soup, tacos, and home
brew. In the spring of 1970, after a tense New Haven rally we were
served brown rice, raisins, and veggies in a Yale courtyard; I remember feeling comforted—both by the free meal and by the
Gothic hug.

Returning in 1971 to Michigan for graduate school, we lived
in a group house, where we met our first macrobiotic. With his
mystical jargon and special food cache, he seemed too self-
righteous and inconvenient. But within two years, we too were
vegetarians, although not macrobiotic. As meat got more expensive
than it was worth, we began to pay attention to others who had
already made the change. Back east my sister-in-law Leni was
provoking loud dinner table arguments by refusing meat and cham-
pioning granola; when her younger sister Marty defected too, family dinners became tense indeed. My own sister, Clare—raised, I
seem to remember, on a steady diet of scrambled eggs and fried
bologna—now subsisted on bulgur and lentils as she toured the
Rockies in an old VW minibus with Dave from upper Michigan,
where vegetarians were scarcer than surfers. My closest cousin,
Chick, was quoting Tolstoy and deploring the corned beef we once
craved as kids. Someone told us about Frances Moore Lappé and
protein complementarity. Another gave us *Uncle John's Bread Book*.
We got an old USDA pamphlet on home pickling and bought our
first dozen Ball jars. Mastering the pressure cooker, blender, canning kettle, and sourdough starter, we felt free, grounded, and
right. For company, we now served soybean stroganoff instead of
chicken with almonds; at Christmas we gave out pints of jam made
from berries we'd picked in July.

7

In Ann Arbor it was getting easier to eat this way. Several of
the dorms and housing co-ops now offered vegetarian options. The
new Sikh restaurant served crispy vegetable tempura and curried
squash soup. Volunteer cashiers at the food co-op (opened in 1970)
toted up whatever price you wrote on the bag of grains that you

weighed yourself. At the radical commune with the loud music near campus you could get your fruits and vegetables really cheap —if you got your weekly order in on time and helped with the bagging. If you stuck around summers you could get a free plot in a community garden and grow your own. In one fading photo from 1973, Amy and I grin proudly amidst our corn patch—our first and best crop ever. Our parents doubted the beans and grains theory but felt relieved that at least we ate cheese. That same year, however, someone accidentally mixed fire retardant in dairy cattle feed; like everyone else who lived in Michigan at that time, we still don't know the full effects of that contamination.

In 1974 we moved to Washington, D.C., and immediately scouted the food supply. Safeway and Giant owned the town, but the best co-op was said to be run by a collective of Nicaraguan revolutionaries; they cleared out at the end of the decade, and the place later reopened as a French bistro, befitting the gentrification of that Adams-Morgan neighborhood. Other exiles arrived—Ethiopians, Indochinese, Salvadorans, Afghans, Jamaicans, Cubans—all making D.C. a much more interesting place to eat. The farmers' market near our Capitol Hill apartment was pretty expensive, so we tried growing our own, which greatly annoyed our landlord —probably, we concluded, because he worked for the CIA. But the prodigious eggplants and peppers did impress our black neighbors, who were the only other people to grow food out front. In 1979 we bought a house in semihip Takoma Park and were able to go organic in peace.

Somewhere in the early 1980s the dinner table schism at family reunions began to mend. The arguments about feeding the hungry in India, the perils of sugar, and the latest chemical threat continued, as did the ritualized barbs, but at least we all ate together. The carnivores tried the tamari-tahini salad dressing and we nuts sampled the admittedly delicious roast beef. Soon the family food fights stopped altogether. Perhaps we were all tired of hearing the same old questions and giving no good answers. Since the discussion just wasn't going anywhere, why ruin dinner? We were becoming more alike anyway: the regulars were eating less meat and the vegetarians were eating more chicken and fish. And the kids of the 1960s were becoming the parents of the 1980s, with our own dinner table struggles and accommodations. At our house, homemade granola gave way to the commercial vitamin and bran-fortified varieties. We bought our grains, tofu, and eight-grain bread from the Takoma co-op, our milk, cereals, and plastic wrap from the conglomerate. We kept chemicals out of our garden, but grew more flowers than food. In summer, it seemed easier to buy organic produce from the pricey local farmers; the rest of the year, like everyone else, we got it from California, Mexico, and, groan, Chile. We still used our pressure cooker and *Recipes for a Small Planet*, but we also stocked frozen pizza and chicken nuggets, and on special occasions, I took my daughter Sonia out for fast food; while she savored her burger and fries, I scavenged the not-so-bad salad bar.

Having shared my memories, perhaps I've jarred your own. I suspect that some readers will recognize the story—if not all the details, then at least the plot: first, a bountiful and complacent time when we didn't worry; then a stressful but energetic time of worry and change; then confusion and compromise. But, you might ask, what's so special about this? How significant are these memories? So far this story sounds simply like another tale of growing up. This is indeed the implicit theme of many embarrassed recollections of the Woodstock generation. Haven't I just described the classic life cycle: innocence, rebellion, "maturity"? Where's the larger drama I promised—the edible dynamic, the connections between palate and power?

I think there's much more to the story, but to get at it, memory must give way to history—quite a different way of recalling the past. Personal memory tends toward the archetypal—the universal, transcendent, timeless, "that's the way it is." Selective and self-comforting, such archetypes help us get over the past, to forgive and, ultimately, forget our youthful dreams and mistakes. Since, according to the archetype, we all sow our wild oats (or brown rice) and then "grow up," we might as well accept what we did and get on with life. If we're confused and compromised now, well, that's life too. History, on the other hand, is less accepting. Seeking understanding rather than comfort, history asks tougher questions: Why did we act that way? Did we *have* to? Could we have acted differently? Did things have to turn out the way they did? Do we have to act this way now?

Being personal, my own memories of the late 1960s and early 1970s are now hopelessly compromised by selective amnesia and nostalgia, so in researching this project I've relied much more heavily on the underground newspapers, cookbooks, guides, and catalogs of that period. Of course, as any historian must acknowledge, my present interpretation of those florid and feverish sources will be colored by my own experiences and interests, but I have worked hard to reconstruct the thinking and atmosphere of that traumatic and exciting time. This reconstruction, in turn, puts my own dietary experiences in a cultural and political context that I was only dimly aware of as I lived it; Diggers, People's Park, the New Left, Vietnam, Earth Day, feminism, the ethnic revival, Richard Nixon, Gary Snyder—all had a lot to do with what was going on in the kitchens of Ann Arbor, New Haven, Berkeley, and many other hip student zones. Indeed, I've found that rather than just being silly or perverse—as our parents and skeptical peers probably thought—we were cooking up something quite serious, ambitious, and, yes, radical: an alternative food system with its own ideology, staples, and supply lines, a countercuisine.

While at the time we were only semiconscious of what we were doing, in hindsight I see how right many of the intuitions were: the need to align private action with planetary needs; the distrust of chemicals and technology; the resanctification of nature, community, and tradition; the ecological and moral qualms about meat; the enthusiasm for small farms and organic methods; the intrinsic delight in whole foods; the sense that a better society might have to be built literally from the grass roots. Yet, even with Thoreau and Gandhi on our side, we failed to change the world— or even ourselves—very much. Despite all the new "healthy" foods, the supermarket is an additive minefield, processors are consolidating rapidly, the farm belt is a disaster area, pesticides are out of control, and we reek with contradictions like everyone else. Later in my narrative, I will blame much of the present mess on the quasi-organized food establishment. But part of the failure stems from the counterculture's original weaknesses: the druggy vagueness, the lack of follow-through, the new-convert insensitivity to "straight" culture, the overestimation of our power and the underestimation of the establishment's. Worst of all, we did not study our case clearly enough so that we'd have our facts straight
10 at the family dinner table. When the inevitable questioning, skepticism, and ridicule came, we were unprepared. Removed from its supportive bohemian enclaves, the countercuisine was highly vulnerable to counterattack by the patriarchal powers who controlled —and still control—the nation's food supply. The moral panic (Part 2) and market exploitation (Part 3) were partly our own fault. We were talking about the right things but we didn't always know what we were talking about.

Of course, since the problems are still there, there may still be time to get the case right. This book may be a rather elaborate way of reviving an old dinner table debate, but we still need to eat, and there's much to fight about.

PART ONE

REBELLION: THE MAKING OF A COUNTER-CUISINE

1 AN EDIBLE DYNAMIC

I f French gourmand Anthelme Brillat-Savarin (1755–1826) was right and we are what we eat, then what does that make us? More than a mixture of nutrients, food is a metaphor for what we like most or least about our society. To marshal self-satisfaction, mainstream politicians use reassuring images like "Mom and apple pie," "milk and honey," "bringing home the bacon," "meat and potatoes," "a chicken in every pot," grits, jelly beans, and pork rinds. Conversely, social critics may consider such staples "unhealthy," "poisonous," or "junk." Indeed, throughout American history, food fights have often accompanied grass roots political struggles. Thus, in the fiercely contentious Jacksonian period (the 1830s), radical vegetarians resisted mainstream medical authorities (who advised a heavy, meat-based diet.) The critique of processed foods during the Progressive era (1900–1914) mirrored widespread concern about irresponsible corporations and dangerous urban-industrial conditions. And in the Johnson-Nixon years (late 1960s–early 1970s), the rediscovery of organic foods and holistic healing accompanied the ecology movement, which was itself a reaction against the wholesale destruction of nature and tradition both here and in Southeast Asia.[1]

To be sure, when the first hippies wandered into health food stores around 1966 they probably were more interested in cheap exotica than in political advice. Indeed, young bohemians often shared the conventional view of "health food nuts" as hypochondriacs who dipped desiccated wheat germ crackers into yeasty carrot juice cocktails. In turn, these genteel, middle-aged health seekers tended to look askance at the hairy, blue-jeaned "freaks" searching for hallucinogenic treats, not sound advice. The veterans often hoped to treat specific diseases and ailments, but the newcomers weren't after medical cures. Young, healthy, well-bred, few considered disease to be an imminent or even remote prospect. While the nuts resisted the ravages of aging, the freaks felt more afflicted by their "sick" society.

Still, differences aside, the older generation did have refreshingly irreverent perspectives to share with the hip tourists. Venturing into a health food store in late 1968, the *San Francisco Express Times*'s food advisor Barbara Garson ("grandma shulman") assumed the manager would be another one of those "proverbial little old ladies in tennis shoes." Yet in explaining why Garson should not eat sugar, the manager recounted the sordid role of U.S. refineries in Cuba since the turn of the century. Previously wary of health food "cults," Garson was pleased—and surprised— that honey, whole wheat, soy noodles, organic raw milk, unusual herbs, and other health food staples could have a progressive context.[2] Other freak explorers of the health food underground reported similar discoveries: dusty copies of Euell Gibbons's 1962 survival guide, *Stalking the Wild Asparagus*; hard-to-find works by critics Adelle Davis, Beatrice Trum Hunter, and Rachel Carson— all dismissed as crackpots and cranks by mainstream authorities; complete sets of *Organic Gardening and Farming*, *Prevention*, and other publications by the much-maligned but indefatigable J. I. Rodale; and assorted pamphlets with utopian, spiritual, and dietary guidance. Writers of such advice commonly dismissed technocratic experts, worshiped nature, warned of impending disaster, and, in suggesting solutions, tended to see connections, to think in whole systems, not parts. In short, the health food stores offered holistic information that might be called protoecological.

The word "ecology" itself was not much used before 1969, when the events at Berkeley's People's Park signaled a major

16

"greening" of the counterculture; at that point the trickle of hip visitors to the health food underground swelled into a steady stream. Before 1969, however, few freaks gave much serious thought to food, healthful or otherwise—except perhaps for the Diggers.

FOOD AS MEDIUM

L ate one afternoon in October 1966, when the Haight-Ashbury was still producing daily surprises, a yellow bus dubbed the Yellow Submarine pulled up to a group of freaks lounging in the Panhandle and unloaded a scavenged feast of day-old bread, tossed green salad, turkey stew, and apples. Yelling "Food as medium," the anonymous submariners—dressed in monk costumes—also handed out mimeographed sheets crammed with political and philosophical speculation. These "Digger Papers" were features in what became regular "Feeds"; their aim, according to Digger Emmett Grogan, was as much to teach as to feed—to use food as a medium to develop "collective social consciousness and social action." The Diggers were in fact so concerned that the medium not obscure the message that they made it hard for the hungry to reach the meal. Thus, to hammer home the point that the food was "free because it's yours," the bus would cruise by several times, deliberately teasing the waiting crowd into a mini–food riot; sometimes the stew container lids were screwed on especially tight, again forcing the hungry to move out of a state of passive receptivity. And to reach their meal, people had to walk through a large yellow wooden Frame of Reference—thus "changing their frame of reference as they did." Such theatrics were soon elaborated in a "free store" decorated with empty window frames, where customers seeking newly liberated food and clothes were greeted with signs such as, "If someone asks to see the manager, tell him he's the manager."[3]

The Diggers were by no means the first to use the dinner table as a springboard—in the Diggers' case trampoline might be more apt—for consciousness raising. The name itself had deep roots. In part it came from the seventeenth-century English levelers who, protesting insensitivity to the poor, planted in the commons of towns and distributed the food free. Also, it alluded to California's Digger Indians, memorialized in Ruth Benedict's *Pat-*

17

terns of Culture, a book well known to the neotribal counterculture. In 1934 Benedict had written that the Diggers were ignorant of "the insides of tin cans and the things for sale at butcher shops"; instead they had subsisted off "the health of the desert"—including roots roasted over mesquite. The Digger Feeds also reflected the role of food in 1960s activism: the symbolic importance of interracial dining in sit-ins at segregated restaurants; the Quaker-led fasts against the war; the consumer boycotts in support of lettuce and grape pickers—the exploited subjects of Edward R. Murrow's 1960 documentary, *Harvest of Shame.*[4] But precedents aside, the Diggers made one critical contribution: they put food at the center of an activist program based on an emerging ecological consciousness.

While other prophets—both stoned and straight—were predicting a leisure-based postindustrial paradise, the Digger Papers sounded a distinctly somber note.

> *Industrialization was a battle with 19th century ecology to win breakfast at the cost of smog and insanity. Wars against ecology are suicidal. The U.S. standard of living is a bourgeois baby blanket for executives who scream in their sleep. No Pleistocene swamp could match the pestilential horror of modern sewage. No children of White Western Progress will escape the cries of people forced to haul their raw materials.*

Anticipating an imminent collapse of an urban-industrial civilization awash in garbage, the Diggers articulated a stark survivalist strategy: cut back, clean up, and clear out. Get back to basics—like feeding the hungry or, better still, growing your own. In "Sounds from the Seed-Power Sitar," one Digger welcomed a "return to the land" as a way "to straighten our heads in a natural environment, to straighten our bodies with healthier foods and Pan's work, toe to toe with the physical world." Moving beyond these therapeutic benefits, the author sketched a decentralized, postapocalyptic utopia nourished by a hip food network: in the cities free stores and co-ops would feed the hungry with food grown by city gardeners and nearby communal farms. While conventional civilization crumbled, this alternative supply system would insure "the healthy, organic, harmonious evolution of the Tribe."[5]

18

For the Diggers, the environmental crisis was both worldwide and very local: acting as what Charles Perry calls a "hip Salvation Army," the Diggers worried about the youthful hordes jamming the Haight for the overhyped Summer of Love (1967). Seeking free food sources and a rural safety valve for overcrowded hip ghettos, Diggers visited communes outside the Bay Area. Formal hip involvement with food production and distribution may date from March 1967, when a delegation of Diggers proposed to pick surplus apples and farm a few vegetables at folk musician Lou Gottlieb's Sonoma County retreat, Morning Star Ranch. When the Haight began to sour that fall, Morning Star filled with hundreds of refugees—including overworked Digger women who did most of the gardening and cooking for the Feeds. Harassed by local police, Gottlieb eventually had to close the ranch. But the Morning Star–Free Store connection was the model for the network of rural communes and urban co-ops that began to take shape in 1969–70. Indeed, when Friends of the Earth issued *The Environmental Handbook* in time for Earth Day, a nationwide teach-in held on April 22, 1970, its call for a decentralized food supply based on cooperative groceries, city gardens, and organic farms sounded much like the 1967 vision of "Sounds from the Seed-Power Sitar."[6]

But there was a three-year gap between "Seed-Power Sitar" and Earth Day. The Diggers were a bit early. In 1966–67 cultural radicals were only just discovering the urban-acid-hip scene and were not ready to flee to Vermont or Sonoma. Charles Perry writes that many in the Haight saw the Diggers as an "anonymous group of stubborn moralists, probably stiff-necked primitive Christians in sackcloth," and for the average street person, a Digger Feed was just a free meal whose moralistic messages had no more impact than the sermons at a skid-row mission. Still focused on the war and civil rights, political radicals were mostly hostile to what seemed a reactionary back-to-nature strategy. By 1969, however, when there would be a more receptive constituency, the burnt-out Diggers had disbanded as an identifiable group.[7] Yet their spirit and vision lived on—especially at People's Park.   19

PEOPLE'S PARK

On April 20, 1969, several hundred members of the ad hoc Robin Hood's Park Commission invaded an empty Berkeley lot owned by the University of California, planted vegetable seeds, trees, and sod, erected a striped swing set, picnic tables and benches, launched balloons, shared fruit, marijuana, and wine, danced to the country rock band Joy of Cooking, and cheered the new sign: PEOPLE'S PARK: POWER TO THE PEOPLE.[8]

Although the Diggers themselves had drifted off into assorted escapes and causes, the action was Digger in spirit. The seizure of public land for the purpose of producing free food and rallying the landless had seventeenth-century precedents. Also, like the Digger Feeds, People's Park was participatory "living theater." Sharing members and ideas with the improvisational San Francisco Mime Troupe, the Diggers treated property, food, and clothes as an array of props and scenery to be taken or cast off at will. Deeply ingrained habits and taboos could be shucked off as easily as a script. The acute relativism of this theatrical model served, along with psychedelic drugs, as a deconditioning mechanism, a tool of liberation. Entering the Free Store you became at once its owner, manager, employee, and customer. As that famous sign read, all roles were open. "No owner, no manager, no employees, and no cash." When the Diggers distributed stolen food with the claim, "It's free because it's yours," they invited recipients to act *as if* it did belong to them. The implication was that if everyone started acting as if food were truly common property, perhaps it would become so.[9]

Similarly, the Robin Hood's Park Commission invited people to seize land and plant seeds everywhere. Publishing the original call to take the park, the *Berkeley Barb* advised, "Nobody supervises and the trip belongs to whoever dreams." When one self-described "agrarian reformer" told a reporter, "We ultimately plan to take over all Berkeley," he almost meant it. In living theater, if enough people played the role, it became real. As a Digger broadside explained in 1967, "First free the space, goods and services. Let the theories of economics follow social facts." Understanding quite well the marshaling power of popular drama, Governor Ronald Reagan called out the National Guard. For two weeks in May, Berkeley was, according to the *San Francisco Chronicle*, an "occupied city," as "revolutionary peasants" and reactionary "Storm Troopers" alike improvised new "social facts."[10]

The theories of economics soon followed, beginning with a teach-in devoted to ecology and politics in America. A widely distributed pamphlet prepared for the teach-in by an American Federation of Teachers local suggested that the confrontation raised "questions about the quality of our lives, about the deterioration of our environment, and about the propriety and legitimacy of the uses to which we put our land." The authorities' violent response to what seemed a harmless bid for green space mirrored both a long-standing American disdain for nature and the current mass defoliation of Vietnam. "It is the way of the world! Trees are anarchic; concrete is Civilization." When seen through the wide-angle lens of ecology, People's Park became a microcosm of American society. Hungry for such perspectives, the crowd was most receptive to Gary Snyder, the Zen-beat poet who had just returned from several years of recharging in Japan and whose earlier work had greatly influenced the Diggers. Likening trees to other exploited minorities—blacks, Vietnamese peasants, hippies—Snyder termed People's Park a guerrilla strike on behalf of the "non-negotiable demands of the Earth."[11]

As the tear gas evaporated, the park stayed closed and the crowds scattered; soon the restless mainstream media departed Berkeley for other stations on their tour of "campus violence." For the underground press, however, People's Park pointed away from violence, toward ecology. "Revolutionaries must begin to think in ecological terms," wrote "Pantagruel" in New York's *Rat*. "An attack against environmental destruction is an attack on the structures of control and the mechanisms of power within a society." In mid-1969 the 500 or so underground papers could not get enough about Ecology Action, Gary Snyder, DDT, trees, and environmentalism. In "Earth Read-Out," the first underground syndicated ecology column, Berkeley Yippie Keith Lampe trumpeted a transition to a "broader, ecologically-oriented radicalism." By November 1969 *Rat*'s "Pocahontas" could observe that "in the six short months since People's Park, the word 'ecology' had been lifted from the dusty academic shelves of abstract scientific definition; it became a powerful breathing consciousness, meaning all things about life, death, and survival that no radical could avoid."[12]

Pursuing the "ecology is revolutionary" dream of 1969, when any urban vegetable patch could seem, in Todd Gitlin's words, a "conspiracy of soil," a *Good Times* reporter visited a Berkeley "People's Garden." For spokesperson J. Channing Grant, an "organic" garden was a model of a peaceful, cooperative society—"a harmony between as many life kingdoms as possible." His collective thus avoided all pesticides, herbicides, chemical fertilizers, and other "poisons, because most all the life is friendly—even neces-

21

sary." Skeptical but sympathetic, the reporter acknowledged the "good vibes" from all those healthy plants thriving where once only weeds had grown. If barren lots could produce free food, he mused, maybe civilization was not doomed after all. The wider implications that Grant drew from his savory spinach were indeed dizzying. A cooperative garden served as an "edible dynamic," a "living medium through which people can relate to each other and their nourishment." By raising food jointly, people could "explore their own roots" and overcome alienation. This sounded like "a digestible ideology," quipped the intrigued but still dubious reporter. "That's just the point," the unfazed Grant replied. "A garden-oriented neighborhood would become a more self-dependent and self-determined group. Perhaps it will lead in other cooperative directions." Local wastes could be recycled into the soil, not lost in sewers. Pooling scientific skills, local gardeners might hybridize vegetables to local growing conditions. The more food grown locally, the less need for energy-wasting, polluting trucks and railroads. Food unavailable locally might be purchased by cooperative buying clubs—food "conspiracies"—that would undercut the commercial "monopolies." Looking ahead, communities might be planned with cooperative gardens in mind, thereby fostering decentralization and setting "functional limits on urban development." All this from a small city garden! [13]

The article, titled "People's Pods," was typical of underground ecological reporting: an earnest yet playful desire to join personal means (organic gardening) with political ends (radical decentralization), and conversely, to have political means (socialized production) yield personal dividends (tasty spinach). The dream was beautiful, and naive, but in the otherwise gloomy atmosphere of 1969, disaffected youth needed new dreams.

ECOLOGY:
THE SUBVERSIVE SCIENCE

Why did ecology emerge as such a powerful buzzword almost overnight? In part, 1968 and 1969 were years when it was hard to feel confident about planetary survival. With the King and Kennedy assassinations, televised mayhem in Vietnam, riots in black and student ghettos, the sieges of Paris, Prague, and Chicago, social order was clearly disintegrating everywhere. The environmental crises peaked in 1969, when an oil spill off Santa Barbara fouled beaches and killed birds, a smog alert paralyzed Los Angeles, and Cleveland's Cuyahoga River caught fire. On top of this came a rash of news stories on DDT, cyclamates, soil erosion, world hunger, and warnings of impending earthquakes and tidal waves. "We must realize that unless we are extremely lucky, everybody will disappear in a cloud of blue steam in twenty years," Paul Ehrlich pronounced in mid-1969. Ehrlich's new book, *The Population Bomb*, had been largely ignored when published in 1968, but in the wake of People's Park, it received more attention in the underground press. In the first chapter, entitled "Too Many People—Too Little Food—A Dying Planet," Ehrlich declared that the age of affluence was over. A combination of overpopulation and misguided agricultural practices—soil erosion, excess use of pesticides and fertilizers—was pushing the world toward ecocatastrophe. Blaming "a record of ecological stupidity without parallel," Ehrlich predicted that the 1970s would witness worldwide famine, rioting, and perhaps even a nuclear war resulting from "runaway food/population pressures." While Ehrlich suggested that ecocatastrophe might take ten or twenty years to develop, hip interpreters often telescoped the time frame: Doomsday was already at hand. Acknowledging the apocalyptic mentality, the Sierra Club's 1970 handbook, *Ecotactics*, quipped, "Some people are beginning to suspect that due to a lack of interest, tomorrow has been cancelled."[14]

The prospect of imminent upheaval may indeed have been one of the reasons for ecology's appeal among the young, especially those draftable males unable to contemplate a future beyond graduation. But even for those not expecting The End, environmentalism was emerging as the left's primary vehicle for outrage and hope, edging aside civil rights, the antiwar movement, and revolutionary socialism. Many who had once rallied to the cause of civil rights had, by 1969, seen the movement taken over by Great Society bureaucrats and exclusionary Black Power advocates. Idealistic entrants into the Welfare State (especially public education and social work) burned out almost overnight; minority groups organizing from the bottom up were increasingly unreceptive to white middle-class young people. The antiwar movement too was in a rut. Peaceful protest seemed ineffectual; under the liberal banner it had become a mild, single-issue plea to "end the bombing," and even this minimal goal seemed unattainable through the

23

electoral process. Antiwar rallies continued to attract large numbers in 1969 and 1970—how could you stay away?—but few participants could feel confident that marching would end the war or solve problems at home. Yet confrontational street-fighting tactics were proving counterproductive. The "revolutionary" left seemed too involved in dubious poses and impenetrable theory. At first, media-savvy leaders had deliberately inflated their rhetoric to gain attention, and stunts like the 1967 "levitation" of the Pentagon had the freshness of Digger Living Theater. But by the time of Columbia and Chicago (1968), Yippie actor-activists seemed trapped in the media/movement script. The hardening and splintering worsened after the disastrous Chicago Democratic convention, which helped to elect Richard Nixon. Former Chicago *Seed* editor Abe Peck recalls that, after Students for a Democratic Society (SDS) split into hopelessly doctrinaire and irrelevant factions at its June 1969 meeting, the *Seed* ran a cartoon "with two screaming demonstrators arguing whether the 'Neo Trotskyist Progressive Socialist Radical Action Club for International Peace' or the 'Socialist Progressive Club for International Democracy Thru Radical Prototrotskyist Action' held the correct line."[15]

Ecology emerged as a fresh oppositional alternative. Moved by Gary Snyder's performance at People's Park to read *Earth House Hold*, former SDS president Todd Gitlin projected onto the poet's "green" message everything that the New Left was not: "tender without weakness, earth-seeking without romance, religious without reverence, combative without cant." For one thing, there was as yet no dogmatic party line. The movement seemed open to diverse opinions and strategies. "Nobody in it is yet on a heavy ego-trip or power trip," wrote Keith Lampe, who had personally witnessed the calcification of the once-limber Youth International Party (Yippies). "There's a good chance such trips won't develop at all; concern for all life forms of the whole nature is inherently religious or disinterested."[16]

One immediate advantage in the repressive climate of 1969 was that environmentalists could not be easily framed as violent deviants. At the very moment that the media disseminated stereotypes of bomb-throwing revolutionaries (SDS), drug-crazed hippies (Charles Manson), and gun-toting separatists (Black Panthers), *Time* could praise environmentalists as "pragmatic protesters [who] are now [1969] firing at smog, waste, and mindless developers." At a time of bitter divisiveness, environmentalism appeared to bring everyone together; even President Nixon praised Earth Day. Marveling how "busy executives and bearded hippies discuss the presence of DDT in the flesh of antarctic penguins," *Time* hoped that "pollution may soon replace the Vietnam War as the nation's major issue of protest." Environmentalists frequently exploited this clean image. "When the environmental revolutionaries on this campus [Wisconsin-Madison] gather rocks, they're for mulching, not throwing," *Organic Gardening and Farming* observed. Environmentalism even seemed patriotic. "No one can say that a man trying to save the American environment does not love his country," argued Marion Edey, who helped found Friends of the Earth in 1969.[17]

But beneath its placid surface stirred potentially disruptive currents. Examining the interrelationship between living things and their surroundings, the science of ecology had been around for years. In libraries its older texts were classified with ornate monographs on wetlands, rain forests, and sand dunes—all models of sublime fragility. In the late 1960s, however, ecology broadened from a baroque branch of biology into an interdisciplinary embrace of the whole earth. Attempting to meet the new student interest, textbook publishers hurriedly turned out ecology anthologies with essays covering everything from population problems in India to pesticide pollution in Nebraska, auto emissions to sonic booms, redwoods to red tide, often spiced with transcendent pieces by poet Gary Snyder, historian Lynn White, and biologist Garrett Hardin. Predisposed by psychedelics to find oneness where straights saw fragments, freaks found scientific reinforcement in ecology's global sweep. Moreover, in the polarized climate of the late 1960s, those who felt rejected by their own country could take heart in being citizens of the Planet. As patriots of this wider polity they could feel righteously outraged by what they saw as the root cause of planetary problems: technology.

Like Frankenstein's monster, industrialism had gone berserk, wrecking the delicate balances of eternity. The notion of technological hubris seemed a plausible alternative to the New Left's now-irritating focus on "Kapitalism." Marxism missed the point, ecologists argued, for modern socialist societies were just as sick. Given the intricacies of the planetary system, simply nationalizing ownership would not work. *Everything* had to be changed. Crime in the streets, racial discrimination, sexual subordination, pollution in Los Angeles, starvation in Calcutta, DDT in milk—all were

25

connected, all were symptoms of worldwide imbalances. Taken to its logical extreme—and this is where many hoped to take it— ecology required total overhaul. "You can't be serious about the environment without being a revolutionary," Gary Snyder warned.[18]

Only a complete scaling down of technology and technocracy could restore balance. We would have to decentralize production, deprofessionalize knowledge, live more simply. Snyder envisioned a return to primitive tribal societies on the American Indian model. The backward-looking aspect of this prescription did not bother young dissidents for whom moving forward meant either quick death in some ecodisaster (or in war) or slow strangulation in the professional-managerial bureaucracy. Moreover, countering the Marxist-Leninist charge that they were decadent bourgeoisie, ecofreaks could congratulate themselves on being the most tough-minded and clear-headed of radicals, for they were calling in a most uncompromising fashion for western civilization to pay its dues. Appearing first in late 1968, *The Whole Earth Catalog* propounded three no-nonsense "laws":

> *Everything's connected to everything.*
> *Everything's got to go somewhere.*
> *There's no such thing as a free lunch.*

Although the logic seemed irrefutable, few in 1969 could envision exactly how the wider populace might be convinced to relinquish their modern comforts. Indeed, the job seemed so immense that just contemplating the scope of the changes needed made ecology seem, as captured in the title of one widely quoted essay collection, "the subversive science."[19]

Along with this transcendent vision, ecology offered immediate personal steps. In electoral politics, you had to wait four years to make changes at the top; in dialectical Marxism you had to wait generations for changes from below. In ecology, however, you could act right away, in your own household. Scale down your attachments to modern technology, Snyder advised; voluntary simplicity would subvert an economy geared to overconsumption.[20]

Metaphorically, living ecologically meant adopting simpler, more "natural" styles, patterned on models that were nostalgic, often nonwestern, non-Anglo-American, or at least nonurban.

26

Whereas the city-based counterculture of the mid-sixties had assumed a future based on postindustrial, universal affluence, the rural-oriented ecoculture at the end of the decade thought in terms of preindustrial subsistence. In fashion, out went the radioactive Day-Glo colors, bright plastics and foils, the mod sophistication that had reflected a more playful view of technology. In came subdued browns and blues, faded cotton and wool, Apache headbands, peasant skirts and shawls. In arts and crafts, out went the ingenious pop art bricolage of the mid-sixties, in came a cultivation of natural materials, especially houseplants, clay, leather, and oak. In music, the louder electric rock of the Haight-Ashbury gradually gave way to softer country rock, acoustic folk blues, and Afro-Cuban fusion. Perhaps the most publicized symbol of the neoprimitivist mood came in August 1969, when over 400,000 freaks retreated to a Bethel, New York, farm. As the movie *Woodstock* reveals, Max Yasgur's proud claim, "I'm a farmer," received thunderous applause, but—in graphic proof of the impatience with activist talk—few objected when Abbie Hoffman was bumped off the stage as he appealed for help for the imprisoned White Panther John Sinclair. Throughout the festival, the political activists' tent, Movement City, was, in Abe Peck's words, a deserted, "desperate Leftist island," while the California commune Hog Farm won universal praise for quietly serving brown rice and vegetables to the hungry crowd.[21]

Brown rice became the icon of antimodernity. In the camp-pop spirit of the mid-sixties, freaks had been game to eat almost anything while searching for experience—even mixing a chemical hallucinogen in an artificially flavored punch, as Tom Wolfe's *Electric Kool-Aid Acid Trip* (1968) documented. Arlo Guthrie's 1967 hit song "Alice's Restaurant" celebrated it for serving "anything you want"—sometimes in tinfoil-lined hubcaps. As late as 1968 *Fifth Estate*'s food columnist passed on recipes for "instant espresso" (instant coffee and cocoa, dash of cinnamon, nondairy creamer) and "bologna knish enchiladas" (fried eggs and onions rolled in bologna slices, then wrapped in white bread and covered with canned cheddar cheese soup sauce).[22] After 1969, however, no countercultural food writer mentioned processed foods—unless in contempt.

Jaded as we now are by commercial phrases like "natural, whole grain goodness," it may now be hard to see revolutionary significance in the eating of unhulled rice and curried carrots, or

27

granola and yogurt. In 1969–70, however, dietary change was one of the more substantial household reforms. Compared to other cultural adaptations, the emerging countercuisine seemed less co-optable because it demanded greater personal commitment. Anyone could wear what *Business Week* called "ecology pants" (Levi's) or listen to country rock, but it took a substantial act of disaffiliation to forgo familiar cooking. Fashion and musical styles changed rapidly, but food habits were imprinted almost from birth, and even in a culture dedicated to perennial obsolescence, food patterns changed slowly. To undo these patterns took considerable effort. Examining and altering one's tastes was somewhat akin to psychoanalysis: a confrontation with subconsciously ingrained values, tastes, and behaviors. Coming out of the confrontation, new converts might experience a sense of liberation and rightness, a therapeutic "high" akin to the psychedelic experience.

The high that came with breaking food conventions stemmed in part from the shock value. As many neovegetarians discovered when they first requested alfalfa sprouts and chopsticks over roast beef and stainless steel, the countercuisine brought the war home to the family dinner table. At first parents and friends might easily dismiss the defection as adolescent perversity—a predictably familiar desire to be different.

But being different in something so basic and taboo-laden as food might lead to being different in many things. This, not generational rebellion, was the implicit agenda of the countercuisine: food was a medium for broader change. If dietary rebels seemed a bit self-righteous, perhaps it was from their renewed sense of moral purity and political consistency. Unlike sporadic antiwar protests, dietary rightness could be lived 365 days a year, three times a day. The New Left had always insisted that the personal was political. What could be more personal than food? And what could be more political than challenging agribusiness, America's largest and most environmentally troublesome industry, with $350 billion in assets (1969), employing 23 million workers and 3 million farmers, selling $100 billion worth of food to 200 million consumers?[23]

28

2 RADICAL CONSUMERISM

The close link between personal life and politics was most evident in the underground food columns, e.g., Alice Waters's "Alice's Restaurant" in the *San Francisco Express Times*; *Good Times*'s "Eat and Enjoy" feature, written first by movement veteran Barbara Garson, then Jeanie Darlington (San Francisco); *Quicksilver Times*'s anonymous "food and fun" (D.C.); *Fifth Estate*'s "Eat It!" by Judie Davis (Detroit); *Kaleidoscope*'s "Politix of Garbage" by "Sally Soybean" and "Annie Avocado" (Milwaukee); the widely syndicated "Grub Bag" by Ita Jones and "Peasant's Pot" by Jay Melugin; and numerous columns titled "Food for Thought" and "You Are What You Eat." Recruiting for the emerging countercuisine, these writers spiced recipes with scathing analysis of agribusiness "rip-offs" and "poisons." Although the data cited in *Rat* and *Good Times* would not have surprised readers of *Time* and *Newsweek*, the language, goals, and context were altogether different. The liberal Naderites spotlighted by mainstream media wanted reform, but radical consumerists wrote direly of primitive survival. Such talk may have been part hype, but to some extent they really believed it, for survivalist imagery accurately reflected the apocalyptic urgency and new-convert certainty of the early ecology movement.

SURVIVALIST STRATEGIES

When using the word "survival" before the doomsday scare of 1968–71, hip writers had not meant it literally, as in life or death. Rather, in line with venerable bohemian traditions, it meant living well without running the rat race. If you got by without getting caught in the 9-to-5 trap, then you beat the system. Price, not nutrition, was the main issue. One boho survival strategy was to seek cheap food at local wholesale markets and ethnic groceries and restaurants—especially those still serving first-generation immigrants in older city neighborhoods. Judie Davis urged Detroit bargain hunters to try the Polish area of Hamtramck for kielbasa on egg bread, then drive over to Greek Town for feta cheese and baklava. Similarly, grandma shulman offered hints for "budget buying" at Bay Area Italian and Jewish delicatessens. San Francisco and New York's underground gourmet guidebooks cataloged restaurants—usually ethnic—serving meals under $2.00. For dinners at home, recipes turned low-grade meat and canned vegetables into standard bohemian fare: spaghetti, curries, stews. A popular student cookbook of the mid-sixties, Jay F. Rosenberg's *The Impoverished Student's Book of Cookery, Drinkery, and Housekeeping* (1965), devoted a chapter to "A Brief History of Horsemeat," which it recommended as a tasty, cheap alternative to beef.[1]

At the end of the decade, however, "survival" had both financial and physical connotations. Widely printed in the underground press, Diane DiPrima's "poem for the summer solstice 1968" expressed a much-shared sense of personal danger in the aftermath of the King riots and the violent student confrontations at Columbia and the Sorbonne—with the Chicago convention debacle yet to come. Predicting that city stores might soon be closed for months at a time, DiPrima urged freaks to hoard nutritious commodities: beans, rice, dried fruits and nuts, whole wheat flour, sea salt. Moreover, DiPrima suggested that with a prolonged crisis near, it might be wise to eat less and stay fit. Thinness would be not so much an aesthetic nicety as a survivalist necessity.

30

> *remember, we are all used to eating less*
> *than the "average American" and take it easy*

before we
ever notice we're hungry the rest of the folk will be starving
and help will arrive, until the day no help arrives
and then you're on your own.

Recommending *Passport to Survival,* one of the first hip-oriented natural foods cookbooks, *The Last Whole Earth Catalog* expanded the traditional boho-student economic rationale: "Emergency procedures and forethoughts stored here will serve you come holocaust, catastrophe, or unemployment." Included was a "survival diet" based on ingredients that would "keep indefinitely when properly stored": whole wheat, powdered milk, honey, and salt. In a late-1968 *Liberation News Service* column entitled "What to Do Until the World Ends," Kerry Thornley predicted that "an economics of chaos" would soon follow an impending "hard rain"— either a revolution or perhaps some natural disaster. "Learn to eat weeds. Edible wild plants, compared to the wilted, handled, sprayed, and artificially fertilized crap you buy in the supermarkets, are health foods. Further, properly prepared, some of them are gourmet delights that can keep you alive when other food sources fail." For the next two years the underground papers were full of such talk: the revolutionary crisis was at hand, it was time to hoard food and water, rally the downtrodden masses, man the barricades—and prepare to head for the hills should the revolution fail.[2]

As it became clear around 1970 that the masses were not ready to rise up and topple the state once and for all, hip food writers sought explanations for the passivity of the oppressed. Perhaps Orwell had been right when he quipped, "We may find in the long run that tinned food is a deadlier weapon than the machine gun." Amerika of the late 1960s had so many totalitarian Orwellian qualities, why not see processed food as one of its weapons? "Violence against people is waged every day in this capitalist state," Berkeley's "Medical Cadre" pamphlet began. The violence was not of the overt kind but through a more subtle and insidious poisoning of the population. "There are two kinds of repression," *Quicksilver Times* agreed. "One is the way the shit comes down on the Panthers and others; that's the kind of repression that's rampant before Babylon's collapse. The other kind is the sort that Babylon's people live with through their lives; this is the sort of repression manifested by the poisoning of the people of Amerika."[3]

31

POISONING AMERIKA

Since seeing broad connections was part of the ecological paradigm, freaks could intuitively grasp the view long held by "health food nuts" that there was a conspiracy of agribusiness firms, medical professionals, and government officials. When "experts" brushed aside Rachel Carson's evidence on DDT, Adelle Davis's qualms about additives, or the Rodale Press's case for organic farming, it seemed clear that a systematic cover-up was in progress. Noting that many defenders of pesticides and additives received lucrative consulting contracts from food corporations, one *Rat* writer concluded: "I feel that these men are in it for the control of men and men's minds. The logic of this is simple—a drugged, poisoned, sick, mentally deranged populace . . . is easier to manage, to intimidate by police force." Citing a "food conspiracy" united to "keep Americans unhealthy," *Good Times* observed that food processors seemed to take "satanic delight" in chemicals; meat producers laced their animals with hormones and antibiotics; the FDA routinely approved all but the most obviously noxious of additives; and supermarket conglomerates kept prices unjustly high. Meanwhile, afraid of competition from preventive health care, doctors ignored nutrition and dismissed food critics as "faddists."[4]

The military-industrial complex was also involved. The same companies producted DDT and defoliants, plastic wrap and napalm; the same army destroyed Vietnam to save it and bulldozed organic gardens in Berkeley; the same government lied about body counts and cyclamates. To feed the troops in Vietnam and to break the farmworkers' strike at the same time, the Defense Department blatantly bought scab grapes and lettuce. The same junk foods that stupefied the American home front were shipped overseas to corrupt innocent peasants. Indeed, everywhere one looked, it began to add up to one health-defying system. "Contemporary food is monstrous," *Good Times*'s "Windcatcher" concluded. "The vested interests of the U.S. are far too strong for them to revalue their approach." In "Cosmic Clinic," *Good Earth*'s Marcia indicted not just the AMA, drug companies, and food manufacturers, but also television, teachers, and parents: "Mind blasted by TV and radio flashes, brainwashed by Marcus Welby and other Video Vampires, spellbound by Zombie parents, teachers and physicians, an Amerikan is programmed into the alienation and death that must result from the vivisection of the mind and body."[5]

Contemplating the power of this foe, food writers urged freaks to go into training, partly for self-protection, partly to speed along the battle. "How can you fight if you don't feel good?" asked *Quicksilver Times*'s "food and fun" columnist. "Thinking concretely," Ita Jones wrote for the *Liberation News Service*, "one can see that to win our healthy minds will need healthy bodies." Borrowing Napoleon's maxim, *Good Times* observed, "An army travels on its stomach. If you don't eat well, you don't have the energy you need. You get sick, both in body and mind." Jones recommended potato kugel, granola, and heavy whole wheat breads because they were nutritionally dense and also portable; easily made in large batches and eaten cold, they could be supplied to those "who know they will be occupying buildings for a length of time." Indeed, Jones added, kugel would have been perfect food for revolutionary Jews fighting the pharaoh in Egypt.[6]

While the apocalyptic sensibility was widely shared, only a handful actually pursued the street-fighting scenario—with disastrous results. Still, paramilitary, survivalist language had broad metaphorical appeal. The difficulty of shifting to environmentally sound consumption patterns, especially in food, should not be underestimated. If Americans were "junk food junkies," it would take quite a fight to break the habit, to "revolutionize our digestive tracts," as *Good Times*'s "bod squad" put it. Given the persuasive power of processed food advertising, *Quicksilver Times*'s Judy Swann could feel realistic in claiming that "eating natural foods is revolutionary in terms of the sorts of crap that people are given in processed foods." Given the economic clout of supermarket chains, it did seem a "conspiracy" to organize a nonprofit food-buying cooperative. Noting the overwhelming authority of AMA doctors and scientific "experts," *Good Earth*'s Marcia had little trouble branding holistic healing, yoga, and herbal remedies as "part of our total revolution." In short, the food underground used the language of struggle not just for hype or paranoia, but also because it *was* a struggle to change and the stakes seemed large.[7]

Countercuisine missionaries also used the rhetoric of struggle to make dietary change seem personally compelling and politically important. Metaphors were particularly useful in telling readers what to avoid. As an adjective, "pig" linked elements of the main-

33

stream food-military-industrial complex: "pig Safeway," "pig police," "pig media." Urging freaks to give up all "pig food," the Red Yogis of San Francisco put the term in broader context:

> *The pigs will rip us off for everything we've got, especially our strength! If we let them. We're all conditioned some by the slovenly habits of the pig culture we grew up in. It's not easy to shake them. . . . Pig manufacturers are like embalmers. Preserving away this dead stuff, shooting it full of chemicals, coloring it up, putting a high price on it and pushing it off on the people as better than the real thing.*[8]

Pig was related to fat—itself a long-standing metaphor for bourgeois affluence, softness, and corruption. In advising readers not to "pig out," food writers were more concerned for readers' minds than waistlines.

FEMINIST ECOLOGY

The rhetorical battle against pigs and fat had special resonance for women, who predominated as writers—and perhaps also readers—of underground consumer columns. The place of women in the countercuisine was ambiguous, spanning both traditional and feminist roles. Traditionally, women served as the primary gatekeepers of family food intake, acting as shoppers, cooks, home economists, dieticians, and consumer activists. In the mid-sixties, housewives organized protests against rising food prices. In the counterculture and New Left of the mid-1960s too, many women still played conventional parts as sexual playmates and as domestic helpmates. SDS and Black Panther males debated strategies; their "chicks" made coffee and tended children. Digger men played front-stage roles as "life actors" in living theater; Digger women cooked backstage. Underground food columns were written by women; men took most of the front-page hard news stories. Marvin Garson edited the *San Francisco Express Times*—financed by the proceeds from his wife's antiwar play, *MacBird*; Barbara Garson served as a surrogate Jewish mom, grandma shulman.[9]

Yet, this very separateness made women front-line warriors in

34

the battle against pollution. Likening the endangered earth to a woman being raped, some argued that ecology was a feminist issue; both did emerge as dominant radical concerns about 1969. Thus, included in the People's Park teach-in pamphlet was a poem by Book Jones:

> *The earth is our Mother the land*
> *The University put a fence around the land—our Mother*
> *The University must stop fucking with our land*
> *The University must stop being a Motherfucker.*

Although many feminists objected to the image of a passive or pastoral earth mother, they agreed that women should have no trouble grasping ecological issues. In "Goodbye to All That," her rousing call for a separate women's movement, Robin Morgan dismissed male ecologists "tripping off women as earth-mother or frontier chicks," yet added that women's bodies were "unavoidably aware of the locked-in relationship between humans and their biosphere—the earth, the tides, the atmosphere, the moon." [10]

For feminist survivalists physical fitness was a necessary self-defense. Appropriately, the front page of the first issue of *It Ain't Me Babe*, a Berkeley women's paper, was devoted to karate. Promoting healthy eating as a feminist priority, writers sometimes advised women to lose weight, although some showed considerable ambivalence about weight control. On the one hand, to diet was to conform to male images of beauty; on the other, women who ate compulsively often felt helpless and powerless. "Fat is a defense against men," Roberta Weintraub wrote for *Liberation News Service*. "But it is also a major source of conflict and unhappiness in women." For Weintraub, the advantages of self-discipline were greater than the disadvantages of seeming to conform to the waist-line fetish. A woman who felt in control of her appetite might also be able to control other aspects of her life. Concluding that "losing weight is a political act for women who have been compulsive eaters," Weintraub urged feminists to form their own weight control groups rather than seek out Weight Watchers or regular doctors. An implicit promise of some 1970-vintage feminist writing about fat was that consciousness raising would make women more comfortable with their bodies, and once they felt more comfortable, they would also be better able to control their appetites. [11]

35

The struggle for self-control and self-defense also led to a generalized attack on a food-medical-industrial establishment guilty of "male-feasance." Male doctors, druggists, government health officials, academic experts, grocers, processors—all stood indicted of exploiting or, at best, ignoring women's needs. The 1970 edition of *Our Bodies, Ourselves,* a very successful "self-health" manual written by the Boston Women's Collective, reasoned, "We want to become physically healthy and strong and enduring, through exercise, proper eating, and training (like karate) and proud of ourselves, proud because we feel good ourselves, not because we look good for others." Noting that almost all gynecologists were male, Robin Morgan advocated a self-examination as a political act: "The speculum may well be mightier than the sword." While the battle against patriarchy could lead simply to calls for more women MDs, it could also lead back to traditional ways of healing that were controlled by women— herbalism, midwifery, witchcraft. By 1973 there were so many self-health, holistic alternatives that they took a large part of *The New Woman's Survival Catalog,* a feminist "access to tools" designed along the same lines as ecology's *Whole Earth Catalog.*[12]

Themes of self-control and self-defense also ran through feminist discussions of conventional cooking. In an article titled "Nothin' Says Lovin' Like Somethin' from the Oven," *off our backs* writer Norma Allen Lesser accused cookbook writers of subtle seduction: promising easy-to-make meals with "gourmet appeal" and "foreign flair," cookbooks exploited housewives' boredom, anxiety, and need for creative accomplishments. "Once again, a product is being subsidized by appealing to the insecurities of women." Extending the exploitation imagery, Atlanta's *Great Speckled Bird* attacked the Pillsbury Bake-Off for now favoring contestants who used convenience foods rather than cooking from scratch; by downgrading older folk recipes, a male-run corporation was wresting power and skill away from women—hence the article's title, "The Rape of Edible Food." The image of violent invasion seemed especially fitting in discussions of food pollution: e.g., cyclamates in fetal chromosomes, DES (a growth hormone used to fatten cattle) in breast tissue, and DDT in mothers' milk. For the feminist press, the long delay in studying and banning DDT was a grim object lesson in the "male-feasance" of a single government-agribusiness-medical establishment. Observing that "the amount of DDT in the breast milk of some mothers tested in the U.S.A. exceeded the limit set by the federal government for DDT in milk for sale," Washington, D.C.'s *off our backs* ran a cartoon of a woman squirting a bothersome fly with breast milk.[13]

NATURAL VS. PLASTIC

Feminist or not, underground advisors distrusted all chemicals. Sometimes the case was as ideological as it was scientific, for few empirical studies had been done. While the toxicological case against DDT was overpowering by 1969—Rachel Carson having broken that ground back in 1962—the scientific jury was still out on most pesticides and additives, and it might never come in. Given the difficulty of testing thousands of food chemicals both as single toxins and in combinations, could anyone prove conclusively what caused cancer and what did not? But despite the still-sketchy evidence, it simply made sense that a sick society would produce carcinogenic food. And since modernity itself seemed the cause of cancer, the prevention seemed equally clear: Think primitive. Avoid anything complex, anything you can't pronounce, anything chemical, synthetic, or plastic.

Of all the adjectives applied to mainstream, processed foods, "plastic" may have been the most apt, for it was both a realistic description of the direction of food technology and a powerful metaphor for the direction of "straight" society. As a realistic label, plastic did describe the decorating and packaging materials predominating in supermarkets and fast-food restaurants. It also suggested links between various elements of the food-military-industrial complex: e.g., pesticides—plastic bags—napalm. Also, the same principles that guided the manufacture of plastic materials were beginning to be used in the food industry. Before World War II food processing was relatively simple and mechanical: e.g., breaking down wheat kernels into still identifiable flour, germ, and chaff or vacuum sealing vegetables in tin cans. But after the war, food technologists began to go much further, breaking raw grains down to their basic molecular structure and reassembling them into foods that bore no resemblance to the raw materials out of which they were fabricated. Prewar margarine and vegetable oils were harbingers of the fabricated wonders to come: Tang, Carnation Instant Breakfast, Pringles, instant puddings and pie fillings, non-dairy creamers, meat analogs spun from "textured vegetable pro-

37

teins." As radical biochemist Ross Hume Hall wrote in *Food for Nought* (1974), food chemists were only just beginning to apply rheology, the study of the "deformation and flow of materials"— the basis of plastics technology. Once mastered, rheology would enable engineers to turn almost any raw material into almost any shape and taste. The age of truly plastic food seemed close at hand.[14]

Defined as "impressionable, easily influenced, malleable," plastic was even more distressing as a symbol of mainstream culture. While plastics had been viewed somewhat ambivalently by the camp-mod subculture of the mid-sixties, by 1968, the year of *The Graduate*, the word was negative. Millions of young people shared Dustin Hoffman's disgust when advised to consider plastics as a career. To his would-be benefactor, the word had a nice high-technology sound. In mainstream ideology, petrochemical processing and manufacturing was one of the "clean," "postindustrial" growth sectors. No more grimy, back-breaking, blue-collar work. To Hoffman's peers, however, plastics suggested the false, saccharine, stagnant life of the much-despised Organization Man, a spineless bureaucrat molded into accommodating shapes by the lever pullers above.[15]

Similarly, "plastic" supermarket food fit a few standardized models—usually with the aid of genetic selection, chemical additives, and glitzy packaging. Sunkist oranges were always a particular orange, red Delicious apples always a certain red, Del Monte canned corn a specific yellow. Waxed cucumbers were always hard, dark green, and the same length, while prematurely picked and gassed tomatoes stayed firm and red for weeks. Oblivious to seasonal or regional variation, iceberg lettuce traveled from California to Rochester without losing a leaf, perhaps crossing paths with cod trucking from Gloucester to Kansas City. Engineered to defy decay, Ritz Crackers were always crisp, colas eternally bubbly, donuts ever gooey, canned peaches invariably cling. Conjuring up the Huxleyan vision of totalitarian stability, chemically preserved, cellophane-wrapped plastic food neither lived nor died; it simply occupied shelf space and generated corporate profits.

Lifeless plastic food also imposed grave environmental costs. Urging freaks to use brown paper bags, one underground cookbook writer argued, "A cellophane bag represents 5,000 years of machine history, inventors suicided by their inventions, eons of garbage dedication, paid for in cancerous wombs, in fallen cocks, in the crazy waste of our fathers." The plastic culture was on the move, and freaks invoked sympathetic magic to ward it off. You are what you eat; if you don't want to be turned into "nonbiodegradable people," don't eat plastic food.[16]

Plastic food caused sickness; natural food meant health, though definitions of natural and healthy were, of course, open to debate. If, as Susan Sontag suggests, illness often symbolizes what's wrong with a society, natural could be invoked to represent what's right with a society—or what it should be like. Given the high ideological stakes involved in the term, natural was a contested terrain, used by both defenders and critics of the food system. The great food debates of the 1960s and 1970s involved contrasting definitions of nature, one from the Enlightenment, the other romantic. To the former, nature was a realm of rational laws and exploitable resources which could be controlled for entrepreneurial gain; all earth resources—including petrochemicals—were "natural"; Wonder Bread and cellophane were as natural as brown rice and tree bark. To the romantic, however, nature resisted human manipulation. The greater the human control and design, the more artificial or plastic; the freer from rational involvement, the more natural.[17] A basic rule for romantic naturalists, then, was to eat "lower down the food chain." The closer to the original source of the food, the better, for it was less likely to have been fouled by human intervention. Celebrating the untamed, some romantics advocated eating just wild fruits, weeds, and herbs— hence the revival of Euell Gibbons's fortunes.

Taking a more pragmatic approach, most advisors moved up the food chain a bit. The ideal was to balance the needs of convenience (some human intervention did increase food yields and save time) and the needs of safety (avoid damage to oneself and the environment). Many thus drew the line not at manipulation per se, or even at mechanical refining, but at chemical involvement. Essentially this meant turning the clock back not to the Stone Age (as some industry defenders scoffed) but rather about forty or fifty years, before petrochemicals had entered the food chain in signifi- 39 cant quantities. Wheat could be planted, tended, harvested, ground (preferably by stones), kneaded, and baked, but no chemical pesticides, fertilizers, or additives should be used along the way. Most agreed that the safest foods were those you grew, raised, and prepared yourself, since you could personally control the inputs. If you didn't have an outside garden, you could at least sprout alfalfa seeds and mung beans in the kitchen. Pinpointing the status of animals in the food chain proved difficult, however. Some refused to eat any animal products, including milk and eggs; others accepted dairy products but drew the line at meat, preferring to eat the feed grains and soybeans before they entered the animals' mouths. Some did consume flesh of domesticated animals, but only if they had been raised without the chemical hormones, antibiotics, and other drugs fed to modern livestock.

As for other store-bought foods, two guidelines proved handy: Don't eat anything you can't pronounce (i.e., no propylene glycol alginate, a stabilizer used in bottled salad dressing) and if worms, yeast, and bacteria grew on it, then it must be natural, for no self-respecting bug would eat plastic. Inverting established notions of spoilage, the countercuisine equated preservatives with contamination and microbes with health. Decay was healthy; the more biodegradable, the better. Many core foods incorporated "friendly" contaminants: brewer's yeast, acidophilus milk, kefir, soy sauce, miso, tempeh. Homemade breads, beer, and yogurt enlisted benevolent "germs," and gardeners put garbage in compost piles, not plastic bags. Strong-smelling cheeses seemed preferable to tasteless and odorless American. Natural warmth was welcomed as an ally of natural decomposition. While mainstream culture insisted on chilling almost everything not preserved with chemicals or cellophane, natural food stores, co-ops, and hip restaurants commonly scorned energy-wasting air conditioning and refrigeration. Just as some in the counterculture swore off deodorants, they were not afraid of the natural odors that came with heat.

Beyond defining the content of food, natural was a liberated state of mind, a symbol of opposition to mass production, efficiency, rationalization, limits. Supermarket names honored security, centralization, and homogenization: Safeway, Grand Union, Giant, A&P. Natural food stores seemed to value diversity, variability, eccentricity: Cornucopia, Back to Eden, Land of Plenty, Erewhon. While Safeway carried just two or three brands of canned baked beans (of unknown variety), Vital Vittles offered sacks of adukis, garbanzos, pintos, black beans, soybeans, mung beans, Great Northerns, and the like. In addition to white and brown rice, the People's Grainery stocked buckwheat, millet, couscous, bulgur, unpearled barley, and rye berries. Even the more processed products at natural food stores had eccentric character that mass marketers, in their search for the lowest common denominator,

40

could not afford: Carque's Creamed Papaya or Apricot Mango Juice, Queen Helene's Cucumber Beauty Creme and Mint Julep Masque, New Pacific's Gotu-Kola and Ginseng Tea. Similarly, at some hip restaurants of the early 1970s, naturalness meant a wildly eclectic assortment of dishes, decorations, costumes, and props. Praising San Francisco's "free form" natural foods restaurants, the *Underground Gourmet* saw a "revolt against a plastic, money-centered, soulless culture and all its trappings." Aesthetically, natural offered adventure, surprise, rich diversity—all in contrast to what Raymond Mungo called the "shallow" America of "frozen food and better ketchup bottles and lousy theater and boredom, boredom." [18]

Yet, paradoxically, even as it seemed to offer a cornucopia of options, natural could also stand for simplicity, humility, lack of pretension, a healthy lack of self-consciousness or sophistication. Even as they disdained the plastic security of supermarkets, freaks sought the time-tested security of enduring, "honest" natural foods. Thus, at some natural food restaurants of the plain, Shaker-esque variety, patrons were offered just one or two simple dishes —usually casseroles—which they ate at spare oak tables, as if in a monastery.

Although defenders of mainstream cuisine liked to point out how ill-defined, indeed contradictory, the concept of natural could be, within the countercuisine the adjective was attractive precisely because it was so expandable. Basically, natural had three reference points: content, time, and attitude. Applied to content, natural food lacked certain ingredients and qualities: preservatives, pesticides, chemicals, packaging. Applied to time, it suggested old-fashioned cooking, whether homespun American, European immigrant, or Third World—anything not postwar suburban, standardized, too convenient or too sophisticated. As a state of mind, it suggested an enchantment with anything that was not too rationalized, predictable, standardized. In all, natural seemed a useful oppositional category because it was defined by what it was not.

41

But negation was a means, not an end. By clearing their minds and bodies of all that was modern and artificial, radical naturalists hoped to start again. Returning to the primitive was a necessary first step, not just an escape. Urging the use of natural materials like wooden chopsticks and reed baskets, *Good Times*'s Wind-catcher defined "primitive" not as "immaturity" but as a necessary prerequisite: "primitive in the best sense of the word, 'primal,' not backward, first, not last." Similarly, in *Getting Back Together*, one of the first sympathetic treatments of the hip back-to-the-land movement, Robert Houriet argued that the retreat to preindustrial roots was but the "first lap in a long journey." After backing out of the "cul-de-sac" of recent history, Houriet argued, hip naturalists "would again move forward, very slowly, careful not to take the wrong turn and keeping to the main road and to the central spirit and consciousness that modern man has lost along the way." Out of the negation process would hopefully come more positive models for rebuilding self and society.[19]

3 RADICAL THERAPY: THE OPPOSITIONAL IDENTITY

The counterculture went natural not only for survival but also for fulfillment. Dietary primitivism would purge and protect you, but it would also make you well—even happy. Like most young leftists, ecofreaks saw no reason why radicalism could not be enjoyable. Like most bohemians, they rejected deferred gratification. What kind of new society could come out of joyless self-denial? The charm—and fragility—of the insurgency was that it honestly believed (or hoped) that you could survive Armageddon, start all over, *and* have fun along the way.

Part of the fun came in romantically relishing the paradoxes.[1] Natural foods were safer *and* tastier; wild greens were hardscrabble staples *and* gourmet treats. Ethnic foods were cheap *and* rich. Vegetarianism seemed ecologically *and* spiritually sound. Exercise and dieting made you a better street fighter *and* lover. Fasting confronted the system *and* made you high. Hip food stores peddled both radical tracts *and* facial creams, wilderness survival manuals *and* aphrodisiac teas. Organic gardening was a medium for self-discovery *and* social integration.

As dour intellectuals lamented, hip vocabulary seemed more than a bit vague, inconsistent, and disconnected—and it often was. When applied to underground cuisine, however, the words had a tangible context and internal coherence. A cuisine consists of a distinct set of core foods and seasonings, preparation techniques, and dining etiquette. Every society derives its cuisine (and culture) out of a much wider range of options. The human race as a whole is omnivorous, but individual societies are picky. By categorizing foods into what's good to eat and what is not, a cuisine helps a society's members define themselves: To eat appropriate foods is to participate in a particular group; eat inappropriate foods and you're an outsider. Like language, a cuisine is a medium by which a society establishes its special identity.[2]

Deviant subcultures are especially dependent on such oppositional language.[3] Reflecting the polarization of the period, the countercuisine offered rebels a rich vocabulary of clear contrasts, e.g., "natural" vs. "plastic." While these polarities had important nutritional implications, the symbolic aspects were initially more interesting. Indeed, only later, after their serendipitous experiences in the kitchen, did some participants turn for theoretical confirmation to the lab and library—as if in fulfillment of the Diggers' hope that subversive theories of economics would follow the social facts of countercultural life.

IMPROVISATION VS. SPECIALIZATION

Paradoxically, the first rule was to improvise. Even as they offered recipes and advice, underground food advisors consistently undercut their own authority by urging readers to experiment. One enduring goal of the 1960s was to upset the rule of "experts." "Deprofessionalization" would return power and dignity to the grass roots, giving ordinary people a sense of worth and importance. Throwing away the few reigning cookbooks and conventional wisdoms, freaks adopted an "anything goes" approach to food.[4]

Drug experiences no doubt reinforced such experimentation. Like the bohemian experience in general, psychedelics simulated a childlike state in which you nibbled here, picked there, sometimes with your hands, and otherwise played with your food. Ita Jones found it easy to add food to the delightful "kaleidoscope of things" rediscovered in hallucinogenic explorations. After detailing the recipe for "Venezuelan head food"—a hash of red peppers, onions, raisins, squash, and noodles—Jeanie Darlington advised, "Cook it straight and eat it stoned, because that's what it's made for." In acid trip's "white light," all connections were valid, all taboos arbitrary. If acid could go in Kool-Aid and marijuana could go into just about anything, why *not* put onions and oranges in the same salad, garlic and zucchini in pancakes, peanut butter in ice cream? It was no coincidence that some of today's superpremium ice cream moguls started out as hip restaurateurs serving zonked customers attuned to strange blends of thick fresh cream, tropical fruits, and crushed candy bars.[5]

National cuisines were mixed and matched without concern for international boundaries or incongruities: bologna knish enchiladas or Irish-Jewish stew. Compiling "unusual combinations flavored with a free hand by stoned culinary adventurers," Lucy Horton's *Country Commune Cooking* (1972) adapted recipes from Tibet, the Ukraine, Hungary, Denmark, Mexico, India, none anthropologically precise—but who cared? Ecologically one-worldish, Horton's recipes leaped continents within a single dish: for example, Sweet and Sour Spaghetti Sauce (from High Lodge Farm, Oregon), Torgerson's Mexican-Italian Blintzes (Crow Farm, Oregon), Armenian Polenta (Morning Star Ranch, California).[6]

Mystical religions and living theater also encouraged trust in intuition. The California-Buddhist authors of *Tassajara Cooking* likened food preparation to the satori-inducing experiences of Zen archery and tea service: zap! something you just *did*. "The way to be a cook is to cook." Don't try to achieve some prescribed standard; just pick up some tools and vegetables and get started.[7] Like the Diggers' Free Store, hip groceries and restaurants were full of props and improvisational possibilities. Recipes were scripts that could be altered at will.

Sometimes dabbling could lead to important results. Thus Frances Moore Lappé dated her food activist career from her recombinant trials in the late 1960s. Discouraged by the antiwar movement and her futile social work job, Lappé turned in 1969 to ecology. As her friends began to go natural, Lappé started playing with all sorts of peculiar foods like tofu, mung beans, bulgur, soy grits, and buckwheat groats. "I remember devouring my first 'natural foods' cookbook as if it were a novel. Barley, mushrooms, and dill together? Cheddar cheese, walnuts, and rice? How odd. What

45

would that taste like?" The new combinations restored a sense of intentionality and contact—key therapeutic goals—to what had previously seemed humdrum chores. "As new types of combinations became more attractive, shopping for food and cooking was no longer unconscious and boring, but a real adventure." As culinary barriers broke down, so did other assumptions. Lappé began to question conventional wisdoms about nutrition and world hunger. At the Berkeley agricultural library, Lappé read about the vast amount of acreage devoted to growing feed grains for livestock: half of our harvested land was planted with feed crops; 78 percent of our grain was fed to animals. Assuming that meat was the best source of protein, most Americans accepted this allocation of resources. Yet Lappé also encountered the theory of protein complementarity: by creatively combining beans, seeds, grains, and dairy products, one could easily meet daily protein needs without resorting to ecologically wasteful meat. There was thus theoretical underpinning for all this seemingly random mixing and matching. Zap! Lappé's career as a food activist was off and running! Her *Diet for a Small Planet* (1971), with its mix of recipes and analysis, typified radicals' faith in the ability to combine personal therapy with political activism.[8]

PROCESS, NOT PRODUCT

Although many of the experiments no doubt wound up in the garbage can—or compost heap—this was not necessarily seen as failure, for the countercuisine stressed process over product. It was more important how you got there—what you learned along the way—than what you actually wound up with. The True Light Beavers' commune cookbook *Eat, Fast, Feast* was "not a book, but a process." *Tassajara Cooking* was "a cooking book, not a cookbook." In her column, "'Bread Bakin': A Garden of Kneadin'," *Northwest Passage*'s "mother bird" gently advised, "Don't be discouraged by a few bricks, or even a lot of bricks—they're all building blocks."[9] Clearly, in Lappé's case the building process *was* productive, but such happy endings were not always so obvious—or even important.

It was in their abuse of the process, in fact, that most manufacturers went astray. Little consideration was paid to how food was grown, manufactured, or distributed. The welfare of farmers,

46

migrant workers, animals, slaughterhouse workers, and supermarket clerks mattered little. All that counted was that it got to the consumer, who had no connection to or responsibility for those in the food chain who sustained him.

Nutritionists collaborated with food technologists by analyzing foods into molecular components that could be rearranged to suit the processors' convenience. Since all that mattered was that the body somehow got its "recommended daily allowance" of basic chemicals, it really did not matter if vitamins and minerals were sprayed on shelf-stable wheat flakes or if sugar and artificial flavors were added to otherwise tasteless fruit preserves. Some nutritionists even boasted of their indifference to the aesthetics of food; taste, color, and appearance were relevant only to the extent that they fooled the mouth into ingesting the daily dose of nutrients. "Plastic" foods were consummately efficient, malleable, convenient—and biochemically "adequate" according to the prevailing nutritional paradigm.[10]

Such exaggerated attention to end over means offended the holistically minded. Thus, mother bird opened her bread column with a much-used quote from Khalil Gibran: "If a man bakes bread with indifference, he bakes a bitter loaf that feeds but half his hunger." Mass-produced, processed food encouraged alienation from nature, society, one's own body. Unfortunately, most consumers seemed to collaborate in their own alienation. "They are content to swallow 'enriched' foods as a substitute for real nutrition, much as a robot might be content to practice artificial insemination," *Quicksilver Times*'s food writer observed. Ita Jones agreed. Anesthetized by the system, Americans ate "as though the object of eating is to fill a pink box called the stomach."[11]

To overcome such alienation and interact with Mother Nature, you had to become fully conscious of every step of the preparation, each ingredient. If the recipes were traditional, you also communed with the past. Like music, sex, and drugs, food was to be shared as a medium of "communication," the counterculture's favorite process-oriented word. The Haight's flower children frequently offered strangers food on the street—an act of "propitiation" that sociologist Helen Perry likened to the practices of primitive people. Similarly, Diggers used food to bind and educate the hip community. In gloomy 1969 one of Diane DiPrima's "revolutionary letters" suggested that the act of sharing food in countercultural gatherings was in itself a healing and subversive act:

47

but don't get uptight, the guns
will not win this one; they are
an incidental part of the action
which we better damn well be good at
what will win
is mantras, the sustenance we give each other
the energy we plug into
(the fact that we touch
share food)
the buddha nature
of everyone, friend and foe, like a million earthworms
tunneling under the structure
till it falls.

Appropriately, *The Last Whole Earth Catalog* put all its food-related entries in its Community section as central to the group-fostering process. Get good cooking equipment for your "cell," editor Stewart Brand observed, for "the best way to attract and keep good people is with outstanding food." [12]

BROWN VS. WHITE

White vs. brown was a central contrast. For *Quicksilver Times*, underground nutrition could be easily capsulized in the admonition: "Don't eat white; eat right; and fight." Whiteness meant Wonder Bread, White Tower, Cool Whip, Minute Rice, instant mashed potatoes, peeled apples, White Tornadoes, white coats, white collar, whitewash, White House, white racism. Brown meant whole wheat bread, unhulled rice, turbinado sugar, wildflower honey, unsulfured molasses, soy sauce, peasant yams, "black is beautiful." Darkness was funky, earthy, authentic, while whiteness, the color of powerful detergents, suggested fear of contamination and disorder. "Only in Amerika," *Quicksilver Times* observed (incorrectly), "could people want their food *bleached* before they eat it. Flour, sugar, rice—all bleached to match the bleached-out mentality of white supremacy." Unlike flabby, devitalized Tastee Bread or Minute Rice, brown breads and rice offered resistance to teeth and digestive tract. White foods were preprocessed, but dark foods left the processing to you. Later research would corroborate the physiological benefits of fiber, but in the sixties, the payoff seemed more immediately sensual: a rush of energy that came from sustained chewing of tougher, sturdier, hardier food.[13]

Whiteness meant blandness. The two main seasonings of white middle-class culture were white salt and sugar, with white saccharin making gains along with the other white powders that went into plastic foods and their wrappers. Spices were generally abhorred, other than perhaps a dash of pepper. But the counter-cuisine favored powerfully dark spices: soy sauce, miso, molasses, curries, chilies. About the only white flavorings used were garlic and onions—sources of terror to the WASP middle class—and yogurt, whose bitterness cut against the mainstream's sweet cream sauces and mayonnaise.[14] Pale, insipid lager beers gave way to darker, frequently homemade ales, bitters, and stouts. Alternative stores sold brown eggs, dark whole wheat noodles, mud-colored unpasteurized apple cider, and a variety of products wrapped in brown paper.

The early countercuisine paid a lot of attention to white and dark breads because bread was a staple—the proverbial staff of life, hip slang for currency, and, in its white form, a longtime symbol of all that seemed banal and mass in Western culture. For Theodore Roszak, who popularized the word "counterculture" in his 1969 best-seller, white bread was a perfect metaphor for the regime of experts and technocrats who, for the sake of efficiency and order, threatened to rob us of all effort, thought, and independence. "Not only do they provide bread aplenty, but the bread is as soft as floss; it takes no effort to chew, and yet it is vitamin-enriched." Linking plastic food to totalitarian control, an ad for *Good Times* listed white bread as a "dangerous drug"—along with work, property, television, and money: "This and similar nonprescription drugs are gobbled almost unconsciously by drug users at nearly every stage of their addiction. Runs down the body and adds to addict's general misery. Psychologically addicting. Signs: general weakness and lack of vitality; 'faded' appearance."[15]   49

Wonder Bread came in for special attack, partly because, having been billed as a builder of strong bodies in "eight ways," it was the best-selling brand. Also, the Orwellian name itself tickled the stoned and invited analogy. The manufacture of this first cousin to the Twinkie aptly symbolized the white flight of the 1950s and 1960s. To make clean bread, ITT's bakers removed all colored ingredients (segregation), bleached the remaining flour (suburban school socialization), and then, to prevent discoloring decay, added strong preservatives and stabilizers (law enforcement). Brown breads had shorter life spans, but at their peak seemed suffused with innate character. The color contrast externalized white radicals' estrangement from sanitized suburban life.

Baking brown bread nicely balanced the personal and the political—a craft and a statement, a first step toward self-reliance. Appropriately, one of the first hip best-sellers was Edward Espe Brown's *Tassajara Bread Book* (1970), which sold 400,000 copies. According to Brown, bread baking was a "ripening, maturing, baking, blossoming *process*." After mastering bread, hip cooks moved on to the *Tassajara Cooking Book* (1973)—and main courses. Similarly, when Carol Flinders apprenticed herself to Laurel Robertson, her first real challenge was to bake bread. For Laurel, bread was the ultimate life food because it was in fact the product of a living process of fermentation; the dough "seemed to come alive in her hands." Bread baking was thus a ritualistic affirmation of membership in a subculture that viewed itself in direct opposition to the plastic death culture.[16]

SLOW FOODS VS. FAST FOODS: CRAFT VS. CONVENIENCE

B aking bread took a lot of time, but that was the point. After first tasting a homebaked loaf, Ita Jones *had* to bake her own, even if it took a whole afternoon—indeed, precisely because it took a whole afternoon. "There's no return to the days when I thought that three cluttered hours were preferable to three, long, calm, warm fragrant ones."[17]

It is a mark of the modern mind to complain that life is moving too fast. Throughout the nineteenth century food reformers struggled against food "bolting" as an unhealthy symptom of urban-industrial acceleration. In the late 1960s the pace seemed especially fast to the young for whom one stressful year could seem like ten. Moreover, as amphetamines became more popular, the phrase "speed kills" had special meaning in the drug culture. Food writers linked this fear of uncontrolled momentum—"bad trips" —with the food they despised. Thus, the Red Yogis Collective likened "shit food" laden with predigested white sugar and white

50

flour to white powdery drugs like speed and junk: "Easy to cop, quick to fix, satisfies your craving for awhile, and destroys your body." Cooking soybeans on the other hand took almost forever. Infant formulas—white powders—were easy to prepare, but these too became addictive drugs—children's introduction to a lifetime's dependence on sugary convenience foods. On the other hand, time-consuming breast feeding was, for Jeanie Darlington, a natural high, "a beautiful, organic experience . . . a feeling of cosmic exchange." Wooden chopsticks took time to master and prevented bolting. "Eating with sticks teaches us to caress food in small enough doses to notice and appreciate a meal," Windcatcher observed. "Metal utensils are simply instruments for shoveling food into our mouths." For "alicia bay laurel," author of the best-selling manual *Living on the Earth*, eating slowly heightened bodily awareness: "To find your own perfect diet, eat very slowly and chew each mouthful as many times as you can. Feel the effects of each food on your stomach, intestines, and throughout your body." Such advice recalled progressive era dietary reformer Horace Fletcher—except that, in true progressive spirit, Fletcher had seen slow mastication as the most rational, efficient way to eat, while for alicia, it was a form of Buddhist meditation and a surrogate for drug-induced self-discovery.[18]

Gardening too had a calming, decelerating appeal. Stephen Gaskin—who led a convoy of Haight refugees to The Farm, a large and enduring Tennessee commune—wrote a short aphorism titled "How to Slow Down": "Find a little bit of land somewhere and plant a carrot seed. Now sit down and watch it grow. When it is fully grown pull it up and eat it." Labor-intensive organic techniques took more time than conventional chemicals, which "put your soil on a speed trip," according to Jeanie Darlington. By taking time to build up compost, cultivate earthworms, handpick predatory insects, you became "part of the living process."[19]

Slowing down could have subversive economic consequences as well, for the prevailing insistence on speed was the very basis of the processed foods business. Slicing, chopping, dicing, pureeing, mincing, pounding, cutting, stewing, fermenting—all this could be done in the kitchen or, for a fee, in the factory ahead of time— part of the bargain by which harried consumers bought minutes from processors. The deal was costly to both budget and health. One reason why refined foods had so much sugar and salt was that natural flavors had been sacrificed for the sake of speedy prepara-

51

tion. Presliced bread may have been, as the cliché went, one of the world's wonders, but at what cost to the palate? For the sake of a few minutes, instant oatmeal was more expensive and less nutritious than the less refined flakes. Moreover, to the mechanical ways of speeding up food production, agribusiness had added a new dimension of chemical acceleration. Speedy agrichemicals damaged soil, water, and, possibly, human health. In the kitchen, instant breakfast bars, stove-top stuffing mixes, TV dinners, imitation juice drinks, and toaster-ready waffles took seconds to prepare, but their ingredients resembled paint formulas. In contents and manner of consumption, these products were virtually indistinguishable from the snacks that were, because of all the packaging and assorted "value added," the processors' major profit area. To Carol Flinders of *Laurel's Kitchen*, the fetish of speed made the home irrelevant. " 'Household' is hardly the word—at this point, when the emphasis falls increasingly on speedy refueling and immediate departure, 'pit stop' might be closer to the truth." The autoracing analogy applied especially well to the roadside fast-food restaurant, with its roots in the disreputable drive-in of the 1950s.[20]

Against this backdrop, writers of the countercuisine called for a deliberate slowdown. For sustained contact with nature, take time to pick your own produce, clean your own chicken, shell your own nuts. At the co-op, weigh and bag your own beans and grains. Instead of the bogus warmth of a can of Campbell's soup—that camp symbol of the 1960s—take time to make soup from scratch. Can your own tomatoes, pickles, preserves. Instead of heating a frozen dinner in a toaster oven, simmer lentil stew in an old-fashioned cast-iron kettle over the stove—preferably of the labor-intensive wood-burning kind.

In confronting the time question, the countercuisine touched an inflamed nerve; the middle class has always worried about the acceleration wrought in large part by their own industriousness and entrepreneurship. As Pierre Bourdieu notes in *Distinction*, the bourgeoisie has long envied the aristocrat's power over time, that upper-class ability to carry on affairs with a sense of complete detachment, civility, ease. To an extent, the bohemian's historic function has been to explore low-cost routes to that upper-class control of time.[21]

Moreover, consumers themselves have sometimes hesitated to sacrifice craftsmanship for efficiency. In the mid-nineteenth century some cooks questioned whether food cooked in timesaving

52

cast-iron stoves tasted as good as the old fireplace-roasted variety; as late as the 1890s, middle-class housewives regarded baker's bread as immoral and "poorfolksy." More recently, immigrant mothers might criticize "lazy" daughters-in-law who fed sons "from a can" or from the freezer. One-stop, self-service chain stores came under attack in the 1920s and 1930s, because they undermined friendly Mama-Papa groceries, just as fast-food chains had to fend off zoning restrictions in the 1950s. Every new gadget has had to run the gauntlet of humor magazines, stand-up comics, ad parodies, and other forms of ritualized ridicule. Furthermore, as Ruth Schwartz Cowan argues in *More Work for Mother*, the very persistence of the home appliance testifies to the reluctance of Americans to surrender completely to centralized production and processing. If convenience were the sole determinant of market behavior, middle-class Americans might eat out all the time or have meals home delivered from commercial kitchens rather than insist on processing food at home—even if only from freezer to micro-wave. In other words, the enduring cult of the private home reflects continued ambivalence about modernization.[22]

But the fact is that, for the most part, Americans have accepted the ideology of convenience, with its aura of liberation, freedom, and choice—some of it grounded in historical experience. Few familiar with the chores of the typical nineteenth-century housewife would doubt that the transition from wood to gas or electric stove was worth making. Still, as Cowan's title suggests, it is possible that many "laborsaving" appliances introduced since the 1920s have made as much work for women as they have saved. Before automatic washing machines, clothes simply stayed dirtier; ditto for rugs and upholstery before vacuum cleaners. But consumers' expectations were raised and there was no going back. Moreover, they liked the technological spectacle. Faced with the trade-off between craft satisfactions and push-button, prewrapped wizardry, consumers generally chose the latter, and the challenge of marketing has been, through creative use of nostalgic themes, to ease the guilt that consumers feel in making the bargain.[23]   53

The countercuisine too sensed the craft-convenience trade-offs. There were times when large batches of portable food needed to be prepared quickly and efficiently. A pressure cooker did save time cooking beans. With a blender, busy students and activists could make nutritious, easily transportable smoothies. Some even defended that ultimate convenience item, the food stamp. Did food stamps release time for "the revolution" or co-opt freaks into "the system"?

Feminists debated whether the priority of craft over convenience was sexist, for women did most of the cooking. On the one hand, rejecting convenience products reasserted female competence and control, much as the revival of midwifery, witchcraft, and other forms of folk self-health was a feminist defense against modern medical patriarchy. On the other hand, cooking without packaged aids and appliances was more work, especially if you were not used to going primitive. There was, moreover, a regressive tone in some of the cookbooks extolling premodern housewifery. The chapter in *Laurel's Kitchen* entitled "The Keeper of the Keys" sounded strikingly Victorian, with its praise of women's traditional role as gatekeeper and spiritual paragon—the person whose inherent cooperativeness and "nurturant impulse" made her best suited to lead the ecological, social, and moral reform that America so desperately needed. Some of this time-consuming work could seem boring or tedious, Flinders allowed, especially for working women who were too rushed to appreciate household craftsmanship. If this required that women reexamine their commitment to business or professional careers, so be it—an uncomfortably conservative critique of the two-career family model that was coming to dominate mainstream middle-class life.[24]

In all, the craft mystique was simultaneously one of the countercuisine's enduring charms and one of its chief obstacles to widespread acceptance. As we will see, overcoming the craft-convenience conflict would be one of the major marketing challenges of the following decade.

VEGETABLE VS. ANIMAL

Sooner or later, every oppositional cuisine confronts the meat question. In the late 1960s this was no small undertaking. If it was hard to give up convenience, the determinant technique in American cuisine, it was doubly hard to give up meat, the core staple. Americans ate about 121.7 pounds of red meat per person a year in 1930 and about 160 pounds in 1970; the greatest gains had been in beef consumption, which rose from 38 pounds a year per person in 1930 to 90 pounds in 1970. Two factors contributed to the gains in beef: the lower cost that came after World War II from feeding America's chemically stimulated grain surplus to cattle and the spread of burger-based fast-food restaurants. The virtually unique availability of cheap, grain-fed beef was a central component of the American ideology of abundance. Vegetables, on the other hand, had a distinctly subordinate role—decorative, supplementary, certainly not sufficient. The basic structure of the American dinner plate was set as early as the colonial period, according to nutritional anthropologist Norge Jerome: "animal meat forming the centerpiece and embroidered with fruits, vegetables, grain products, dairy products, legumes, sweetmeats, sugar, and alcohol." And the soybean—well, it might be fit for animals and Orientals, but certainly not for Americans! [25]

To turn all this around was indeed an ambitious task, and even the countercuisine was uncertain about the wisdom or viability of doing so. Many tried giving up meat, but since the reasons for doing so were ideological, not traditionally religious or even physiological, it was easy to lapse. At first few worried about cholesterol, fat, or animal antibiotics—or animal welfare either. [26] Confronting meat eating was part of the consciousness-raising process, a bit like taking a course, and even those who remained committed to meat felt compelled to attend classes and take the exams.

Pursuing the holistic search for connections, some first tried macrobiotics, a complex Japanese import that was, in the late sixties, only poorly understood. By the late 1970s macrobiotics would earn grudging respect as a viable therapy for certain types of cancer[27]; a decade earlier, however, its appeal lay largely in its ambitious unification of diet, Eastern religion, and a variety of academic disciplines, including psychology, physics, geography, and biochemistry. Literally translated as "large life," macrobiotics was as interdisciplinary and paradigmatic as ecology, for it offered both a comprehensive world view and a program for individual action—with a healthy vegetarian diet as the key link. [28]

Drawing on Taoist thought, macrobiotics divided not just foods but all matter into yin-yang categories. Health—i.e., wholeness—came by reconciling these opposites. To find the right balance, one had to understand the larger environment. This became complicated, for the precise ratio of yin and yang forces bearing down on, say, a twenty-year-old white Christian male in Berkeley, California, was different from the ratio affecting a forty-eight-year-old black Muslim female in Kaduna, Nigeria. Macrobiotics was thus considerably more personalized than conventional

55

dietetics, which tended to reduce health to a statistically averaged standard of U.S. RDAs. Since the correct macrobiotic diet aligned individual need, environmental influences, and transcendent forces, getting there required systematic study and guidance.

Few new converts in the late 1960s got past the first stages, which involved simplifying one's sources of yin and yang foods to a few basic grains, beans, sauces, and vegetables. The word circulated that meat was "too yang," whatever that meant. Although macrobiotics advised eating locally grown and seasonally available foods, in the 1960s young converts gravitated toward brown rice and soy sauce. It was, after all, hard to find strictly localized foods in an economy based on nationalized distribution. Also, perhaps simplifying one's diet to a few "Oriental" staples symbolized solidarity with poor but spiritually strong Vietnamese peasants. The soybean was a particularly expressive oppositional staple for ecological reasons as well. As Peter Farb and George Armelagos have noted, eastern civilizations discovered early on that soy was well adapted to a society pressed by growing population, limited land, and scarce energy—the very opposite of the American core food, the burger, which took so much land and energy to produce and distribute. The cheap soybean was indeed a miraculously flexible bean. Soaked in water, it could be left to sprout into a nutrient-rich vegetable that could be eaten without any expenditure of energy; pureed, it could ferment on its own into soy sauce and miso. Simmered, it turned into curd (tofu). It could also be processed into oil and flour.[29]

Macrobiotics also offered a tidy reconciliation of opposites. If, as one popularizer put it, "everything is the differentiated manifestation of one infinity," then perhaps there was hope for brutally polarized America. Eventually, however, most found the yin-yang idea to be either impenetrable or simplistic.[30] The numerous misinterpretations in underground columns invited ridicule and backlash. Still, with its emphasis on integrating individual and environment, macrobiotics did serve as a congenial rest stop on the path to Frances Moore Lappé's more secular version of ecological vegetarianism.

An extension of a one-page handout that Lappé had circulated among her fellow improvisers in Berkeley, *Diet for a Small Planet* (1971) soon became *the* vegetarian text of the ecology movement, selling in the next ten years almost two million copies in three editions and six languages. The argument was straightforward and well-presented. By feeding vegetable protein (grain, soy) to animals rather than directly to humans, Americans were wasting scarce protein resources at a time when much of the world went hungry or had serious nutritional deficiencies. A grain-fed North American steer ate 21 pounds of vegetable protein for every pound of protein it delivered to the steak eater. This inefficient process required vast quantities of land, fertilizer, water, pesticides, and herbicides. An acre of land devoted to cereals for direct human consumption produced five times as much protein as an acre devoted to feedstuffs; an acre devoted to legumes was ten times as productive of protein, an acre of leafy vegetables, fifteen times as much protein. Conversely, if Americans ate the protein directly in grain and bean form, they would free up large amounts for redistribution elsewhere. Lappé calculated that of the 20 million tons of protein fed to U.S. livestock in 1968, only 2 million tons were retrieved for human consumption; 18 million tons were lost—90 percent of the yearly world protein deficit, enough to provide 12 grams of protein a day to every person in the world! To cap her case, Lappé showed that, popular beliefs notwithstanding, a vegetarian diet was nutritionally adequate because creative combinations of beans, nuts, grains, and dairy products would produce more than enough protein.[31]

The argument had been making the rounds in underground papers even before the book's publication in 1971. But Lappé was the first to put it down at length in a readable, accessible way. In characteristically countercultural style, she merged the political and the personal by combining economics and autobiography, consumerism and therapy, sober biochemistry and tasty recipes. Like most ecologists, she thought in terms of a single world system transcending petty national boundaries and of the interrelatedness of all species. A shopper's decision at the meat counter in Gary, Indiana, would affect food availability in Bombay, India. She understood well the counterculture's need for a language of inversion to overcome its sense of alienation and disbelief. Noting that most Americans ate far more protein than they really needed, Lappé asked who were the real "heads"—hip vegetarians or "respectable" meat eaters parasitically overdosing on protein? Pointing out that beef was a relatively recent addition to the human diet, Lappé questioned whether the real "faddists" were those who were now returning to timeless grains and legumes.

She also did not flinch from the subversive implications in her

57

program. Global economic interests were involved in America's meat-oriented diet, which was itself a reflection of a much larger "cultural pattern of waste." Even if Americans gave up meat, major changes in world distribution would be necessary to insure that feedgrains were released to the needy overseas. In later editions and other books, Lappé became even more explicit in her advocacy of worldwide revolution. At the same time, she seemed to back away from her original implication that eating soybeans and rice in America would feed the hungry in the Third World. Instead, she claimed that the Third World did not need American food, but could feed itself—if the existing economic and political order were overhauled. But Americans should still stop eating meat, partly to relieve the ecological and economic burden on American agriculture and partly to change their own ideas about food and politics. At the same time as she advocated radical political change, however, she also promised personal adventure, growth, and liberation through culinary adventure.[32]

The book also avoided the usual mystical prose. There was no mention of karma, yin, or yang. If meat was nutritionally dangerous, it was due to DDT, not "bad vibrations," in the fatty tissues. Much holistic literature relied on faith, not research. But in explaining protein complementarity, Lappé stuck to amino acids and NPU (net protein utilization): biochemistry, not meditation, showed that if you ate, say, soybeans and rice together in the same meal, you would gain more protein than if you ate them separately. The whole *did* total more than its parts, and Western science proved it![33]

Indeed, Lappé took pains to distance herself from her more spiritual comrades by claiming that she was not really a vegetarian (in the traditional sense of disdaining flesh). If meat weren't so ecologically wasteful to produce, she'd eat it; cattle and chickens raised economically on the open range were acceptable, though hard to find in this age of feedlots and chicken factories. She also accepted beef raised on a diet of urea, a nitrogen-containing compound derived from the animals' own urine—the wonders of recycling! In her insistence on efficiency she certainly did not sound like a stoned hippie.[34]

There was also a strong meat-eating strand in the countercuisine. In her tour of communal kitchens, Lucy Horton found that only half were vegetarian, and that most of those were in California, Lappé's territory. For many in the more Marxist East, the issue was strictly economic: if you had the money you ate meat, if you didn't, you resorted to beans and other substitutes. For these rationalists, vegetarianism smacked of extremism, holier-than-thou "purism," even fascism. Underground defenders of meat often pointed out (incorrectly) that Hitler was a vegetarian. Economic determinists noted that many in the Third World did eat meat if they could afford it, and it was possible to stretch meat cheaply in stews and curries.[35] As the ecological paradigm gained ground in the early 1970s, however, some meat eaters felt compelled to defend their habits, and in so doing, they invoked rationales similar to those of vegetarians.

For example, Ita Jones explored the meat issue in several of her *Liberation News Service* food columns, which were reissued by Random House as *The Grubbag* in 1971. Like Lappé, Jones believed in conscientious consumption, i.e., taking responsibility for the full implications of one's actions. The problem with modern diet was not its use of meat, but its alienation from death itself. By cleaning your own meat and fish, she argued, you could regain the more primitive sense of respect for basic life forces.

> *Sitting at the kitchen table yesterday, I cleaned and shelled a pound of fresh shrimp—the pink and white soft bodies stripped of the transparent flower-like shells, the gut system knifed out, the heads chopped off. I felt murderous, yet a calm feeling was settling like a snow on me. I didn't feel stranded from nature as I do when I open a box or can, and stare at the bloodless, diced, dried, powdered, unrecognizable "food" which permits us to look neither life nor death in the face.*[36]

Such determination induced some rural communards to attempt butchering their own meat. Reviewing an old manual for home butchering, *Last Whole Earth Catalog* editor Stewart Brand wrote, only half ironically: "One advantage of doing your own butchering, you get to thank the animal personally, and see him personally all the way through what you're doing together. There's nothing abstract about it." Some communes even ritualized the process. Guided by a USDA pamphlet, "Let's Butcher a Hog," one Pacific Coast community collected wood, built a huge fire, and paraded "Siegfried" to the slaughtering place. After much singing and chanting—and squealing by the recalcitrant Siegfried—the pig was reduced to elemental flesh, blood, and bones. Drinking a mix of homemade wine and Siegfried's blood, one stoned celebrant felt "energized and clear, disconnected and numb, fearless, and in touch with my inner self." [37]

Although there would seem to be extreme differences between the vegetarian and carnal wings of the countercuisine, in therapeutic and political terms, the ritual butchers were not so very far removed from Frances Moore Lappé. Both saw diet as a way to transform consciousness, to reintegrate mind and body, to overcome personal alienation, and to take social responsibility. Ecologically, a society where people had to slaughter and butcher their own meat would probably be a society where people ate less meat (and thereby wasted less protein—Lappé's concern) since it would take so much time, effort, and emotional energy to prepare. The problem with modern American society was that it was so easy to get meat—disembodied and prewrapped in plastic—so easy to forget the killing. The same disconnection had produced the Vietnam War, where politicians and their constituents could so blithely approve saturation bombing because they did not have to see the consequences. The modern fragmented mind had become anesthetized to death—and thus callous to life. Either response— whether avoiding flesh or drinking fresh blood—involved resensitizing, seeing connections, understanding whole systems.

Ultimately, however, neither extreme prevailed, in part because the philosophical purity of either was hard to maintain. Why stick to rice and beans in order to feed the hungry when it was clear that, if given a choice, most of the Third World preferred meat too (just as it liked white rice and breads)? Moreover, as Lappé herself wrote in the mid-seventies, it was not at all clear that growing less corn for hogs in Iowa would automatically put grain on the table in India. Since India could grow its own food, perhaps the hunger problem was India's, not ours. As for the humanitarian argument against flesh, wasn't it murder to eat a seed before it sprouted, to pull weeds or kill bugs that through no fault of theirs interfered with your own predatory needs or social conventions? Wasn't it inherently imperialistic to tame vegetable species? Were those who kept animals for dairy products so free from blame? Wasn't the domestication of animals similar to the subjugation of women in households? How could a vegetarian support abortion? On the other hand, weren't the blood-ritualists glorifying a sadomasochistic fantasy: a timeless "intimate experience," a sensuous indulgence of our "animal side"? When stoned communards chanted, "Kill the pig," as they slaughtered Siegfried, were they that different from Charles Manson's comrades shouting the same thing in Beverly Hills? Cultism aside, would inexperienced amateurs with knives really be more humane than slaughterhouse professionals with stun guns and buzz saws? [38]

In all, like so much in the early countercuisine, the meat debate was a learning process that illuminated but did not necessarily resolve basic conflicts.

ETHNIC VS. WASP

Before the late 1960s, vegetarian cookbooks suffered from terminal drabness, perhaps reflecting classic vegetarianism's puritanical edge—that ascetic drive to purge the mind of the taste not just for flesh, but for all sensual distractions. For Tolstoy and Gandhi the need for food in general, not just meat, was an annoying reminder of human frailty and imperfection. Typical of the precountercultural cookbooks was the Institute for Mentalphysis's spare but efficient *Food for Thought* (1954). Printed on undecorated white paper, the text presented simple, nutritious, tasteless dishes that might be prepared quickly between bouts of meditation. The names of the recipes were generic: cottage cheese patties, summer squash in sour cream, walnut-cheese loaf, squash-chestnut soup. Recipes were wholesome, relatively easy to prepare, and boring. The boredom factor was probably one reason why precountercultural "health food nuts" were branded as humorless fanatics. [39]

The design and tone of vegetarian guides changed in the early seventies, however. Printed on colorful thick paper, full of line drawings, calligraphy, occasional nudity, political analysis, and silly puns, *these* books were fun! And the recipes were ecologically and nutritionally correct, and usually ethnic, or at least ethnic inspired. 61 Thus, Frances Moore Lappé's *Diet for a Small Planet* had recipes for Roman Rice and Beans, Masala Dosai (Indian Filled Pancakes), Curried Rice, Sukiyaki, Enchiladas, and Brazilian Feijoada. True Light Beavers's *Eat, Fast, Feast* had recipes for meatless tzimmes, Colleen's Tacos, and Joan's Tabbuleh Salad. *Laurel's Kitchen* had Green Beans Hellenika, Greek Cauliflower, Ratatouille, and Chillaquillas (a Mexican egg dish). Anna Thomas's *Vegetarian Epicure* had numerous dishes with vinaigrette, curry, and chutney.[40]

To a small extent, these dishes reflected the wider neoethnic revival. Inspired—or repulsed—by Black Is Beautiful, white ethnics were reasserting an immigrant heritage that they had been all too ready to forget a decade before. In particular, second- and third-generation "core" ethnics—those who had objective, genealogical, historical ties to a specific land or region outside the United States—resented the angloconformity of Kraft, Campbell's, and Howard Johnson's. In 1972, *Commentary* writer Robert Alter chose food metaphors to convey his rejection of the "depersonalized face of the new corporate America." "The alternative to Little Italy or Little Warsaw, with their networks of close kinship and distinctive custom, is usually not the riches of individualism, but a fresh-frozen life in some prepackaged suburb, Howard Johnson's on Sundays, Disneyland vacations, the cut-rate American dream of happiness out of an aerosol can." Asserting pride in heritage, Michael Novak's "unmeltable ethnics" dusted off old-world recipes, rediscovered specialty stores in declining immigrant neighborhoods, and patronized restaurants and festivals that featured traditional dishes.[41]

While Alter and Novak sounded a bit like the countercultural critics of WASP cultural imperialism, the similarities were superficial. Unlike "hard hats" and "core ethnics," hippies were as interested in other people's heritage as in their own. Indeed, the more *other* the better. Moreover, Novak's neoethnicity was conservative, almost antiquarian, but in hip theater, ethnicity provided the props for the improvisational, liberationist performance. Freaks adapted ethnic recipes, but rarely copied them. Novak's ethnics sought to get out of the melting pot, while hip cooks were ready to throw almost anything (but WASP) into their oppositional stew.[42]

There was, however, some method to the apparent madness; the choice of ingredients was not entirely random. Urban hip/ student ghettos were frequently located in or near immigrant neighborhoods, with their ready supply of cheap, picturesque restaurants and Mama-Papa groceries. At a time when co-ops and natural foods stores were rare, ethnic groceries often had the unprocessed, unpackaged bulk commodities—rice, beans, grains, pastas—unavailable in conventional supermarkets, and they provided service and advice too. Indeed, in some minds ethnic foods *were* health foods, because foreign cuisines often lagged behind

62

America's in the use of prime beef, chemical additives, frozen or canned produce, and plastic wrap. Conversely, most old-world, lower-class cooks had long ago learned to stretch scarce or inferior ingredients by skillful use of stews, soups, and powerful spices— an obvious attraction to those scraping by in group homes. Highly spiced fare also went well with drugs and cheap wine, particularly the fruity kind popular among hip youth. Such romantic "peasant cuisine" also seemed closer to the earth, nature, life, and death, along the same lines as brown vs. white. Many ethnic breads were of course dark, filling, and cheap. Yet, interestingly, despite the obvious propinquity and political romance, black American cooks were not often discussed or recommended in white underground columns and books. While soul food was oppositional for blacks, at a time of rising tensions between black and white radicals, it may have been off limits for whites.

On the other hand, French dishes, despite the long-standing elitist associations, *were* adapted for underground use—especially quiche, crepes, fondues, and soufflés. To attract converts, some vegetarian cookbooks went overboard with rich gourmet staples, especially cheese, cream, and eggs. Also the hip appropriation of what was conventionally understood to stand for "high class" and "good taste" may have seemed, in its underground context, de-lightfully ironic and consummately bohemian. Here was a way of saying that despised deviants knew how to live well on so little. This at least might explain an otherwise puzzling contradiction in the *San Francisco Express Times* of 1968, that dreadful year: on the front pages, increasingly hysterical reporting and street-fighting rhetoric; on the back page, Alice Waters's exquisite recipes for vichyssoise, mushroom escargots, and chocolate mousse. Take, for example, the July 3, 1968 issue: on page 1, "War Declared" as troops gassed protesters in Berkeley/ page 14, marinated tomatoes. Or August 7, 1968: "FBI Agents Finger Hoover"/pâté maison.

This flirtation with French cuisine also reflected hip fascina-tion with regional country cooking. Most of the French recipes found in countercuisine guides were of the simple, "peasant," variety, rather than of the flashy, overly fussy type found in all too many urban French-American restaurants: more provincial *cassoulet* than metropolitan *velouté*. In France, young, insurgent chefs were abandoning the pasty white sauces, canned truffles, and predict-able frills of Paris for the seemingly plainer but fresher home cook-ing of the countryside. The countercuisine's premier adapter of

63

this "nouvelle" style, Alice Waters, traced her fascination with locally grown ingredients and regional specialties to personal experiences in Provence and her reading of Elizabeth David's *French Country Cooking*.[43]

In celebrating the local and unpretentious, food rebels were continuing the long battle between the cultivated and vernacular streams in American culture. While the former aped upper-class European and eastern metropolitan standards, the latter sought to preserve indigenous, grass roots culture. Historically, this struggle has been strongest at times of democratic ferment—the American Revolution, the 1830s and 1840s, the Progressive era, 1930s, and 1960s–70s. This most recent populist wave was strong enough that even mainstream food critics railed against formalized "second-rate Escoffier" and called for a return to "honest home cooking" using regional ingredients.[44]

In part, hip neoregionalism was born of necessity. When the counterculture moved out of cities into the countryside, survivalist considerations dictated local, seasonal produce. *The Last Whole Earth Catalog* listed fourteen books that classified edible wild plants. Forced to scrounge in unfamiliar territory, many did arm themselves with Euell Gibbons's *Stalking the Wild Asparagus* (1962) or Bradford Angier's *Gourmet Cooking for Free* (1970) and learned to identify fiddleheads, daylilies, wild mushrooms, gooseberries, and other indigenous "weeds." In *Living Poor with Style* (1972) Ernest Callenbach seemed to anticipate California cuisine as he advocated baking seaweed over an open driftwood fire on the Mendocino coast: "It tasted like those thin, salty crackers they serve at cocktail parties." Even better were the local mussels simmered over a campfire with wine, butter, and lemon. For those on the East Coast, Angier recommended Sea Moss Blancmange—sun-dried Irish moss cooked in milk and vanilla, topped by wild strawberries. From arcane pamphlets hip homesteaders also learned that the much-overlooked goat was cheap to keep and provided a delicious rustic cheese; in grazing preferences, the goat was in fact the animal equivalent of the hip survivalist—a rather undisciplined, easily bored deviant who preferred scavenging wild berries to clipping carefully tended lawns. ("Lesson one about dairy goats . . . [they] don't care much for grass. . . . If your interest in goats is a well-mowed lawn, we suggest sheep instead.") Every hip survival manual also had folk recipes for canning, pickling, and smoking.[45]

Indeed, in learning to cope with what was cheap and avail-

64

able, the countercuisine recapitulated the survivalist origins of many great cuisines. After attacking the "gourmet plague" in *The Taste of America* (1977), John and Karen Hess wrote:

> *One trouble is that Americans have forgotten how to be poor. Not that hard times were ever fun, but people coped better. In fact, the history of cookery is largely the triumph of housewives making do with what the gentry wouldn't touch. Eating high on the hog meant eating the fancy marketable cuts; the poor would get the jowl, the chitterlings, the feet, the tail, and with them would make fine food. All the great tripe, snail, and sausage dishes are their inventions, and all the chowders. What is* bouillabaisse *but a chowder that Marseilles women made of the trash fish that their husbands couldn't sell?*[46]

The Hesses therefore had much praise for the voluntarily poor of the counterculture who were rediscovering folk wisdom, though they worried that far too many were reinventing the wheel rather than consulting those who already knew how to make do. But reinvention was, after all, part of the therapeutic process.

LIGHT VS. HEAVY

The ethic of "living lightly" crystallized the countercuisine's sense of separateness. Opposed to "heaviness," the meaning was more metaphorical than dietetic. "Heavy" stood less for a set of foods than for a state of mind, an attitude, a frame of reference. Its etymology reflected the transition from the antiwar to ecology movements at the end of the 1960s. In their "Lexicon of Folk-Etymology" (in *The 60s Without Apology*), Ralph Larkin and Daniel Foss note the increasingly negative connotations of the word "heavy." Derived from black speech and popularized by Black Power, the word originally described someone who was respected for his or her admirably weighty ideas and charismatic leadership. By 1969, however, it meant "one of a bunch of people who think they're the whole movement and only talk to each other so they can spout Marxist bullshit." By the early 1970s it came to mean any crazy or deviant person, as in "you're too heavy."[47] The turn to ecology was a rejection of such heaviness, a determination to break free of the left's acute gravitational drag.

Applied to food, "heavy" contrasted with a counterculturally derived notion of "common sense." Underground food writers repeatedly advised against embarking on any "heavy food trips," i.e., extremes in diet. Every cuisine seems moderate and balanced to its practitioners. Advocates of the countercuisine were no different. If the meat-centered diet of most Americans was an extreme, so too were the fringe diets that prescribed too much of one thing —say, vitamins or fruit or brown rice. Even macrobiotics—itself an example of self-defined balance—was attacked underground as a "Zen hustle," a "fad," "weird," a "heavy food trip." Such heaviness violated the improvisational ethic.[48]

The "light" ecological antidote to leftist political analysis may have been *The Whole Earth Catalog* which, with its short pieces, breezy tone, and stoned epigrams, was lighter reading than *Capital.* Yet it did provide, in its own words, "access to tools" for more systematic thought. Thus, in the September 1969 issue, Gary Snyder incorporated the Indian edict to "walk lightly on the land" into his environmentalist program of voluntary simplicity:

> To live lightly on the earth *[my emphasis], to be aware and alive, to be free of egotism, starts with concrete acts, but the inner principle is the insight that we are interdependent energy fields of great potential wisdom and compassion—expressed in each person as a superb mind, a beautiful and complex body, and the almost magical capacity of language. To these potentials and capacities "owning things" can add nothing of authenticity. "Clad in the sky with the earth for a pillow."*

66 At the same time as he called for voluntary poverty, however, Snyder cautioned against excessive self-denial: "Learn to break the habit of too many unnecessary possessions—a monkey on everybody's back—but avoid a self-abnegating, anti-joyous self-righteousness. *Simplicity is light, carefree, neat, and loving—not a self-punishing ascetic trip* [my emphasis]."[49]

Snyder's version was actually a straddling of two opposing

traditions of lightness. On the one hand, lightness can suggest a certain bubbly effervescence, hedonism, self-indulgence, as in John Milton's *L'Allegro*:

> *Come and trip it as you go*
> *On the light fantastic toe.*

On the other hand, when compounded in "enlightenment," "lucidity," or "illumination," light could suggest a transcendent consciousness best attainable through self-sacrifice, abstinence, and renunciation. Ascetic sages had long advised that to see the light, one needed to travel light. Earlier truth seekers thus usually gave up hedonism for enlightenment, fleshly pleasures for spiritual insights, but not so in the 1960s. In the hip pastorale, there was a middle ground that might be reached at once—a way simultaneously to have fun and live conscientiously, to get high and stay close to the earth. And the place to begin, Snyder suggested, was with food. "Simplicity and mindfulness in diet is perhaps the starting point for most people." But unlike most schemes of dietary simplification, this time there would be no self-mortification, no sacrifice.

This, then, was the charm and fragility of the countercuisine. As David Shi illustrates in *The Simple Life: Plain Living and High Thinking in American Culture*, the dream of a "broad and middle way" between orgiastic and monastic extremes was by no means new. And as in previous waves of "high thinking," there were hopes that maybe this time the dream could come true, that the contradictions would not take their toll.[50]

4 ORGANIC FORCE: AN ALTERNATIVE INFRASTRUCTURE

T o be self-sustaining, a cuisine needs more than ideas about food; it also needs the food itself—and a separate infrastructure to supply it. As the countercuisine evolved, the ideological changes often came first, sometimes accidentally and experimentally, sometimes drug-related, sometimes tied to apocalyptic or mystical visions. Experiments in radically different ways of growing, distributing, and retailing food came next—along with numerous books hoping to publicize and perpetuate the initial gains. These efforts were at once realistic and utopian: realistic because they were determined to do the hard work of coming up with practical alternatives, utopian because these alternatives frequently posited fundamentally subversive ways of doing business and constructing society. Here was the countercuisine at its most ambitious—and also at its most conflicted and vulnerable.

THE ORGANIC PARADIGM

The key word guiding these reconstruction projects was "organic"—an oppositional concept that I have deliberately left for last because it straddled so neatly the three strands of therapeutic self-enhancement, consumerist self-protection, and alternative production.

In its therapeutic context, organic suggested integration, wholeness, health—all in direct contrast with the prevailing fragmentation, alienation, dis-integration. Living organically meant experiencing basic processes of growth, change, renewal. Embracing enduring life processes such as natural childbirth, breastfeeding, bread baking, and gardening, the organically inclined saw nature as an ally rather than as a nuisance or conquest. In a quasi-mystical, quasi-practical column on organic gardening, the San Francisco *Oracle*'s Elsa Gidlow glowed with her newfound sense of oneness and cosmic camaraderie: "We are returned to mystery and the power of cooperating with life—rather than, as so often now, working against it." [1]

The DDT scare of 1969–72 reinforced interest in the "organic foods" sold in health food stores, places that had been warning about pesticides and other chemical contaminants for years. In this consumerist, antichemical sense, "organic" resembled "natural" —and they were sometimes used interchangeably in the early years—but, strictly speaking, organic had wider implications. Natural addressed factory processing—the shunning of preservatives, flavorings, other additives—while organic referred to what actually went on at the farm. As we'll see, it was possible for the existing food industry to remove a few additives and call a product natural, but organically *raised* food required a completely new system of food production and distribution, and with that, major social decentralization.

There was nothing particularly new about farming without 69
chemicals—it was the only way until very recently. Nor was there anything new about intellectuals' fascination with decentralized agrarian societies. But Jefferson never used the word "organic." An explicitly organic model was first applied, according to Raymond Williams, by nineteenth-century conservatives who thought modern industrial society to be too atomistic, disorganized, artifi-

cial, and democratic; on the other hand, medieval society, with its landed aristocracy and deferential peasants seemed more cohesive, i.e., organic.[2]

In the early twentieth century the concept took a more progressive turn with the work of Sir Albert Howard (1873–1947), whose 1940 monument, *An Agricultural Testament,* was reviewed and extolled by organic farmer-poet-agrarian philosopher Wendell Berry in *The Whole Earth Catalog.* A well-respected agronomist who was knighted after his return from nearly thirty years in India, Howard combined a scientist's careful research and observation with a mystic's disdain for western-style fragmented, analytical approaches. Like Tolstoy and Gandhi, Howard admired the peasantry not as a reactionary resisting democratization but as a populist seeking ways for a colonial society to develop without relying on western technology or social organization. In countries rich in labor but poor in capital, it made sense to adapt to local strengths rather than to impose western models. "The poor of the world cannot be helped by mass production," Gandhi wrote, "only by production by the masses." Such ideas seemed particularly apt to those interested in the peasant revolutions of China, Indochina, and Cuba, and to those who likened America's own beleaguered farmers to a peasant class in need of land reform.

Drawing on western-style scientific methods as well as peasant wisdom, Howard conducted hundreds of experiments in nonchemical farming at his Indore station. His most noted contribution was in the area of soil maintenance. Believing that nature itself provided models of "self-renewing" agriculture, Howard wrote of the need to cooperate with, not conquer, natural forces. In language reminiscent of Thoreau and anticipatory of Gary Snyder and the *Oracle*'s mystics, Howard advised farmers to emulate the delicately complex forest, which, through careful rotation and avoidance of overspecialization, "manures itself."

70

Mother earth never attempts to farm without live stock; she always raises mixed crops; great pains are taken to preserve the soil and to prevent erosion; the mixed animal and vegetable wastes are converted into humus; there is no waste; the process of growth and the processes of decay balance one another; the greatest care is taken to store the rainfall; both plants and animals are left to protect themselves against disease.

A protecologist, Howard deplored the "fragmenting" tendency of analytical chemists to break down soil to its basic components—nitrogen, phosphorus, and so on—and then attempt to reconstruct it in chemical fertilizers. He advocated instead looking "at the wheel of life as one great subject and not as if it were a patchwork of unrelated things." According to Berry, Howard "saw that the soil was more a *process* than a substance, that its life was more important than its analyzable contents, that its health was not a matter of inert proportions but a balance of live forces"—especially the enduring cycle of growth and decay. Harnessing this natural cycle, Howard essentially *grew* compost by layering green matter, manure, earth, ground limestone, and phosphate rock in a well-aerated heap. His "Indore Method" is still the cornerstone of organic gardening.[3] Yet Howard did not specifically use the word "organic"—that was left to his American popularizer, Jerome Irving (J. I.) Rodale (1898–1971).

One of eight children of a grocer on New York's Lower East Side, J. I. Rodale was a weak child who, through body building and self-improvement courses, convinced himself that he could do anything—and he did try many things: accounting for the IRS, manufacturing electrical equipment, publishing a humor magazine, and writing plays and assorted treatises. In 1940 he purchased a farm in Emmaus, Pennsylvania, and began to experiment with Howard's theories, which Rodale integrated with his own nutritional beliefs and insights into an argument for the health benefits of organic foods—i.e., those raised according to Howard's methods of soil building. An enthusiastic convert, Rodale wasted no time publicizing his discovery: in 1940 he started *Organic Farming*. He failed, however, to interest American commercial farmers, who were in the 1940s being bombarded with government and chemical industry advice to increase, not decrease, their reliance on artificial means. So Rodale repositioned the magazine as *Organic Gardening and Farming*. But even this was not an economic success until it was picked up by the counterculture in the late 1960s. Until then, its readership consisted mostly of small-town and suburban backyard gardeners, many of them first-generation immigrants. A so-called health food nut, Rodale did make money publishing *Prevention*, which combined consumerist and therapeutic advice. Routinely dismissed as a quack by the medical and agricultural establishments, Rodale did not appear that unhappy with his marginal status as intellectual gadfly. In 1960 he turned over his publishing duties to his son, Robert. While J. I. pursued his main

71

intellectual interests—writing plays, attacking the medical experts, studying foreign languages, and collecting humorous items about the Soviet Union—the Rodale Press continued to lose money on *OG&F*.[4]

In 1969, with the hip turn to ecology, however, *OG&F*'s readership suddenly broadened. At first, the younger Rodale cautioned his "middle-aged frustrated farmers" against reacting too negatively to the weed-eating "social rebels"; they meant well and at least they were nonviolent. Many of the older "nuts" no doubt suspected the "freaks" of being more interested in the mystical word "organic" than in the rather mundane advice about worms, mulches, compost, and canning. The magazine certainly had none of the countercultural style of, say, *Mother Earth News* or Jeanie Darlington's 1970 hip *Grow Your Own*. Still, the tips did get read, and the word was passed on in the underground press. Thus, reviewing Rodale publications for *The Whole Earth Catalog*, Gurney Norman commented,

> *It has occurred to me that if I were a dictator determined to control the national press*, Organic Gardening *would be the first publication I'd squash, because it's the most subversive. I believe that organic gardeners are in the forefront of a serious effort to save the world by changing man's orientation to it, to move away from the collective, centrist, superindustrial state, toward a simpler, realer one-to-one relationship with the earth itself.*

By 1971 *OG&F* claimed 700,000 readers—up 40 percent in just one year. Adapting to the new converts, the editorial content became more explicitly ecological and utopian; supported by new wealth, the Rodale organic farm in Emmaus, Pennsylvania, became a haven of organic experimentation.[5]

72   The organic idea began—but did not end—in the farm or garden, executive editor Jerome Goldstein wrote. "Begin with the soil, get into the compost heap, natural cycles, the need to return garbage, sludge, and wastes back to the land, the hazards of pesticides and artificial fertilizers, and the personal health benefits that result from eating quality, nutritious food." From this base, Goldstein sketched a blueprint for an ecologically balanced, radically

decentralized, humanely pastoral society. The deceptively humble backyard garden, compost heap, and Mama-Papa organic foods store were "symbols of the new American Revolution."[6]

The argument went this way: Capital-intensive monoculture was destroying the independent family farm. Obsessed with economies of scale, conventional agriculture relied increasingly on specialization, mechanization, irrigation, chemical fertilization and insect extermination, and exports of the resultant surpluses. As soils depleted, chemically reliant farmers had to invest more and more to get the same results. As Barry Commoner noted, the productivity of nitrogen fertilizer was dropping steadily through the 1960s: between 1950 and 1959, corn farmers added 26 pounds of nitrogen per acre and harvested an additional 16 bushels per acre (.62 bushels per pound of fertilizer); although they added another 71 pounds of nitrogen per acre between 1960 and 1970, corn yields increased only another 27 bushels per acre (.38 bushels per pound of fertilizer). Similarly, some questioned whether the steadily increasing dose of pesticides and herbicides was improving productivity, as nature had a way of adapting to each chemical so that it took ever-stronger fixes to produce the same effect. When petrochemical prices soared in the early 1970s, the productivity gains seemed even more dubious. Since overproduction kept food prices low, the only way to survive according to conventional advice was to get even bigger—i.e., take on more land, more equipment, more chemicals.[7]

Organic methods, on the other hand, inverted the bigger-is-better formula. Composting, soil building, and biological control of pests were best practiced by smaller, labor-intensive, diversified farmers. Until they attracted the right mix of "beneficials"— friendly insects and birds that ate predators, such farms might experience somewhat higher losses to bugs, but these costs would be offset by the lower capital costs. In the short run crop yields might also be lower without chemical fertilizers, but here too farmers would benefit from lower costs, and in the long run, after several seasons of careful soil building, their yields would increase. 73 Because it was best practiced on a small scale, organic agriculture would restore rural employment opportunities for those recently pushed off the land and into urban ghettos by the industrialization of agriculture.[8] Rural areas would repopulate, urban unemployment, crowding, pollution, and unrest would decline.

Organic agriculture also threatened the existing food distribution system, which was increasingly centralized and dependent on long-distance transportation. To get vegetables from the highly specialized giant farms of California to the rest of the country required considerable energy, processing, and corporate management. Chemical-free (and thus more perishable) foods, on the other hand, had to be distributed locally. They might be hybridized, however, to suit local growing conditions—the rule that prevailed before the Californization of produce. The ideal would be a ring of organic truck and dairy farms around each metropolitan area. Having farms near every city would provide an incentive for cities to recycle sludge—a partial solution to the urban waste problem. Since almost any soil and climate could yield an amazing variety of vegetables through careful husbandry, there would be less need to rely on distant specialized producers. Indeed, labor-intensive methods could transform cities themselves into food producers; think of all the energy saved if city dwellers grew tomatoes in abandoned city lots, along expressways, in backyards. A family of four could grow almost a year's supply of produce on a forty-by-sixty-foot plot. Through canning and reliance on root crops they could live on locally available produce year round; careful seed selection might extend local growing seasons too.

To be sure, a system of small-scale local suppliers raised the trust problem that had given rise to the brand-name processors in the first place. Who would guarantee that a local farmer's produce was indeed fresh or wholesome? Ideally farmers and customers would deal directly with each other, in farmers' markets, or through relatively straight channels: farmer to Mama-Papa grocer to customer. Such direct links would restore the face-to-face intimacy lost in mass-scale supermarkets and mass society in general. In conjuring up the neighborhood grocery and vegetable stand, Rodale editor Goldstein invoked a nostalgia that Americans had felt ever since the advent of the supermarket age. In a direct marketing system, if prices seemed high one season, the producer could explain firsthand: a drought, a cold snap, or whatever. Eliminating misunderstanding and distrust, direct marketing might result in alliances between producers and consumers against the true villains in most radical analyses of the food system: predatory corporate middlemen, the processors and distributors. Eliminating the middlemen would leave more money in the hands of farmers, thus making it more economically viable to be small and diversified rather than to go the large-scale monocultural/conglomerate route.

Consumers would benefit from healthier food that might also be cheaper once there were enough organic farmers to supply the demand.

Such a transformation would require changes in values and expectations—but what economic revolution could go on without a cultural one? No more demand for plastic tomatoes in January, more self-reliance, better consumer attention to food quality—and a willingness to pay for it. Farmers would have to be viewed as long-term trustees of a living soil, rather than as short-term miners of chemically interchangeable nutrients. Food would have to be viewed not merely as a commodity to be rationalized or a set of nutrients to be metabolized, but as a medium of communication, a symbol of a whole way of life, an edible dynamic. And the idea that small is beautiful would have to be reinforced and reworked for modern times—a job performed ably by neo-agrarians such as E. F. Schumacher and Wendell Berry in the early 1970s. Organic living meant "thinking little," accepting limits, seeing, in Berry's words, "that man's only freedom is to know and faithfully occupy his place—a much humbler place than we have been taught to think—in the order of creation."[9]

So carried away were some new converts with this larger utopian vision that they often overlooked the more mundane details of gardening itself. For example, a 1971 special edition of *Northwest Passage* was titled "Compost Power." Inside, an article entitled "Heap Good Garbage . . . The Story of Compost" began, not with a discussion of mulches or microbes, but with a diatribe about Vietnam, bad schooling, and social disintegration. "This is a story about reconstruction," Frank Kathman continued. "This is a story about compost. So why am I wasting all this space ranting about schools and politics and money. Because it is the very framework of thinking and living which is the very reason why most people are NOT making compost today. It is the reason war is now being waged on the earth and on us by the profit-mongers and their quite willing consumer cohorts, the 'silenced majority.' "[10] There was no better illustration of the "everything is political" mindset than in the organic gardeners' determination to enlist earthworms in the cause of worldwide revolution.

The Rodale Press thus provided some of the details lacking in the decentralist suggestions of the Diggers' "Sounds from the Seed-Power Sitar" and J. Channing Grant's "People's Pods." There was a key difference between underground and Rodale ver-

75

sions, however: while Rodale invoked long-standing yeoman farmer/village shopkeeper ideals, the counterculture linked organic agriculture with a more utopian or "New Age" model of society. Along with Wendell Berry, the Rodales were Jeffersonian, dreaming of a nation of little businesses—but the countercultural model would do away with business altogether. The radical vision extended the organic farmer's cooperation with nature to a cooperative model in human relations as well. This could be seen in its vision of communal farms and cooperative groceries.

COUNTRY COMMUNES

Multiplying fivefold between 1965 and 1970, 3,500 or so country communes put the counterculture into group practice.[11] What better way to find nature than to move to the country? What better way to identify with brown-skinned peasants than to live in a peasant village oneself? What better way to experience organic interrelatedness than to live in a tribe where everyone spoke the same deviant language? Being a "health food nut" in the family dining room or school cafeteria conferred identity, but it could be a lonely undertaking. In commune life one went beyond personal protest to build a cohesive model community.

To be sure, not all communards had such dreams. To an extent the revolutionary communal ideal simply made a virtue of what seemed a necessity in the late 1960s: escape. Many hippies fled to the countryside because tourists, reporters, police, shopkeepers, and unfriendly neighbors were making urban slum bohemias uninhabitable. These refugees just wanted to be left alone in peaceful coexistence with plants and animals. Some political activists too went to the country, not with fully formed utopian plans but rather for therapeutic rest and recuperation. Some also saw the country as the only refuge from the nearing catastrophe; perhaps by buying a cheap homestead in some depopulating area, they might be able to live off welfare for a while and hope that it would all blow over. Mark Kramer described his move from New York to Vermont as "a doomsday decision. . . . It turns out that a farm with friends is a very pleasant street corner to hang out on while waiting for the bomb to fall." Yet Kramer did more than just "hang out." He worked hard at his organic garden; his experiences

76

and insights later produced an influential gardening column in the Boston *Phoenix*. It might seem paradoxical that those awaiting the Big One would take the time to care for a large garden, yet, as Wendell Berry observed, the connection between an apocalyptic sensibility and communal craftsmanship had its precedent in the Shakers: "Asked one day why the Shakers, who expected the end of the world at any moment, were nevertheless consummate farmers and craftsmen, Thomas Merton replied: 'When you expect the world to end at any moment, you know there is no need to hurry. You take your time, you do your work well.' "[12]

Traditionally, utopian communities had looked to food production and crafts for long-term survival and growth. For precedent in communal subsistence-through-crafts, *The Whole Earth Catalog* cited the Bruderhof and the Macedonia communities, both of which made expensive toys for cash.[13] Hip communards seeking ways to sustain the organic "tribe" could also look to the Diggers, who grew vegetables at Morning Star Ranch to supply their San Francisco Feeds and Free Store. This model appealed especially to those refugees who felt guilty about seeming to cop out of the revolution. The flight or fight issue was debated intensely in the countercultural press between 1969 and 1972. The more dialectical, less pastoral activists tended to agree with Tom Hayden that "there is no escape—either into rural communes or existential mysticism—from this dynamic of world confrontation." Those who favored a more confrontational strategy warned that a rural trend would disperse and dilute the movement.[14]

But as urban activism appeared to reach a tactical and rhetorical dead end, the defenders of rural communes had their own ammunition. British Columbia communard "Mason Dixon" insisted that *someone* had to feed the troops. While shipping vegetables to Vancouver for free distribution by Yippies, Dixon made contact with farmers who were commonly dismissed as red-neck reactionaries by urban activists. After seeing hippies working hard in the field to overcome the same obstacles—insects and climate —these straights were less likely to criticize "lazy hippies." The Rodales' tentative admiration for freak organic gardeners was one sign that such respect was possible. Similarly, the editor of *Northwest Passage*'s "Compost Power" issue observed that, despite the cultural clash, "remarkable" things happened when "the freaks and the farmers" got together at local co-ops to discuss prices and techniques. Dixon saw good potential to develop a rural power

77

base by joining harassed farmers against developers, grain companies, power companies, and agrichemical producers. The search for rural alliances made sense at a time of hostility between the white left and labor and blacks. In Dixon's view, therefore, the country commune was a bit like a Maoist cell that, through quiet cooperation with the local peasantry, might battle the capitalist empire.[15]

While the peasant coalition analogy was perhaps too ambitious, the relatively isolated rural commune did facilitate group process. Of most interest to observers—especially journalists— were communal experiments with sex and drugs; ironically, both eventually proved most destructive of community. Communal food practices received somewhat less notice from the sensation-seeking press, yet they were probably more successful in bringing people together in the short run and in raising awareness for the long run. "It's a delightful joke on the press, I think, that most rural 'hippie communes' should prove to be centered not on lurid sex or violent politics, but on food," Lucy Horton wrote. In most communes, another observer concluded, the kitchen was the social center—the place where the community came together not just to eat food but to talk about it—and, given the ideological connotations of every foodstuff, there was a lot to talk about.[16]

On the surface, the reasons for food's central role were obvious and simple: you could go without almost everything else— certainly sex, drugs, and politics, even a roof and clothes (in the summer at least)—but you needed to eat every day. The challenge of daily sustenance became more complicated, however, when all the countercultural culinary expectations were toted up. In *Celery Wine*, a frank memoir of four years on a California farm, "elaine sundancer" wrote:

78

> *We want to eat food that has the things our bodies need to grow, food that hasn't had all the goodness processed out of it, food in its proper season. And we'd like to eat food that has been grown and picked and cooked with love, by people who enjoyed what they were doing, food with good vibes in it. We want to stand in a good relation to the soil—to feed it well, so we will be fed by it. We're not fanatical about any of these things, but that's the general shape of what we want, and we think it's possible to have it.*[17]

Even though sundancer's group was determined to be as primitive as possible, it discovered that even the bare prerequisites were considerable: an organic garden large enough to provide most vegetables, a truck that ran to haul manure, a well-maintained private access road and bridge to get the truck to the garden, a new well to provide water for the garden, assorted tools (all manual), a wood-burning stove, cooking equipment (again, all manual), canning jars and kettle, table and chairs, and, to announce the communal meals, "a gong that rings in summertime to announce the cutting of a watermelon." [18]

Such equipment could be had—although not without some sacrifice of self-sufficiency, as communal members dipped into savings or took menial jobs in town. More vexing (and instructive) however, was the relentless introspection, the constant exploration of the gaps between organic theory and practice. When everything was connected and everything was political, everything became an issue. When everything from religious rituals to waste disposal had to be improvised and reinvented, dilemmas and soul-searching could arise almost anywhere. And in the food cycle there were many places—store, garden, kitchen, dinner table. Was it better to save a half-eaten peach for someone else—at the risk of spoilage—or feed it to the worms in the compost? Making jam from wild raspberries was clearly righteous, but where was the sugar to come from? If the aim was to be self-sufficient and simple, was there really any difference between buying white sugar (condemned) and buying soy sauce (approved), white flour (taboo), and brown rice (okay)? If, as some maintained, it was cowardly to buy meat in the market but honest, even holy (according to the blood ritualists), to kill your own, then who was going to do the tedious work of raising, cleaning, and butchering the hog? If you didn't buy sugar, meat, or other supplies from the local grocery, what would happen to the Mama-Papa storekeepers who were the backbone of the decentralist dream? Wouldn't the rural economy deteriorate further?

Of course, no commune could grow all its food; who pressed their own oil or grew their own rice, cocoa, bananas? Shopping trips to town were inevitable. But this meant further ideological difficulties. Was it permissible to throw the skin from a nonorganic orange or banana into the compost heap? More troubling, to make up their budgetary deficit, many relied on government surplus and food stamps. Given the start-up and maintenance costs of raising your own animals, it was cheaper to buy your dairy products com-

79

pliments of Uncle Sam. Until 1972, this was a legal entitlement. Yet, the "everything's connected" mindset was distressed. True, food stamps improved children's diet, but they also linked users to agribusiness, capitalism, and the touchstone in almost every radical analysis during this period, the war. "We want to drop out," elaine sundancer noted, "but we're buying our food with money that comes from the same government that is fighting the Vietnam war. I want good vibes in my food, but I'm eating Vietnam for breakfast. What were we doing here, anyway?" [19]

How much convenience *was* permissible? Was there any real difference between, say, using a store-bought knife or rotary beater and using an electric blender or grinder? Where was the line between a hoe and a gasoline-driven rototiller? If a truck was necessary to haul manure—an alternative to chemical fertilizers—then why not use a tiller that made it less necessary to kill weeds with deadly herbicides? And if a tiller, why not a tractor? Indeed, if a commune's goal was to feed urban comrades, wasn't it better to use chemicals to boost immediate yields, rather than to accept initially lower production through organic methods? How did you distinguish between expediency and idealism, necessity and luxury? The journal of one male member of a Pacific Northwest community illustrated the common tension between wanting to "feed the people" with full attention and feeling out of energy: "Today, sick of being in the kitchen—its physical space oppressive, making the most-times joyous routine of preparing onions for sauté a drag. Feeling rushed to get it over with, mechanically going through the motions of the Chinese quick soup, knowing it'll be good anyway, but if I don't feel good, what's it for? Enjoy cooking or get out of the kitchen!" [20] Was every dinner to be considered a ritual "feast" in which every member participated "joyfully," or were most dining occasions simply "meals" that tended to be assembled by the same people, usually women, without much support?

Few communes successfully resolved these questions. Yet, according to the process model, it was the search for answers that mattered. "One reason we promote communes," *Whole Earth Catalog*'s Stewart Brand wrote, "is that there's no better place to make all the wishful mistakes, to get your nose rubbed in your fondest fantasies." Ideally the lessons of failure, however painful (and seemingly inevitable in retrospect), would prove good for the long run. "Sometimes a mistake works; that's gravy and an obligation." [21] While individual experiments faltered, those with communal educations sometimes went on for postgraduate training.

What *was* learned? Most important, the joint production and consumption of organic food was not enough to sustain harmonic oneness. Although food-related issues frequently created ideological schisms, many colonies ultimately succumbed not to dietary squabbles but to more deep-seated interpersonal tensions. In her postmortem for Freefolk, a small anarchistic commune that lasted just 1½ years, Patsy Richardson observed that the enterprises that best brought people together—the garden and the kitchen—were not enough to maintain the community when, down deep, its members did not really like each other anymore. Deep-grained individualism overwhelmed impressive but basically superficial gains in food production. Paul Williams left Apple Bay after a year, a refugee from a lovers' quarrel. Looking back from 1976, he saw that the subsistence gardening had been physically rewarding but beside the point. "Make no mistake: living in the wilderness, with all its deprivations and hard work, is easy; it's living with people outside of those safe unreal structures of city life, that kills us every time." Down deep, the commune was perhaps too innocent, too prepubescent. With improvisatory playfulness communards often saw themselves as children resisting the grown-ups outside, but that innocence was intensely self-conscious and artificial. After gushing about his "kids" frolicking in Vermont meadows, Raymond Mungo admitted, in a telling aside, "It is awfully hard to be nine once you'll never see nineteen again." [22]

Particularly disheartening were the experiences of communal women who learned the hard way how sexist the 1960s organic tribe could be. Although some in the New Left and counterculture of the 1960s did care about developing new gender roles, free sex was no doubt more important to many men. As one Berkeley communard put it, for many men the best way to "smash monogamy" was to sleep with several women. A distinctly feminist orientation emerged only at the end of the decade, partly in reaction to the sexism within the movement. "Digger women have had it with puttering over all that brown rice while the guys go off to create the free new world (just like in Scarsdale after all)," Robin Morgan 81 wrote in explaining why left women had begun to act separately. [23]

For all too many hip women, the escape to the country meant further isolation and a return to the drudgery of the nineteenth-century homestead—with the added burden of having to be sexually accessible as well—frontier chicks/earth mothers, as Morgan put it. In one widely reprinted recollection of her experiences at two rural communes, Vivian Estellachild wrote that, at The Farm in Oregon, men did the odd jobs, wrecked the tractors, drank, and "fucked a lot," while women did all the cooking, cleaning, and child care. There was no time for reading, music, or poetry, just bread baking, gardening, feeding chickens, and so on. Men would not allow her to drive the tractor because she was not fast enough, they claimed, though later on she learned. Moving on to The Outpost in Minnesota, she found the same situation, which worsened as the commune attracted many hip tourists. "The men visitors would never really do anything but sit and wait for their meals and treat the commune as a summer resort." Macrobiotic dinners for thirty guests were especially difficult to prepare on the commune's inefficient wood-burning stove. [24]

Here the counterculture seemed doomed to repeat the mistakes of earlier utopians. In *The Simple Life*, David Shi writes of Fruitlands (1843), where males "tended to spend more time cultivating their conversations than their crops," while Bronson Alcott's wife, Abigail, and daughters wound up doing most of the work. Yet it has been the injustice of history that men frequently get credit for such noble experiments in plain living. One temporary resident, Anna Page, sardonically observed that "a woman may live a whole life of sacrifice and at her death meekly says, 'I die a woman.' But a man passes a few years in experiments of self-denial and simple life, and he says, 'Behold I am a God.' " [25]

Just as such liberal male hypocrisy heightened feminist consciousness in the nineteenth century, so too did the dissatisfaction with the counterculture strengthen the women's movement in the 1970s. Wondering why women let themselves be used so badly at both communes, Estellachild concluded that at least the communal work brought women together. Moving into all-female communes, some women found they *could* drive tractors, dig ditches, swing axes, butcher hogs, and otherwise do quite well without men. In such separate "free spaces," they explored lost or misrepresented skills, particularly herbal healing and midwifery. Being "natural" could mean being a "witch" (originally "wise woman"), not a "frontier chick." Early communal disappointments raised curiosity about the world of farm women in general. By the mid-seventies, according to Sally Hacker, enough historical and rural sociological studies existed to help women find "a life closer to the soil, where physical, social, and mental work again form an integrated organic whole." Of particular note was *Country Women* (1973), an explicitly feminist periodical devoted to helping women

82

go back to the land without surrendering to the earth mother model.[26]

Such fruitful spin-offs supported Stewart Brand's case for "wishful mistakes." The organic farming movement too learned from initial failures in communal agriculture. By the end of the first summer, it was clear that going organic did not mean simply letting nature do its own thing—a fact to which any long-term subscriber to *Organic Gardening* could attest but which, given the information vacuum in which so many hip youths operated, had to be discovered by doing. The decline after 1972 in the number of new communes devoted to organic farming could be seen not as a defeat but as a necessary pruning after a particularly lush first season. As it became clear that America would not decentralize overnight, specific aspects of the organic ideal received more careful treatment. As Robert Rodale cautioned in 1975, not only would organic farmers have to think small, they would have to be satisfied with small incremental steps.[27] One clear lesson of this early lyrical stage was that Albert Howard's labor-intensive Indian version of organic farming was unsuited for American conditions: the long-standing scarcity of rural labor and the decidedly uncollectivist values of the American "peasantry." Feeling that the problem lay in the communal aspect, not the organic methods, some ex-communards stayed in the country, bought or rented individual farms, and worked quietly on developing skills and local distribution channels.

Under the rubric of Appropriate Technology, organic devotees worked on laborsaving ways to nourish crops, replenish soil, and control pests and weeds without resorting to expensive, resource-wasting chemicals and heavy machinery. At a former dairy farm on Cape Cod, the hip dreamers of New Alchemy began in 1971 to investigate ways to make small-scale farming viable through solar heating, aquaculture, windpower, biologic pest control, and solar-aided composting; aware of early communal sexism, the New Alchemists also sought ways to reconcile feminism, the back-to-the-land ethic, and food preparation. By the early 1980s New Alchemy had 2,000 contributors, a model farm, and an affiliate in Costa Rica. Its research budget fattened by booming subscriptions to *Organic Gardening* and *Prevention*. The Rodale Press conducted experiments at Emmaus, instituted a program to certify organic produce and reduce fraud, kept track of successful organic farms worldwide, and in 1978 started a magazine of "regenerative

83

agriculture," *New Farm*, "dedicated to putting people, profit, and biological permanence back into farming." To improve public relations, Rodale discarded the "organic" label when applied to commercial farming—but the vision was the same, only more sophisticated, more sure of facts and viability. Pitched to small independent farmers, not peasant communes, *New Farm* presented valuable tips for a *gradual* changeover from chemicals and heavy machinery.[28]

As organic proponents studied and regrouped, other sympathizers investigated conventional agriculture. The writing career of Mark Kramer illustrated this transition from apocalyptic to analytical interests: first a *Boston Phoenix* column on subsistence organic gardening, next a communal memoir (and critique), *Mother Walter and the Pig Tragedy* (1972), and then, in 1980, *Three Farms*, case studies of family farms using conventional methods. Jim Hightower's blistering attack on agribusiness, *Eat Your Heart Out* (1975), was an outgrowth of the short pieces first syndicated underground through the *Liberation News Service*. In instinct and background, Hightower was more populist than hip communard, but his defense of small-scale organic farming and regionalism bolstered the movement's morale and informed a wider audience. Indeed, for every person who actually tried agriculture there were many more who, in the food-sensitized climate of the early 1970s, wanted to read about it. That these critiques were often distributed by major publishers was also evidence of awakening commercial interest in the countercuisine.[29]

The communal experience also spawned a host of books devoted to household techniques. The initial impulse had been to ignore written advice and to learn by doing. Thus, elaine sundancer noted that even though her commune had Scott Nearing's guide to subsistence living, they still felt compelled to learn— often through disaster—the subtle rules of cooking with wood. One clear lesson from communal kitchens was that improvisation had to be balanced with skill, intuition with consistency, creativity with efficiency. To aid in achieving that balance, experienced communards passed on recipes, advice, and moral support.[30]

The most lucrative of communal guidebooks was *Living on the Earth*, a pastiche of "celebrations, storm warnings, formulas, recipes, rumors, & country dances, harvested by alicia bay laurel," the pseudonym of a veteran of Wheeler's Ranch, a spin-off of Lou Gottlieb's Morning Star. First issued in 1970 by Bookworks, a

84

small Berkeley "movement publisher," it was immediately listed in *The Whole Earth Catalog*, where it was noticed by Random House's Bennett Cerf. Mindful of the extraordinary commercial success of Theodore Roszak's *The Making of a Counter Culture* (1969) and Charles Reich's *The Greening of America* (1970), Cerf paid laurel a large advance for the national distribution rights. As a large-format Vintage paperback, *Living on the Earth* became the classic of what was soon a rather sizable genre: brown paper cover, line drawings of skinny long-haired nudes, roughly handwritten text. By avoiding capital letters, alicia exuded a tone of seductively self-deprecating innocence. She also "harvested" a *lot* of information —on gardening, canning, cooking, baking, clothes making, shelter building, herbal medicine, backpacking, astrology, midwifery, ceramics. Intentionally dropping a table of contents, she hoped her readers would flow through the book as if on a life cruise, starting with a salute to the sun and ending with tips on cremating bodies in the forest. Perhaps at the publisher's insistence, laurel *did* append a useful index and bibliography for impatient readers unwilling to undergo the process.[31]

The publicity accorded *Living on the Earth* illustrated the widespread fascination with country communal culture, ca. 1971, as well as the ironies and pitfalls awaiting anyone bridging the gap between countercultural and mainstream media. Underground papers treated it as a useful guide to rural communal living. The mainstream press, on the other hand, hyped laurel the celebrity. A backgrounder filed in *The New York Times*'s Food/Fashions/Family/Furnishings section described laurel as the dropout daughter of a wealthy Los Angeles plastic surgeon. Although the book itself had no photographs, the *Times* presented a picture of the barefoot author on the steps of her simple hut—with long-sleeved white blouse, long dark skirt decorated with stars, long dark hair, radiant smile—the very model of countercultural fashion. Although the book was dedicated to those who wanted to subsist off the land, the article ironically noted that the royalties would buy groceries for everyone at the commune. While the sketch did a fair job of 85 describing alicia's dedication to her "open land church" and to countercultural ideals of voluntary poverty, it ended on a comfortably domesticated note: the twenty-one-year-old alicia had just broken with her social-register boyfriend because she wanted marriage and babies and he didn't. While the *Times* seemed determined to find middle-class conventionality beneath the hip pose, other interviewers looked for opposite caricatures. Thus, one television talk show host asked about her connection to the Manson family, while another tried to make her out as a stereotypical country hick, "a country innocent in the big city, looking at the tall buildings." [32]

Yet this city-bred artist-musician was no innocent; she was, on the contrary, quite capable of using the mass media to further her own countercultural aims. In her Random House contract she insisted on maintaining her original Bookworks design, because otherwise, in her words, "the New York publishers would have fucked it up." To the Manson question she responded that "a lot of criminals wear business suits, but not all men in business are criminals." And the *Times*'s backgrounder notwithstanding, laurel did not become a suburban housewife but, rather, stayed on at her commune, where she collaborated with another veteran, Ramon Sender, on *Being of the Sun*, another large-format paperback that was, if anything, more esoteric than the relatively practical *Living on the Earth*. [33]

Similar paradoxes accompanied other mass-distributed guidebooks of this period. Was it possible to use the media for movement ends, as a way to publicize the food underground through channels inaccessible to the righteous alternate press? In Ita Jones's case, no. There was no cookbook more explicitly political than Ita Jones's *The Grubbag: An Underground Cookbook*, issued by Random House six months after its Vintage edition of *Living on the Earth*. Underground reviewers liked the politics, but disliked the recipes, which were not natural and vegetarian enough to suit the trend. The *Times*'s reviewer, on the other hand, liked the recipes but not the politics, which could be ignored anyway, the writer concluded, for the sake of understanding "young people's ways of cooking." Frances Moore Lappé was somewhat more fortunate with *Diet for a Small Planet*. To get her message across, Lappé chose Random House's mass marketer, Ballantine, over a local Berkeley press. As a result, *Diet* became a widely accessible text, but Lappé did have to undergo the trials of the talk shows, where she was frequently treated condescendingly as the "Julia Child of the Soybean Circuit." Still, like laurel, Lappé was unstoppable, dodging largely irrelevant questions about weight control and sticking to her agenda. She used the royalties to finance her more explicitly political food activism. [34]

Publisher interest in communal guidebooks seems to have

86

peaked in 1972, the year of Lucy Horton's *Country Commune Cooking* (Coward, McCann & Geoghegan), True Light Beavers's *Eat, Fast, Feast* (Doubleday), and Crescent Dragonwagon's *The Commune Cookbook* (Simon and Schuster). Although rural communal membership and general reader interest in communes declined after 1972, 1972–75 were years of sophisticated analysis of the food system and decentralized alternatives: e.g., Judith Van Allen and Gene Marine's *Food Pollution, The Violation of Our Inner Ecology* (1972), Jim Hightower's *Eat Your Heart Out* (1975), Jacqueline Verrett and Jean Carper's *Eating May Be Hazardous to Your Health* (1974, on FDA negligence), Ross Hume Hall's *Food for Nought* (1974, a critique of mainstream nutritional science), E. F. Schumacher's *Small Is Beautiful* (1973), and Ernest Callenbach's fictional compendium of New Age ideals, *Ecotopia* (1975). The shift from "how to" to "why" books thus broadened the information infrastructure; the formal theories of economics were indeed following the improvised social facts.[35]

FOOD CO-OPS

Much of this information was first disseminated through co-ops —neighborhood outposts of the countercuisine. In addition to linking producers and consumers, co-ops provided advice, moral support, and living examples unavailable through regular media and markets.

Here again, one model came from the Diggers, whose free stores inspired a wave of cooperatively run, free or "open" clinics, theaters, galleries, schools, legal services, and housing. But the Digger stores distributed mainly surplus (and stolen) food and clothing—more like the Salvation Army or Goodwill—and, due to a scarcity of goods, organizational burnout, and police harassment, they rarely lasted beyond the first season.

Freaks often rejected another precedent: the New Deal era co-op. Although co-op groceries were scarce, almost 40 million Americans belonged to some other form of 1930s-vintage cooperative institution—credit, electric, farm, telephone, housing, health, burial society. Since all were designed to supplement, not subvert, capitalism, they seemed too materialistic, too one-dimensional. "The old cooperatives are still trying to get people to consume more," one "new wave" co-op worker observed. "We want people to consume less." There was little opportunity for therapeutic learning by doing or of living theater in an older co-op managed by paid professionals whose main responsibility to consumers was to return annual refunds. Nor did older co-ops meet the countercuisine's widened definition of consumerism, for they often sold processed "plastic food" and seemed insufficiently concerned about additives and pesticides. The same could be said, of course, about the rural cooperatives that helped conventional farmers buy chemicals and market their very unorganic products.[36]

While the older co-ops were cheap but insufficiently healthy, the commercial health food stores were healthy but expensive. Especially suspect were the newer stores established in the late 1960s by hip capitalists. According to the author of "The Age of Acquireous," "the difference between straight and hip capitalism is roughly the same as between a butcher's knife and a switchblade." Dismissing San Francisco's organic food merchants, *Good Times*'s Windcatcher wrote, "They traffic in something too essential to be trafficked in."[37]

At first many communes and households simply banded together to buy food wholesale, dubbing their buying clubs "conspiracies." The subversive side of such informal networks appealed to those already entangled in extralegal dope distribution. Indeed, heads could pattern conspiracies after drug-buying arrangements: to get a lower price, they got together with friends to pool a bulk order, contacted a wholesaler, brought the stuff home, subdivided the haul—only now the little bags contained grains, cheese, and vegetables, not grass, peyote, and mushrooms.

Another context was more explicitly anticorporate: buying clubs facilitated boycotts of nonunion grapes and lettuce. In mid-1966 Berkeley activists had targeted Safeway, the largest supermarket chain, for carrying scab products, but would-be boycotters were at first hard-pressed to come up with alternatives, for all chains—even the large but old-style Berkeley co-op—acted pretty much the same. With the rise in 1969 of conspiracies, the boycott movement took on new viability, for now there seemed a clear-cut nonprofit alternative. Some storefront co-ops were also called "conspiracies"—at least until city health department inspectors began to scrutinize such blatantly nonconformist outlets with extra care. After the first round of citations and closings, it seemed wiser to use the more neutral "co-op" name—and to pay closer attention to the plumbing, screens, and refrigeration.[38]

88

Impelled by these dual needs—to find nonprofit food sources and to fight corporate capitalism in quiet, nonviolent ways—co-ops boomed in the early 1970s. Boosters hoped that these nonprofit distribution channels would serve organic farmers unable to reach markets through regular middlemen. With more outlets, more farmers would be encouraged to go organic, supplies would increase, and prices would go down. As co-ops helped to increase the number of producers, they would also expand the base of consumers by serving as neighborhood outposts of the countercuisine. Through bulletin boards, book racks, and word of mouth, co-ops would provide advice and moral support unavailable through the mass media.

Some hoped that co-ops would serve not only dietary rebels, but also poor and working-class constituencies distrustful of white middle-class hippies and protesters. Through quiet example, co-ops might bridge the gap between neighborhood people and the nonviolent left, and thus serve as cells for spreading the most basic sort of participatory democracy. And with many inner-city stores looted and burned out, the need for such alternative retailing was obvious.[39]

No doubt co-ops did achieve some of these goals. At a time when commercial health food stores were plagued by charges of fraud and hucksterism, co-ops were no-frills sources for counter-cuisine staples such as brown rice, whole grain breads, herbal teas, and soy products, all of which could be purchased in bulk. As sources of health information and moral support, the co-ops were indispensable. Sympathetic journalist Daniel Zwerdling observed "an almost religious spirit that seeks to satisfy the human needs forgotten in the plastic-coated world of a corporate supermarket. Some of the people who work and shop at co-ops seem almost starved for a sense of communion with the earth and with their food, and co-ops help provide it."[40] Communion aside, working in a co-op—visiting warehouses, unloading a truck, cutting cheese, ringing cash registers—quickly demystified the food business.

Shoppers too saw food in a new way. Instead of being bombarded by endless aisles of elaborately packaged, prepriced brand names, co-op consumers found a relatively limited array of staples which they bagged, weighed, and oftentimes priced on their own. Complementing the low-tech decor, the restricted inventory, with its lack of impulse items, embodied the "small is beautiful" philosophy that sought to align wants with needs. At a co-op you

89

learned to live on less. As an educational model, the *Environmental Handbook* cited the Cambridge, Massachusetts, co-op established by Boston Ecology Action, where bags and containers were returnable, soaps were biodegradable, many products were handmade from recycled materials, and the staff was "always available for household ecology counseling." Similarly, Madison's Whole Earth Co-op was renamed in 1970 the "Whole Earth Learning Community."[41]

For sure, what co-ops lacked in packaging, they made up in counseling. While regular food processors did not yet have to list ingredients on labels, some co-ops pinned explanatory cards above bins telling customers not only of ingredients, nutritional content, recipes, but also of the political situation where this fruit was grown or this egg was laid. Or, the newcomer might be initiated and advised through informal contact within the store. Such was the case when Carol Flinders—already thinking about changing her diet—wandered into the Organic Foods Co-op in Berkeley.

> *Tubs of beans, all colors and shapes, surrounded me, and barrels of noodles—buckwheat, whole wheat, soy, and spinach. Everything was beautiful: earthen-colored and completely free of cellophane wrappers, alluringly tactile. But no packaging meant no cooking instructions —and no visible means of getting the stuff out of the store. My stomach sank.*

Then she heard the familiar voice of Laurel Robertson, whom she had met briefly years before. Taking her in hand, Laurel showed her the paper bags, told her how to soak beans, cautioned her about handling fragile whole wheat lasagna noodles, and introduced her to her first kohlrabi, kefir, and dried figs. From there it was on to the cooking lessons that led eventually to *Laurel's Kitchen.*[42]

Flinders's experience was an almost too perfect example of a co-op acting as a recruitment office for the countercuisine. But co-ops did involve far more people than communes, rural or urban, and may very well have been the most successful of the alternative institutions developed by the repositioned left in the 1970s. According to the Cooperative League of the U.S.A., between 5,000

90

and 10,000 new wave food co-ops were established between 1969 and 1979; such outlets grossed about $500 million a year. Moreover, as supermarket prices soared in the mid-seventies, co-ops spread beyond university and hip communities into much-prized working-class areas.[43]

But growth posed major challenges and exposed important divisions in co-ops' strategies. Since co-ops, like communes, were devoted to the participatory process, such differences were often discussed to the point of exhaustion and schism. With everything connected—food, health, politics—it was hard to establish priorities. The chief problem lay in balancing economic and idealistic goals, price and ideology, pure shopping and pure revolution. If the co-op's aim was to bring healthy food to people, then perhaps price should be a secondary consideration, since, given the present high demand and low supply, organic prices were bound to be high. When some complained that organic produce was not only costly but also of poor quality—blemished, wilted, spoiled—they were chastised for being impatient, even disloyal; for the sake of the long-run goal of favoring organic farmers, shoppers should cheerfully accept immediate shortcomings and be willing to wait for supply channels to be established. In a sense, co-ops needed the "voluntary socialism" of Lake Wobegon, Garrison Keillor's small town—an uneconomic fidelity to the "pretty good" village grocer who might not stock everything and was often more expensive than the supermarket at regional centers. Yet, unlike Ralph's, co-ops were located in larger cities where people tended to shop comparatively. Ironically, members of Depression era co-ops tended to be more loyal mainly because they received their discounts only at the end of the year, while shoppers at new wave co-ops wanted tangible benefits each shopping trip. Frustrated by bargain shoppers who bought only sale items at the co-ops, one worker urged supporters to suppress "Middle-Class Greed" for the sake of political loyalty: "They should understand that if they support the store now politically it will serve them better in the long run."[44]

A similar argument was made by those who saw co-ops first of all as arenas for group therapy and education. For example, at a 1970 meeting of a San Francisco conspiracy, *Good Times* reported the general consensus "that cheaper food was not the main issue. Food is our common denominator, but the people working with and for one another toward a common goal of self-help was the most important issue." Those who wandered into a Bay Area co-op mistakenly looking for bargains were urged to go down the street to Safeway. Journalist Daniel Zwerdling did just that when he compared prices at D.C.'s Fields of Plenty co-op and the nearby Safeway. Safeway's chicken, detergent, and prunes were cheaper; Fields had more grains and its produce was cheaper—but also "battered and wilted." Behind such indifference to price and quality, Zwerdling detected the agenda guiding many who actually worked in co-ops: "Selling food seems almost like an excuse, an organizing tactic to bring the community together for future political projects." [45]

But *which* community, hip or straight, middle or working class? An emphasis on process over product was appropriate in relatively small conspiracies whose membership was culturally homogeneous, where everyone worked, and where a major goal was to overcome alienated work and foster group solidarity. Indeed, in highly politicized communities like Berkeley and Cambridge, it was not uncommon for conspiracies to break down into even smaller block units to facilitate the participatory process, even if such decentralization hindered the sort of bulk buying that would lower prices. Boston's *Old Mole* reported that at the weekly block meetings of Cambridge area buying clubs, food buying issues frequently gave way to talk about media work, a drug program, antiwar actions, community events, International Woman's Day, the local leftist bookstore. But members were almost exclusively "freaks, students, and movement types." [46]

On the other hand, those who saw co-ops as a way to attract the masses were more interested in improving efficiency to lower prices and improve quality. While hiring a manager raised the specter of bureaucracy and authority, such employees tended to be ideologically compatible anyway, for who else would work for the low wages? Other stores sought to balance democratic participation with retailing efficiency by restricting management to a small collective of like-minded workers. Since fewer people had to be consulted, such collectives might run more smoothly, yet they too could become beset by internal arguments, especially over what kinds of products to sell to the wider public. Should all products be healthy and ecologically correct, i.e., a relatively restricted stock of natural foods, nothing plastic? Most agreed on boycotting iceberg lettuce and nonunion grapes, but what about bananas from Central American dictatorships? Should everything be organically

92

grown, or was it enough to avoid obviously bad preservatives and additives? Some even argued that it might be wise to stock supermarket-style "junk" foods as a way to attract workers suspicious of "health food." Of course, the more white bread and canned goods, the more like the older co-op supermarkets, the less of a countercuisine identity. It was the classic crossover dilemma: the more you stretched to accommodate mainstream tastes, the more likely you were to alienate your original customers. On the other hand, if you didn't grow, your small size made it almost impossible to get lower wholesale prices from food jobbers, who dealt in trailer loads, not cases. Who could come up with the credit, or the space? A typical Safeway had 50,000 square feet, a co-op under 2,000. The basic fact of life in the food industry was this: the big got bigger, the small got out.[47]

The challenge of the mid-seventies was to overcome the organizational and scale disadvantages that, in the first stage, had made co-ops charming but frustrating places to shop. Organizationally, most co-ops did move toward a system of using at least one paid employee to keep things running and coordinate the volunteers. Forced by health department inspectors and picky consumers to treat food as an end, not a means, the best-run co-ops paid closer attention to the quality of perishables, although organic produce remained a problem throughout the decade. As for scale, most co-ops had little option but to remain small, since there was virtually no credit available for large-scale purchases or expansion. Supermarkets thus remained almost unaffected by co-op competition. For example, in 1974 Washington, D.C., co-ops grossed $2 million, 1/80 of what Safeway sold in D.C. alone—at a time when Safeway was reducing its inner-city presence there. Still, co-ops could improve their price situation somewhat by banding together in local networks of community warehouses, trucking cooperatives, and bakeries. Unable or unwilling to compete in the realm of "junky foods," co-ops became nonprofit specialty stores supplying countercuisine staples to the already converted.[48] Their long-term prosperity depended on the growth of health consciousness, the idealism of the low-paid work force, and their ability to compete against the profit-making specialty stores that, in the early 1970s, constituted a growing sector within the countercuisine's infrastructure. In other words, like all little businesses, co-ops faced the uncertainties of shifting consumer demand, labor morale, and competition. Forced by the dictates of efficiency to become more

93

businesslike, co-ops found themselves emulating those who *were* businesses.

HIP ENTERPRISE

H istorically, bohemian businesses have performed vital functions as safe havens for industrious nonconformists and as advanced testing stations for larger-scale corporate involvement. A bridge between the underground and the establishment, the hip business sector reflected both the countercuisine's maturity and its vulnerability.[49]

Despite the underground press's distrust of hip capitalists, many early hip food businesses were barely distinguishable from communes and co-ops. Just as some commune members wrote memoirs and cookbooks to support their groups, others sought— and occasionally achieved—a bare subsistence by baking bread, retailing vegetables, or serving meals. And, like co-ops and communes, they hoped to perform community service at the same time.

The romance of service was especially strong in hip restaurants, which, in effect, attempted to institutionalize the communal culture. If food was a medium for "communication," much of the deviant dialogue was first carried out privately in communes and dorms, and then, as the first generation of converts aged and had more to spend, in public commercial spaces. According to Alice Waters, Chez Panisse began in 1971 as an extension of the home-cooked meals that she had been preparing for Berkeley radicals. Similarly, the other, initially more famous Alice [Brock], of "Alice's Restaurant" fame, started out as a sort of surrogate earth mother for the hippies of western Massachusetts, and her restaurant served as an important community center. Even when she, like Waters, became too famous and too expensive for her original clientele, she continued to see herself as a hip therapist whose loving attention, homey fare, and communal atmosphere helped diners battle everyday "alienation."[50]

Brock and Waters were also businesswomen in an industry (and world) dominated by men. The feminist model was even more explicit in restaurants created *for* women. Thus Jill Ward, a management consultant, and Dolores Alexander, a journalist, opened New York's Mother Courage Restaurant in 1972 "as the idea of creating a social milieu where women could get together over good food, where THEY would set the tone, not male waiters, owners, customers—a place badly needed by the New York feminist community." And both women were anxious to find ways of making a living "outside the male-dominated business world which, as committed feminists, they were finding increasingly intolerable and oppressive." Unable to get bank credit, they got loans from friends in the women's movement. (Waters too was financed by radical friends.) Two years later they were still open —remarkable enough in the restaurant business—and were praised as a model of collective financing.[51]

There were many examples of the communal-restaurant theme. After living in several rural communes in western Massachusetts, Elliot and Katherine Blinder moved to their own farm and in 1974 opened the Home Comfort Restaurant in Greenfield. Visitor Raymond Mungo noted the name was derived from the stove at Total Loss Farm, as was the quiche and curry menu and the log cabin–woodsy atmosphere. After living in a New York commune and writing *The Commune Cookbook*, Crescent Dragonwagon took her advance from Simon and Schuster and invested in a group farm in the Arkansas Ozarks, where she hoped to set an example of organic living and to serve the local hip community.[52]

Similarly, in 1972, Mollie Katzen and twenty friends established Ithaca, New York's Moosewood Restaurant as "a community project." In collective operation and nostalgic atmosphere, the highly successful restaurant was virtually indistinguishable from a co-op. Like communal organic gardeners and co-op workers, Katzen's group saw itself as a vital link in an alternative food chain, as well as a model of the participatory process. In her preface to the *Moosewood Cookbook* (1977) Katzen noted that workers participated in "almost all aspects of running the restaurant, from deciding policy (at mandatory monthly meetings, with the job of chairperson rotated) to planning menus to changing light bulbs." Appropriately Diggerish, there was "no singular owner and no 'boss.' " Profits were "recycled" among workers or back into the restaurant. Reinforcing the improvisational ethos, the ever-changing menu was posted on blackboards—a countercultural norm. As in other commune cookbooks, Katzen's text was hand-lettered, chatty, and somewhat disorganized; the index was so inaccessible that readers might rightly wonder if, as with the True Light Beavers's *Eat, Fast, Feast,* they were encountering "not a book but a process"

95

each time they sought a recipe. The menu was eclectically ethnic, with whole grains and rich desserts, a Lappé-style lesson in how to live well without wasting the earth's protein resources.[53]

Although Moosewood made enough money to endure—as long as workers accepted minimal compensation—one suspects that, like co-ops, the aim was as much educational as entrepreneurial. It may have been a coincidence that Moosewood was located in an abandoned school building, but there was a didactic quality in the blackboards, the Shakeresque straight chairs, library-style tables, and quietly coercive notices found in so many hip restaurants. Since Brattleboro, Vermont's collectively run Common Ground restaurant had no "private" spaces, patrons were "encouraged" to share tables with strangers. Founded in 1973 by a collective dedicated to showcasing the simple life, the Communion Restaurant in San Francisco charged only 60 cents for an all-you-can-eat, self-service vegetarian meal. (The original price of 80 cents was lowered after the group found that they were making more than they could use.) But the customer had to be willing to *learn* while enjoying such a cheap meal. Although customers were free to take as much as they wanted, they were politely urged by not-so-discreet signs to "take only as much as you need. There is a difference between want and need. Want is all ideas and need is real." For further self-examination, customers made their own change at the open cash register. And finally, to keep the pupils intent on their lessons, the restaurant enforced a "No talking" rule. By doing away with useless talk as well as "distracting" music and wall paintings, Communion hoped "to let people have a chance to learn how their bodies feel about food—how to pay full attention to their food and their eating."[54]

Even individual entrepreneurs claimed disinterested, non-profit motives. By nourishing the health-oriented consumer and encouraging the organic producer, they too hoped to support and expand the countercuisine. And just as co-ops found themselves acting like businesses, businesses acted like co-ops. One of the earliest hip entrepreneurs, Jerry Sealund opened a Haight-Ashbury health food store in 1966. Although his Far-Fetched Foods was criticized by the Diggers, who wanted all food to be distributed free, Sealund was praised by *Organic Gardening* for organizing employees as a commune, for taking only $20 a week for expenses, and for selling only nutritious foods. Avoiding the expensive vitamins and dietetic items found in older health food stores, Sealund

96

sought new sources of supply, especially organic truck gardens. (Charles Perry reports that after being robbed twelve times in the Haight, Sealund closed the store, worked for the All Saints bread-baking operation and the Black Panthers' free breakfast program, and then opened another organic grocery in the more tranquil Santa Rosa.)[55]

Similarly, although Fred Rohe's New Age Foods was sternly condemned by *Good Times*, Rohe characterized himself as a devout Buddhist who provided valuable nutritional and spiritual guidance to the hip community. A former chemicals salesman and part-time producer of rock concerts, Rohe opened his first store in the Haight district in 1965. As his clientele shifted from older people to flower children, Rohe repositioned accordingly. In addition to organic foods, Rohe's first store sold Rodale Press books and rock albums, and offered a meditation area complete with altar. By being so overtly countercultural, Rohe's well-stocked store filled the gap between the older drugstore-type health food store and the limited-inventory new wave conspiracies, and his sales increased tenfold in four years. From his original Haight store, Rohe established outlets in Santa Cruz, San Anselmo, and Palo Alto. Even Rohe's critics had to allow that he did not exploit his workers and that there was some merit in his argument that by expanding, he might improve his economies of scale and thereby lower prices. To foster bulk purchases and to maintain organic standards, Rohe joined with other Bay Area merchants in establishing a wholesale cooperative. What looked suspiciously like a cartel to some was defended as a "tribal council" whose aim was to establish a viable "alternative to poisoned, processed, and synthetic foods of the not-so-super markets."[56]

The troublesome overlap between counterculture and capital-ism was illustrated by two successful food purveyors, Erewhon and Celestial Seasonings, both of which generated considerable ambiv-alence within the food underground. Founded in 1966 to supply Boston-area followers of macrobiotics guru Michio Kushi, Erewhon was in its early years virtually indistinguishable from a co-op. Its tiny, informally run Back Bay store became a haven for those in search of organic foods, advice, and support. Fueled by its early success in meeting basic needs, Erewhon expanded both horizon-tally and vertically in the early seventies, opening new retail stores in the Boston area and on the West Coast, and becoming a major wholesaler and processor as well. Pursuing the organic ideal of

97

regionalized agriculture, Erewhon sought out local organic growers even when these were more expensive and riskier than California sources. Noting that Vermont's Champlain Valley used to be the "breadbasket of New England," one manager claimed Erewhon's mission was to "turn New England agriculture around to growth rather than decline, to polyculture instead of monoculture, to agricultural self-sufficiency instead of leaning on areas outside of the region for 80 to 90 percent of its food, and, of course, to natural, rather than chemical ways of growing food." To cultivate consumer demand, Erewhon published pamphlets on food and worked closely with another Kushi-related project, *East-West Journal,* a monthly devoted to nutritional advice, alternative medicine, and New Age politics.[57]

But as Erewhon grew it became apparent that it was not just a particularly successful co-op. Like any profit-making food business, it took the normal 25 to 35 percent markup. Moreover, as a privately held company with close ties to the apparently imperious Kushi, management was hierarchical and policies were imposed from above. Throughout the seventies the firm was plagued by labor-management disputes that were reported in much of the alternative press but not in *East-West Journal,* which acted as an advertising outlet for Erewhon. According to David Armstrong, the antiunion Kushi attributed workers' dissatisfaction to personal health problems, not poor working conditions. (Kushi's heavy hand was felt most directly at *EWJ,* where his insistence on macrobiotic purism eventually drove several staff members to establish in 1974 a more eclectic, multipurpose monthly, *New Age.*) By the late 1970s, the company had weathered several boom-bust cycles, but at a cost. One visitor to its huge new warehouse found a "seductively serene" atmosphere full of hanging plants, split-bamboo blinds, and eastern-mystical decorations, but the company no longer permitted meditation breaks and the era when the day's receipts were toted up on an old envelope had long passed. Indeed, Erewhon now had "many trappings of any midsize corporation: a computer, inventory control, market test programs, 160-odd names on the payroll, and a comptroller who simply loathes natural foods." Perhaps appropriately, when Raymond Mungo attempted in 1978 to interview an Erewhon executive for his largely boosterish study of hip businesses, *Cosmic Profit,* he was unable to get through the "secretarial barriers."[58]

Mungo was more successful, however, in reaching Mo Siegel,

98

president of Celestial Seasonings. Beginning in 1970, at age twenty-one, Siegel built his Boulder, Colorado, herbal tea company into one of the best known of hip enterprises. By 1978 Celestial Seasonings employed 200 people and grossed over $9 million a year. Siegel's teas were righteously ecological and healthy: non-caffeinated, additive-free, organically grown, or gathered by hip youth in the wild. Each box was a minimasterpiece of countercultural communication, covered with naive art, health advice, a more-than-full ingredient label, spiritual sayings, and sketches of medicinal plants. Employees of Siegel's "cosmic spiritual community" received free lunch, T-shirts, and a shareholding plan.[59]

Yet, despite its hip trappings, workers there made less than the going Boulder wage. Employees were encouraged to discuss the nutritional and political implications of each ingredient, but Siegel had the final word. Siegel even admitted to Mungo that his aim was to "defeat the unions by providing more and better benefits for his workers than any union could"—yet the benefits were more spiritual than material. Like Kushi, Siegel deflected workers' complaints with religious sermons. Professing great admiration for IBM, Siegel dreamed of rapid expansion. In a pamphlet advertising the company's "guiding principles," Mo's first was "to do the will of our Heavenly Father"; his seventh was "to develop within the next decade a sales volume of many millions of dollars per year, employing many people and distributing products that will directly aid the health and wealth of the planet."[60]

Fitting an old business text distinction, Siegel was not a "little businessman" who, for the sake of independence, was determined to stay little, but rather a "small businessman" who hoped one day to be big. In the later seventies Siegel pursued his stated goal of replacing Coke with Red Zinger as the national drink by investing in new overseas supply lines, production facilities, and distribution outlets. His ambition inevitably led him in directions that seemed disloyal to the alternative food network. Thus, in 1977 the company took its advertising away from its own in-house publicity department, Celestial Reflections, and gave it to a mainstream San Francisco agency. Soon after, the company stopped dealing exclusively with co-ops and health food stores and began shipping to supermarkets. In 1984, Siegel sold the company outright to Dart & Kraft, Inc., for a reported $8 million to $10 million. Agreeing to keep Siegel on as chairman-president for at least two years, the food giant—with $6.7 billion in sales in 1983—apparently had its eye on a prize much bigger than Celestial's estimated 40 percent share of the $100 million herbal tea market. Rather, analysts guessed that the maker of Velveeta, Miracle Whip, and Parkay hoped to use the Celestial name and aura as a way to authenticate Kraft's entries into "the booming health food area." At Kraft's direction the company instituted an invasive drug-testing program —so much for the "laid-back" image. Even so, Kraft was disappointed with the acquisition, and in 1987 tried to sell Celestial to the tea industry giant, Thomas J. Lipton, Inc.—a capitalist variant on the mystical theme "what goes around comes around." [61]

LIVING IN THE CRACKS

The paradoxes, inconsistencies, and contradictions were common to all countercultural enterprise, whether tiny or, as in Celestial's case, just small. To a certain extent, these businesses were firmly based in the countercuisine and reflected its major consumerist and therapeutic tenets. Dedicated to providing safe, healthy, ecologically sound products, they saw themselves as the necessary infrastructure for an ongoing alternative community, a role as much cultural as economic, designed to change minds *and* to supply goods and services. Packaging, decor, and advertising were generally nostalgic and playful. Self-consciously "educational" advice was freely and copiously offered—whether on painstakingly handwritten wall signs, in countless pamphlets, or on cereal and tea boxes. "Honest pricing" was practiced through round numbers—$8.00 instead of $7.95—and, in some concerns, open books. As in any good commune, every decision was cause for protracted discussion of the full ideological implications. In line with organic ideals, workers saw themselves as members of a family or tribe, not as employees; hence the often bitter labor disputes when owners or managers asserted authority. And many proprietors saw themselves not as classic entrepreneurs seeking small margins but rather as New Age pioneers whose service to the community would also provide a therapeutic high, a sense of "joy," a growth experience.

Since such therapeutic benefits were thought to be compatible with the larger goal of social reconstruction, many hip businesspeople hoped to make their own "cosmic profits" without hurting others. Indeed, the wider market was viewed not as a zone for

100

intense competition but rather as an opportunity for cooperation, "sharing," or "networking." Like other alternative institutions of the seventies—alternative media, radical law collectives, free schools, food co-ops—hip enterprises grouped themselves along what David Moberg has called the SPIN model: "segmented, polycentric, integrated through a network." One of the largest networks was the Briarpatch Community, comprising over 300 alternative organizations and businesses in the San Francisco area which, starting in 1973, pooled information, tools, expertise, and resources through workshops, reciprocal consulting, and a journal, *The Briarpatch Review*.[62]

In tone, the *Review* attempted to ennoble hip proprietors caught between the "capitalist exploiter" label conferred by the left and the "huckster" tag used by the mainstream media. The key was "right livelihood"—simple living. By earning only as much as you absolutely needed to stay independent and viable, you would profit personally without hurting anyone. The less income you needed, the more successful you would be in business. "If we are not in business for a large return," contributor Andy Alpine reasoned, "then our prices don't have to be as high, our employees can be treated more humanely, and our customers are not looked upon as dollar bills."[63] Low expectations would mean low costs and virtuously modest profits. Through an ascetic lifestyle and honest pricing, one might keep one's economic *and* spiritual books in balance.

Also, according to Briarpatch founder Dick Raymond (of *Whole Earth Catalog* fame), smallness meant survival in the hard times that seemed ahead. Given the likelihood of a major economic collapse, only those enterprises least visible and closest to the ground would withstand the crisis and start the reconstruction. Raymond derived the Briarpatch name from a "postapocalyptic" vision of thorny briar bushes thriving on little water or soil in a devastated urban landscape:

> *The larger industrial culture, with its monolithic pyramidal structures, is going to find itself in the middle of an earthquake—cracking when it becomes too much out of tune with people's values. These will be difficult times. Those who survive will be the ones who can live in the cracks that open up. Weeds survive in the cracks; as*

101

concrete breaks apart, here comes the weed, or briar bush,
which can survive on much less. In the Briarpatch we
can survive on much less and enjoy life much more.[64]

The Briar philosophy, then, was to stay small, lie low, and wait. Yet, staying small, however healthy for some future apocalypse, was no easy trick in the present. Like all entrepreneurs, hip businesspeople faced the challenge of finding credit, supplies, labor, and customers in an imperfect world where small was definitely not yet beautiful. While the *Review* argued that these steep odds offered great potential for self-education through failure, others worried less about the education of the proprietor and more about the welfare of the customer. Accustomed to urban efficiency and options, the public wanted products, not process, service, not sharing. Given the disadvantages of scale and inexperience, hip goods and services seemed doomed to be expensive and thus available mainly to elites.[65]

Some also feared that, rather than disintegrating, the "monolithic" corporations would invade hip turf and, using their own scale advantages, crush the small independents. Some hip proprietors thought that to survive they had to grow large enough to battle the giants in open field. As early as 1970 when most hip food businesses were barely sprouts, much less bushes, Erewhon's Roger Hillyard argued that companies like his needed more visibility, not less, for unless the public learned about "real health foods," the major food manufacturers and grocery chains would within ten years be marketing "plastic health foods." To increase its visibility Erewhon attempted nationwide manufacturing and distribution—an exceptionally ambitious multifront campaign for an infant retailer. Defending Green Mountain Grainery's decision to reach far beyond its base as a Boulder, Colorado, natural foods store, one executive argued that the natural foods industry had to "invade the supermarket shelves *before* the regular companies can come up with more ersatz natural food like those breakfast cereals with outdoorsy names and logos and a ton of white sugar in 'em." [66]

102

There was a built-in logic to expand, whether through internal reinvestment (as in Celestial Seasonings), acquisition of other firms (Erewhon), or networking (Briarpatch). Because each path involved considerable coordination, rationalization, and, above all, stress, the individual had to be ready to surrender a certain amount of spontaneity, craftsmanship, and self-determination. Yet it was the desire for these advantages that had led many into business in the first place. The desire to maintain control over operations has been a central managerial imperative in all capitalistic enterprise, and especially so in a subculture that prized individual independence. Even those hip proprietors who were comfortable with corporate growth fought to keep personal control, sometimes through a quasi-religious cult of leadership and a fierce hostility to unions. The prospect of government intervention also seemed threatening to proprietors' control. Given the very real harassment of hip food businesses by local police and health inspectors, some paranoia was certainly in order. But some New Age entrepreneurs sounded like reactionary New Rightists in their denunciation of federal regulation of advertising, processing, and labor practices.

As a hip entrepreneur undertook a growth strategy there was danger of alienating the original subcultural market, just as some countercultural celebrities found themselves cut off from their radical base. Mo Siegel probably angered many co-ops and co-op shoppers as Celestial Seasonings cut deals with Safeway. Siegel's strategy did produce higher profits, but not so for Erewhon. Erewhon's decision to sell to the largest retailers at a very low profit margin undercut many smaller-scale outlets and ultimately damaged Erewhon itself, for it frequently found itself unable to supply its large customers while its older small ones stopped ordering. This New Age company made a very old mistake: it attempted to be both a large-scale manufacturer *and* distributor when it barely had the capacity to do one, much less both.[67]

Another hip variant of an old story was that of Steve's Ice Cream, a funky Somerville, Massachusetts, ice cream store that specialized in just the sort of all-natural, high-quality, hand-cranked, fruity ice cream adored by area heads. Popular far beyond his original low-key expectations, Steve Herrell soon tired of the business, sold out cheap ($40,000) to local franchisors, and moved to western Massachusetts, where, using his last name, he attempted to sell ice cream the original way. Herrell found himself competing with a much larger Steve's that used his own picture— a bit the way "Colonel" Harlan Sanders lost control of his name, image, and recipe to Kentucky Fried Chicken. Indeed, the same ultimately happened to Erewhon. Forced to file for bankruptcy in the early 1980s, Michio Kushi sold the firm to Nature Food

103

Centres, a chain of vitamin-oriented health food stores which kept Kushi on as a figurehead chairman for two years.[68]

UNCERTAINTY: GENTRIFICATION?

Like all businessmen, hip entrepreneurs were challenged by uncertainty. Where were supplies to come from, and at what price? Were there enough workers who, for the sake of an unusual work environment, were willing to accept lower wages? What would the competition do? The government? And, most unclear, how large was the market? What was the state of the countercuisine relative to the mainstream cuisine in the mid-1970s? To use a marketing term, where within its "product life-cycle" was the healthy foods business in the mid-seventies—introduction, growth, maturity, or decline?[69]

Given the crises of the 1970s, Dick Raymond's notion of hip Briars surviving in the cracks was a good metaphor, and certainly more realistic than talk of "revolution now." But *whose* cracks, that of a seemingly doomed establishment (as Raymond argued) or that of a crumbling counterculture? Would the big earthquake ever come, or were these "alternative" entrepreneurs simply subsisting in the shallow troughs left by a minor bohemian tremor?

Although I have argued that countercultural food beliefs, practices, and infrastructure constituted a coherent "cuisine," the countercuisine certainly did have its own fault lines. Indeed, the contradictions probably made the cuisine romantically attractive at the start, i.e., ca. 1968–73. By the mid-seventies, however, the question was whether this challenging array of beliefs and practices had enough power for the long evolutionary pull, or was it more a one-shot eruption, a fad? Was the countercuisine internally strong enough to surmount the obstacles posed by a hostile external environment?

The internal weaknesses were intellectual, organizational, and demographic.

Intellectually, the oppositional language of the countercuisine —natural vs. plastic, white vs. brown, process vs. processed, fast vs. slow, light vs. heavy—was exceptionally fragile. Depending so much on their overall context, these words were easily misunderstood and misused when taken out of it. The very vagueness and evanescence of these terms made them vulnerable to co-optation,

104

and for this the counterculture's hostility to intellectual discourse was partly to blame. A strong anti-intellectual strand spanned the whole period, from the Diggers' fierce attacks on New Left theory in 1966 to the *Briarpatch* editor Michael Phillips's 1976 outburst, "I love business! I find that the people who are happy in their work and do well in business don't place an undue value on ideas, routine, or 'talking' about things." [70] Yet informed conversation was really needed. It was one thing to reject rigid sectarian rhetoric or liberal academic complacency, but it was another thing to be so oblivious to the historical precedents for so many of the therapeutic, consumerist, and agricultural experiments of the time. It might have been helpful, for example, to know more about earlier utopian communities, the fate of nineteenth-century vegetarian reformers, or the high failure rate of small businesses. To be sure, much of the scholarly spadework of the later 1970s and 1980s was inspired by the improvisation early on, but a lot of time—perhaps too much—was wasted. Some of the most useful studies and proposals came after the organizational means to implement them no longer existed.

As the record of communes, co-ops, and hip businesses indicates, the organizational problems of building and maintaining alternative institutions were enormous. How to balance the often competing needs of men and women, management and labor, control and cooperation, efficiency and experimentation, ideological purity and pragmatic compromise, personal growth and organizational stability? Inevitably participants went through cycles of exhilaration and depression, swinging between what Daniel Zwerdling called "illusions of grandeur and burnout." From the therapeutic standpoint of "learning through failure," such cycles had educational value. But when applied to food production, volatility was dangerous and self-defeating. Small farms, groceries, and restaurants are not like other alternative institutions, which sociologist Paul Starr calls "high-intensity, low-commitment" organizations. [71] Rather, food-related organizations require precisely the reverse ratio: a low-key fidelity to an almost endless series of dull, repetitious chores and a stubborn commitment to slow, steady, modest gains over a very long run. One problem with the counterculture was most of its members were too young and profession-minded to feel fulfilled as stolid peasants, cooks, or shopkeepers.

105

Demographically, being young, white, and middle class was both a strength and a weakness. By sheer force of unprecedented numbers, this cohort demanded and won attention. But these characteristics also posed significant problems. Some treated their countercultural experience as an interesting semester abroad in a program that inevitably led back to school and managerial-professional status. As the war faded, so did some of the deviant-group solidarity of the antiwar coalition. The self-destruction of the Nixon administration in the Watergate affair, leading to a liberal democratic surge in 1974, softened the sense of alienation from established political institutions. The lack of any spectacular ecological disasters in the early seventies further eroded the group-survivalist imperative; to be sure, the environmental news was still bad—but for the long run, not for tomorrow. Instead, the mounting economic crisis encouraged more immediate, individualistic solutions. Rapidly rising food, housing, and land prices made dropping out into cheap communal living more difficult. As it became clear that the apocalypse was not at hand, thoughts naturally turned to training and career, marriage and family, home and neighborhood—and to ways of coping creatively with urban professional life's ambiguities, frustrations, and tensions.[72]

In *A Trumpet to Arms*, his narrative history of the alternative media, David Armstrong notes the rise in the mid-seventies of slick urban weeklies that catered to this "gentrification" of the Woodstock generation. In a chapter appropriately titled "Ten Great Places to Find Croissants After Midnight," Armstrong documents how much of the life-style advice was still phrased in survivalist terms, but now "survival" meant ameliorating the stresses and strains of renovating a house, finding sturdy oak antiques, staying thin, meeting like-minded singles, or holding a two-job marriage together with interesting dinners at unusual restaurants. Visiting Boston's New Earth Exposition of Appropriate Technology in 1978, political scientist Langdon Winner encountered "devices and techniques that can alleviate the kinds of pressures that normally befall professionals toiling in banks, insurance companies, and bureaucracies." Hundreds of bearded inventors and entrepreneurs hustled a startling array of ecologically virtuous jogging shoes, racing bicycles, hot tubs, backpacks, hang gliders—but no political programs. "Rather than attempt to change the structures that vex them young Americans growing older have settled on the quest for exquisite palliatives." Boston area seekers of edible palliatives had to go no further than the *Real Paper*'s "Out to Lunch" column, written by "Mark Nadeau," the pseudonym of Mark Zanger, who in the earlier 1970s was the *Real Paper*'s "Red Chef." As Red Chef, Zanger had reviewed restaurants known mostly for their cheap, abundant fare and resolutely proletarian atmosphere. His reviews were of course spiced with revolutionary exhortations and political advice. As Nadeau, however, he focused far more on "authenticity" and "taste"—the classic gourmet concerns. In 1978 Nadeau's recipes were collected in what he fittingly called "a survival guide." Since Zanger pronounced that there were "no great restaurants, only great dishes," his would-be survivors had to be prepared to do a lot of browsing. And there certainly were plenty of places to browse—all those cracks filled by hip Briars.[73]

While disappointed radicals deplored the "gentrification," other observers shrugged off as "inevitable" the transition from youthful rebellion to adult capitalism; the hippies were finally "growing up," "maturing." Countless "where are they *now?*" articles rejoiced in the radical-capitalist convergence: hairy revolutionaries had now become prosperous consultants, evangelists, therapists, politicians, merchants, investment bankers, music moguls, fashion designers, and gourmet chefs. The counterculture was thus dismissed as yet another ironic example of sowing wild oats before the inevitable "settling down."[74]

But did the counterculture really "settle down"? The "aging" analogy was deceptive. For one thing, although the Woodstock cohort was entering adulthood, there were many more baby boomers yet to come—a huge pool of potential recruits who loved rock 'n' roll and hated plastic. Also, not just the young cared about radical reform; many critics and role models were already quite grown-up—e.g., Robert Rodale, Barry Commoner, Gary Snyder, Ross Hume Hall. And growing up did not necessarily mean giving up youthful ideals. Hippies left communes for graduate school, but some of them wrote rather radical dissertations. Some wound up on congressional committees and in federal regulatory agencies investigating corporate abuses. Even many of those who went into "straight" careers remained concerned about peace, justice, and ecology. Reports of the counterculture's demise—or worse, "maturity"—may have been premature.[75]

It would be wrong, moreover, to focus exclusively on the movement's internal dynamics. The mainstream was changing too. *Time* and the *Real Paper* began to cover the same crises. People of all kinds were now against the Vietnam War; they were concerned about pollution, food quality, inflation, energy shortages; they re-

107

sented unresponsive central authorities and institutions; they felt nostalgic for a simpler, cleaner life. And, addressing those concerns, mass marketers were proliferating a variety of apparently natural, ethnic, lite, and otherwise healthy foods. Granola, yogurt, sprouts, even tofu were found in ordinary supermarkets.

Still, gentrification did happen in the late 1970s and early 1980s. Food co-ops lost their leases to French bistros; communal farms became weekend retreats. The oppositional grammar lost its context and power. Words like "macrobiotic," "organic," and, indeed, "revolution" became cause for embarrassed reminiscence— along with strobe candles, psychedelic bananas, and other undergraduate follies. "Natural" had no real meaning, while "living lightly" meant microwaving a low-calorie TV dinner. Only the more affluent consumers showed much interest in the healthy foods market. And many of these changes were problematic: the granola came as candy bars; the yogurt was laced with sugary jam or came frozen, artificially flavored, and topped with sprinkles.

To understand the countercuisine's ironic fate, we need to examine the external environment against which food rebels struggled and which they hoped to transform. How much of their message got through to the wider public? How much didn't, and why?

PART TWO

PROCESSING IDEOLOGY: THE MORAL PANIC

5 THE ORTHODOX DEFENSE: THE WAR OF THE METAPHORS

The food industry zeroed in its big guns on the insurgency right away. If the countercuisine functioned through networking, so did mainstream cuisine. A loose alliance of agribusiness firms, government agencies, scientific authorities, and mass media writers, this food establishment helped to distinguish what was considered "healthy" from what was considered "faddish," "balanced" from "extreme," prudent from foolish, safe from harmful. In the 1970s there was a lot of mopping up to do.

The ideological heavyweights generally agreed that organic force was dangerous—and it was! As critic Jim Hightower put it in 1975, although the $500 million organic foods business posed no immediate competitive threat to the $160 billion food industry, the very existence of naturally produced alternatives might cause people to wonder about all the brand-name stuff they were buying. Beyond calling unwanted attention to food manufacturing, the organic paradigm questioned conventional science, challenged the prevailing system of food distribution, and advocated a radical decentralization of population and power. Confronting the organic menace, the food system went into a full-scale "moral panic" in the early 1970s. In *Folk Devils and Moral Panics* (1972) Stan Cohen says:

> *Societies appear to be subject, every now and then, to periods of moral panic. A condition, episode, person, or group of persons emerges to become defined as a threat to societal values and interests; its nature is presented in stylized and stereotypical fashion by the mass media; the moral barricades are manned by editors, bishops, politicians, and other right-thinking people; socially accredited experts pronounce their diagnoses and solutions; ways of coping are evolved or (more often) resorted to; the condition then disappears, submerges, or deteriorates.*[1]

The fierce counterattack did force organic proponents to lay low through the late 1970s and early 1980s. Although organic research and development went on, it was done quietly, out of the sight lines of the food industry's heavy artillery.

The food wars of the 1970s showed how dominant forces combat deviant ideas. Yet, however lopsided, such hegemonic contests are never one-sided. According to Antonio Gramsci, hegemony is a "moving equilibrium," an ongoing process of adjustments, shifts, and accommodations by the dominant culture.[2] In the food-ideological battles of the 1970s, radicals scored points too, forcing adjustments and compromises. To maintain overall control, the establishment would have to give a bit by 1980. But the dominant culture gave, not out of any benevolent spirit of fair play or noblesse oblige, but because the food establishment was itself weakened by internal debates: How safe and fulfilling *was* the food supply? Was chemistry a friend or foe? Had modern agribusiness produced the best of all cuisines? While some diehards fiercely defended the status quo, others in government, the media, and business saw the need for some changes. But which or how much? Just when food-related stories were big news, the public was treated to the discomforting spectacle of scientists, journalists, and politicians disagreeing among themselves. The cracks that gave hope to the Bay Area's Briars and other alternative organizations widened in the later 1970s, leaving the public even more worried

112

and confused about food quality. The struggle to fill the cracks posed major ideological and marketing challenges: to what extent would the fissures be occupied by the countercuisine's alternative organizations-in-training, and to what extent would they be patched by the food industry's new adhesives?

TRUE BELIEVERS

F irst the hard-core defense.

Ideological conflicts are as much a clash of metaphors as of economic and political self-interest. While countercuisine partisans saw themselves as heroic rabbits struggling to establish healthy niches in a survivalist briarpatch, many in the food establishment acted more like complacently plump suburbanites whose cocktail party is invaded by voracious rats. How could this have happened? After having been so careful for so many years! While some hippies might wonder if rodents were so terrible, the industry rushed to mobilize the fumigators.

The fierce counterattack was no surprise to radical critics, who viewed the food industry's ideological apparatus as a powerful and sophisticated equal of the better-known defense establishment. In power-structure analyses with titles like "Boston's Agri-Biz Academics" and "Professors on the Take," left investigators chronicled the "interlocking directorate" between the "Green Monster" and its kept intellectuals and politicians: elite university nutritionists, land grant college agronomists, chemical engineers, newspaper and magazine food and health writers, school dieticians, medical school professors, government researchers and managers, agriculture committee members in state and federal legislatures, and so on. A favored target was Dr. Frederick Stare, who had chaired Harvard's Department of Nutrition ever since founding it in 1942. Stare was a dedicated defender of just about every staple of modern processing—additives, sugar, white flour, fortified cereals—and he did not hesitate to voice his scorn in the most direct and colorful ways. Like another professorial spokesman for the food industry, USDA Secretary Earl Butz, Stare was a master of pithy positivism. In *Panic in the Pantry* (1975), a full-scale defense of the status quo written with fellow nutritionist Elizabeth Whalen, Stare argued that "food additives are like friends. We need and depend on them and often take them for granted. . . . Eat your

113

additives, they're good for you." Dismissing as "totally unfounded" concerns about the chemical cuisine, Stare called the
back-to-nature "mania" a "hoax, perpetuated by opportunists who
are intent on taking advantage of nervous and very gullible consumers." Stare was formidable because he really got around, testi-
fying before congressional committees, writing for the whole
gamut of academic and popular periodicals, speaking on dozens of
panels, sitting on food industry boards of directors, and, most important, serving as a standard "source" for mainstream journalists
in need of a quotable reaction to the latest food scare. Such journalists rarely quoted Stare's critics, who alleged that the inventor
of Special K (and consultant on the Pop Tart) was simply a hired
gun. Stare repeatedly denied that he personally benefited from
industry largesse, but he did acknowledge that his own department received numerous research grants from food corporations.
Harvard's Nutrition Department was also the base of another
much-quoted expert, Jean Mayer, who had served on the Board of
Directors of Monsanto and Miles Laboratories.[3]

Establishment defenders frequently ridiculed the "conspiracy
theories" of underground journalists, and indeed cited such "paranoia" as evidence of the pathological marginality of countercuisine
"quacks." Dismissing these "food neurotics" and "food Mc-
Carthyites," a *Vogue* writer wondered how so many scientists "with
the most impeccable credentials" could all be "in league with the
devil." Such was the line in the more popular magazines, but
behind the scenes, in industry trade journals, food corporations
were actively setting up "information programs" that relied on
friendly academic experts to reassure and "educate" an increasingly alarmed public. Thus, to the extent that these allies had
helped the food industry in the past and were asked to do so again
in the battles of the 1970s, the radicals were not unnecessarily
paranoid. Someone *was* out to get them.[4]

To read just the titles, credits, and bibliographies of articles
in *Food Technology* is to appreciate how widely cast was the food-
industrial-academic net. A three-page assault in 1974 on "Organic
Foods" by the Institute of Food Technologists' Expert Panel on
Food Safety and Nutrition had forty footnotes, citing diverse and
impressive-sounding journals like the *Annual Review of Plant Physi-
ology, Journal of Nutrition Education, Journal of Agricultural and Food
Chemistry, Bulletin of the Entomological Society of America, Journal of
the American Dietetic Association,* and *Journal of Home Economics.*

114

Mixed in were articles from parascientific periodicals tied to specific industries: *Food Product Development, Dairy Council Digest, Chemical and Engineering News.* Expanding the interdisciplinary net were references to *Scientific American, Natural History, Science, Farm Bureau, Today's Health, Nutrition Today, Ladies' Home Journal,* and assorted publications of the USDA and FDA. The article's experts were in turn quoted, paraphrased, and otherwise invoked in mass-market publications like *Time, Life, Seventeen, Vogue,* and *House Beautiful.*[5]

Reiterated in this and dozens of similar articles was a defense of the assumptions and metaphors upon which the food industry had long depended for popular support. Challenging the sharp contrasts drawn by the countercuisine, the defenders offered their own interpretations of key concepts—especially "natural," "organic," "chemical," and "moderate."

WHAT'S NATURAL?

For the countercuisine, "natural" stood for a subversively preindustrial and romantic world—something very different from the status quo. On this the orthodox defenders agreed: "natural" was a dangerous concept that might seduce the public into romantic antimodernism and thereby undo many years of propaganda on behalf of high-tech food production and processing. Determined to nip any natural trend in the bud, the food industry's ideological warriors were bold—especially in the early 1970s, when they still assumed that they had history on their side. Rather than bend to any public softness for nature, the zealots made two self-serving but somewhat inconsistent arguments: that everything, including additives, pesticides, even plastics, was natural; and that modern technology was superior to nature.[6]

The "everything's natural" argument simply defined away all conceivable conflicts. If man, birds, food, cars, and Carnation Instant Breakfast were all assembled from the same relatively finite array of chemicals, then they were all related! The logic recalled high school chemistry class: Remember those periodic charts that used to hang up front, over near the window? All those elements are natural! Remember our friend carbon, letter C? Well, since everything that has the letter C in it is organic, just about all pesticides and processed foods are "organic." So much for Mr.

115

Rodale! Conversely, "natural" foods were actually composed of chemicals. Like the back-row wise guys in tenth-grade lab, some defenders delighted in playing practical jokes by scaring their squeamish victims with a tongue-twisting list of chemical compounds and then revealing, after a chuckle or two, that these were the ingredients in "natural" eggs, coffee, green beans, or an apple. Presenting a paragraph-long partial listing of the ingredients in breast milk, Kraft's chairman, William Beers, mused that food technology's public relations problem was one of semantics, not science: the public was simply frightened by all that technical language.[7]

But it shouldn't be, the defense continued; a chemical is a chemical is a chemical. Contrary to the claims of holistic fetishists, it did not matter whether you ate whole wheat bread or fortified Wonder, since, in molecular terms, the nutrients were the same. Similarly, a plant could derive its nitrogen equally easily from synthesized fertilizer or "organic" compost; nitrogen was nitrogen. Nor was there any difference between applying a store-bought pesticide, like DDT, or some biological control, like rotenone. Both were chemicals. "Chemical pest control is neither foreign nor incompatible with nature," American Cyanamid's pesticide manager explained to a 1970 convention of outdoor writers. "Animals and plants are chemical factories. They regulate their growth, reproduction, and relations within their environment by chemical signals and exchanges."[8]

In what transmuted into a sermon about the eternal and universal oneness of life, those who questioned chemicals stood accused of denying their own essence. Marveling at this breezy reductionism, Michael Jacobson, of the Nader-inspired Center for Science in the Public Interest (CSPI), caricatured it this way:

People, natural foods, air, and water are made of chemicals.
All of these things are safe.
Food additives are chemicals.
Therefore food additives are safe.[9]

116

Overplayed, the "everything's natural" tautology probably failed to ease anxiety, for it offended common sense. If everything was natural, then nothing was artificial—and this just did not seem right to those who, while perhaps rusty in high school chemistry, felt sure that only *some* things were natural, and, moreover, that some chemicals *were* dangerous. The real issue was *who* should control *which* chemicals and for whose benefit and at what costs? These were questions for policymakers, not dictionaries.

The second case against natural foods was stronger because it confronted the policy questions directly. Rather than relying on an etymological sleight-of-hand, it acknowledged that there *was* some difference between nature and chemistry, and it was a good thing too, the argument went, for chemistry was superior. Cut the nostalgia; nature has never been a friend to mankind. Without science and engineering, we'd starve. Measured against the job performance of Mother Nature, food technology's benefits far outweighed its risks.

The portrait of nature as a poor provider was archetypal, used whenever would-be civilization builders needed mythic support. The Greeks, for example, invoked Prometheus, who, to feed and warm mankind, stole fire from the gods, who would have preferred that we suffer in an apparently frigid state of nature. At some cost to Prometheus's liver (even in the Golden Age there was no free lunch), humans defrosted, learned to roast, bake, and fry, and ultimately mastered the world. Elaborating on that ancient case for better living through chemistry, the modern-day Swiss Prometheans of the food industry spelled out the ways that Mother Nature grossly neglected her human offspring, especially in the field, at the cash register, and in the kitchen.

First, in agriculture, "nature" meant plagues, pestilence, and famine. The defenders of high-tech agribusiness wrongly equated "organic" with laissez-faire and somberly warned of the dire consequences of "doing nothing" and "leaving everything up to nature." (In fact, organic farming entailed a supervigilant, labor-intensive manipulation of nature in nondestructive ways.) Nature has never been in balance, they argued; ruthless competition, not serene harmony, is the universal and timeless rule. To Exodus's frogs, gnats, flies, cattle anthrax and boils, hail, locusts, and dust, they added 10,000 other species of insects, 1,500 species of parasitic nematodes, 1,500 parasitic plant diseases, 80,000 species of fungi, and 600 kinds of harmful weeds—all eagerly awaiting any sign of Americans letting down their shield of 45,000 brand-name insecticides, fungicides, herbicides, rodenticides, defoliants, nematocides, miticides, desiccants, and plant-growth regulants. Organic researchers questioned whether all these pesticides had actually increased yields in the relatively short time that they had been applied; there was some evidence that the percentages of crop lost to pests had remained about the same, but at vastly increased costs. But chemistry's defenders commonly avoided matters of productivity and effectiveness. Rather, they tended to cite the same statistics and anecdotes: the incredible reproduction rates of the ordinary house fly, the potato blight that devastated Ireland in the mid-nineteenth century, Texas's great grasshopper plague in 1864, DDT's role in fighting malaria, yellow fever, or sleeping sickness. That there possibly were less toxic alternatives to these chemicals (as became clear after DDT was banned in 1972) was rarely admitted.[10]

Similarly, defenders of petrochemical fertilizers repeatedly misrepresented the case for natural substitutes. While every organic gardener from Albert Howard on knew that the heat generated within a well-tended compost pile made it sterile, establishment spokesmen wrote as if compost were fresh night soil and thus more dangerous than any synthetic fertilizer, even with the acknowledged chemical runoff problems. "While organic foods may escape chemical pollution," Harvard's Jean Mayer asserted, "biologically speaking they tend to become the most contaminated of all. Organic fertilizers of animals or human origin are obviously the most likely to contain gastrointestinal parasites."[11]

Mayer & Co. warned that organic farming would bring both Third World sanitation problems and, by doubling food costs, Third World poverty and famine. While radicals hoped that, with improved techniques, wider distribution, and increased demand, organic food prices would decline, industry defenders assumed that organic prices would remain high forever, doubling the 16 percent of family income said to be spent on food. This statistic was repeated constantly, even after the USDA admitted that it applied only to families of four with household incomes of $20,000 —about one-fifth of American families in the early 1970s. Jim Hightower estimated that the average "working stiff" spent up to 60 percent on food—a figure he attributed to the high costs of oligopoly.[12]

Nature would also impoverish the farmer. Without the strong chemical fix to which they were now addicted, farmers would go bankrupt. In dismissing "impractical" compost and manure, no one acknowledged the possibility that decreased yields might be offset by lower costs, and that even these losses might be made up, in time, through careful husbandry. Instead, the trade-off was invariably drawn between mass starvation and mass affluence. Virtually every attack on organic ideas dutifully quoted Earl Butz's categorical declaration: "Without the modern input of chemicals, of pesticides, of antibiotics, we simply could not do the job. Before we go back to an organic agriculture in this country, somebody must decide which 50 million Americans we are going to let starve or go hungry." "Natural farming is perfectly all right," went an advertisement by Pennwalt Corporation, a maker of agricultural chemicals, "as long as you believe in natural famine." That millions of Americans were already hungry or that American farmers had been overproducing long before the widespread application of these chemicals did not enter into the debate. Frances Moore Lappé's argument that world hunger was a political and distribution problem, not a matter of a problem of production, received no attention from those whose livelihood depended on heightened production. Rather, the choice was between "doing nothing" and the status quo, with no possibility of change, except for farmers to get big or get out. The small family farm was just one small step above Mother Nature in mankind's evolution from barbarism to civilization.[13]

Similar arguments abounded for chemicalized food processing. Life without preservatives meant botulism, salmonella, and dysentery; without fortification, rickets, pellagra, and scurvy; without fabrication, starvation; without artificial flavors and dyes, boredom. Not only did chemicals fight germs and build strong bodies, they could be less toxic than many "natural poisons." "As a physician and a student of nutrition for the past 30 years," Frederick Stare announced, "I am convinced that food additives are far safer than the basic natural foods themselves." In *The Consumer's Right to Know*, a consumer newsletter distributed by the Kraft Food Company, Michigan State University nutritionist Dena Cederquist testified to the horrors of a natural diet: "I was raised on an Iowa farm, and grew up on natural foods. Now I have prematurely gray hair, wear glasses, and have all my teeth filled. I had undulant fever as a child from drinking raw milk, and I've had major surgery for cancer. So, I'm delighted that milk is pasteurized, and that our food supply is of consistent, safe quality." If the argument be believed, some of the deadliest toxins were in foods commonly thought to be healthy: spinach and rhubarb (oxalic acid), peanuts and corn (aflatoxin), celery (nitrates), potatoes (solanin), lima

119

beans (cyanide), almonds (prussic acid), cinnamon (hallucinogens). The natural food store, with its unprocessed wheat germ, raw milk, and herbal teas, was a minefield of rancidity. Almost as dangerous as Mother Nature was the human mother who persisted in old-fashioned ways. Home-canned beans were potentially more deadly than anything concocted by Del Monte; moldy home-baked brown bread could not compare in safety with store-bought, plastic-wrapped, artificially preserved white.[14]

Here again, the strategy was to neutralize the critics by making everything equal, toxins in cereal and toxins in celery—everything's natural, everything's deadly—and thus to finesse the question of control. The average consumer could monitor his personal intake of potentially deadly spinach, but could he regulate the amount of coal tar dyes in Jell-O? Obviously not. But trust us, the defenders argued, *we* know how much to put in. Why would we want to poison you? "Why would the food industry want to destroy its consuming public?" Dr. Cederquist asked. "I'm sure they'd like to keep us consuming for as long as possible." And if economic self-interest and inherent good were insufficient to safeguard the public, there were always the experts at the FDA, with its list of additives Generally Regarded As Safe (GRAS). Whereas chemicals were scrutinized by federal watchdogs, nature roamed unregulated, free to maim and kill, as the *FDA Consumer* observed in an article entitled "Natural Poisons in Food": "There are toxicants present in naturally produced foods that would never be permitted by FDA if offered as food additives." If the FDA was negligent, some processors argued, it was in tolerating the Mama-Papa natural foods business.[15]

Beyond being a life-threatening pest, nature was a poor chef. Additives enhanced the palatability of packaged foods. Without the sodium in baby food, how would baby eat her carrots? Without the food coloring, artificial strawberries, and sugar in otherwise bland cold cereals, how would Mom get her kids to drink their milk? One flavoring manufacturer urged its processor-customers to "think of putting in a little something for Mother. The delicious, pure flavors that will help give her children the health and body-building foods they need." In nutritionists' terms, processing enhanced the "nutrient availability"; in other words, processors bribed otherwise picky eaters to take their vitamins and minerals.[16]

Such bribery would be even more necessary in the near future, food technologists argued, for without artificial flavor, how

120

would people down their seaweed patties? Like many in the late 1960s and early 1970s, scientists worried about overpopulation and worldwide food shortages. But for solutions technologists looked not to redistribution (as Lappé advocated) but to new feats of chemically aided production. Especially promising was the fabrication of pseudo-chops, burgers, and sausages out of substances previously thought inedible—algae, fish meal, textured vegetable proteins, wood pulp, and petroleum by-products. In a 1974 report to a U.S. Senate committee investigating world hunger, an "availability panel" of nutritionists, M.D.'s, and food executives chaired by Jean Mayer strongly recommended that food processors be "encouraged to create new foods as new technologies and new resources provide opportunities, especially new foods that will improve the nutritional status of malnourished people in lesser developed areas of the world." [17]

This servant-savior mantle was enthusiastically welcomed by food technologists who, to enhance a product's acceptability, carefully engineered its "hedonics"—taste, flavor, mouthfeel, texture, and color. The frontispiece to a standard textbook, *Flavor Research: Recent Advances*, gave a poetic version of this mission to "feed the hungry":

> *To researchers who analyze taste*
> *We dedicate this opus in haste,*
> *We salute all your labors,*
> *Devoted to flavors,*
> *And your efforts to minimize waste.*
>
> *With so many people to feed,*
> *Of every religion and creed,*
> *We have no recourse,*
> *Than to use each resource,*
> *To meet man's nutritional need.*

121

Noting that the cost of protein processed directly from waste effluents was only three cents a pound—one-third the cost of agriculturally produced animal protein—one flavoring industry marketing consultant concluded that "the challenge to the art and science of flavoring is quite clear." [18]

Despite this rhetoric of public service, critics suspected business self-interest. For one thing, as the food chemical ads themselves showed, artificial flavors were far more predictable than Mother Nature's. Thus, Durkee's Synthesized Tomato Flavor enabled sauce makers to "quit hassling nature's fickleness—crop failures, labor costs [apparently a natural plague too], supply problems, quality fluctuations." Moreover, "feeding the world" could be a euphemism for "expanding exports of processed foods" to the Third World. Although there might be merit in investigating the protein potential of waste effluents, algae, fish meal, and soybeans, food industry critics and defenders alike knew that for the foreseeable future any edible analogs would be far too expensive to feed the poor. As insurgent nutritionist Joan Dye Gussow quipped in an essay, "Who's Going to Eat the Breakfast of Champions"—a reference to a Kurt Vonnegut novel in which petroleum was the main food source—the new food analogs were "more likely to end up as Baco's than as survival rations." In the near future, the industry hoped to ship what it was already making. For example, one Nabisco executive confided that, to offset the growing public concern at home about additive-ridden "junk foods," Nabisco hoped to expand its exports of Oreos and Ritz Crackers to Latin America. "It's fine to talk about nutrition, but when people are really hungry, what they really need is calories. Our products are good supplies of basic calories and a certain amount of nutrition." To quibble about natural ingredients thus seemed a frivolous self-indulgence at a time of global calorie shortage.[19]

CHEMICAL LIBERATION: THE IDEOLOGY OF CONVENIENCE

The case against nature was logically consistent with the long-term thrust of consumer capitalism: for at least half a century, mass marketers had been struggling hard to propel consumers out of their earthbound, preindustrial ruts and up into a weightless realm of perpetual nowness and newness.[20] But perhaps aware that messy tradition still had a residual gravitational tug, food technology's defenders also sounded the venerable theme of equal opportunity: Modern agriculture and processing freed farmers and housewives from drudgery, created time for more noble pursuits, and, through lowered costs, raised everyone's standard of living.

When applied to convenience goods and services, the ideology of equal opportunity had long served to reconcile democratic val-

122

ues with mass production. The original mass producers of cheap cars, cigarettes, and entertainment were all hailed as democratic liberators. Similarly, in *The Americans: The Democratic Experience*, Daniel Boorstin recounts the way early innovations in food processing were promoted as ways to overcome the constraining inequities of season and region.

> *The flavor of life had once come from winter's cold, summer's heat, the special taste and color of each season's diet. The American Democracy of Times and Places meant making one place and one thing more like another, by bringing them under the control of man. The flavor of fresh meat would be tasted anywhere anytime, summer would have its ice, and winter have its warmth, inside and outside would flow together, and men would live and work not only on the unlevel ground but also in the homogeneous air.*

In the 1850s Gail Borden offered his condensed meat biscuit and milk as invaluable aids to westward migrants in desperate need of portable meals that could be consumed safely and quickly anywhere; the same rationale sold fast-food burgers a hundred years later. In 1924 a historian of the canning industry boasted that canning gave every American family—even in the worst tenements— "a kitchen garden where all good things grow, and where it is always harvest time. There are more tomatoes in a ten-cent can than could be bought fresh in city markets for that sum when tomatoes are at their cheapest." Virtually the same words pitched refrigerated meat in the 1880s, frozen beans in the 1930s, and irradiated pork in the 1980s: in each case, a commercially controlled technology was hailed as an important step forward in what Boorstin terms Americans' democratic drive to "level time and place." [21]

123

To this basic theme the ideological warriors of the 1970s added a timely variation: processed convenience foods were allies of feminism and environmentalism; only a society as widely blessed with affluence could afford the luxury of such life-style insurgencies. This assertion was familiar enough during the political battles of the late 1960s, when rebellious youths were portrayed not as champions of the disadvantaged but rather as spoiled by-products of an overly generous mainstream society.[22] In the food wars of the 1970s, processors themselves took credit for creating the affluent prerequisites for rebellion.

The notion that packaged foods and electric appliances liberated women from kitchen slavery was not in itself new, nor was it completely inaccurate, but what was relatively novel was the assertion that the revived drive for women's rights in the late 1960s was caused by the blender, toaster oven, and instant pudding mix. As recently as the 1950s food ads and articles in women's magazines had implied that convenience goods helped to preserve dependence and domesticity; relieved from drudgery, housewives would have more time to drive children around and look pretty for husbands. It was the overworked wife, such literature warned, who would be less able to maintain her spouse's sexual interest or who might be tempted to abandon the nest herself. By the late 1960s, however, manufacturers offered themselves as accomplices in women's drive for independence. For example, one executive argued that more and more women were entering the workforce because, with all the new convenience foods and tools, they no longer had to spend so much time in the kitchen. Thanks to these aids, he continued, women were freer to augment their family income. Along the same lines, Jean Mayer suggested that the additives in convenience foods were a precondition for the women's liberation movement:

> *The women's liberation movement became possible when labor-saving devices freed adult females from many of the drudgeries of housekeeping. Refrigerators eliminated the need for daily food shopping, modern stoves and dishwashers reduced somewhat the time associated with the preparation of meals. The development of convenience foods, however, was the major quantum jump in freeing the housewife from the need of spending hours every day being the family cook. . . . Food additives have played an indispensable role in the development of these time-savers.*

124

More a nutritionist than an historian, Mayer overlooked the rise of feminism in the early nineteenth century—long before the introduction of laborsaving appliances and packaged foods by supposedly benevolent male manufacturers.[23]

Such explanations also tended to reverse cause and effect. Historians of housework have shown that some household appliances and prepared foods did reduce drudgery—especially at the turn of this century—but they did not necessarily reduce labor. Historian Ruth Schwartz Cowan observes that American housewives worked about as many hours a week at home in 1980 as in 1910—fifty. Rather than cutting time, the new tools often introduced new standards and tastes that, if anything, created new tasks and also new income needs. When women went to work it was not because they now had spare time, but rather because they needed the additional income to pay the higher capital costs of the ever more mechanized household. In turn, with two jobs, women now had even less time, and thus came to rely even more on gadgets and processed foods—a cycle of dependency hard to break. The recent revival of feminism stemmed in part from resentment at the failure of household mechanization to free women's time and spirits, and partly from women's need to make more money to pay their bills. Convenience goods manufacturers had little to do with women's "liberation"—except as targets of mounting criticism. In fact, in their own trade periodicals mass processors frequently acknowledged that many women resented being dependent on products increasingly perceived to be nutritionally and aesthetically inferior to homemade.[24]

In addition to asserting patrimony of women's liberation, food establishment defenders also attempted to portray the rise of consumerism and environmentalism as inevitable offshoots of mass-produced prosperity. With all this extra money came extra time to worry about every teensy risk. "At the present time," a food researcher for the right-wing Hudson Institute announced, "the abundance of our food supply permits the luxury of trying to avoid any and all risk." Fretting about trivialities like preservatives and pesticides was a bit like some bored, pampered teenager crying about a split fingernail or a misplaced curl. Branding as an "extreme self-indulgence" what was a very moderate food labeling proposal by the FDA, one industry ally observed, "In no place in the world where food is in short supply could one imagine a regulatory effort of this kind. . . ."[25]

Having progressed so far, soft Americans had quickly forgotten to whom they owed it all. "Please note that it is our new

125

wealth which gives us the luxury of being able to reassess our relation-ship to our environment," one General Foods market researcher asserted. "While we were scratching for enough calories to main-tain our body weight, environmental issues didn't seem very important." To enhance the point, food industry defenders com-monly claimed that life before processing was barely worth living. If these historical portraits be believed, as recently as the early twentieth century America was little different from Bangladesh, a world where rickets, scurvy, and kwashiorkor were the norm. Having conquered these dread diseases through modern medi-cine and food processing, narcissistic Americans of the Me Dec-ade seemed to be enjoying "the luxury of worrying" about the maladies of affluence: heart disease, cancer, stroke, hypertension, and diabetes.[26]

Like moralizing parents badgering picky children to remem-ber the starving in India and clean their plates, the food establish-ment urged balky consumers to ponder pellagra and gobble down their additives, sugar, and fat. To some extent, such reasoning simply reflected cultural lag on the part of nutritionists and doctors still fixated on nineteenth-century deficiency diseases. Operating within the prevailing paradigm of "nutritional adequacy," studies found that most—but by no means all—Americans now ate enough of the "basic" nutrients: protein, calories, vitamins, and minerals. But it was no coincidence that this argument served the self-interest of food processors oriented to "adding value" to oth-erwise inexpensive raw foods. Conquering the familiar deficiency and food bacterial diseases had been easy for them, for it required the addition of ingredients; battling the newer "diseases of afflu-ence" was much harder, for it involved taking out ingredients that made products manageable and palatable. In the vitamin boom after World War I, major manufacturers profited nicely by replacing some of the nutrients lost in the processing—and then charging for the extra step of "fortification." So too, defeating mold and sal-monella meant more preservatives, more packaging, more han-dling, more fees. But how to "add value" by doing less in the first place?[27]

126

STAKING THE CENTER

After ridiculing reformers, misrepresenting organic farming, slandering nature, belittling Mom, and caricaturing history, the defense then attempted to occupy the democratic middle ground highly desired in a public debate. Here again, as with "natural," the middle was more rhetorical than scientific.

The vocabulary of attack was classic. First, the critics were relegated to the undesirable fringe. Like health reformers before them, food radicals were subject to a variety of well-worn epithets: "faddish," "cultish," "quacks," "lunatic," "nuts," "reactionary," "hucksters," "hogwash," "superstitious," "medieval," "witch-hunting," "fraud," "dupes," "zealots," "anti-intellectual," "emotional," "hysterical," and perhaps the most damning in a supposedly postideological age, "ideological." Reductio ad absurdum was a particularly favored tactic: if the radicals "had their way," we would return to "the pickle barrel era," plagues and pellagra, "mass starvation," "caves," "the trees," and so on. Hopelessly naive "do-gooders" were a frequent target—as in American Cyanamid's T. J. White defense of pesticides before the 1970 conference of the Outdoor Writers Association of America:

> *Pesticides are pollutants in some degree or another. But what isn't a pollutant, including you and me? You may have read of Goodwyn Goodwill, whose only desire was to leave this world a better place for his having passed through it. He was a happy man until he took up the study of ecology. Goodwyn Goodwill became so concerned he was harming the ecology of our planet that his only solution was to drop dead. He did, was cremated, and his ashes were scattered. Alas, most of his remains became smog and the 10 parts per million of DDT in his ashes floated back down to earth.*

127

So if the mischievous radical was one pole, the overly credulous public was the other. Ignorant, confused, or just plain lazy, the average citizen—Goodwyn Goodwill—was letting himself become unduly alarmed by left extremists. Since life was imperfect and imperfectable, the best that one could hope for was that men of "good sense" would make "sound judgments." And who would these "reasonable" people be? The "experts" in industry, government, and research—the food establishment.

The soothing vocabulary associated with these authorities was as centrist as the harsh description of radicals was polarizing: "reasonable certainty," "knowledgeable," "scientific," "informed," "responsible," "constructive solutions," "best scientific judgment attainable," "generally recognized," "pragmatic," "balanced," and, to be sure, "moderate." [28] But how meaningful were these labels? As Benjamin Disraeli wrote, "There is moderation even in excess." Advocates of radical reform also counseled moderation. In *Small Is Beautiful*—the crystallizing textbook of appropriate technology, voluntary simplicity, and the Briarpatch philosophy— E. F. Schumacher characterized his "Buddhist Economics" as "the Middle Way between materialist heedlessness and traditionalist immobility." [29] To the countercuisine, this meant avoiding "extremes" such as fast food on the right and misunderstood macrobiotics on the left; co-ops were the sensible middle ground between supermarkets and health food stores. Confident that common sense resided in a time-tested, minimally processed "natural" diet, underground food writers expressed contempt for overnight wonders, whether the latest instant toaster breakfast from Pillsbury or the latest mystical import from Asia. Suspicious of "heavy" dogma, rhetoric, and rules, they advised readers to steer what they saw as a cautiously flexible course between "poisons" and "fads."

Still, the countercuisine's "sound judgment" was quite different from that of the establishment. Who would do the judging? The conflicting definitions of "common sense" were most clear when it came to the question of "evidence." Both sides recognized that, because little sustained research had been done on the thousands of food chemicals introduced in the past thirty years, there could be "little evidence" of an ingredient's harmfulness or safety. For critics like Beatrice Trum Hunter, scientific ignorance dictated an abstemious approach: when in doubt, throw it out. For defenders like Emil Mrak, former chancellor of the University of California (and frequent board member of various food corporations and federal agencies), our lack of knowledge meant that we should "quit worrying about food safety, practice moderation, and

128

enjoy life." When the critics cautioned, à la Franklin, "never leave that till tomorrow which you can do today," and "a little neglect may breed mischief," the defenders seemed to urge consumers, with Ecclesiastes, to eat, drink, and be merry—and forget tomorrow. When one side was skeptical about anything that might be risky, the other side shrugged that this was silly, since it was probably more dangerous to cross the street. As with so much of the debate, it boiled down to a conflict between doubt and trust.[30]

To bolster trust, the food industry stepped up its "nutrition education" efforts. The young in particular needed to be reminded about plagues and pellagra. With relish, major food corporations distributed free pamphlets to schoolteachers ever grateful for colorful material. At a 1977 hearing before the House Subcommittee on Domestic Marketing, chairman Fred Richmond (D-NY) found most corporately sponsored "nutrition education" to be "self-serving." Of twenty-five samples of corporate literature, seventeen examples were "highly promotional." Observing that "under the guise of nutrition education, they are promoting their products to captive audiences" of students, Richmond warned that the classroom was in danger of becoming "the new frontier for advertising." Sheila Harty's *Hucksters in the Classroom* (1979), a Nader-related study of industry propaganda in the schools, reached a similar conclusion: it was hard to distinguish nutrition education from product advertising in publications such as KraftCo's "Guide to Cheese Nutrition," Kellogg's "Stick Up for Breakfast Campaign," "The Campbell Cookbook," the Manufacturing Chemists Association's "Food Additives: Who Needs Them?", McDonald's "Nutrition Action Pack," and "Mr. Peanut's Guide to Physical Fitness."[31]

Given the "lack of evidence" about food chemicals, such materials had little that was new to tell students. Instead, they warned against "faddism," and charted the standard three-squares, basic-four formula for a "balanced diet": Three times a day eat selections from the four basic groups: meat, dairy, vegetables and fruits (one group), grains. Reflecting the older war against deficiency diseases, this protein- and vitamin-rich diet also testified to the power of the meat and dairy interests, who got 50 percent of the responsibility for a "balanced" diet. In this equation, a vegetarian diet seemed to lack protein and was thus "imbalanced"; the macrobiotic diet was particularly dangerous because it lacked both meat and dairy. Grains—whether whole wheat, corn flakes, or refined starch—were considered sources of carbohydrates but not

129

of protein or fiber. Ice cream fit nicely under dairy as a fine source
of calcium—along with American cheese. The sugar in the ice
cream and the additives in the cheese did not enter into consideration, which was fine by the food processors. But where would
soybeans and other legumes fit—with lettuce, apples, and other
fruits and vegetables?

Despite such jurisdictional dilemmas, the standard advice was
quite inclusive, not exclusive. By eating a "wide variety" of foods,
consumers would spread the risks, acquire as-yet-unidentified nutrients, and, happily for food processors, feel free to sample the
10,000 or more foods available in modern supermarkets. The last
consideration was of special comfort to snack-food makers whose
products were full of sugar, salt, and fat, but were rather meager
in any of the "basic fours" and were not generally consumed during the "three squares." In responding to the charge that junk
foods did not even satisfy the conventional formula, such manufacturers relied on what were the standard defenses of every questionable product, from beer to cigarettes to potato chips: crossing the
street is probably more risky; don't overdo it; who said that X
(chips, beer, candy bars, cola, or the like) is the only thing you
should eat? Blaming the consumer for imbalances, individual manufacturers hoped that shoppers would make up dietary shortcomings not by restricting purchases of junk foods but by eating even
more widely. Addition, not subtraction, was the key to business
prosperity.[32]

Although there was little new in the content of such "education" or in what it revealed about nutritionists' congenial ties to
food manufacturers, what *was* significant was that these campaigns
had to be waged at all. A more secure establishment would have
had to say nothing. As sociologist Paul Starr argues in *The Social
Transformation of American Medicine* (1982), persuasion (or force) is
needed only when authority breaks down; when authority is secure, reasons are assumed or taken on faith, and do not have to be
stated. The 1970s were years of widening doubt, however, when a
lot of reasons had to be stated—and restated.[33] For the food industry as for Starr's medical industry, the erosion of authority was
worsened by the fact that the doubts were felt within the power
structure. The network was beginning to unravel. That food processors felt compelled to endow their own "research" and "educational" institutes, councils, boards, centers, and bureaus was
evidence that the normally unpaid, quasi-autonomous channels of

130

information and reinforcement were no longer so dependable. Indeed, in the mid-seventies, as the diehards struggled for the desired middle ground, their list of purported "extremists" lengthened to include "zealots" at the FTC, "ideological" liberals in Congress, "arbitrary" regulators at the FDA, "ill-informed" scientists at elite universities, "huckster" physicians, the "sensation-seeking" media, and—perhaps most distressing to true-believing food engineers—the "hypocritical opportunists" at major corporations who were beginning to market "natural" and "healthy" foods, the party line notwithstanding. In turn, these would-be compromisers distanced themselves from the "reactionaries." Thus, as the orthodox dug in, they deepened the cracks that threatened the whole edifice.

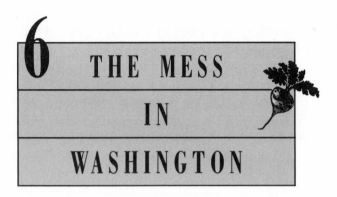

6 THE MESS IN WASHINGTON

While radicals had little use for central government—and certainly not for the Nixon administration—mainstream consumers had grown accustomed to looking to Washington for help in deciding questions of food system safety and control. Most now accepted the Progressive/New Deal argument that private individuals could not oversee the economically elaborate and geographically elongated route from farm to dinner table. Barring a radical shift to the intimate, localized commissariat of the organic paradigm, public officials would have to scrutinize hidden practices of food production and processing. Given this impossibly complex food chain, the public needed to feel that *someone* in Washington knew what was going on, particularly when conventional assumptions and practices were being questioned.

During the food debates of the 1970s, however, federal policies satisfied no one—neither radicals nor orthodox true believers nor the general public in need of clear answers. Rather than fostering confidence in the food supply, the government was itself a bundle of contradictions, inconsistencies, and vacillations. Reinforcing public anxieties, the government augmented the noise level of the debate without offering itself as an authoritative mediator. The resultant "mess in Washington" set the stage for the neoprivatism of the 1980s, when the public sector would have little to offer those seeking relief for food system problems.

AGRIBUSINESS'S FRIENDS

To be sure, at the onset of the moral panic, orthodoxy had more friends in Washington than did the radicals. In particular, the Department of Agriculture (USDA) and the Food and Drug Administration (FDA) were valued defenders of the agribusiness paradigm: that only through a highly chemicalized, capital-intensive food production system would Americans be able to meet their responsibility to "feed a hungry world."

The USDA had long been the principal federal overseer of the system's chronic surpluses and inequities. Through its information and research facilities, the USDA helped farmers produce more, while through its market intervention programs it attempted to deal with the overabundant fruits of that efficiency. During the relatively liberal 1960s and early 1970s, the glossy yearbooks of agriculture routinely celebrated overproduction as a form of foreign aid; to meet world hunger, American farms needed to grow bigger and grow more. The mandate to expand seemed especially clear after the 1969 White House Conference on Food, Nutrition, and Health, which certified that tens of millions were hungry. Also of interest to the detente-minded Nixon were repeated crop failures in the USSR.[1]

Aiming to feed the hungry and bolster the Soviets, Nixon's USDA encouraged farmers to take advantage of relatively cheap credit, buy land, machinery, and petrochemicals, and, in Secretary Earl Butz's words, "plant fence row to fence row." American grain exports increased 70 percent between 1970 and 1973. A decade later, however, it became clear how shortsighted this policy was, as grain production abroad recovered, world demand slackened, energy and credit costs skyrocketed, and land values plummeted, leaving many farmers vastly overextended. In the mid-eighties, the farm crisis was so bad that at least one Reagan administration official grudgingly proposed studying small-scale, diversified, regional farming—virtually the essence of the organic model.[2]

During the moral panic, however, Earl Butz was an especially

133

colorful critic of organic farming as a formula for mass starvation. Butz was also a good example of the "interlocking directorate": former dean at Purdue University, former director of Ralston Purina, Stokely Van Camp, J. I. Case farm machinery manufacturer, and the International Minerals and Chemicals Corp. Like many establishment economists, Butz scoffed at radical calls to curtail demand, which he viewed as morally and politically messy. Against the Lappé suggestion that Americans eat less meat in order to free up resources for more efficient sources of protein, Butz insisted that Americans were incapable of changing their eating habits. "Americans are not going to eat one less hamburger per week. They are going to eat one more hamburger per week. Furthermore, they need have no sense of guilt as they do so." For America's small farmers facing the conglomeration of agriculture, Butz's view of the alternatives was equally blunt and uncompromising: "Adapt or die; resist and perish." Similarly, Butz applauded the trend toward higher-cost convenience foods because they added value and profit for processors upon whose prosperity everyone else depended, in his view. At the same time, his department's vast informational machinery regularly defended additives, questioned natural foods, and advised housewives how to maximize their use of convenience foods.[3]

Perhaps even more influential than the USDA's literary output were its two major feeding programs—school meals and food stamps—both of which expanded greatly during the Nixon years in line with the mandate to "feed the hungry." Serving 30 million breakfasts and lunches a day in 1971, the school lunch program grew into a massive entitlement for just about every public school child in the country; what was a $300 million program in 1970 was a $3 billion program in 1980. While there is little doubt that the program did improve the nutritional status of the very poor, it also represented a great marketing opportunity for processors. Not only were schoolchildren socialized in the mainstream convenience food cuisine, but the USDA also opened the school lunch program to experimentation in the use of vitamin-fortified and soy-extended products beloved by food technologists. For example, with USDA encouragement, ITT Continental Bakeries developed fortified Twinkies for the lucrative school feeding program. In a high-tech variation on a Lappé theme, nearly fifty major food companies experimented with Ralston Purina's soy isolate to develop low-cost, high-protein substitutes for hamburgers, eggs, and fish.

134

Administering these experiments was Rutgers nutritionist Paul LaChance, another well-quoted defender of the prevailing paradigm. "Schools have the tightest economics of any feeding system," LaChance advised processors. "If you can make a go there, you can make a go in any market."[4]

While the school lunch program beckoned as a rich potential market, a more immediate boon to the food industry was the reformed food stamp program—the Nixon administration's response to media reports of widespread malnutrition in America. Instead of receiving outright grants of surplus commodities, the poor now shopped at regular stores. While there was a humane side to this mainstreaming of the poor, critic Jim Hightower argues that the enthusiasm of grocers actually had more influence in the final decision: industry reports showed that the poor could buy more processed goods with greater "value added" than the low-margin basic commodities of the previous program. Here again, a policy idealized as a redistributive measure worked well to bolster the existing system of distribution.[5]

The other main federal ally of the food industry was the Food and Drug Administration. The story of the FDA was a classic case history of how a Progressive era reform (1906) in the name of efficiency and professionalism could result in an agency with cozy ties to the industry it was supposed to police. In a 1973 article in the *Progressive,* Michael Jacobson and Robert White reported that twenty-two of fifty-two top FDA officials had "worked for regulated industries or organizations that catered to those industries." According to Ross Hume Hall, however, the FDA's service to industry resulted not so much from the revolving door as from a shared worldview—its assumption that a "safe" food was one for which the toxicological evidence was lacking. Yet even in 1906, Hall argues, technological advances in food fabrication were outdistancing the fragmented, one-variable-at-a-time approach of analytical chemistry. Knowing that it was impossible to test the long-term effects of *every* food chemical, the FDA stuck to investigating only the most notorious—and even then only after years of almost hysterical outside lobbying. To prod the FDA into action, Congress passed the so-called Delany Clause in 1958, which required the FDA to ban any additive that caused cancer in laboratory animals—regardless of the size of the dosage. But the same act also grandfathered in existing food chemicals by allowing the FDA to establish a list of almost 1,000 substances Generally Recognized as

135

Safe. This GRAS list exempted almost all known additives from testing. New chemicals were routinely granted provisional certification while being tested—a long, arduous process. From 1958 through 1969 only two substances were banned by the FDA—a carcinogenic weed killer used on cranberries (1959) and, after much delay and equivocation, cyclamates (1969). In 1955, before Delany, about 400 million pounds of additives went into food; in 1970, 1.06 billion, or five pounds per capita. On the whole, the GRAS list served mainly to validate the existing food supply. In the public debate, technologists could point to the list as evidence that additives were safe and that the government was taking care of everything.[6]

Meanwhile, the FDA proclaimed a higher mission to patrol the dangerous natural universe of bacteria, spinach, heavy metals, and vermin; even this claim was tarnished a bit by the 1971 General Accounting Office report accusing both the FDA and the USDA of inadequate inspection of food processing plants and slaughterhouses. Not only were these main federal watchdogs lax in addressing the relatively recent chemical threats, they were unable to meet the more rudimentary responsibilities envisioned by Harvey Wiley and Upton Sinclair back in 1906. Thus in 1972, the FDA admitted keeping a secret list of "acceptable contaminants" —insect fragments, rodent hairs and feces, larvae—in processed foods.[7]

While accepting rat turds in commercial sausage, the FDA came down hard on health food manufacturers. Although the FDA humbly (and rightfully) cited lack of "clear evidence" concerning most food chemicals, it dogmatically dismissed the therapeutic and consumerist claims of the countercuisine. For example, the FDA's 1975 label regulations prohibited claims that relatively unprocessed natural products were superior to the regular variety; that organic fertilizers produced more nutritious plants; or that a conventional diet lacked adequate nutrients. Worried that megavitamins implied a lack of faith in processed foods, the FDA proposed in 1974 to limit vitamin dosages. Flooded by mail protesting this attempt to hinder self-medication by ordinary citizens, Congress voted to limit the FDA's authority. Barred from overt interference, the FDA resorted to the traditional "educational" route: a chemical was a chemical; a "healthy" diet meant the basic-four, three-squares formula; processed foods were healthy; anyone claiming the superiority of "natural foods" was a quack.[8]

136

CRACKS:
BUREAUCRATIC TURF BATTLES

With all this support from the USDA and FDA, why did the food industry become increasingly anxious, indeed angry, about government intervention, especially in the mid-1970s? Where were the cracks?

There is a simple explanation and a more complicated one. The simple one is that industry instinctively worried about even the most compromised regulation because it feared worse down the line. Hence the fierce resistance to the Delany Clause, however rarely invoked, and to ingredient labeling, however limited. This "give 'em an inch, they'll take a mile" reaction was the reductio ad absurdum weapon in every true believer's rhetorical arsenal.

The more complicated explanation is that "government" was not a single ideological force, but rather a collection of "governments" with varying agendas, outlooks, and proposals, some favorable to orthodoxy, some not.

The most obvious inconsistency was between Republican and Democratic administrations. Jimmy Carter certainly did employ more liberal activists than Richard Nixon or Gerald Ford. But the complaints about federal harassment began *before* Carter's election. The reason had something to do with the time-warp nature of policymaking. Presidents do not operate solely in the present; they all inherit the programs of previous administrations and seek to co-opt those of future opponents. Thus, a law passed in the Eisenhower administration (Delany) forced Richard Nixon's FDA to confront substances studied by Lyndon Johnson's agency (cyclamates, DES, food colorings, mercury) and to initiate other reviews that came due on Jimmy Carter's watch (saccharin, nitrites, BHT). Moreover, in an effort to head off the liberal competition anticipated for 1972, the ostensibly conservative Nixon expanded government involvement (EPA, food stamps, labeling), while the supposedly activist Carter switched to a deregulatory approach in anticipation of a conservative swing in 1980. Further complicating the picture were turf battles among agencies, cabinet officers, congressional committees, and White House advisors. If the public became increasingly confused by the "mess in Washington," it was

137

because Washington *was* a mess. A flurry of food-related activity from scattered government players created a sense that something was being done at great expense; by the end of the decade, however, it was unclear whether much had been accomplished after all —except to toss the ball back into private hands.

EPA AND DDT

The memoirs of two Nixon administration officials concerned with environmental policy, Robert Sansom and John C. Whitaker, show how the time-warp factor along with bureaucratic infighting shaped the 1972 decision to ban DDT.[9] Personally and ideologically, Nixon was probably as friendly to pesticides as was John F. Kennedy, whose administration had categorically dismissed Rachel Carson's eloquent indictment of DDT in 1962. In 1969, however, a study by the U.S. Department of Health, Education, and Welfare—a department somewhat more oriented to human health than the USDA—legitimized concern. The USDA's response—a minor ban on DDT use on tobacco, on shade trees, in households, and in aquatic areas—did not satisfy critics, but it did anger manufacturers concerned that any DDT restrictions would lead to wider controls (the inch/mile reflex). Although DDT was actually being replaced by other, less overtly problematic pesticides, the campaign to ban or save the pesticide became a symbolic contest during the first environmentalist surge of 1969–70.

Personally, Nixon sneered at the "bird and bunny crowd" and felt most comfortable with the pro-industry, antiregulatory forces in government. But his chief political advisor, Attorney General John Mitchell, was worried about the 1972 election. Lest his boss be dubbed "Dirty Dick" in a contest against "Ecology Ed" Muskie, Mitchell backed the creation of a separate, seemingly interest-free department, the Environmental Protection Agency, first headed by William Ruckelshaus, known for his "Mr. Clean" image. From December 1970 through November 1972, Ruckelshaus was given a relatively free hand to expand his own territory. Of particular importance was the shift of pesticide regulation from the USDA to the EPA. No bureaucracy likes to lose ground, and when agriculture secretaries Clifford M. Hardin and Earl Butz warned of imminent catastrophe if pesticides were restricted, they were in part licking wounds after losing the early rounds of an ongoing turf battle with Ruckelshaus.[10]

138

After hearing the DDT debate, Ruckelshaus announced a near total ban on domestic use of DDT by December 31, 1972. Although experts disagreed on the long-term effects of DDT, it was clear that the pesticide was being stored in fatty tissues. It seemed to Ruckelshaus that any "prudent" person would want to avoid a substance "that may ultimately have serious effects on his health." Ruckelshaus's decision was a good example of how scientific uncertainty and "prudence" could be used either way in a matter of policy: one could either allow use, pending absolute proof—which would take generations—or one could ban use as a precaution. Although Ruckelshaus's reasoning outraged farm interests, his ban was moderated by a gradual phaseout and by the exemption granted a few industries where there was no known alternative chemical—green peppers, onions, and sweet potatoes. The ruling did not cover exports of the pesticide or imports of food from countries still using DDT. For these loopholes, Ruckelshaus was condemned by activists seeking an immediate and total ban. After 1972, with "Ecology Ed" safely out of the way, Nixon put the brakes on environmental activism and even returned some pesticide oversight to the USDA. The increasingly frustrated Ruckelshaus left for the Justice Department, from which he was fired during the Watergate crisis.

Symbolically and materially, the battle over DDT was an important event. The level of DDT measured in animal and human fatty tissues did decline significantly in the mid-seventies. But although agribusiness lost the battle, it may have won the war, for overall pesticide use actually increased steadily. At the EPA, Ruckelshaus's successor Russell Train managed to ban just four more major pesticides. But each ban required considerable time, money, and political capital—the inherent costs of the fragmented, one-at-a-time approach. With the resources to review only about twenty-five chemicals a year, the EPA would need the rest of this century just to test the other 600 active ingredients in 50,000 pesticides approved for use before 1972. As the EPA fell way behind, one 1986 *Newsweek* story confirmed what Rachel Carson had insisted back in 1962: "Nature fights back." Despite an increase in pesticide use from about 200,000 pounds a year in the early 1950s to 1.1 billion pounds in 1986, approximately one-fifth of the nation's crops were being lost to pests—about the same percentage as in 1945. As Sansom argued, the public had been led to believe that "billions" were being spent to test and limit dangerous chemicals, whereas in fact only a few were subjected to the full review

139

process—and with what effect? Lacking a comprehensive plan for pesticide use in general, the federal government seemed to be spinning its wheels and getting nowhere. Even DDT resurfaced as a media story in the mid-eighties, mostly because of the import and export loopholes in the 1972 ban.[11]

FDA AND ADDITIVES

Another source of confusion was the FDA, which, despite its traditional amiability toward chemicals, was virtually compelled to confront a number of them in the mid-seventies. Here again, the time-lag factor was partly responsible: studies begun in earlier administrations were concluded under Nixon and Carter. Indeed, saccharin was studied first under Roosevelt—Theodore Roosevelt. Yet certain things had changed. Advances in laboratory techniques —the pride of the food technologists—made it harder to avoid invoking the Delany Clause, for now it was possible to find carcinogens at previously undetectable levels. Also, increasingly vocal critics were making it harder for the FDA to offset possible chemical risks with business benefits. As former FDA scientist Jacqueline Verrett pointed out in her best-selling exposé of government negligence, *Eating May Be Hazardous to Your Health* (1974), "The intent of the law is unequivocal: the FDA is mandated by Congress, representing all consumers, to make decisions solely on the basis of whether an additive is safe—not whether it has any economic benefits."[12] In the mid-seventies assertive liberal Democrats in key oversight committees pressed the FDA to focus strictly on those risks, however small or economically inconvenient. And now that these risks were detectable in previously unseen amounts, the FDA simply had to go public.

And go public it did, not against chemicals in general—as the countercuisine urged—but against particular chemicals, one at a time. In 1969 the FDA banned the use of MSG in baby foods after certain tests indicated possible brain damage in baby laboratory animals. Again in 1969, after two studies found that cyclamates caused cancer in laboratory animals, the FDA banned what was then the sole artificial alternative to saccharin, a sweetener already in disrepute. (The total ban came only after Congress prevented the FDA from allowing cyclamates to be sold over the counter.) Since both MSG and cyclamates had been on the GRAS list, the

140

ban brought the whole list into question. In 1970 the FDA warned against using too much canned tuna, which was found to have unsafe levels of mercury. In 1971 it was the hexachlorophene in infant baths. In 1972, DES, diethylstilbestrol, a growth hormone in cattle feed—a move delayed by the courts. In 1973, violet no. 1 —used to color various beverages and candy. In 1973, three more food colorings plus kepone found in fish in Virginia's James River. In 1977, saccharin. In 1978, the agency warned that the nitrites used to preserve bacon might turn into carcinogenic nitrosamines when fried, a fear that was soon extended to many charcoaled meats, including the iconic backyard hamburger. Although in retrospect not very many substances were banned, at the time the drawn-out announcement process led many to believe that "everything causes cancer." Yet at the same time, because the Delany Clause required the FDA to act only if a substance caused cancer in test animals, many understandably wondered how close humans were to laboratory rats—especially considering that these rats were often fed very large doses of the chemical in question.[13]

In a sense, the FDA was telling people more than they wanted to know (small amounts of carcinogens are found in many everyday foods), and yet not enough (what are my chances of getting cancer?). This contradiction came to a head in 1977, when the FDA proposed to ban saccharin after a Canadian study showed that it caused bladder cancer in rats. Rather than being greeted by public praise for its decisiveness, however, the FDA was scorned for going too far. For one thing, as the agency itself noted, the Canadian rats had been fed high doses equivalent to drinking 800 cans of soft drinks a day. Buried by letters from consumers worried about the lack of any alternative to sugar, Congress delayed the FDA's ban for eighteen months pending yet another study—by the National Academy of Sciences. The NAS study agreed with the Canadian report, but was uncertain about the relevance to humans. While such hedging was well suited to the inherently agnostic world of basic science, in the politically charged world of applied science, it was an enormous escape clause. Since there were no long-term studies of saccharin's impact on humans, the incontrovertible "proof" was lacking. Given public exhaustion with possible dangers, there was little protest in the 1980s when the FDA drifted back to letting economic benefits outweigh carcinogenic risks, Delany notwithstanding.[14]

141

FDA AND LABELS

In labeling too the government agency undertook cautious reforms that wound up angering both critics and the industry, yet did not really satisfy the general public either.

The drive for nutritional labels had long been a part of the consumer movement, which, valuing the "public's right to know," believed that a properly informed consumer would make the right choice in the marketplace. Through the early 1970s food products did not have to carry ingredient labels if they conformed to federally mandated "standards of identity"—meaning, for example, that all mayonnaise had the same basic ingredients: eggs, vinegar, vegetable oil. In effect, these standards reinforced the status quo: the USDA's minimum of, say, meat in corned beef hash was based on a simple averaging of industry practices. Moreover, government standards changed to meet industry needs. As Ralph Nader's 1969 campaign against the "fatfurter" disclosed, the USDA was prepared to allow hot dogs to contain 33 percent fat—a ratio that had doubled in just fifteen years as a cost-saving measure. The requirement also had loopholes. For example, additives Generally Regarded As Safe did not have to be identified individually but might be lumped together as "artificial flavoring"—no help at all for those with allergies and special concerns. While theoretically the list was public information, in practice it was hard to find. In publicizing such inadequacies, consumer activists like Ralph Nader and Michael Jacobson were joined by allies in Congress. For example, Utah Democrat Frank Moss, chairman of the Senate Consumer Subcommittee, liked to point out that it was easier to get information about the nutritive value and ingredients of canned dog food than of certain canned meats for humans. As such stories made news, pressure mounted for a mandatory listing of all ingredients on labels. In addition to this ingredient list, activists wanted a nutrient list of vitamins, minerals, protein, fat, calories, and so on. While the former would signal possible chemical dangers, the latter would educate consumers in their basic daily nutritional needs.[15]

142

Just as the Nixon administration felt compelled to accommodate environmentalism, so too did it grudgingly move to answer the consumerists. The FDA's response was about as minimal as it could be. Although it never agreed to a complete disclosure of every ingredient and its purpose, it did require ingredients to be listed in descending order of weight—a tip-off to the vast amount of sweeteners in many processed foods. (These could be subdivided, however, into corn syrup, brown sugar, and dextrose, and thus moved down the list a bit.) But the standards of identity remained: enriched white bread remained exactly that rather than the 1½ pages of small type revealed by Michael Jacobson in *Eater's Digest*. Only those relatively few products making specific nutritional claims—e.g., "high protein," "low calorie,"—had to list nutrients.[16]

Most of the food industry opposed even any mandatory labels, however vague and incomplete. A list of the forty-three ingredients in General Mills's Breakfast Squares took away space from the sort of consumer education preferred by processors: recipes and promotions. They also feared the "opening wedge." At what point would radical consumerists get what they really wanted: full explanation of every ingredient? Invoking the reductio ad absurdum ploy, one Cooke and Castle, Inc., executive complained, "A label just isn't big enough to have an appendix, an index, and a bibliography. Everything would have to be packed in a giant-sized can." A "consumer affairs" vice-president at Oscar Mayer, Inc., warned direly of "Big Brother leading us down the supermarket aisle." Manufacturers feared having to spend enormous sums analyzing products—another element in the conservative backlash against "the high cost of regulation."[17]

Although the food industry had many reasons to worry privately about a possible spread of the labeling virus, its most commonly aired public critique was that food labels would unnecessarily confuse the consumer. "Unquestionably a food product package should provide a description of its contents," KraftCo's deceptively accommodating chairman allowed, "but the current emphasis on technical language and scientific terminology defeats this purpose. The average person is more frightened than helped by language he does not understand." Indeed, although vast majorities of those polled continued to back labeling in principle, in practice only the more affluent seemed to read labels regularly, and even these seemed to make very limited use of them: mainly to check vitamins, protein, and calories. The technical names of additives did confuse people. Respondents frequently complained that one needed a biochemistry degree to

143

understand them. To the industry such responses seemed to confirm the utter uselessness of label laws as a significant market force. But, said activists, labels were confusing only because they did not indicate the uses of the chemicals. And at any rate, only 10 percent of supermarket products bore them in 1980.[18]

Caught in the middle of the debate were many citizens who, by the end of the decade, remained in favor of labels but were increasingly dubious about extending complex regulations that seemed to increase costs and confusion. Exploiting such doubts, the Reagan administration backed the sort of voluntary educational efforts preferred by manufacturers. Rejecting a proposal for fast-food labels, both the USDA and the FDA commended fast feeders who provided informational booklets to the relatively few consumers who troubled to request them. Just about the only labeling advance in the 1980s was the inclusion of sodium in nutrient lists, and even this could be turned to a manufacturer's advantage. Thus, in 1981, FDA Commissioner Arthur Hayes argued that potato chip bags should voluntarily list nutrient content because chips were in the lowest one-third of all processed foods in sodium content. When Frito-Lay accepted his invitation, its packaging used the nutrient label to show that one ounce of potato chips had less sodium than two pieces of bread, and fewer calories than eight ounces of whole milk. In other words, potato chips could be advertised in the "healthy snack" category! So much for the "consumer's right to know."[19]

Agreeing that labels *were* rather complicated, biochemist Michael Jacobson saw the need for professional help: "Somebody who has a Ph.D. in chemistry can know a lot about food from a label. Someone should be looking out for everyone else."[20] In a sense, the food industry agreed—but who was that "someone"? Both sides agreed that the government had to serve as a watchdog, but who would hold the leash—consumer activists or food manufacturers? In the labeling controversy, the industry wound up with the leash, at the end of which napped a rather timid hound, the FDA. A similar contest developed over the role of two other government watchdogs: the Federal Trade Commission (FTC) and the Senate Select Committee on Nutrition.

144

FTC

Charged with promoting "free and fair" competition, the FTC has always been one of the more potentially subversive federal agencies, since its mission clashes with the oligopolistic tendencies of corporate capitalism. Riding the anticorporate, decentralist wave of the late 1960s and early 1970s, the FTC's staff had leeway to study market concentration and advertising practices. Although the agency failed to follow through in forcing major divestitures, its studies were released to the press. The countercuisine's consumerist literature was full of references to FTC reports on the food industry. In the 1970s, the FTC staff focused on an area of vital importance to the food industry: breakfast cereals. Overpriced and overhyped, cold cereals were both lucrative and "educational." Through cold cereals children were introduced to the processed cuisine, a tight net linking imaginative packaging, television advertising, sugar and additives, and oligopoly. In 1970 the FTC released a study indicating that the top four companies—Kellogg's, General Mills, General Foods, and Quaker Oats—had achieved a "shared monopoly" of 91 percent of the market. Were the industry more competitive, cereal prices would be 25 percent lower. Rather than compete through price, however, cereal manufacturers expended enormous sums on advertising and promotional gimmicks that exaggerated trivial differences and glossed over nutritional inadequacies. The latter received a lot of media attention that same year when nutrition advocate Robert Choate told Senator Moss's subcommittee that two-thirds of dry breakfast cereals were nutritionally worthless and that children were being exploited shamefully. Moreover, the most heavily advertised cereals were the least nutritious, while those with some benefit were promoted the least.[21]

Cereal makers defused the uproar by adding vitamins, but they faced difficult years nevertheless. FTC staffers continued to build the case for divestiture—a very long process—and also began to investigate cereal advertising. Proposals languished, however, until 1977, when Jimmy Carter appointed the Senate Commerce Committee's chief counsel, Michael Pertschuk, as FTC chairman. With Ralph Nader's principal legislative facilitator at the helm of one of the most powerful regulatory agencies, consumer activism

145

seemed on the brink of a major breakthrough. According to *Food Engineering*, Pertschuk's staff was so imbued with "radical 1960s antibusiness attitudes" that 20 percent of its 700 ongoing investigations concerned the food industry.[22]

Of these, none was more controversial than a 1978 FTC staff proposal to regulate children's television ads. Confirming Choate's charges, various researchers had established that most of these ads were for highly sugared cereals and snacks, that young children did not distinguish programs from ads, and that children who saw a lot of these messages tended to equate sugar with good nutrition. In 1977 representatives of CSPI and the self-described "militant mothers" at Peggy Charren's Action for Children's Television met with the new FTC chairman to suggest that such a pattern might (under an activist interpretation) be considered "unfair" advertising and thus subject to FTC control. After a nine-month investigation, Pertschuk's staff made three proposals: a ban on all advertising (much of it for cereals and candy) on programs seen by children under the age of eight; a ban on ads for highly sugared foods for anyone under age twelve; and a requirement that advertisers pay for public service nutritional ads.[23]

The proposals were condemned by industry-oriented researchers but endorsed by pediatricians and dentists. Analytically, the proposals pleased those urging government to look at the big picture, particularly a whole system of early childhood socialization. But politically, the target was perhaps too large, threatening not just the cereal industry—large enough—but also candy, snack and toy manufacturers, fast-food chains, and the advertising-dependent mass media. Facing a long process of hearings and reviews, the opposition had time to coalesce. Action for Children's Television reported that broadcasters, advertisers, and targeted manufacturers raised a $30 million "war chest" to fight the FTC in the courts, in the FTC oversight committees in Congress, and through political advertising. Editorial writers joined with food technologists in deriding FTC activism, which, according to the classic reductio, threatened "to turn us all into children." Advertising and network officials cried "Censorship!" Meanwhile, behind the scenes, lobbyists undertook a multifront strategy—accusing Pertschuk of being biased, urging sympathetic congressmen to cut all funds for the investigation, and attempting to block ACT's participation in the hearings. In 1980 they succeeded in getting Congress to pass the FTC Improvement Act, which eliminated the

146

FTC's power to rule on "unfair" advertising and which subjected all FTC actions to a congressional veto. Although the veto was eventually declared unconstitutional, the commissioners got the message and sidetracked the whole investigation. The FTC's final report concluded that, based on the available evidence, food advertising did harm children, but the only meaningful response would be to ban or severely limit all advertising, and this would be both politically impossible and aesthetically undesirable. As one FTC lawyer—clearly on a strategic retreat—remarked, the agency did not want to "straightjacket advertising into a dull information mode." [24]

The FTC's opponents won not only because they had a large war chest, but also because of waning public support for regulatory activism—as evidenced in the saccharin episode. Bombarded by "too much, too soon," people withdrew into the protective shell of extreme skepticism: they wanted "more evidence." While more than half of those surveyed in 1980 wanted the government to continue to test for harmful ingredients and to publish more information, only a third wanted government to regulate advertising of possibly harmful foods—a considerable decline from earlier polls. [25] If people doubted the connection between saccharin and human cancer, they had even more doubts about the damage caused by television ads, whose impact could never be proved with absolute certainty under laboratory conditions. To an extent, these doubts simply licensed people to go on as before—before the "experts" began to make trouble by interfering with important consumer needs. Just as weight-conscious people needed saccharin, carcinogenic or not, parents needed children's television, counternutritional or not. Attacking the advertising proposals, the *Washington Post* scolded the FTC for trying to be the "national nanny," but in fact television was baby-sitting the kids, and many parents resented having to feel guilty about that. [26]

In a way, the FTC proposal was a victim of bad timing. Had an immediate ban been imposed in 1977—or better still, just after Watergate—it might have won wider support, for the electorate 147 was still in a self-critical, problem-solving mood. But by 1980 many citizens had heard enough about all the dangers in the everyday world. Ronald Reagan was especially effective in flattering voters by arguing that they, not the "bureaucrats," knew what was best and worst for them. Thus, in a letter to one cereal executive, Reagan wrote that "the cereal [industry divestiture] case is but another example of a bureaucratic crusade undertaken in the premise that the bureaucrats rather than consumers can make rational choices." As Reagan rode the antigovernment wave toward nomination and election, the White House pressured Pertschuk to drop even the more focused and well-documented investigation of cereal industry concentration. On the eve of the election, Vice-President Mondale declared that forced divestiture was "inconceivable" and went on to welcome legislation that would bar the FTC from forcing a cereal industry breakup.[27]

But the food industry did not relax until after the election. An editorial in *Food Engineering* hoped that Reagan's FTC would serve as a "protector" of business, not just of consumers. Pertschuk's successor as chair, James Miller, enthusiastically agreed that the consumer needed less help. At his first news conference, he pronounced, "Consumers are not as gullible as many regulators think they are." Such simplicity sounded soothing after several years of officially sponsored worrying, and there was little outcry as Miller cut the FTC staff by 34 percent in his first eighteen months. In food advertising, as in labeling, additives testing, and pesticide control, the old dictum *caveat emptor* reigned.[28]

McGOVERN'S LAST STAND

After 1980, the FTC fell back on the hope that government might take a more dynamic "educational" role—and some of that hope rested on the USDA's new "Dietary Guidelines for Americans," a pamphlet based largely (but incompletely) on the work of George McGovern's Senate Select Committee on Nutrition and Human Needs.

The "Dietary Guidelines" story showed the progressive potential of government-sponsored information; it also revealed the limits wrought by the fragmented nature of policymaking.[29]

Established in 1968, Senator George McGovern's Select Committee on Nutrition and Human Needs first focused on hunger and malnutrition—issues compatible with the conventional "plagues and pellagra" paradigm. Soon after McGovern's resounding defeat in the 1972 presidential elections, however, the committee's staff began to shift its worries to the overfed. Its hearings in the mid-seventies served as a forum for consumer activists and health researchers claiming a link between diet and major killer diseases—

148

especially heart attack, stroke, and cancer. In 1977 the committee staff issued the first draft of "Dietary Goals for the United States."

By no means did the report recommend radical changes. Still, in its own moderate-reformist way, it undermined the orthodox defense. Questioning whether modern Americans were indeed the best-fed people in history, the report compared an average diet for 1976 with one from the early twentieth century—the period supposedly little different from the Dark Ages according to food technology's defenders.[30] The results were alarming: although protein levels were relatively constant, Americans were now getting a lot more of it from fatty meats, eggs, and dairy products and a lot less from whole grains rich in fiber and micronutrients. With their increasingly sedentary life-styles, they needed fewer calories but were actually consuming more—thanks in particular to the refined sugar in soft drinks, snacks, and virtually every processed food. Whereas in 1909 Americans had derived 40 percent of their calories from fruit, vegetables, and grains, in 1976 they were getting only 20 percent from those sources, the rest coming from fat and refined sugars. In addition, they were consuming unprecedented quantities of sodium and untested additives.

The report explicitly linked this dietary decline to current health problems—thus indirectly legitimizing the countercuisine's nostalgic thrust. Of the ten leading causes of death, six seemed related to diet (heart attack, stroke, arteriosclerosis, cancer, cirrhosis of the liver, and diabetes); and these constituted about half of all deaths. Eating, it concluded, could be as deadly as smoking. Previously, such definite connections had been made mainly by so-called quacks, as the medical-nutritional establishment took a more agnostic position behind the "lack of clear evidence." Moreover, the report's recommendations strayed from conventional notions of "balance." Whereas the basic-four, three-squares formula permitted eaters to sample just about anything in the supermarket, the McGovern report proposed specific dietary changes that would bring Americans back to the supposedly healthier standards of 1910. To meet this goal, Americans should cut consumption of eggs by 50 percent, sugar and sweets 50 percent, animal fats 16 percent, and meat, poultry, and fish 20 percent and increase consumption of whole grain products by 66 percent, fresh fruit and vegetables 25 percent, and skim milk 12 percent. Breaking with the "everything's natural/ a chemical is a chemical" model, the report preferred sugars "naturally occurring" in fresh fruits to "re-

149

fined and processed sugars" found in soft drinks, snacks, and most convenience foods. Fresh produce was both healthier and cheaper, the report argued. As with the cholesterol-heart connection, the link between additives and cancer was not fully proved, but as a precaution the amount of additives should be reduced. Reflecting other critical arguments, the report pointed out the high ratio of television ads for junk foods, the industry's oligopolistic tendencies, and the processors' value-adding rationale for supplementing cheap raw materials with sugar, salt, and additives. Its government policy recommendations also were at the liberal leading edge: complete and compulsory food labeling, federal funding for research into safer techniques in food processing and food service, and much more money for government-sponsored nutritional research and education.

With its push for major government programs to be channeled mainly through the USDA, this was certainly no decentralist document. Still, it clearly threatened both the friendly-chemical paradigm and the well-being of major producers and processors. As McGovern went on the talk show and convention circuit, "Dietary Goals" became a best-seller at the Government Printing Office, sparking a heated public debate. A year later the staff had received well over 1,000 pages of printed rebuttal, some from industry, some from within the committee. For example, one pro-agribusiness group pointed out the potentially disastrous results if consumers actually bought more fresh fruits, vegetables, and whole grains: manufacturers of canned, frozen, formulated, and dehydrated foods would suffer from "major adjustment problems." Cutbacks in fatty animal protein might mean a "severe negative regional impact" for the Corn Belt. In a dissenting forward, ranking minority member Charles Percy (R-IL), suggested that, given the "inadequacy of food data," especially about the cholesterol-coronary connection, perhaps the goals and recommendations were premature.

As in so many safety issues at this time, the "lack of evidence" could be used to counsel either alarm or confidence. Like William Ruckelshaus on DDT, McGovern leaned toward preventive caution, while Percy insisted on adding this statement in bold type: "The value of dietary change remains controversial and science cannot at this time insure that an altered diet will provide improved protection from certain killer diseases such as heart disease and cancer." While the industry pushed for a stronger retreat to the

150

vague, all-inclusive notions of "balance," the committee attempted a compromise. It toned down the historical comparisons, deemphasized additives, and hedged a bit on the cholesterol connection. Even so, it continued to recommend that certain foods be increased or decreased.[31]

Despite the modifications, the revised (1978) McGovern report did not mollify industry diehards. Indeed, coming at the same time as the saccharin and cereal controversies, the McGovern report reinforced the food industry's determination to fight back. While the anti-FTC campaign looked mainly to conservative allies in Congress, the anti-McGovern campaign was fought at the USDA, which was charged, in cooperation with HEW, with turning the committee's recommendations into an official element of government "nutrition education."

Despite its historic friendliness, the USDA was not completely trusted by agribusiness. In the bowels of the government's largest civilian department labored researchers whose work was potentially subversive if it ever caught the light of day. Thus, the McGovern committee's historical comparisons were based on data developed by the USDA's Economics, Statistics, and Cooperatives Service. FTC-style studies of food industry concentration were published in the department's *National Food Review*. And in Mark Hegsted, head of the USDA's Human Nutrition Center, George McGovern had a colleague who agreed that, given the high death rate due to heart attacks, hypertension, and diabetes, the government could not wait for all the evidence to come in before taking a dietary stand. But what sort of stand?[32]

Hegsted's office certainly had no lack of advice. On the right were various reports disputing *any* significant connection between health and diet. On the left was the first McGovern draft. The middle course chosen by the USDA was assertive enough to scare many producers but considerably weaker than even the revised McGovern position. Bowing to orthodoxy, the 1980 "Dietary Guidelines" did not make any historical comparisons with 1909–12 standards or set any statistical targets. Also, fearful of making any "quack-like" claims that a particular diet would actually prevent disease, the USDA secretary emphasized that the recommendations were "purely advisory," "not a prescription," "not immutable or permanent." This equivocation was apparent in the title, where the word "guidelines" replaced the stronger "goals." Also gone were any references to additives or food industry eco-

151

nomics. Three of the seven McGovern goals had concerned fat and cholesterol; the pamphlet compressed them into one. This *was* controversial, but the text took pains to stress that only certain people seemed at risk, while most could continue to eat eggs, whole milk, even liver "in moderation." Whereas McGovern had urged everyone to "decrease" and "reduce" sugar, sodium, and fat, the USDA pamphlet used the softer and vaguer "avoid too much." The USDA made no distinction between "naturally occurring" and "refined sugars," but it *did* recommend less candy, soft drinks, ice cream, and salty processed foods. The recommendation to "eat foods with adequate starch and fiber" specified whole grain breads and cereals, fruits and vegetables, but made no distinction between "fresh" and processed sources. The final guideline—to drink less alcohol—was not found in the McGovern goals and was perhaps a gesture to those arguing that alcohol abuse was a greater health danger than anything concocted by the food industry.[33]

The 1980 "Guidelines" were in fact so compromising that, just before they were released, USDA Secretary Robert Bergland was overheard to ask, "Is that all we're going to say? Why, I was taught that much back in elementary school in Minnesota." Yet, in the most general way, this was a turning point. The U.S. government was now on record recommending that people eat less, not more, of substances that were vital to the processing industry —a distinct shift away from the basically upbeat, confident assertiveness of the basic four, three squares. Reflecting a determination to conquer deficiency diseases, that paradigm had licensed overindulgence—a badge of middle-class security for those raised in deprivation. With the 1980 "Guidelines," fat lost its propaganda value.[34]

Furthermore, as the affected industries complained, the cholesterol, fiber, and sodium recommendations came out before all the evidence was in. Indeed, the "Guidelines" threatened to divide the food lobby just as it was mounting its strongest opposition to government intervention. While the meat, dairy, and egg interests were livid, cereal manufacturers, bakers, and vegetable growers immediately exploited the good news for fiber-rich whole grains, potatoes, and produce. Makers of fabricated substitutes for butter, eggs, and meat also saw great opportunities. The pages of food industry periodicals were full of acrimonious debate between technologists rejecting the "Guidelines" fully and marketers allowing that they could probably work within them. The cracks were widening.[35]

152

To the diehards' alarm, there had been a slow shift of opinion. As Bergland remarked when releasing the original pamphlet, the "Guidelines" represented a "consensus" which, while by no means as radical as the countercuisine's or even George Mc-Govern's, was somewhat to the left of the orthodox defense. To nutritionist Jean Mayer, who replaced Harvard colleague Frederick Stare as the most widely quoted establishment expert, the "Guidelines" seemed "perfectly reasonable." That is, they had become the model of a centrist, "moderate," "balanced" diet—a model so established that even the most blatantly pro-agribusiness administration in recent history had to stick to it. The Reagan administration rolled back virtually every other federal involvement—pesticide control, labeling, additives testing, advertising and antitrust investigations, alternative agriculture research, school lunches, food stamps, meat and poultry inspections—but it could not change this one. The Reaganites were able to abolish Hegsted's Human Nutrition Center and turn other nutrition education programs into showcases for processors and producers, but the "Guidelines" survived. "All of us have changed a little bit in our thinking," Reagan's Agriculture Secretary John Block admitted.[36]

The question then arises, if even John Block—"Butcher" Block to his environmentalist foes—could learn to live with this Carter era achievement, what had changed and why? How was it that the political culture of the early 1980s seemed to tolerate just about every federal cutback but this one? Partly, the "Guidelines" stuck because they did not constitute much of a federal commitment. Sidestepping the pressing problems of additives and pesticides, they seemed to put the responsibility for a healthy diet squarely on the individual—a position quite in line with Reagan's privatization policies and the public mood.[37]

Still, the recommendations had unsettling implications for major segments of the food industry, especially Block's own hog-farming friends. Who was responsible for worrying the public and shifting the consensus away from the basic four, three squares? Many diehards had no doubt who was to blame: the press.[38]   153

7 THE PRESS: SHIFTING THE CENTER

No wonder everyone cursed the press. In the ideological battles of the 1970s, every contender needed it badly. The countercuisine needed and used the press to gain attention, converts, and resources. Orthodoxy needed the simple metaphors, colorful anecdotes, and snappy prose of *Vogue, Good Housekeeping,* and *Life* to dramatize the otherwise drab arguments of *Food Engineering, Nutrition Reviews,* and *FDA Consumer.* The government needed the press to foster an aura of control and confidence, expertise and order.

The target of all this information—the consuming public— also needed the media. The traditional sources of nutritional wisdom—mother, friends and relatives, word of mouth—had been under steady attack for most of this century as scientists, progressive reformers, journalists, and advertisers had fought for "professionalism" and against "common sense." Public opinion surveys indicated that the campaign against folk wisdom was won long before the 1970s. As health and nutrition counselors, the media ranked second only to physicians. And since most medical information dealt with weight or acute health problems (like diabetes), the mass media were the principal source of advice and information about the more generalized issues of the time: food chemicals, agriculture, inflation, prevention, the overall norms for "moderation" and "balance." [1]

In interpreting the food battles of the 1970s, the press sought the high middle ground of conservative reform. On the conservative side the mainstream media echoed "expert" opinion in ridiculing much of the countercuisine, especially the organic paradigm. Radical words were taken out of context, gestures became caricatures, claims became hype, spokespeople became celebrities, partners became followers, movements froze into snapshots. Yet the defense was not quite of the orthodox variety, for the press rejected both "extremes," radicals and diehards— hence livid orthodox complaints about liberal media. Indeed, by highlighting scientific controversy and political confusion, the press exposed and deepened the establishment's cracks. Publicizing the worst cases of corporate abuse, professional malpractice, and bureaucratic bungling, the press absorbed some of the rationale for change and helped to push public opinion toward the privatistic, negative model of the 1980 "Dietary Goals." [2]

DEBUNKING THE COUNTERCUISINE: ORGANIC FRAUD

First the conservative side.

Given media dependence on advertising, few critics of the food industry expected a fair hearing. Over two-thirds of newspaper space and one-fifth of television time was devoted to carrying the advertising that paid for the rest. Judith Van Allen estimated that 65 percent of newspaper revenues in 1972 came from food advertising. According to Robert Choate, over 50 percent of television's revenue in 1973 came from the grocery business. The McGovern committee report estimated that only 25 percent of all TV food ads were devoted to "nutritious groups" like bread, cereals, pasta, soups, fruits, vegetables, and dairy. And the McGovern percentages were generous, since they included as "nutritious" products that were highly refined or processed. To this nutritional damage, Jim Hightower added food advertising's economic impact: by favoring companies with the largest market-

155

ing budgets, mass media advertising raised the costs of entry and fostered oligopoly.[3]

Despite their economic clout, food advertisers rarely interfered directly with editorial content, however, for such interventions could backfire. In *Deciding What's News,* Herbert Gans cites a 1970 NBC documentary exposing exploitation of migrant workers at Coca-Cola's Florida citrus farms. When Coke complained, the network made some changes, but the clumsy confrontation became a news item in itself, heightened interest in the subject, and actually embarrassed both corporations.[4] Most advertiser influence was more subtle. Journalists might shape a story to avoid a potential conflict, or, more commonly, they were not even aware of what they were editing out because they had so completely internalized the dominant ideology. Although such self-censorship did not always protect individual companies or politicians accused of egregious abuses, it helped to support the overall system, which was held to be generally sound. The same was probably true of ads: they might not persuade a particular customer to buy a particular product, but they did reinforce the overall environment conducive to a consumption-based economy.

Commercial media had long supported mass consumption, especially of convenience foods. Starting at the turn of this century women's magazines devalued cooking from scratch, first by stressing that brand-name packaged goods were safer than bulk commodities. According to Kathryn Weibel, *Woman's Home Companion*'s 1911 exposé of the "dirty grocery store" "resulted in increased prestige for packaged, trademarked, and thus advertised products. In 1912 *Good Housekeeping* invented its Seal of Approval, perhaps the most potent device of its type for making the consumer feel good about buying advertised products." Once the sanitary campaign was won, the pitch for convenience targeted women's marital anxieties. In *Perfection Salad* Laura Shapiro shows how women's magazines urged wives to work more on sex appeal and less on household drudgery, especially elaborate, laborious cooking. For example, the 1953 *Ladies' Home Journal* feature, "Can This Marriage Be Saved?" held one hardworking homemaker responsible for her husband's infidelity because "she never took time to be a wife." "Standard domestic skills were only a secondary component of wifeliness," Shapiro observes, "which was a service occupation calling for the competence and cajolery of a Mata Hari."[5] Furthering these sexual companionship goals, the 1953 TV dinner seemed to release women from the kitchen so they could snuggle up to husbands on the couch as they watched even more perfectly feminine TV wives avoid the kitchen altogether. Hollywood's physically splendid performers led such busy, exciting lives that they had no time to cook, yet seemed very well nourished (but still slim), did not suffer from hypertension or constipation, and never went to the dentist. The relatively few women portrayed as housewives were either clowns (Lucy Ricardo) or saints (June Cleaver), and neither type actually peeled an onion or scrubbed a roasting pan.

As mass entertainment glamorized the convenience-consumption ethic, it also mystified—or simply ignored—the details of food production. The classic cowboy drama had about as much to do with cattle raising as soap operas had to do with dishwashing—maybe less. The Hollywood farmer did work hard to get by, but he never suffered from pesticide poisoning. With the exception of an occasional, low-rated documentary or TV movie, entertainment programming shunned the slaughterhouse, industrial bakery, and suburban supermarket.

Given the relative importance of entertainment media over news media, it might not have mattered had journalists devoted all their space to critical stories, for such stories might have been lost in the otherwise supportive atmosphere. But the mainstream press was reluctant to criticize business in general, even as it publicized the unavoidably glaring transgressions of individual firms. Reporters might expose business extremes such as the slavelike treatment of migrant workers in Maryland or the unusually high percentage of arsenic in certain chickens in Alabama, but they were less likely to describe a less spectacular but more pervasive *pattern* of abuse. As self-styled moderates and skeptics, newspeople routinely dismissed as "conspiracy theories" radical stories about a *systematic* poisoning of the food supply. Similarly, the Hightower case against the daily, routine oligopoly went virtually unreported. At the same time, the news highlighted crop failures, store lines, and high food prices behind the Iron Curtain—an indication of "free enterprise's" superiority over central planning and communal production.[6]

The media's goodwill toward capitalism was matched by an uncritical softness for elite professionals, who served as efficient sources for general reporters who had neither the time nor background to research issues in depth. This faith in "impeccably cre-

157

dentialed experts" made the press a congenial outlet for the orthodox counterattack during the moral panic.[7] But much of this information was outdated. Nutritionists were still stuck with the "plagues and pellagra" paradigm that focused on deficiency rather than overabundance. Toxicologists were still testing chemicals one at a time. As we'll see, the social scientists consulted by journalists were rehashing well-worn anecdotes about "food faddism." The well-publicized assault on organic farming also had little recent research to go on. During the 1930s, the USDA had done some work on labor-intensive, diversified, nonchemical techniques, but those reports went out of print after World War II, when capital-intensive, highly chemicalized farming became the official policy. No American study on the comparative nutritional quality of food raised with and without chemicals had been conducted since 1951. In the 1960s, German and Swiss scientists had found organically grown vegetables to be nutritionally superior, but such studies were not taken seriously by American scientists, who dismissed European methods as too inefficient and expensive for American agriculture, with its mission to "feed the hungry." The Rodales had been experimenting with nonchemical practices for years but were not considered reliable witnesses in the mass media debate.[8]

Lacking recent evidence, the press did have powerful "frames." Frames are explanatory shortcuts. Like stereotypes, they are quickly grasped, and their efficiency endears them to busy reporters and audiences. With their powers of inclusion and exclusion, they set the "agenda" for what is considered a legitimate discussion and what isn't. Based on the already familiar, the agenda they set is conservative and difficult to change. And because of the media's glitzy dramatic techniques, frames are what modern journalism can do very well.[9]

Given the multidimensional aspect of the organic paradigm—encompassing radical production, distribution, and consumption—several frames were needed.

To package the complex array of nonchemical techniques being attempted by the Rodales and others, the mass media used a simple frame: "compost and ladybugs." Urbane, congenitally cynical (and usually male) reporters were hard-pressed to consider seriously horticultural techniques said to be practiced previously by "little old ladies in tennis shoes" and the "lunatic fringe." To an extent the first generation of hip converts compounded this oversimplification by assuming that organic meant letting nature "do its thing"—i.e., throw a few seeds in the ground along with some compost, release a few beneficial insects, and then just sit back. The inevitable failure of such gardening was often spotlighted in media articles on "squalid" rural communes. The communal garden depicted in *Easy Rider* was an early film version of the news theme: a few pitifully scrawny plants tended by stoned, filthy, hungry misfits. That surviving communes often took a more systematic approach the next time around received little or no press attention, for reporters rarely returned for follow-ups. As for the commercially successful organic farmers supplying co-ops and health food stores, media wags suspected they were probably spraying the orchards secretly at night when no one was looking.[10]

The frame of organic farmers as cheats well suited the press's traditional suspicion of self-styled purists. *Newsweek*'s headline "Rotten Apples" subtly recalled Progressive era campaigns against "dirty" local groceries and for the sanitary, standardized name brands of nationwide chains and processors. Cheerfully cynical was another *Newsweek* heading, "Dead Bugs," in a discussion of the way one merchant verified whether celery was truly organic: if it had live insects, it was okay, but if it had dead bugs, it was sprayed. Indeed, the huckster frame went back beyond the Progressive era campaign for honesty and efficiency to the medieval roots of the word—"a pettily mercenary fellow" who "hooked" the unwary by "hawking" products of dubious quality. In applying the label to both organic farmers and merchants, the media noted two abuses. Organic produce either looked bad because it wasn't sprayed, or it looked too good because it was sprayed. Either way, according to media punsters, entrepreneurs taking this "fresh approach" were reaping "healthy markups" and "wholesome profits," and their numbers were "mushrooming."[11]

Largely anecdotal, the fraud stories sometimes sounded like a Bob Hope or Johnny Carson monologue. *Business Week* cited one California retailer who diluted organic pineapple with canned (in what, fruit salad?). Another was said to buy regular produce and label part of it "organic," at a 30-percent increase. Having cited two cases, the article mused that misrepresentation and fraud constituted "a combination to make the most rabid food faddists brood over their sesame seeds." A well-publicized 1972 investigation by New York State Attorney General Louis Lefkowitz provided still more anecdotes: "organic flounder" caught in the Atlantic selling at a 50-percent premium, "organic eggs" at $1.00 a dozen (vs. the

159

regular 69 cents), "organic" chuck selling for three times the regular chuck price. Most damaging was a state lab examination of fifty-five "organic" products: 30 percent had detectable pesticide residues.[12]

While this evidence did get reported widely, other, more positive testimony did not get reprinted. For example, at the same hearings, Lester Brown, a well-known writer on world food problems, noted how new and untested most high-tech methods actually were and praised organic agriculture as a "way to keep our ecological options open." Another witness argued that labor-intensive organic farming was a way to keep rural people on the land and out of overcrowded cities. Another made the Lappé argument for the ecological efficiency of vegetarianism. Another discussed the benefits of organic methods for soil conservation. Indeed, judging from the overall testimony, one observer concluded that there was a legitimate demand for organic products, that more research needed to be done, and that the cases of overcharging and fraud resulted inevitably from the shortage of supply.[13]

Ignoring the other testimony, however, the mainstream press focused almost exclusively on the fraud problem, which it interpreted not as a short-term supply problem but as evidence of archetypal human greed and folly: that is, these health food entrepreneurs were simply performing in the huckster tradition of snake oil salesmen and charlatan faith healers. That Rodale was "a very prosperous health freak" seemed to merit the proselytizing-profiteer label (even though he was well off *before* going organic in the late 1930s). A 1972 *Harpers Bazaar* article, "The $2 Billion Health Food Fraud," quoted Frederick Stare to the effect that the "Rodale interests" were making a "fortune." The article was typical of those ridiculing "food faddism," although the price tag was higher than most. Since media conventions required a dollar appraisal of movements considered socially significant, almost every article in 1972 mentioned a $400 million figure; perhaps in line with capitalist conventions requiring steady increases, this amount 160 went up annually—to $500 million worth of "fraud" in 1974 and $600 million in 1975. The most negative articles—especially Stare's—had the highest dollar estimates, perhaps because they had the greatest ideological case to prove: the more money "wasted" on organically grown food, the more proof that nonchemical agriculture would be too expensive, a frivolous self-indulgence at a time when America should be lowering costs to feed the hungry overseas.[14]

While the mainstream media routinely mentioned that the number of profit-making health food stores had "sprouted" (or "mushroomed") from 500 in 1965 to over 3,000 in 1972, no major newspaper or magazine dealt with the even more spectacular increase in nonprofit outlets. According to the Cooperative League of the U.S.A., between 5,000 and 10,000 food co-ops were established during the 1970s, with estimated sales in 1975 of $500 million—just $100 million under *Newsweek*'s estimate for the profit-making sector that year. Although such figures were unreliable for both sectors, the point is that the mass media chose to focus only on one and not the other.[15]

Responding to the moral panic, the Rodale Press blamed organic fraud on short supplies and lax regulation. Supplies would take time to catch up, however, for the conversion from chemical to organic methods needed at least five years. (In fact, some organic farmers tested positive for chemicals because residues lingered on from previous years—or blew over from neighbors' fields.) Meanwhile, the movement faced a public relations crisis. Declaring in 1972 that "we don't want this important industry ruined by a few charlatans," Robert Rodale hired an independent laboratory to visit self-described organic farms to test soil for humus content—a good indication of compost use. Those with at least 3 percent humus content received a Rodale Seal of Approval that could be displayed at the grocery store or farm stand. But because certification was voluntary, it would not catch the most unscrupulous. For mandatory national standards, some growers and distributors lobbied the FDA and FTC to accept the simple Rodale definition of "organic" as produce grown in soil containing at least 3 percent humus content. But the FDA stuck to the standard "everything with carbon is organic" line. Passing the buck, the FTC urged self-regulation by manufacturers and consumers.[16]

To this de facto government policy of "buyer beware," the media added "beware the buyer." That is, if people were silly enough to buy fraudulent "organic" food, the problem lay not only with profiteering hucksters, but with their gullible followers.

Attempting to explain "the booming health food business," *Vogue*'s James Trager identified three customer "types": those seeking fresher, more interesting food; environmentalists worried about pesticides, herbicides, and fertilizers; and "people consumed with anxieties about their appearance and well-being, which they link to what they eat." Although the first two gave health food sales their sudden spurt, Trager deemed the last to be

161

the largest in size and "fervor." Seeking "supernatural powers" in so-called natural foods, these pitiful neurotics were susceptible to being proselytized by "cults" whose "patron saints" were Adelle Davis, Carlton Fredericks, Gaylord Hauser, J. I. Rodale, "and other legatees of that progenital American food faddist, Sylvester W. (Graham cracker) Graham." [17] This rhetorical link between postmodern angst, religious sects, and nineteenth-century reformers was a common one, and illustrated the alliance between journalism and academia. Quoting elite university chemists, agronomists, and biologists on issues of food production, the mass media referred to social scientists for perspective on food consumption, particularly its more deviant varieties.

From historians came old stories about the "faddist" followers of Sylvester Graham, John Harvey Kellogg, Horace Fletcher, and other "nuts" and "flakes." Such stories tended to treat radicals as intemperate extremists who added little more than a smattering of comic relief to the great centrist, anti-Communist tradition. What made these radicals so humorous was that they seemed in fact so "long-winded," so self-righteous, so sober. (Temperance was indeed usually part of the nineteenth-century reform program— though certainly not that of the 1970s.) Quoted out of context, these ultraserious people seemed to damn themselves before fading into history as quaint curiosities. In line with the huckster-profiteer frame, Graham was linked to the Graham cracker, Kellogg to the corn flake—ironic evidence of how impossible it was for deviants to stay out of the mainstream. Their followers emerged as victims of the same middle-class "status anxiety" and "alienation" that, according to Richard Hofstadter and Christopher Lasch, drove marginalized intellectuals to seek therapeutic relief in moralistic, unpragmatic crusades. That organic food consumers were willing and able to pay such high prices seemed to confirm the elitist nature of the countercuisine. [18]

Serving—along with "fruit" and "flake"—as one of the ironic puns describing health food consumers, the "nut" frame also illustrated the cross-fertilization between history and pop psychology. Journalists instinctively distrusted radical warnings about ecocatastrophe and the counternutritional food system. Trager's *Vogue* article opened by putting the health food boom in the context of growing "indignation, angst, melancholy, even acute paranoia." Even Ralph Nader—generally approved by the media—was singled out as responsible for contributing to the "currently fashionable mystique" that "they're out to poison us." [19]

162

Like many journalists, Trager reflected—and perhaps drew on—the pop psych ridicule of conspiracy theories found in reigning nutritional textbooks. In *Fundamentals of Normal Nutrition* (1968), Drexel University nutritionist Corinne H. Robinson belittled the paranoid "charlatan" who distrusted commercially added nutrients and who, supposedly without evidence, berated "the chemical and drug manufacturers, American agriculturalists, and foodprocessors for a deficient food supply." Further betraying emotional instability, the "charlatan" accused "the American Medical Association, the Food and Drug Association, physicians, and dieticians of being in league with the big business of food productions, and of campaigns to persecute him for his 'life-giving' ideas and products." These paranoids in turn seduced those with "hypochondriac tendencies" into trying "special food preparations," according to *Living Nutrition* (1973), by Frederick Stare and Margaret McWilliams. In *Nutrition, Behavior, and Change* (1972), Helen H. Gifft and Marjorie B. Washbon pronounced that "food faddism stems from acute or chronic psychological aberrations, including psychosis." Special claims for honey, molasses, wheat germ, and whole grains had little scientific veracity and had "overtones of magic." The compulsion of some people to embrace such delusions probably indicated "their need for emotional support when coping with worries about food." [20]

While some nutritionists hoped to "cure" patients of their delusions, others did take a more positive, if still clinical, view: while of dubious nutritional value, health foods did at least help shore up the faddist's "ego defenses" and "self-realization." *Vogue*'s Trager thus granted the "placebo power" of some health foods. Such benevolent condescension was soon popularized in the movie persona of Woody Allen, especially in *Annie Hall* (1977), and in the Tom Wolfe essay "The Me Decade" (1976). In both cases, the theme was how, in a difficult age, the "therapy junkie" was a laughable but basically lovable—or at least harmless—lunatic. [21]

While journalists might tolerate vegetarianism as neurotic behavior akin to nail biting and hair pulling, all treated macrobiotics as a form of psychosis far beyond the range of liberal tolerance. In this they echoed established medical opinion. Thus, according to the Council on Foods and Nutrition of the American Medical Association, a "zen macrobiotic diet is one of the most dangerous dietary regimens, posing not only serious hazards to the health of the individual but even to life itself." [22] For evidence, nutrition

163

textbooks, scientific papers, and mass media articles all referred rather vaguely back to the case of one woman who, in the mid-sixties, had supposedly come close to death as the result of a "macrobiotic diet." Although it remains unclear whether this woman actually died, whether she was from New Jersey or Greenwich Village, or whether she was in fact following a *correct* macrobiotic diet, the story was a keystone in the moral panic. Just as organic was reduced to "compost and ladybugs," macrobiotics was reduced to "brown rice." Although many thousands of young people were "eating brown rice" for a while, the only (possible) death reported was the same one from 1965—before the countercuisine. However stale, the anecdote served as the reductio ad absurdum for the whole trend: if this thing kept going on, the nation's white middle-class children might all wind up dead. Health foods might be neurotic placebos, but brown rice was an instrument of suicide.

What made matters worse was that people were "going macrobiotic" in groups, suggesting a specter of lemminglike *mass* suicide. Here the "neurosis" frame of pop psychology blended into the "cult" label that pop anthropology often applied to unauthorized religious "sects." Since the health food hucksters were branded as "gurus," "high priestesses," "missionaries," "crusaders," and the like, their followers were called "devotees," "cadres," "converts," and "true believers." Quoting Brillat-Savarin, Claude Lévi-Strauss, and a hip rabbi, *Time* branded macrobiotics "The Kosher of the Counterculture." That the countercuisine was a bizarre religious cult seemed borne out in the sayings of its adherents. According to one "Hollywood macrobiotic enthusiast," food was a way "to attain the order of the universe." "Fruit is probably the most spiritual food there is," observed another mystical Southern Californian. Dressed in long white robes, the owner of The Source, a well-known Los Angeles health food restaurant, told *Seventeen*, "If God had wanted us to eat things out of a can he would have made them that way." Lacking "technical credentials," she could offer no "corroborative evidence" of her claim that "when you eat meat, you make your body a graveyard for dead animals." It was at this "decidedly mystic" restaurant that Woody Allen would order a plate of alfalfa sprouts and "mashed yeast" in *Annie Hall*.[23]

164

Such spiritual claims unnerved reporters who, unaccustomed to aligning the universe at lunch, also noted that the more outlandish quotes tended to come from Southern California. While Los

Angeles was not as important a center for the countercuisine as the Bay Area or Boston, it was an area long fascinated with health therapies—imparting a certain continuity to the "nut/fruit" frame. Moreover, as the entertainment capital, it offered another explanatory frame: perhaps the health food fad was just another by-product of the mass culture to which this generation of youth seemed particularly susceptible. Since, as many articles noted, John Lennon and Yoko Ono were "doing it," perhaps impressionable youth were following just to be "with it." At its best, therefore, the macrobiotics/organic cult might be relegated to the frame of teenage ephemera, along with white bucks, Hula-Hoops, and bell bottoms; at its worst, however, it smacked of two other California events suggesting that the counterculture was running amok in late 1969: Altamont and the Manson murders.

Perhaps the final frame was of the food itself: weird tastes for weird people. Here, as elsewhere, a hurried snapshot substituted for an experimental process, caricature for context. Before the moral panic took hold, an occasional photospread in *Life*, *Seventeen*, or *Good Housekeeping* might almost do justice to the broad variety of whole grains, beans, breads, salads, fruits, and juices. One particularly sensual full-color *Life* essay on "The Move to Eat Natural" actually applauded the brown-earthy motif, the nostalgia for "small, country-style stores," the revival of the "old art of bread making" and its corollary, the rejection of the "instant world of brown-and-serve." Writing in late 1970, the author hoped that the countercuisine would be able to overcome the health food stereotypes that were old long before most of the current practitioners were born: "Despite natural food's broadening popularity, a large part of the public still believes that it's just wheat germ and molasses all over again, ingested chiefly by body builders and other exotics." More often, however, authors rested content with the "wheat germ and molasses" frame—or with other time-tested symbols of faddism: carrot juice, desiccated beef liver, sea salt, dandelion soup, pumpkin seeds, cider vinegar, brewer's yeast, peppermint tea, and endless variations on a theme of spinach. 165 Indeed, in an editorial reversal that indicated the extent of the negative turn taken, a 1972 *Life* follow-up aggressively titled "What's So Great About Health Foods?" repeated the orthodox case against the countercuisine. Running through a list of "basics" —"from parsnip juice to sea salt"—it found no redeeming value at all. Granola had too many calories, brown rice meant starvation, seeds and nuts were high in fat, honey had "no significant nutritive value," and so on.[24]

Not only were these fad foods outrageously expensive and of dubious nutritional benefit, they also tasted strange. In "The Kosher of the Counterculture," *Time* sympathized with the hungry guests at one macrobiotic wedding forced to eat "a feast of brown rice, nituke vegetables, and Mu tea." That people would spend so much money on "tricky nuts and dreary lentils" was a source of amazement and amusement, especially in the business press. In an article titled "What Tastes Terrible and Doubles in Sales Every 60 Days?" the *Wall Street Journal* found granola to be "something a horse might be fond of. It's made of rolled oats, wheat germ, sea salt, sesame seeds, coconut, brown sugar, and soy oil, all mixed together. Even when soaked in milk it's about as chewy as leather —and not quite as tasty." The title of a follow-up on yogurt captured the seeming perversity of the health food consumer: "Oh No, Not Yogurt! Many People Hate It, Yet Many Now Eat It."[25]

After 1976, the volume of ridicule tended to taper off, although the images stuck—hence the persistent equation of health foods with "nuts and twigs." As the counterculture dispersed out of its communal base into seemingly normal households and professions, the perceived threat to mainstream values seemed to diminish as well. In influencing that dispersal, the mass media played their historic role of identifying and destabilizing an "extreme." In *Scenes,* a study of deviant subcultures, sociologist John Irwin argues that the media's role is to make bohemian activities and life-styles "available" for scrutiny by a broader public hungry for novelty, otherness, and vicarious amusement. The longer it takes for the mass media to find a new bohemia, the longer that subculture has time to establish its separate identity and strengthen its defenses. Because the Southern California surfer scene had been around for at least ten years before its "discovery" in the late 1950s, it was able to withstand and outlive the sudden publicity. In the case of the Haight-Ashbury counterculture of the 1960s, however, the exposure came too soon and was devastating. Barely two years after the Haight-Ashbury's founding as a distinct scene (ca. 1964), a glut of articles were attracting new converts, police intervention, and editorial condemnation. Within four years the scene had gone through the full life cycle: Golden Age (1966– 67), Expansion (1966–69), Corruption (1968–69), Stagnation (1970–71).[26]

166

The countercuisine had even less time to get established. The turn to ecology and dietary reform was the counterculture's own internal attempt to deal with the media-instigated corruption phase of 1968–69, but this shift was indeed "discovered" almost as soon as it got started (ca. 1969), and by 1970 it was already feeling the unsettling effects of too-rapid expansion and editorial condemnation—the moral panic. Through relentless freeze-framing of the countercuisine's playful improvisational process, the media helped to create a distorted, if not downright embarrassing, picture, thereby impeding recruitment and encouraging committed practitioners to lay low. In particular, by 1974, key words like "natural" and "health food" had been severely discredited, while "organic," "macrobiotic," and "holistic" were rendered, at least temporarily, beyond the pale of decent discourse.

I say "temporarily" because later on, as new perspectives and personnel entered academia, food reformers were studied more seriously. Taking a new look at Sylvester Graham, historians found valid nutritional advice and telling social criticism, not laughable quackery. Moving beyond the "cult" label, anthropologists found the countercuisine to be both a "social revitalization movement" and an "alternative health maintenance system." Even Frederick Stare had good words for macrobiotics as a useful diet for some cancer patients: "The macrobiotic diet, as we've known it for the past three or four years, is a healthy diet." [27] But these revised views were not widely publicized, for the "moral panic" was over and the press was not all that interested.

Probably the most damaging impact was on organic agriculture. The favorable evidence did begin to come in, yet since it was poorly publicized, few consumers, voters, or farmers could learn about it. A 1980 USDA report giving organic agriculture grudging respect was a frustrating example of "too little, too late." Motivated by the energy crisis to explore less expensive technologies, a USDA team had visited organic farms in the United States, Europe, and Japan. The report cited numerous instances of successful operations—even on a fairly large scale of 1,500 acres—and suggested further study. Ironically, the hippie/kook stereotypes had become so ingrained that the USDA had to dismiss the misconceptions of its own making: "Contrary to popular belief, most organic farmers have not regressed . . ." but were in fact using modern machinery, and sophisticated methods of crop rotation, pest control, and soil management. Reacting to this about-face, one organic

167

farmer quipped, "You know, if all this keeps up we're all going to have to wear underwear."[28]

The report was said to stem in part from a 1978 visit by Carter agriculture secretary Bob Bergland to the successful organic farm of his Roseau, Minnesota, neighbors, Paul and Dale Billberg. But Bergland was soon replaced by Reagan's John Block, who pronounced organic research "a dead end" and closed the one-man organic office. In 1983—at the start of the worst farm crisis in recent history—the *Washington Post*'s new agriculture reporter and part-time organic farmer, Ward Sinclair, profiled Delmar Akerlund, a Nebraska grain and cattle farmer who had prospered without chemicals since 1967 but was unknown to farmers reliant on mainstream information sources. Four years later, the unusually sympathetic Sinclair wrote virtually the same article: while Akerlund continued to do well, his neighbors were going under in unprecedented numbers. Again bemoaning the lack of publicity, Sinclair blamed the persistent old frames—"the popular image of the organic farmer as a freakish health-food nut who is checking out of the twentieth century." Such images discouraged conventional farmers from investigating alternatives. Although even Reagan's USDA began to sponsor a dash of "low-input" research in the mid-1980s, valuable years (and thousands of family farms) had been lost.[29]

Although many journalists had happily joined the charge against "organic fraud," at the time the press actually seemed quite moderate. Disdaining "extremes," newspeople saw themselves as representatives of the broad middle of traditional values, common sense, and adult responsibility. But to claim the center, they had to reject *two* extremes, radicalism *and* orthodoxy. If J. I. Rodale was a quack, then perhaps Frederick Stare was also a bit too hotheaded and unbending. If Beatrice Trum Hunter was "paranoid" about additives, well, maybe the FDA was too lax in its approval procedures. Granola was too expensive and tasted terrible, but Kellogg's Sugar Smacks did have too much sugar and not enough vitamins. Rachel Carson seemed "hysterical" in her blanket condemnation of pesticides, but to defend them all seemed equally extreme. It was wrong to be "obsessed" about food safety, but it also was wrong to be too complacent. Almost daily a news story showed that something was wrong with the food supply and something—though not very much—had to be done about it. Perhaps some cutbacks, like those recommended in the 1980 "Dietary

168

Guidelines," were in fact needed. In short, to the diehards' dismay, what had once served as the status quo—the orthodox defense—was now becoming the extreme offsetting the countercuisine.

SOMETHING'S WRONG

The disagreements with orthodoxy were based in what Herbert Gans calls the news's "enduring values"—a collection of deep-seated journalistic beliefs and assumptions which took hold, Gans argues, during muckraking campaigns of the Progressive era. The most important enduring value was that of "responsible capitalism"—a hope that businesses would not openly exploit consumers or workers.[30] Rooted in the muckrakers' crusade against abusive monopolies, this "responsible capitalism" value framed the food stories of the 1970s in several ways. While the oligopolistic tendencies of the food processors were underplayed, there *were* cases of gross exploitation. Following Edward R. Murrow's exposure of barbaric migrant labor conditions back in 1960, the struggles of the tiny farm workers union to organize western fields and orchards merited press sympathy. The Choate breakfast cereal hearings gained coverage, not so much because of industry concentration, but because of the apparent exploitation of innocent children. Such business abuse stories were usually linked with a call for better enforcement of laws passed during the Progressive era. Thus the FTC's investigation of children's advertising was interpreted as appropriate only to the extent that it uncovered outright deception—the FTC's initial mandate; when the investigation began to push into the relatively new territory of defining "unfairness," however, many editors joined the *Washington Post* in accusing the FTC of trying to act like a "national nanny." The food additives scare was usually framed as a failure of the Food and Drug Administration to fulfill its existing obligations, ca. 1906. Similarly, when a 1973 ABC News special, "How Green Grow the Profits," exposed the use of arsenic to promote chicken growth in Alabama, it ended with a call on the USDA to hire more meat inspectors and to enforce the laws passed in the wake of Upton Sinclair's *Jungle*.[31]

Even such a limited exposé was enough to give affected food corporations fits, however. So too, the food industry could feel

169

threatened by media support for labeling. Labels seemed consistent with "the public's right to know" and "the free flow of information." Moreover, for the free market to work well under responsible capitalism, consumers needed to be able to make rational choices. The corollary of this was that many health problems were the result of ignorance—a position not all that different from the industry's rationale for "nutrition education": if people were not eating well, blame the people, not the industry. But to their credit, journalists at least followed through logically to its implications: they welcomed complete, government-mandated labeling. The food industry, on the other hand, wanted "education" on its own terms—a stance that, when publicized, seemed childish and greedy. This unwillingness to make any concessions did not play well in the press, which held that capitalism worked best when everyone gave a little, like "responsible" adults.[32]

Consumer activist Ralph Nader skillfully exploited this journalistic vision of responsibility when he battled the conglomerates. As one of the world's largest and most secretive corporations, General Motors was an excellent foil. Indeed, GM twice played Goliath to Nader's David—first as the subject of his Corvair exposé, *Unsafe at Any Speed* (1965), and second as clumsy sponsor of private investigators looking for dirt on Nader. After besting GM, Nader went on to publicize other abuse/exploitation stories: the use of monosodium glutamate in baby food, excessive fat in hot dogs ("among the most dangerous missiles this country produces"), inadequate meat inspection ("We're back in *The Jungle,*") as well as DDT and cyclamates. Although Nader had a personal agenda that aimed at comprehensive reform, his celebrity status probably derived from the way he fit so well into the beloved Harvey Wiley–Upton Sinclair mold: the relentless crusader against impurity. He also recalled the Depression era campaigns against fraud and deception, as in Frederick Schlink and Arthur Kallet's 1933 best-seller, *100,000,000 Million Guinea Pigs.* To this was added the obvious Capra-esque touch—the rumpled, plainspeaking lawyer standing up to the plutocrats. Living in a cheap furnished room, paying his scrappy "raiders" a bare subsistence, Nader embodied the populist version of "small is beautiful": the heroic individualist who bested the corporate moguls and government bureaucrats and then refused the perks of success—the outer office, the limo, the retirement plan.[33]

At the same time, despite his asceticism, he was no bohemian.

170

With his short hair, dark suit, and plain tie, Nader was like Eugene McCarthy, who inspired youthful dissidents to "go clean," to "work within the system." (Just as the genteel-academic McCarthy was one of the first liberal politicians to call for an end to the bombing, the Princeton- and Harvard-educated Nader served as the establishment's early warning system in the domestic sphere.) To *Time*, Nader was "a symbol of constructive protest against the status quo. When this peaceful revolutionary does battle with modern bureaucracies, he uses only the weapons available to any citizen—the law and public opinion. He has never picketed, let alone occupied a corporate office or public agency." No radical, Nader focused on single issues and steered clear of apocalyptic "paranoia," "mystical" therapies, and organic "hucksterism."[34]

In short, he seemed, at least initially, the model moderate reformer, the balance between offsetting extremes. Cover stories in *Time* and *The New York Times Magazine* thus enthused that Nader was anathema to both businessmen and "New Left revolutionaries." "The U.S.'s Toughest Customer," Nader seemed the classic bourgeois: ultrarationalistic, out to get his money's worth, skeptical of frippery, a fitting successor to Ben Franklin's Poor Richard, the quintessential Sears patron. Appropriately, the notion of democratic "responsiveness" was inscribed on Nader's door: The Center for Study of Responsive Law. Who could be against responsiveness, a central tenet of free market faith? And who, in this age when students seemed more interested in barricades than books, could be against study?[35]

Responsible capitalism also entailed grudging respect for hip enterprise—although the framing was at best ambivalent. While health food entrepreneurs smacked of hucksterism, they also seemed somewhat heroic in their willingness to start at the bottom and buck the corporate giants. At the very least, hip businessmen were relatively harmless. Rather than throwing bombs or plotting demonstrations they were busy tracking inventories and scraping to meet payrolls.[36] In the 1980s the portraits became more ironic: former revolutionaries were now wearing suits, installing computers, talking about the bottom line. Thus a *New York* magazine spread on "Restaurant Madness" welcomed the dizzying array of menu items invented by "the boutique generation"—all those "freaky people from the sixties," who, once the noise died down after Woodstock, opened expensive restaurants: e.g., Alice Waters (Chez Panisse), Jonathan Waxman (Jams), Ed Schoenfield (Pig

171

Heaven). Despite male corporate domination, the restaurant business seemed open to nonconformists after all. The "unstinting variety" of exotic peppers, greens, and fruits at one Southern California organic produce market testified to the option-maximizing efficiency of small businesses. Spectacular success stories like Celestial Seasonings could be framed as examples of capitalist pluralism and flexibility. If Nader was Ben Franklin's Poor Richard, Siegel was Horatio Alger's Ragged Dick. When Siegel was ultimately bought out by Kraft, capitalism seemed to be operating at its responsible best by rewarding the brightest.[37]

Related to the press's sympathy for small business was the enduring value of "small-town pastoralism"—an affection for craftsmanship, villages, and country traditions. Such nostalgia revealed considerable anxiety about issues of scale and control in the modern urban-industrial world. Life in relatively small agrarian societies had a "human scale"; individuals seemed better able to control events.[38] Viewed through this nostalgic lens, large-scale high-tech conglomerates did not fare well, especially when they seemed unable to control their chemical staples. And there were many visible signs of the loss of control: e.g., the Cuyahoga River on fire, dying birds fluttering helplessly on a beach after an oil spill, dead fish washing up poisoned by DDT, infants grossly deformed by DES, pedestrians in Los Angeles wearing surgical masks to counteract smog, Michigan cattle killed en masse by a fire retardant (PBB) accidentally mixed in their feed, and, later on (1984), thousands of Indians killed by a leak at a pesticide plant in Bhopal.

The strongest news stories involved visible disasters, for it was harder to dramatize the long-term privately experienced effects of less intense contaminants. But there *was* a ritual surrogate for the "dead birds" story: the news conference or hearing at which some official, expert, or critic identified yet another disaster in the making—red dye no. 2, mercury, sugared cereal, advertising, saccharin, nitrates, cholesterol, sodium, and so on and on. Although this one-scare-at-a-time rhythm hindered a comprehensive overview of the food system, its very fragmentation probably enhanced the media effect. If all the danger stories had come out in one week rather than over ten years, they might have been forgotten quickly. By publicizing one danger at a time, however, the media fostered a more lasting perception of technology out of control. The standard chemical danger story began with the orthodox dis-

172

claimer: most chemicals are beneficial, but . . . There was always a "but"—the latest exception to the rule. After a while, the familiar disclaimer might be skipped over, and only the "but" got heard. Mounting up over the decade, the drumroll of "buts" could seem deafening.[39]

Making matters worse was the inability of scientific and political authorities to restore order. According to journalism's Progressive era heritage, once disorder appeared in public places, it was to be studied and resolved by our modern-day village elders—the officially certified, morally unimpeachable "experts."[40] In the 1960s and 1970s, there was certainly enough public disorder to be studied, but the leaders themselves were increasingly disorderly, especially in the later 1970s.

Yet equivocation and conflict were inevitable, as findings were often exposed prematurely and incompletely. Prodded by the alternative press and pulled by public concern, the mainstream media printed more information than ever about food, but many of the data were only half-baked, in the form of tentative hypotheses based on limited studies. Scientist A found some evidence of liver tumors in his rats, while B's results were "inconclusive." C found some correlation between cholesterol levels in 400 middle-aged men and heart disease; in a different population, under different circumstances D found no statistically clear connection. In the relatively restricted academic context of paper giving and writing, such information was treated as scholarly suggestion; when summarized in the mass media, however, suggestions hardened into declarations—seemingly dogmatic statements that often contradicted what other experts were declaring.

Conflicts surfaced within the government too, especially in the Carter years, as newly appointed liberals in some offices fought holdover conservatives in others. The battles over food advertising, cereal industry concentration, the "Dietary Goals," labeling, and saccharin were fought both internally among agencies and externally by lobbyists claiming that government was doing either too much or too little. Public officials generated masses of documents: 173 hearings, proposals, regulations, reports, and the like—and to what effect? More reversals, more inconsistencies, more bureaucratic bungling.

The "battle of the experts" became a major news frame. Having long advocated that ordinary citizens suspend private judgment and yield to certified professionals, journalists now lamented that the experts could no longer deliver. With all the contention, they mused, it was no wonder that so many people were turning to fads or simply giving up in exasperation. After a rash of findings concerning cholesterol, *Post-Newsweek*'s "moderate" voice, Meg Greenfield, confessed to a bad case of anti-intellectual nihilism. The latest "new findings," Greenfield mused, came from the same "They Institute of America" that, over the past fifteen years, kept telling us "to take huge doses of whatever it is we had just succeeded, with much personal agony, in eliminating from our diet." First "they" told us to eat lots of meat, eggs, and dairy products, then "they" told us to eat less of those and more fish, but then "they" told us to eat less fatty fish (due to mercury in fatty tissues), and now "they" were telling us to eat more fish, *especially* the fattiest variety, for fish oils seemed to reduce cholesterol. Wearied by the barrage of conflicting advice, Greenfield observed, "Nothing lasts. No assertion has a shelf life of more than 11 months." Indeed she was sure that, just around the corner, "they" would be telling us to eat more fatty beef, eggs, and whole milk. Newsmagazine covers announced Nixon was "back"; could the Twinkie —with extra salt—be far behind? Hence the title of her essay: "Give Me That Old-Time Cholesterol." Such humor testified to the weakening of what Paul Starr calls cultural authority—a clear, unequivocal, centrally constructed, and widely accepted view of reality.[41]

Of course, columnists had ironic license unavailable to beat reporters in need of a more sober stance. Earlier the standard recourse might have been to call, in Progressive fashion, on public officials to coordinate and rationalize all the advice. The late 1970s and early 1980s were not conducive to more red tape, however. A more common approach was to rely on the profession's inveterate moderatism: look for common denominators in all the advice being offered from all sides. These common denominators were largely negative: a loss of faith in expert authority, a pervasive uncertainty about what was healthy, and a gnawing sense, as one *Time* cover put it, that "Eating May Not Be Good For You." This negative thrust was capsulized in the 1980 "Dietary Guidelines' " key verbs —"avoid," "reduce," "limit," "decrease." Such "negative nutrition" was appropriate to a time beset by what Jimmy Carter called a "malaise," but it dominated the Reagan years too. Noting all the dangers that had mounted up in the seven years following the "Guidelines," a *Washington Post* writer advised wary eaters to follow First Lady Nancy Reagan's antidrug slogan: "Just Say No."[42]

174

NEGATIVE NUTRITION

T he countercuisine certainly had its negative side too. I have argued that this negation was as political as it was nutritional— a reaction to the foreign and domestic crises of the time. The loss of confidence in America's political superiority was matched by a loss of faith in its food habits. But it is useful to repeat that this negation and asceticism were balanced by an affirmative, indeed hedonistic, component. As Gary Snyder put it, "living lightly" did not necessarily mean living in self-denial. In a communal context, it could be joyous. Small might be beautiful if you were involved in the social complex of alternative production, distribution, and consumption: country and city communes, organic gardens, co-ops, alternative restaurants and stores. Forsaking mainstream foods was not simply a negative escape; ideally it was to be balanced by entry into an alternative society. A brown rice diet was boring, if not downright dangerous, only when you attempted it alone. Soy products were virtually inaccessible unless you consulted the right sources, and these were available mainly within the countercultural community. The staples of the countercuisine tended to be low in fat, calories, and additives, but they were rich in nutrients, taste, and symbolism when understood and used in the social environment.

In the mass media, however, mostly negatives came through —stripped of the larger countercultural context. It was fine to reject white bread or to worry about DDT as long as you did not go off the deep end into organic mysticism. It was even all right to stop eating meat, but only for negative reasons—cutting cholesterol; to want to save the world or your soul was still considered nonsense. A 1980 *Consumer Reports* article on vegetarianism dismissed all "faddist" claims concerning spirituality, politics, and longevity, and found "little evidence" that it was either particularly bad or good. Just about the only certainty was that vegetarians did not suffer as often from constipation and also weighed somewhat less. Still, since scientists were so uncertain about what constituted a good diet, you probably could "get by"—as long as you took precautions to get the right vitamins. Although this was a less hostile treatment than vegetarianism might have received ten years before, it was not exactly a ringing endorsement for a comprehensive nutritional program.[43]

175

When it came to disease prevention, mainstream food advisors urged modest, piecemeal cutbacks. Overloaded with inconclusive chemical scare stories, the news agenda shifted subtly to the more certain dangers addressed in the "Guidelines": cholesterol, sodium, sugar, calories. To the extent that these dangers were more easily monitored by the individual than the more hidden chemical dangers, this shift was consistent with the antigovernment turn. It also represented a backward step from a concern about cancer, a relatively recent and poorly understood problem, to concern about somewhat more familiar problems: heart disease, stroke, diabetes, and obesity. Indeed, the only part of the "Guidelines" addressing cancer was that advising people to eat more whole grains and vegetables. Here the cancer danger came not from too much of an industrial pollutant but from too little of a natural ingredient: fiber.

The focus on fiber was itself a perfect case of the narrowing process. With the countercuisine, there were a variety of metaphysical, ecological, therapeutic, hedonistic, and political arguments for whole grains and vegetables. But now the virtue was negative: more fiber might prevent certain disorders of the colon. Although the orthodox protested even this extremely limited concession, there was in fact very little new about it, for constipation and colitis had been the concern of health reformers since Sylvester Graham. All that had changed was that fiber now had official standing—but not accompanied, of course, by the moral and social reform that Graham had associated with his diet.[44]

FIGHTING FAT

Reducing even further the plethora of expert opinions, one *Newsweek* article counseled a "green and lean" approach.[45] If "green" meant fiber and vitamins, "lean" meant dieting—perhaps the most widely practiced and least revolutionary component of negative nutrition.

176   The second dietary guideline—"Maintain ideal weight"—was nothing new, even as the affected food industries protested vehemently. What had changed, however, were the medical and social risks attributed to being overweight. Medically, many of the "experts" did seem to agree that obesity increased the risks of certain diseases. Yet only a small percentage of dieters were in fact so obese as to be medically at risk. More compelling were the social

risks of weighing more than the mass media's ideal, which was considerably lighter in 1980 than in 1960. Thinness was a relative concept. In the 1950s and early 1960s, the ideal female form—thin in the waist but full in the bust and hips—had approximated that of a woman in her mid-twenties, who, after having a baby or two, had lost some weight but had not recovered her premarital size. Such a norm was appropriate to a culture idealizing early marriage and childbearing.

Beginning in the late 1960s, however, the mass media model was decisively younger—perhaps not quite adolescent, but certainly prematernal. Thus, one analysis of the measurements of *Playboy* centerfolds and Miss America contestants found a statistically significant decrease in bust and hip sizes between 1959 and 1978. Moreover, the gap between women considered most beautiful and their contemporaries was widening. In 1959 *Playboy* centerfolds weighed 9 percent less than other women their age; in 1978 they weighed 16 percent less than the average weight of women their age. In 1959 Miss Americas weighed 14 percent less than the average; in 1978, 23 percent. The winning Miss Americas of the 1970s also weighed significantly less than other contestants. In line with the thinning down, the five most popular women's magazines published twice as many articles on dieting in the 1970s as in the 1950s. A 1979 advertisement for Bloomingdale's summer line exaggerated only slightly the new ideal: "Bean lean, slender as the night, narrow as an arrow, pencil thin, get the point?" Many apparently *did* get the point. Anorexia nervosa and bulimia, virtually unreported before 1960, became familiar news topics in the 1970s. Since, by some measurements, Americans actually ate and weighed more in the 1970s than they had in the 1950s, the need to diet seemed disproportionately greater.[46]

The slimming down of the ideal may have related to the way the media isolated the gestures, accoutrements, and look of youthful rebellion: to be energetic, fun-loving, and, ultimately, sexy, one had to be as fit, single, and ultimately, thin as an eighteen-year-old student/hippie protester—the eternal child.

177

This began with the treatment of blue jeans in the late 1960s. Underground, jeans were both practical and symbolically rich—representing a wide range of deviant attitudes, experiences, and groups: bikers, protesters, rhythm-and-blues fans, and the like. Easily purchased, stretched, modified, and personalized, they could accommodate virtually any body size, whim, or need. When the fashion industry took jeans aboveground, however, their ads depicted lean, sexy youth, the "weekend swingers," who, according to one fashion magazine, wanted to appear "hip but not hippy." Levi Strauss was well-known for its ads associating blue jeans with psychedelia, youthful irreverence, and casual sexuality. Even political protest could be sexualized in some jeans ads, as in the case of a full-page 1970 ad for Tads, which invited the fashion-conscious to "Do Something Revolting in Tads." Six slim female models wearing headbands, tight bell bottoms, and nothing else, appeared to be marching up the steps of a university administration building carrying placards reading IF YOU'RE A SEX OBJECT—OBJECT! DOWN WITH THE MALE CHAUVINIST PIG! and IMPEACH MISS AMERICA! [47]

Such ads merely caricatured the associations found in editorial content. *Playboy* consistently ran photo spreads of nude models in hip communal settings, both urban and rural. The *Saturday Evening Post*'s features on hippies differed mainly in degree, not kind: Its subjects had more clothes on, but they too had the "look." [48] Dressed or undressed, Hollywood's hippies were invariably young, sexually adventurous, and thin. Nudity *did* have a role in the counterculture—a way to shock the bourgeoisie and subvert convention, a declaration of one's affection for nature and wholeness, as well as a vehicle for the sexual freedom that was itself a political, cultural, and hedonistic cause. In the mainstream media's soft-porn version, however, nudity simply signaled promiscuity.

Similarly, mass magazines highlighted the "hip but not hippy" features of the countercuisine, especially svelte sensuality. As I've already suggested, weight control did have some underground context: an ascetic badge of living lightly, a rejection of bloated affluence, a tool of self-discipline, a way to train for the long struggle ahead. Aboveground, however, the dietetic kernel was extracted from its deviant chaff. Touring the talk shows, Frances Moore Lappé wanted to talk about the world food crisis; her hosts, however, wanted to discuss *Diet for a Small Planet* as a weight-loss manual. A *Harpers Bazaar* article entitled "Beauty Sense and Nonsense" distinguished between "sensible" healthy foods—of the kind long used by Hollywood stars—and the "wrong way"—macrobiotics, with its spiritual and ecological associations; indeed the article was liberal enough to allow there was "nothing gimmicky about 'organic' eating" as long as you did it simply to stay young and beautiful. Two months after blasting "those mushrooming food fads," *Seventeen* suggested that vegetarianism enhanced dating marketability:

> *Your brother phones from college to announce that he's bringing his roommate (a great guy) home for the weekend. "And by the way," he says, "Dan is a vegetarian." Until recently vegetarians were either physical fitness nuts in space shoes or seekers of the fountain of youth; some restricted their diets for religious reasons. Now lots of kids are into vegetarianism. They're not freaks, but part of a new way of life that welcomes experimentation instead of blindly accepting things as they've always been.*

While the text at least acknowledged some wider deviancy in vegetarianism, the overall context—a magazine devoted to exploiting female adolescent anxieties—offered a more pragmatic message: it was chic to try out these recipes for black bean soup, eggplant Parmesan, green rice, and crisp salad. More to the point were *Vogue*'s photos of "sun-kissed young health food nuts" and "attractive bouncy girls" drinking fruit juices at a California beach. To the usual quips about sprouts and mushrooms, the title punned, "Health Is Busting Out All Over."[49]

Later in the decade, lithe, sexy figures were even more exposed. Stuffed into fashion jeans, T-shirts, leotards, maillots, and jogging shorts, lean bodies dominated television, movies, and advertising. Under attack for excessive violence, television network programmers substituted "T&A" ("tits and ass"); filmmakers concerned about box office slippage discovered that newly liberalized obscenity enforcement allowed them to "get away" with a degree of exposure previously attempted only in the underground and pornographic media. Fashion models followed Ali McGraw, Farrah Fawcett, Cheryl Ladd, and Tom Selleck in moving from Madison Avenue to Hollywood. Formerly anonymous cover girls now owned the lines they promoted. Like the dancers, gymnasts, and swimmers who gained celebrity status in the 1970s, many models were downright skinny. Twiggy (5'7", 92 lbs.) had been a novelty back in 1966, but Brooke Shields became an obsession. Moreover, a perverse modification of the double standard turned skinny male torsos into commodities too. In the mass media's version of fem-

179

inism, men were equally entitled to be treated as sex objects. In fashion spreads—if not also in the streets—men and women worked out in body-hugging "activewear" and then relaxed in snug, color-coordinated "leisurewear." Even the baseball uniform, once the baggy emblem of folksy homeliness, tightened up.[50]

Ironically, while mainstream articles in the early 1970s had dismissed the countercuisine's apocalyptic fantasies, a decade later fighting fat had distinctly survivalist overtones—although more Darwinian than Aquarian. With oil shortages, foreign policy defeats, toxic waste, and nuclear accidents, the world seemed increasingly dangerous, with government unable to tame the dangers. Aiming to take some control over their destinies, Americans were donning sweat suits and going into training—or so it appeared in the media. In a 1981 *Time* cover article entitled "America Shapes Up," J. D. Reed posed this timely question: "how to survive an increasingly imperfect, not to say hostile environment?"[51] Voting for politicians who promised to "cut waste" and "trim fat," they personally aimed to be lean and mean. One media model for the time was the marathon runner: gaunt of build and strong of heart, a long-distance survivor. Another, more grotesque version was that of the anorexic or bulimic hunger artist—a disorder found especially among young women trying to break into the professional-managerial world glamorized in upscale magazines.

Time (like *Newsweek* and the national network news) serves as a useful bulletin board for mainstream media agenda items; its table of contents reflects what establishment journalists consider important (and, by default, not important). Reed's 1981 *Time* cover was thus a measure of how far—yet how little—the mass media had come in a decade. On the one hand, the article suggested changes from the early 1970s, when *Time* had relegated so much of the health consciousness to a lunatic fringe status—as in "The Kosher of the Counterculture" (1970) and in its framing of Adelle Davis as the "High Priestess of Nutrition" (1972). Indeed, using the classic straw man technique, Reed exaggerated the contrast: In the early 1970s, only mystics and deviant intellectuals were interested in fitness; now just about "everyone" seemed to be a health food nut. "One need not be a granola and bean-sprout faddist now to question processed foods. In the 1960s, when Adelle Davis preached against the dangers of good old American 'enriched' white flour, she seemed no more than another village crank." But now the nation seemed "obsessed" with food quality

180

and was on an exercise craze. In 1960 only 24 percent of adults did meaningful exercise; by 1980, 50 percent. On the other hand, when the specific changes were actually discussed and totaled up, they amounted to quite a lot of money being spent in traditionally individualistic ways. Indeed, in summarizing the overall trend, Reed framed it within the venerable American cult of youth, rebirth, and "do-it-yourself salvation." Such was the dynamic of ideological domestication: readers were reassured that despite the appearance of unsettling change, down deep it was all just good old Americanism.[52]

Still, despite the conservative continuities, the changes were unsettling enough to induce segments of the food industry to expend considerable amounts of money lobbying for a rollback even in the modest "Dietary Guidelines." Despite the apparent backlash against chemical scare stories, the contributors to *Food Technology* and *Food Engineering* in the early 1980s were, if anything, more paranoid than before. Judging from the bitter wails emanating from the orthodox camp, the radical activists were winning the debate, and the cracks in the food establishment were widening, notwithstanding the mass media's ameliorative function or Reagan's deregulatory policies.

Since, in fact, the activists were in strategic retreat ca. 1980, who *was* creating this despair among the orthodox true believers? Much of the anger was of course directed at the mass media for simply covering the controversies, however conservatively. But there were other culprits too. Voicing a common complaint, one embittered food technologist blamed "hypocritical" processors who were reinforcing the scare mentality—and widening the cracks—by serving up new lines of "natural," "organic," and "healthy" foods even as they insisted that the regular foods were perfectly safe.[53]

Support for this charge was offered by *Consumer Reports*—not usually an ally of *Food Technology*—in an article on the health foods business entitled, "It's Natural! It's Organic! Or Is It?" As the title implied, most of the article reiterated the now-familiar orthodox defense: everything's natural, everything's organic, a chemical's a chemical. Indeed the rebuttal was probably more unbending than that found in the mainstream media—or, for that matter, the USDA's 1980 organic agriculture report. But where the article did break new ground was in its discussion of the "deceptive" practices themselves. Exactly *who* was exploiting the "natural" and

181

"organic" label? Ten years before, such an article would have focused strictly on the "healthy profits" being reaped by "hucksters" in the food underground. In 1980, however, the companies said to be having "a promotional field day" with these "deceptive" concepts included Pillsbury, Quaker Oats, Gravy Train, Anheuser-Busch, Kraft, W. R. Grace, and Nabisco. The "hucksters" were none other than the largest companies of the food industry![54]

PART THREE

MARKETERS: HEALTHY PROFITS

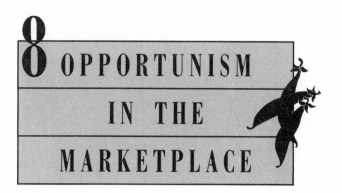

8 OPPORTUNISM IN THE MARKETPLACE

CORPORATE CRACKS: ENGINEERS VS. MARKETERS

What the true believers in the laboratories and research divisions were preaching was indeed being subverted by the sales-oriented executives in the front office. As *Food Technology* defended friendly chemicals and blasted Mother Nature, *Advertising Age* chronicled the latest additive-free, "all-natural" rollouts. Throughout the 1970s, food engineers berated food marketers not to give in to what seemed a press-driven "hysteria." *Any* compromise with faddism might increase fears, encourage further government regulation, and divert resources. The worst thing, diehards warned, would be to add even just a few new products that were low in additives, sodium, fat, or whatever, for such concessions might call into question all the other products, which were not low in these ingredients.[1]

By 1980, however, the internal battle seemed lost. "Rather than standing firm on facts," Nabisco scientist Bruce Stillings complained, "industry often perpetuates unfounded perceptions by flagging 'all-natural' ingredients in advertising." Indeed, according to *Consumer Reports*, Stillings's own company, with its trade ad, "A

Natural for Profits," was one of the more outrageous hypocrites. *CR* wondered whether advertising Nabisco Sesame Wheats as " 'a natural whole wheat cracker' might raise a few eyebrows among thoughtful consumers of Nabisco's Wheat Thins and Cheese Nips, which contain artificial colors, or of its Ginger Snaps and Oreo Cookies, which have artificial flavors. But Nabisco has not suddenly become a champion of 'natural' foods. Like other giants of the food industry, the company is merely keeping its eye on what will produce a profit." Included in *CR*'s analysis of the "tactics of deception" were:

- "the indeterminate modifier": In Pillsbury's Natural Chocolate Flavored Chocolate Chip Cookies, the "natural" modified only the "chocolate flavored," not the "cookie," which contained the chemical antioxidant BHA and artificial vanilla flavoring.

- "innocence by association": the box for Life Cinnamon Flavor High Protein Cereal used the word "nature" four times and "natural" once during a lesson for children entitled "Nature," but the ingredients list itself included BHA and artificial color.

- "ingredients you'd prefer to avoid": Quaker's 100% Natural cereal had no preservatives, but it did contain 24 percent sugars, vs. the 7.8 percent sugars in Kellogg's "regular" Corn Flakes.

- "the negative pitch": Jam labels proclaimed "no artificial preservatives" even though they'd never had them; similarly margarine ads touted "no cholesterol"—an ingredient never found in these otherwise highly processed vegetable oils.

- "the best defense": Simply assert, don't defend. Thus, "natural" notwithstanding, Anheuser-Busch's Natural Light Beer had numerous additives.

Blasting such "hypocrisy," one of the staunchest true believers attributed orthodoxy's retreat to "opportunism in the marketplace." The technologists' bitterness notwithstanding, such marketing tactics continued unabated through the 1980s and became a standard feature of the "Food Porn" column that graced, like a newspaper's comics, the last page of *Nutrition Action*, the consumerist newsletter.[2]

The antagonism between food technologists and marketers is widespread in the business world. Engineers often like to think of

186

themselves as disinterested, "pure" researchers rather than as sub-
ordinates of salesmen, yet a fact of life in industry is that "science"
is usually subordinate to sales. In his widely used textbook, *Marketing Management,* business professor Philip Kotler examines the
built-in tensions between engineering and marketing departments:
From the engineer's perspective, engineers like long design lead
times; marketers think in the short run. Engineers prefer to make
a few, well-designed models; marketers seem to like subtle, often
trivial differentiations to extend the company's reach. By temper-
ament engineers value technical quality, cost economy, and manufacturing simplicity, while marketers seem to keep adding on
expensive, cumbersome "bells and whistles." Even more alienated from marketers are scientists and technicians in research and
development departments. Down deep, R&D people see themselves as pioneers, explorers, leaders who would guide public taste
in an enlightened direction, while marketers seem unimaginative,
compromising hucksters who pander to existing public tastes. The
mistrust is mutual, of course. Marketers pride themselves on being
hardheaded, bottom-line pragmatists and view R&D people "as
impractical, long-haired, mad-scientist types who don't understand
people at all." Naturally, engineers prefer to work in what Kotler
terms "R&D dominated companies"—e.g., aerospace, pharma-
ceuticals, computers—where they are encouraged to look for
"major solutions" and "technical perfection," with less concern
about short-run failures or high costs. In "marketing dominated
companies," however, R&D people feel compelled to concoct lots
of superficially "new and improved" extensions of the same old
things.[3]

Applying Kotler's distinction, it is clear why the food technologists were so bitter, for the food industry had become decidedly
"marketing-dominated," especially in the economically troubled
1970s. In the 1950s and 1960s, there had been an outburst of
genuinely new convenience products incorporating new technologies: e.g., Kool-Aid, TV dinners, salad dressing mixes, toaster
pastries, nondairy creamers. Whether these products were truly   187
necessary could be debated, but such innovations did at least keep
R&D people busy. Moreover, the marketers' role seemed relatively minor, for such products did not have to be heavily promoted. According to *Everybody's Business,* an encyclopedia of
corporate history, the large, homogeneous middle-class market of
the fifties seemed to love "technological bravado and novelty," so

new goods almost sold themselves. "Consumers would try any-thing once, and if the new convenience foods (notably TV dinners) didn't taste anything like what mother used to make, no matter." To the technologists, therefore, 1950–1970 was the golden age to which they constantly referred and hoped to return.[4]

But in the seventies, the food companies got scared. For one thing, there was the space crunch. Many executives wondered if the human stomach could hold more than the 1,400 pounds of food products people ate annually; this total had increased only 5 per-cent in the 1960s and held virtually stable through the 1970s and 1980s. "People will buy only so much food," complained one Na-bisco executive in 1973. Also, there was less room on supermarket (and kitchen) shelves for completely new lines, and grocers were becoming far more selective in taking new products. Moreover, in a time of rapid inflation, many consumers were balking at expen-sive innovations like Pringles Newfangled Chips, and higher ingre-dient and labor costs were cutting into processors' profit margins. To top it off, consumerist pressure was forcing the FDA to take a harder look at some of the chemicals going into new food products. For the already cautious managers of food companies it seemed logical to seek growth not through costly internal R&D but through other, less risky channels: acquisitions of the most profitable smaller companies, overseas trade, school lunch programs, making essentially minor modifications in existing lines, and stretching out the "life cycle" of successful items.[5]

In explaining this conservative strategy, industry executives cited poor profit margins, but according to one USDA study, in-creasing concentration within the food industry was a major factor. Released in 1980, the report by economist John M. Connor proba-bly reinforced business world paranoia about Carter administration activists. According to Connor, in 1950 the largest fifty food com-panies had owned 6 percent of all food manufacturing assets, in 1963, 42 percent, and in 1978, 63 percent. As a result of such decreased competition, the food industry's profit rates increased by 50 percent over twenty-five years. Between 1973 and 1978, the number of food companies declined almost a third; not coinciden-tally, the number of new items introduced annually into supermar-ket distribution dropped 27 percent from 6,770 to 4,900. Of these, virtually all were simple line extensions and minor improvements in flavorings, colors, storability, and packaging, rather than com-pletely new products. As a corollary, food industry R&D was ex-

188

ceptionally low: food industry research and development expenditures constituted less than 1 percent of sales, as contrasted with 3 to 7 percent in drugs, and much higher in the cutting edge, high-tech fields beloved by engineers. Of seventeen major industries, food ranked fourteenth in R&D, and of this, according to Connor, 80 to 90 percent was devoted to product differentiation rather than research on substantially new food. In short, to be a food technologist was to work in one of the stingiest, least interesting industries around.[6]

Connor's report was not well received by food executives, but food technology journals reported it fully. After all, technologists had been complaining about this for years. If their companies really wanted to get into healthy foods, they argued, they should fund basic research that might lead to major technological breakthroughs, rather than the transparent frauds described by *Consumer Reports* and *Nutrition Action*. Throughout the 1970s the technology journals ran enthusiastic pieces about the R&D potential inherent in textured vegetable proteins (to substitute for meat), biotechnology (to engineer pest-resistant plants and thereby bypass chemical pesticides), aseptic packaging (to lessen the need for preservatives), and fortification (to enhance nutrient content). Genetic engineering might also lead to superior mushrooms, peppers, even sprouts. The soybean—icon of the countercuisine—could be fermented, extruded, reformulated, and otherwise reshaped into myriad nutritious products. Biochemists might work on saving the micronutrients currently lost in processing. Even the much-maligned demand for "natural" flavors could lead in interesting research directions. For example, one Campbell's flavorist suggested that "fresh orange volatiles" could be recovered from the "citrus waste streams used in processing the fruit," then distilled and refined into an "aqueous essence" that would "actually be closer to the natural orange flavor than the old expressed from the peels"—in all, a truly natural flavoring that was actually better than Mother Nature! There were also distinct growth possibilities in "flavors produced by the enzymic modifications of foods"—a natural process. Of course, such schemes fit well with orthodox hopes of conquering world hunger with algae, seaweed, fish by-products, wood pulp, and other natural wonders.[7] But more R&D was also needed for more genuine advances. Since, by all accounts, most of the countercuisine's tenets needed "more evidence," there was plenty of testing work to go around.

189

In fact, however, the food companies generally cut research through the 1970s and 1980s (except perhaps for the most problematic alternatives to chemicals: genetic engineering and irradiation). While Connor blamed oligopolistic complacency, industry spokesmen claimed that government regulations were forcing food companies to devote scarce resources to purely defensive research. Indeed, when attacking the Carter administration, conservatives used this antiregulatory argument as an excuse for the poor R&D performance of American industry in general.[8]

But when R&D continued to lag during the staunchly probusiness Reagan administration, it was not quite so easy to blame excess regulation. In a 1982 *Food Technology* analysis, James J. Albrecht, a Nestlé research director, pointed his finger directly at the engineer's nemesis: the marketing department. "The marketing specialists like to talk about new products, so industry spends billions of advertising and promotion dollars convincing customers that products are 'new and improved,' rather than spending significant dollars to make superior products." The food industry had only to look to Detroit, he warned, to see what happens when technological innovation is subordinate to cosmetic changes. Such somber predictions seemed borne out four years later, when the *Wall Street Journal* reported that the American food industry—a vital factor in the nation's world trade status—was losing ground abroad and at home. American agriculture was in shambles and food processors were threatened by imports. Not only was agribusiness failing to feed the world's hungry; the United States was on the verge of becoming a net importer of food. Among the explanations was the familiar engineers' chant: domination by marketing managers with little understanding of factories and technology, and less R&D than Japan and Germany.[9]

Thus the engineer-marketer conflict over dubiously "healthy" foods was more than just another turf battle between often incompatible departments. In a wider context, the fight reflected an ongoing debate over the deindustrialization of America. By hawking superficially "new and improved" products over more substantial innovations, were marketers leading the country into industrial decline?

190

What *was* behind the food marketing strategies of the late 1970s and early 1980s? Was it mainly, as both consumerists and technologists alleged, a case of dishonesty, indeed "hucksterism," in the executive suite? If a huckster is someone who knowingly makes fraudulent claims, then evidence certainly was available—

e.g., the grammatical smoke and mirrors of those Natural Chocolate Flavored Chocolate Chip Cookies. There was an almost nostalgic familiarity in such "food porn" anecdotes, which conjured up the days of cigar-chomping drummers swapping tales about gullible suckers and marks as they hustled between vulnerable villages in smoky Pullman cars.

But few marketers would admit to such a portrait, for they, like technologists, had their own self-flattering ideology of public service. Adopting populist rhetoric, they frequently portrayed themselves as dutiful servants of the dominant popular will. Although personally they had no problems with the status quo, marketers confessed, they felt duty bound to cater to popular tastes, however confused. If "natural" was what "they" wanted, then natural was what they'd get. This rationale was characterized succinctly by a speaker at a 1974 board meeting of the National Canners Association: "The American consumer, in a democratic society, is a bit like the end result of crossing a tiger with a parrot —you may not like what the creature says, but when it talks, you had better listen!" Many consumers "wrongly" considered processed convenience foods to be "junk," a Hunt-Wesson executive observed, but marketers had to cater to "perceived consumer desires" as well as "real ones," for "the consumer is never wrong." If customers insisted on being "nonrational," indeed "paranoid," how could marketers fail to respond? [10]

Such rationalizations accurately accorded consumers more power and marketers considerably less than did the "huckster" model of food company behavior. The consensus about what constituted good nutritional sense was shifting, and marketers knew they would have to respond. Yet the "consumer sovereignty" defense was also a bit *too* self-effacing, for marketers were not simply passive pawns of the popular will. Neither hucksters nor populists, food marketers responded to some people's needs more than to others, and in doing so, they developed only those products that were also convenient to the food industry.

191

UPSCALE/DOWNSCALE

In evaluating what "the people" actually wanted in food, market research was clear throughout the 1970s and 1980s: At best only a large minority were actively engaged in pursuing healthier foods. True, substantial majorities—often as much as 90 percent of a

sample—regularly testified to being "very concerned" or "concerned" about food quality; it would have taken an unusually irresponsible (or honest) shopper to profess otherwise. Yet, when it
came to actually buying products with some alleged health benefit
—however superficial or minor—estimates rarely ran above 40 percent, frequently less. If, in 1980, 7 percent of all supermarket
items were in some way labeled "natural," 93 percent were not.
If, that same year, 31 percent reported buying products labeled
natural, then 69 percent did not.[11]

Why would mass marketers bother with such a troublesome
area when, at any time, the majority of consumers seemed content
to purchase the regular, i.e., unhealthy, goods? The explanation
for this had to do with the new exploitation of "demographics"—
a marriage of technological convenience and business imperative.
Computer-aided survey techniques made it easier to identify small
"taste cultures" at precisely the moment when changing economic
conditions made such discrimination highly attractive.[12]

Until it began to fragment in the 1970s, the broad "middle
market" had been the target of most mass marketers. After the
Second World War, aided by unionization and American industrial
superiority, blue-collar workers began to move en masse into the
lower middle class. As Barbara Ehrenreich suggests, the conform-
ist, male-dominated culture of that time assumed that every male
"breadwinner" deserved a "family wage" sufficient to support a
wife and several children at home in a suburban cottage made
accessible by exceptionally cheap energy, transportation, credit,
and real estate. Although many Americans—particularly minorities
—remained excluded from the dream, business and political leaders generally invoked the "family wage" model as the route to
capitalist utopia. During the expansionist years of the 1950s and
1960s, a middle-class life-style of the sort idealized in the TV
sitcoms of the period seemed within the reach of most Americans.
Making up for the deprivations of the 1930s and 1940s, American
consumers kept marketers busy as they purchased the basic accoutrements of that life-style: a home and furnishings, a family car,
television, kitchen appliances, the latest convenience foods, an
occasional dinner at a family restaurant, a summer vacation.[13]

As the economy slowed down and inflation heated up in the
1970s, however, it increasingly took two jobs to achieve the middle-class life-style once supported by one wage earner. Those with
two jobs in the professional-managerial sector did well, although,

192

as we will see, they complained about the strains of such arrangements. But many middle-class blue-collar Americans lost ground as the economy seemed to give up on high-paying unionized manufacturing. The increase in service jobs did not make up for the loss in factory wages. American class structure began to skew toward the ends; as the upper 40 percent prospered, the lowest 20 percent worsened, and the other 40 percent stagnated or declined. Economist Barry Bluestone dates the decline of the blue-collar middle class from about 1977–78—about the same time that marketing journals and texts were predicting "a widening gap between the haves and have nots." By the early 1980s, Ehrenreich observes, no one invoked the old "family wage"–middle-class ideal anymore. It did not seem to matter whether every family had enough income for a moderate level of consumption; it mattered only that some "upscale" households earned enough money "to consume at a level of gluttony. Not, perhaps, a color television in every home, but *some* homes with wall-sized television screens, video games, home computers, and central air-conditioning." By 1986, according to Ehrenreich, America had become a "two-tier society."

> *The middle is disappearing from the retail industry . . .*
> *Korvettes is gone, Gimbels is closing. Sears, Roebuck &*
> *Company and J. C. Penney are anxiously trying to re-*
> *position themselves as more "upscale" to survive in an*
> *ever more deeply segmented market. The stores and chains*
> *that are prospering are the ones that have learned to*
> *specialize in one extreme of wealth or the other: Bloom-*
> *ingdale's and Neiman-Marcus for the affluent. K-Mart*
> *and Woolco for those constrained by poverty or thrift.*
> *Whether one looks at food, clothing, or furnishings, two*
> *cultures are emerging: natural fiber vs. synthetic blends,*
> *hand-crafted wood cabinets vs. mass-produced maple,*
> *David's Cookies vs. Mr. Donut.*[14]

193

This view was not confined to radical analysts like Bluestone and Ehrenreich. In 1983 the president of Wienerschnitzel International admitted that his hot dog chain's fidelity to the blue-collar, "budget-conscious" market was definitely out of step with trends in fast food and retailing in general. There was "one hell of a market out there" that preferred hot dogs to salad bars, but no one wanted to serve them anymore. "The problem is that everyone wants to be like Bergdorf Goodman and no one wants to be like K-Mart." The relative attractiveness of one class over the other was symbolized that same year by the decision of some vending machine suppliers to seek out white-collar workplaces where they might stock "so-called nutritious foods." Blue-collar workers wanted the same old snack foods—high in salt, fat, and calories—but the vendors saw the need to follow the shift "from a smoke-stack economy to a service economy." [15]

One job of market research is to serve as an early-warning system for emerging tendencies, shifting perceptions, possible trends. In the mid-1970s some demographic surveys were already detecting the fragmentation of the middle market into upscale/ "healthy" and downscale/"regular" components. For example, studies in 1973 and 1975 found that younger, college-educated shoppers were much more likely to understand Recommended Daily Allowances and read labels than were those of low "socioeconomic status." Also in 1975, those most worried about additives tended to be higher educated, with middle to upper-middle income, aged between twenty-five and forty. Appropriately, higher income households were doing a lot more home canning and preserving in 1976 than in 1964, while the poor were doing a lot less —food inflation notwithstanding. In other words, upscale concern about nutrition, not price, was the main reason for the shortage of home canning supplies in the mid-seventies. Capsulizing these findings, a 1975 study concluded that the wealthiest quartile of households were most likely to buy foods "highly correlated with nutrition concern." [16]

The statistics remained remarkably constant through the late 1970s and 1980s. Thus, in 1986, contrary to the Yuppie stereotype, 60 percent of baby boomers (born between 1946 and 1964) had no regular exercise program; of the general adult population, only 20 to 25 percent exercised as much as twice a week—hardly enough for even minimal fitness. A Rodale survey found that 30 percent of adults were "moderately committed" to "self-care" life-styles— mainly better nutrition and exercise; 70 percent were not. Such indifference was not necessarily related to ignorance of health issues. Of those polled in a 1980 USDA study, only a third said they would stop using a food product even if scientists could clearly

194

prove that an essential ingredient caused cancer or heart disease. Despite the "Dietary Guidelines' " well-publicized injunction to eat more fiber, the vast majority of Americans did not eat whole wheat bread, fresh fruit, or broccoli. The all-around favorite vegetable remained the tomato, with iceberg lettuce the most popular (and least nutritious) leafy green.[17]

At restaurants only 40 percent of adult customers reported making some concession to the changing nutritional consensus; i.e., 60 percent did not. The cholesterol news notwithstanding, steak and prime rib were still the most popular restaurant dinner entrees, with the burger the takeout favorite. While red meat consumption declined 6 percent between 1975 and 1985, the total was still higher than in 1965, thanks largely to the continued popularity of fast food. While 40 million adults were said to be more "careful" about how much they ate in 1985, presumably the other 100 million adults were not. That the "less careful" were also less affluent was confirmed by a Los Angeles county study showing poor males to be more likely to die of heart disease. Similarly DuPont found that, over a twenty-six-year period ending in 1983, the incidence of heart disease declined 37.6 percent among its salaried employees, 18.2 percent among hourly workers. Both groups had the same health insurance benefits, but the blue-collar worker tended to smoke more, exercise less, and "eat more junk foods than his more affluent contemporaries."[18]

In the early 1980s, new "psychographic" studies further focused the profit center. Developed by SRI International, the VALS typology—"Values and Life Styles"—supposedly transcended dreary class-dominated demographics and classified people by character traits. Even so, the segments were clearly stratified by income, with the lower 56 percent—which comprised "survivors" (4 percent), "sustainers" (7 percent), "belongers" (35 percent), and "emulators" (10 percent)—less health-conscious than the upper "achievers" (22 percent), "I-am-me's" (5 percent), "experientials" (7 percent), "societally conscious" (8 percent), and "integrateds" (2 percent). Such analysis was of course quite flattering to the upper 40 percent, and especially to the latter four "inner-directed" groups. Only the affluent, it seemed, possessed personalities. These were also the people who tended to buy exercise equipment, like classical music, have cable TV, try exotic ethnic dishes, count calories, buy natural foods, and eat broccoli and zucchini. As psychology or sociology, VALS was gross carica-

195

ture, but it did offer marketers an alternate vocabulary with which to rationalize their pursuit of the upper half, or more precisely, 40 percent.[19]

Although such data were clearly class biased, marketers did not necessarily have to shed their populist rhetoric of serving "the people." Since news reports often equated the upscale segment with all of "America," food executives who scanned the mass media for health trends could easily forget the Other America altogether. *Time* headlined "America Shapes Up," when in fact most Americans did not; reporter Reed claimed that label reading was "not the passion of a literary or political elite," when in fact it still was (and is). A 1984 *Newsweek* article, "America's Nutrition Revolution," announced "a sweeping transformation of old patterns that has penetrated every corner of the United States"—when in fact market research was revealing a far more circumscribed change. Herbert Gans found that, in announcing national trends, newsweeklies often reported phenomena that journalists saw in their own families, neighborhoods, and workplaces. A reporter seeking data on the "youth culture" might interview his children's friends. Similarly, perhaps in announcing a "national obsession" with dietary health, journalists were reporting on what was emerging in their own upper-middle-class professional subculture.[20]

Although the business press tended to be more precise in pinpointing the health-conscious upper 40 percent, their headlines too tended to blur class lines. For example, a Gallup restaurant poll found 60 percent *not* to have changed their menu choices for health reasons, yet the trade paper headline went: "Diners are more nutritionally aware." Two years later the identical 40–60 split was reported under the headline: "Nutrition Plays Strong Role in Dining Decisions." Often the favored minority did not even total 40 percent. Although only 13 percent of adults were reported to be watching sodium intake, 8 percent cholesterol, and 18 percent calories, the accompanying headline went: "Health Hot." Observing similar statistics, a restaurant journal headlined: "Patrons Seek Healthier Foods."[21]

196

Leaving aside the headlines' blindness, was the market research itself right? Did that many people really remain indifferent to food reform, even to the very moderate changes recommended by the "Dietary Guidelines"?

There are good reasons to doubt some of those surveys. People might say one thing and do quite another, or do contradictory things over the course of a day, year, or decade. Most people may in fact have worried about health but were confused about what to do about it, hence the gap between the large percentages express- ing "concern" about food quality and the much smaller ratios ac- tually doing something about it in the grocery store, restaurant, or kitchen. Moreover, when people indicated to market researchers that they were indifferent to health-oriented products, it did not necessarily mean that they were resistant to health in general. Perhaps they did not like the researcher's questions, style, or the products available at that time. Consumers who shunned so-called natural cereals may have had reasonable doubts about the truthful- ness of the "natural" claim. Or maybe they were simply unable to afford the premium prices such products commonly demanded.

Then again, there were strong reasons for not caring. First, some people enjoyed appearing indifferent to personal danger— particularly males aged eighteen to twenty-four, with less than average education. Such men were prime military recruiting ma- terial and also the most ardent consumers of fast-food hamburgers —the bargain-basement restaurant segment most skeptical of di- etary reform. But "hardguts" bravado could also cut across class and gender. Some middle-class people did not want to appear too middle class, i.e., too worried about safety, security, health. In- deed, before the counterculture went healthy in the late 1960s, bohemians often dismissed health as boring or "square." Similarly, in the 1980s some "punk Reaganites" projected a callous indiffer- ence to the natural, which they associated with the older, Vietnam generation. "I want food with artificial additives," one new wave teen told an *Advertising Age* columnist; "that kind of food tastes good." It should be emphasized, however, that such rebels were less affluent than the health-conscious "Woodstock generation." [22]

Less consciously oppositional—and perhaps more pervasive —was the feeling that what was "good for you" could not "taste good." According to nutritional anthropologist Norge Jerome, many people distinguish "food" from "nutrition." "Food" is what "tastes good," while "nutrition" is what's "good for you." You get "food" in supermarkets and restaurants, "nutrients" in drugstores, usually in vitamin pills. You "eat" food throughout the day, while you "take" nutrients once a day to compensate for dietary sins. [23] So ingrained was this distinction that many old-school food execu- tives continued to believe that "It's good for you" was just about the worst thing that could be said about a product. The same

197

attitude guided auto manufacturers insisting that "safety does not sell"—and if they still had been selling to the earlier unsegmented mass market, they might have been right.

The media's treatment of health issues may have compounded skepticism about "good for you." As the food scare stories kept appearing, it could easily seem that "everything" caused cancer—so why bother at all? If the food establishment had deliberately set out to confuse people, it could not have done a better job. Although such confusion was voiced throughout the population, those least familiar with the style and inconclusiveness of scientific debate may have been more likely to adopt a nihilistic attitude toward safety issues.

Longer-run gender, ethnic, and class patterns may also have played a role. On the whole, men seemed less interested in health reform, perhaps because diet-related professions—especially nutritional science—had been feminized in the late nineteenth century, thereby relegating them to marginal status in a patriarchal culture. Moreover, in many working-class and ethnic subcultures women subordinated their own nutritional concerns to the less healthy preferences of husband and children; the act of serving a rich food, however "unhealthy," was a form of gift giving.[24] Pierre Bourdieu suggests in *Distinction* that the lower classes are less likely to defer immediate satisfactions for health's sake based on a pessimistic appraisal of the future. "The propensity to subordinate present desires to future desires depends on the extent to which this sacrifice is 'reasonable,' that is, on the likelihood, in any case, of obtaining future satisfactions superior to those sacrificed." Thus at restaurants, while white-collar consumers ordered ascetic salads, blue-collar customers seeking immediate gratification filled up with foods that, however unhealthy, tasted good. Overindulging in the present was also a way of celebrating escape from past scarcity. While the middle-class countercuisine venerated ethnic and folk foods that fit within the wider paradigm of "living lightly"—voluntary poverty—people with poor backgrounds were less willing 198 to give up the culinary symbols of affluence: sugar (long an emblem of "the sweet life," according to Sidney Mintz), fats (as in "fat cat" and "fat of the land"—Genesis, 45:18), highly refined white flour, and meat, especially well-marbled "prime beef." While affluent people could afford more of these emblems, they took them more for granted and were perhaps more secure in cutting back voluntarily.[25]

Region too was a variable. Surveys consistently reported that people on the coasts and in larger metropolitan areas were somewhat more health-conscious than those in the middle and southern states, smaller cities, and rural areas. Compared to other regions, southerners were poorer and less educated, knew the least about nutrition, and, conversely, were the most avid consumers of fast food—a tendency also found in rural areas everywhere. The meat culture was most firmly embedded in areas economically reliant on growing feedstuffs and raising livestock—the rural Midwest and transmountain West. For marketers hunting new trends, however, people in the less health-conscious regions counted less. It was commonly assumed that trends began on the coasts and in big cities, and that those living in areas of apparent cultural lag would eventually catch up. So too it seemed likely that others in the unhealthy majority would sooner or later come around to the views of the upper-income "opinion leaders." [26]

A good ethnographer might easily argue that such elitist assumptions failed to do justice to the complexity and richness of grass roots life. Yet, to mass marketers assessing the implications of the changing nutritional consensus, the demographic pattern was probably clear enough: those people not interested in health-related products were less interesting to business. To be sure, as Michael Schudson shows, market research often generates answers that marketers already want to hear. [27] In this case the research may have reinforced what, at a time of economic stagnation, the food industry was already predisposed to accept: serving regular processed foods to the traditional "mass" markets might no longer suffice to insure growth.

199

9
STRADDLING
THE
CONTRADICTIONS

T he demographics of health consciousness were established
by the mid-seventies, but it took the rest of the decade to
define and categorize the extent and nature of that concern.
It was not enough to know that the affluent were more likely to
buy health-related products. Marketers also needed to know more
precisely what these affluent people were worried about.

Always a business fact of life, uncertainty seemed especially
prevalent in the 1970s. The scientific debate over food safety was
leading nowhere except to greater doubt. Would the experts, bureaucrats, and politicians ever agree? Would exasperated voters
push for more government intervention or less? Would confused
consumers retreat into a shell of nihilistic indifference toward
chemicals, or would they become radicalized into organic "freaks"?
How concerned were people about these chemicals anyway? Could
"good for you" ever supplant "tastes good" as the principal determinant of food choice? Was this all just a passing "fad," as the
diehards insisted, or was it a "trend," a deep-seated and lasting
change? Given the high development and promotional costs asso-

ciated with any new product, mass marketers hesitated to gear up for fads, however affluent the market; on the other hand, it did pay to respond to trends. Through most of the 1970s, the jury was still out.

By the end of the decade, with the "Dietary Guidelines," a rough consensus did emerge: although it was dangerous to be an extremist, concern about nutrition was not just a fad. While the moral panic had done a good job of associating "health food" with "nuts" and "flakes," respectable people were showing interest in "healthy foods." Crystallizing by 1980, this "health foods"– "healthy foods" distinction was crucial. As one retailer put it, "health foods" seemed to connote strange remedies, as in eating bananas to cure psoriasis. "Healthy foods," on the other hand, were neither bizarre nor inaccessible. Indeed, by counting all the foods that people considered nutritious, one 1982 analysis estimated that "healthy foods" constituted 36 percent ($44.5 billion) of supermarket sales in six major categories: breads, cereals, and grains; dairy; produce; meat, poultry, and fish; beverages; and snacks. The implication was that the existing food system could cater to nutritional concerns.[1]

TOO MUCH/
TOO LITTLE/TOO MODERN

The trick, however, was to pin down exactly what people wanted to achieve—or avoid. Here market surveys confirmed what journalists were concluding: negatives were more clear than positives. These negatives were threefold: some processed, mass-marketed foods had *too much* of something "bad for you," some had *too little* of something "good for you," and many were also *too modern*. Conversely, a healthy food in some way counteracted at least one, preferably more, of the negatives.[2]

The exact components of the *too much* complaint had evolved gradually over ten years or so, reflecting the dynamics of mass media exposure. Through most of the 1970s, as the chemical scare stories mounted, one by one, the primary negatives were additives and pesticides. Around 1978, however, when the saccharin and nitrate stories hit, the overload phenomenon seemed to take over. While concern about chemicals did not disappear in surveys, it no longer seemed to be growing. Instead, anxieties focused on other negatives—calories, fat, cholesterol, sodium—all targeted in the "Dietary Guidelines." Through the 1980s these were the primary negatives in most consumer surveys. And of these, calories remained preeminent. Marketers trying to understand "healthy foods" could thus feel reasonably confident about dietetic products.[3]

Some consumers also feared that highly processed foods had *too little* in the way of basic nutrients, which John and Karen Hess called the "subtractives." Yet this "too little" concern was vaguer than the "too much" worry, perhaps because the scare stories had done a much better job of eroding confidence than of offering solutions. One response was to fall back on the time-tested Recommended Daily Allowances and take dietary supplements. Another recourse was to return to earlier beliefs that fresh produce was inherently more nutritious than processed. By midcentury food processors had almost convinced many middle-class Americans that processed fruits and vegetables were "fresher than fresh." In the late 1970s, however, more traditional notions of freshness returned, especially among those not bothered by the fact that canned peas or frozen spinach could be significantly cheaper. Reinforcing the regression, the original McGovern "Dietary Goals" of 1977 specified fresh produce (and whole grains) as a source of dietary fiber—another subtractive in processed foods. Although later versions dropped the "fresh" to mollify the processors, canned and frozen fruits and vegetables never regained credibility or the growth levels of the fifties and sixties.[4]

By negatively comparing the American diet of 1976 with that of 1910, the original McGovern report also expressed the third element in negative nutrition: the dissatisfaction with a diet that seemed *too modern* in its reliance on timesaving, mass-marketed convenience foods. Part of this complaint overlapped with the other two: whether bought in a supermarket or at a chain restaurant, convenience food seemed especially saturated with contaminants and devoid of nutrients—in short, "junk food." But the concern also extended to a more generalized lament about modernity itself: a rushed, cluttered existence that left little time for the good things. As *Consumer Reports* observed in its 1980 critique, the demand for natural foods went way "beyond fear of specific chemicals." "There is a mistrust of technology," taste researcher Howard Moskowitz told *CR*. "There is a movement afoot to return to simplicity in all aspects of life." Another food industry spokesman added, " 'Natural' is a psychological thing of everyone wanting to get out of the industrial world." A predominant theme in both the counterculture and the mass media, nostalgia revealed itself in food marketing surveys as a growing demand for roots, nature, tradition, family warmth and togetherness, local color, and craftsmanship. While *CR* could warn consumers against "acting out such vague, undefined feelings," for food marketers these nostalgic impulses became a fact of life.[5]

THE DEMOCRATIZATION
OF PERSONHOOD

For mass marketers contemplating entry into healthy foods, identifying the negatives was a necessary first step; the second was less clear. Of the three desirable components, nostalgia was the most troublesome, for it seemed to conflict with distinctly modern trends that had dominated consumer culture since World War II. Even as many Americans appeared to look backward politically, they were breaking new ground in sex roles, sexuality, domestic arrangements, and the therapeutic sensibility. The split between political conservatism and cultural modernism was one of the more striking and problematic features of the late 1970s and early 1980s. Voting for candidates who embodied small-town pastoralism and promised a general return to the imagined simplicity of earlier times, they were also adopting some of the styles and practices of the deviant avant-garde. The adaptations ranged from the superficial to the significant. In appearance, the casually hip (but not hippy) appearance favored by fashion designers in the 1970s was gaining widespread acceptance, in part because it was genuinely less inhibiting, in part because it also seemed sexier. Sexual practices also seemed more casual and overt than ever before. People displayed their bodies more freely and fully, went to bed more frequently with strangers, and began to live with unrelated housemates in a state of unmarried domesticity previously unheard of in 203 "square" society. For reasons both economic and cultural, women stayed in school longer, married later, and worked outside the home more.

As more people learned the rhetoric of self-actualization, the cultural vocabulary turned increasingly relativistic, therapeutic, even mystical. Seeking wholeness and battling alienation, more people than ever insisted on the individual's right to "do your own thing." Although the quest for individualized fulfillment was ancient, an unprecedented crowd was now signing up for the trip, which historian Peter Clecak dubbed the "democratization of personhood": "the substantial extension of the many facilitating conditions for fulfillment of the self." Or, in Tom Wolfe's memorable 1976 caricature, the emerging motto of the "Me Decade" seemed to be "If I've only one life, let me live it as a ————!"[6] When it came to filling in those blanks, exponents of living theater and credit cards alike sensed that the possibilities were endless.

As these remarkable trends appeared in both mass media and market research, food marketers struggled to appraise the opportunities. Given the ever-intensifying sexual heat, the growing demand for weight control products seemed clear enough. Beyond dietetics, however, the implications were vague, often contradictory. The new household arrangements among young adults suggested important changes for mass marketers attuned to conventional, one-earner nuclear families. As General Foods's chairman put it, "For better or worse, 'Ozzie and Harriet' have been replaced by 'Three's Company.' "[7] As people delayed marriage and childbearing, they often had more disposable income to spend on indulging their own tastes. The "Three's Company" segment was more health-conscious and experimental than the "kids around the house" types: more salads and quiche, less canned spaghetti and hot dogs. At the same time, however, both swinging singles and two-career couples (later called "dinks"— double income, no kids) did not want to spend a lot of time in the kitchen and therefore needed more convenience foods. Yet, their dependence on such "junk" appeared to conflict with their health consciousness. Moreover, in line with Clecak's "democratization of personhood," they would not want their takeout or frozen pizza to be too standardized, too "mass."

Thus was posed a major challenge to conglomerates reliant on highly rationalized production and distribution. After having fueled the fast-food boom as teenagers in the 1960s, middle-class baby boomers loomed through the 1970s and 1980s as the food industry's largest and most puzzling adult segment—with disturbing and persistent countercultural impulses. As early as 1971 Marriott Corporation president G. M. Hostage predicted that catering to the surging, free-wheeling "Aquarius Generation," with its antibusiness, antistandardization values, would require chains to adopt a "nonchain" look. The "Hungry Generation" was *Nation's Restaurant News*'s 1971 label, with "hungry" standing for needs both physical and spiritual. "You know they're demanding choice and participation. Informal. Looser. Brutally honest. Impatient with formalism and tradition. Derisive of *your* standards. Refusing to be regimented. Rejecting those that would order them about. Distrustful of the big corporation and the industrial machine. Flaunting their own options, demanding their own thing, refusing to respond to your thing." Serving this "last big market" would entail significant changes in the mass production mentality, *NRN* warned, since the "Woodstock Generation" seemed to value, above all, "openness, involvement," wildness, experimentation, a "do-your-own-thing philosophy." Translated into food service, this entailed open kitchens (to project "at least a *sense* of reality, of made-for-you-cuisine"), salad bars (to enhance "involvement"), finger foods (for "spontaneity"), and outrageous, ever-changing decor (to "un-chain the chain"). In 1974 a new word was added to *NRN*'s characterization of this irreverent theatricality: "funky," which in restaurant operations meant a collage of styles, flavors, props, and gestures.[8]

Even as the Woodstock cohort aged, prospered, and sobered, market researchers still detected tastes that disrupted food industry conventions. According to a 1976 follow-up, the "Hungry Generation" had now grown up to become "new values people"—attracted to "honesty," still distrustful of authority, decidedly eclectic, concerned about health and environment, generally single or married but childless, with strong "interests outside of home and hearth." Similarly, that same year, an American Can Company survey found that young single adults and childless two-career couples were "dietary individualists" who rejected the standard three-meal pattern and viewed eating as "secondary to self-realization." As these better educated, more affluent young adults had children, according to another 1976 study (for General Mills), they tended to become "new breed parents," who were far more permissive, "self-oriented" than the "traditionalist" majority. Committed to "self-assertion," they were unlikely to indoctrinate children with conventional feeding habits. At home, "new breed" family members frequently ate different foods and at different times; at restaurants, they ordered individually and unconventionally.[9]

In the early 1980s another term would be applied to such unorthodox, peripatetic eating patterns: "grazing"—a self-indul-

205

gent sampling of a variety of small dishes, rather than a steadfast commitment to just one or two menu items. According to *Advertising Age*, grazers prefered a "highly mobile, autonomously oriented kind of family environment," spent freely, but were totally unpredictable, with "very little brand loyalty and very little retailer loyalty." [10]

Such pickiness and orneriness exasperated many marketers, who did not know how to live with or without the boomers. It was far more difficult to serve these "dilettantish," "fickle" consumers than the older, more straightforward "traditionalists." According to one marketing professor, the "traditional consumer" had been raised in the Depression and was thus "more concerned about getting than spending, less worldly yet more optimistic, more self-supporting but naive and acquiescent." In other words, a fine prospect for the Sears–mass market approach. The baby boomers, however, were "hedonistic, free spending, demanding, and slightly spoiled." Restaurant consultant Joe Baum despaired of satisfying such "highly individualized tastes." In 1971 Baum had urged a "greening of the restaurant industry"—more honesty, "community," and "delight in cooking"; by 1984, however, the baby boomers seemed permanently "skeptical of any promises made by large concerns." "There's a whole generation of people out there who just don't trust us," Baum observed. Catering to nutritionally aware young adults was tricky, one Long John Silver's executive agreed, because they were "cynical, savvy, frustrated, and bored." [11]

YUPPIES

The bored-cynical-spoiled image was most intense in the portrait of "yuppies"—young urban professionals—emerging in the mid-eighties. For about two years, 1984–86, yuppie bashing seemed everyone's favorite game, both in the mass media and the business press, although for very different reasons. In the mass media, conservatives like George Will saw superaffluent yuppies as confirmation of what they'd attacked all along: the inherently elitist, antipopulist selfishness of 1960s youth. Embarrassed liberal-left commentators either chastised their peers for selling out or argued that true yuppies were actually somewhat younger than the Vietnam generation and more representative of reactionary

206

Reagan youth. And centrist columnists saw the inevitable main-streaming of deviants. In America, it seemed, everyone sooner or later came home to an upper middle-class life-style: large, nicely decorated homes, high-performance cars, distinctive clothes, touristic tastes, a turn inevitable and, in the long run, for the best. Despite the differences, each slant reflected the media's overarching frame of the 1980s as strongly neoconservative. Also, each view projected onto younger professionals a long-standing ambivalence about consumer culture, materialism, and upward mobility. After all, what was new about acquisitiveness? [12]

The business press went yuppie hunting too, but along somewhat different lines. Many articles simply viewed the yuppie as the quintessential affluent customer, the culmination of the up-scale trend of the past ten years. Highly educated, mobile, discriminating, materialistic, with lots of disposable money but not a lot of time, the yuppie seemed the best customer for convenience goods and services with a classy appeal and price tag. But other portraits, especially in cartoons and humor columns, betrayed second thoughts about this privileged, indeed "spoiled," consumer. *Advertising Age*'s regular column of "yuppiegags" revealed considerable resentment at the yuppie's stereotyped interest in high technology, fitness, and unusual foods. In one *AA* contest, readers were asked to submit their ideas about the next yuppie food, whose parameters were defined as: "innumerable snacks made with tofu, Perrier, sushi, or all three together, overpriced and understated, suitable for microwaving." The winner—"Eggs 'n' toast: caviar and melba toast snack pack"—captured the contradictory impulses of those who wanted rich taste and low calories, convenience and class all at the same time. [13]

Would marketers ever be able to pin down such capricious tastes long enough to run off a few years' worth of products? For consumer capitalism, obsolescence had long been a challenge—both as a marketing opportunity and an engineering inconvenience—but clarifying yuppies' tastes could seem a nightmare. Moreover, the fact that most of *AA*'s contestants were themselves yuppies showed how hard it would be to keep up with them, for, predictably, they were already turning against themselves. As the *Village Voice* quipped in a "special report" on "The Feeding Habits of Yuppies," "The Yuppie is always someone else." To be a yuppie was to be a valuable player in the upscale-consumer sweepstakes, but part of the game was to avoid being spotted. It was one

207

thing to search for identity, but to be identified as a seeker was like being It in a game of tag. One study therefore warned advertisers that yuppies were congenitally skeptical of any pitch that categorized them as a group. True, they might all buy Cuisinarts and pasta makers, wear mink coats and jogging shoes, but as soon as you pointed out the pattern to them, "they would very much resent it and say, 'I'm much more of an independent thinker than that.' " No wonder then that they seemed "spoiled"—they did not have the maturity to face up to who they really were.[14]

Business ambivalence also stemmed from uncertainty about the precise size of this market. After the initial wave of hype, doubts about the group's significance began to creep in. Defined by SRI—inventor of VALS—as "25–39-year-olds earning more than $40,000 in professional or managerial positions," yuppies added up to 4 million (just 1.2 million actually living in cities), out of 78 million Americans born between 1946 and 1964. When, in a gushing cover article, *Newsweek* dubbed 1984 as "The Year of the Yuppie," these statistical realities tended to get buried amidst photographs of fit-and-trim junior executives and silly anecdotes about silly people struggling to "get by" on $200,000 a year. But these statistics had to give even the most VALS-conscious marketers pause. Perhaps the baby boom was not as good a target as it was cracked up to be. Even *Newsweek* gave a few lines to a demographer who pointed out that the median income for families in the 25-to-34 age bracket fell 14 percent in constant dollars between 1979 and 1983. According to *American Demographics*, some 62 percent of male boomers and 90 percent of female boomers earned less than $20,000 a year. According to the *Lempert Report*, a marketing newsletter, there were 33 million "yuffies"—young urban failures—earning under $10,000 a year. In a counterstereotype, yuffies—like Couch Potatoes—were said to get most of their exercise going to the kitchen during commercial breaks. One advertising executive cautioned that yuppies were far outnumbered by "poppies"—plateaued-out plain people who preferred pot roast to yogurt.[15]

208 Still, market analysts cautioned against going to the opposite extreme of dismissing yuppies entirely. Although those making over $40,000 a year constituted only a market sliver, a much broader slice shared many of the concerns about health, quality of life, and personal identity. New labels emerged to cover these "would bes" and "psychographic yuppies"—people who thought like yuppies but lacked the cash flow. According to Market Facts,

a Chicago-based market research company, the true yuppies were just the tip of an iceberg composed of people who watched "Cheers," "St. Elsewhere," and "Hill Street Blues," and aspired to grind fresh coffee beans, drink imported beer or wine, own a personal computer, and use automatic teller machines. Furthermore, when a couple worked—the norm in baby boom marriages —they commonly had a higher-than-median household income. More complex segmentation analysis revealed that the older boomers—in their thirties—were significantly more affluent than those in their twenties, and also significantly more attuned to health, ecology, liberal causes, and New Age values. Moreover, there was also some evidence that those age 35 to 49 ("muppies") were proportionately more affluent and health-conscious than the famous yuppies.[16]

In short, the market was clearly smaller than the whole baby boom generation (almost one-third of the population), yet probably larger and older than the stereotyped core yuppies. Perhaps what made these consumers seem so hard to gauge—so fickle and spoiled—was that, like the hyperdiscriminating yuppies—they seemed to want it all. Apparently inheriting the countercultural love of contradictions, they seemed bent on overcoming opposites once deemed irreconcilable. They wanted food that was both healthy ("good for you") *and* fun ("tastes good"), both substantial ("not junk") *and* convenient ("easy to use," "saves time"). And finally, since most were not superrich, they wanted all of these apparently incompatible virtues at a mass-market price ("a deal"), yet without a mass-market image ("classy")!

Catering to negative nutrition, then, was no easy matter. "In surveying the consumer scene," *Fortune* observed in 1978, "food companies see mostly crosscurrents and disorder. Widespread calorie-watching somehow coexists with an increased willingness to try new, and rich, ethnic delights. The public expresses a heightened awareness of nutrition, and then marches in droves to the fast-food emporiums for a Big Mac or a Whopper. A gourmet-cooking craze supposedly rages, even as frozen food sales continue to leap ahead." Two years later, the picture was no more clear. "The same working mother who repairs to McDonald's three times a week may settle down on the weekend for a bout of gourmet cooking. Diet sodas with pizza, health food for lunch, and junk food for dinner—the trends are precisely as consistent as the eating habits of Americans."[17]

209

Facing such complex needs, marketers could at least flatter themselves on how adventurous their daily work actually was, for the contradictions could seem overwhelming, the risks great, and the successes small.

CORPORATE CONSERVATISM

Further complicating matters was this: if consumers seemed to want it all, so did food mass marketers. In meeting corporate goals, they too had to balance contradictions and find happy middles. Demographically, the ideal consumer was upscale, but not too elite: a market slice, but not a sliver. Marketers also needed to balance a healthy image with healthy profits. For middlemen, profit margins increased as foods moved up the food chain. Aggravating this need to add value was the supermarket shelf-space crisis; since grocers were not able to expand easily, processors had to get more price out of the same cubic volume of cereal box, frozen dinner, or cookie package. Fast-food restaurants faced a similar road-space crisis: as cheap suburban real estate became more scarce and as saturation loomed, the industry felt compelled to maximize revenues per unit of space. Yet this imperative to elaborate contradicted emerging health images. According to negative nutrition, the simpler and less processed, the closer to raw commodity, the less likely a food was to suffer from the problem of too much, too little, too modern. Clearly, then, the challenge for food marketers was to develop products that *seemed* to be far lower down the food chain than they actually were.

A cautious, short-run approach thus seemed necessary. While marketers were more sensitive to trends than engineers, they were still basically conservative. Heavily invested in established technology, strategies, and perspectives, marketers sought to appear forward looking without actually repudiating past and present practices. Rather than spend freely on research and development of 210 totally new products, it was safer to try time-tested strategies with lower costs and lower risks. Escalating in degrees of risk, these strategies ranged from simple institutional advertising to repositioning, acquisitions, line extensions, and, as a last resort, genuine breakouts.

Aiming to sell a company rather than a specific product, institutional advertising was the easiest way to respond to consumer concerns, partly because the major companies were already very adept at mass media self-promotion, and partly because such advertising did not really offend the orthodox true believers within the industry. Presented as "consumer education," such advertising was often pitched to convince the public that the status quo was indeed healthy: i.e., that canned peas were no less natural than fresh, that manufacturing frozen breakfast toaster pastries was no more processing than frying an egg, that it was possible to eat a balanced meal at a fast-food restaurant. Such propaganda persisted well into the Reagan administration, when it received official backing. For example, in 1984 the USDA sponsored a Food and Fitness Fair at which the American Meat Institute handed out brochures entitled "Facts About Sausage" and "Pork: The Most Misunderstood Health Food." Campbell Soup gave children a brochure suggesting this "School Lunch to Go": a thermos of Campbell's Chicken & Stars soup, a sandwich of bologna and processed cheese on Pepperidge Farm white bread, two Pepperidge Farm chocolate cookies, some grapes, a Vlasic dill pickle. (Both Pepperidge Farm and Vlasic were Campbell subsidiaries.) The sodium content totaled out at 3,304 mg—more than the absolute maximum adult daily consumption recommended by the National Academy of Sciences.[18]

While institutional advertising proclaimed the "concern" or "involvement" of the whole company, repositioning did the same for specific lines or brands. A sexy marketing buzzword of the period, repositioning was basically old-style sales promotion: rather than redesign a product to suit the needs of consumers or society, just redesign the consumer's perception of the product. This could be the only recourse with unchangeable commodities high in cholesterol, calories, or caffeine. Attacked for peddling *too much*, producers offered remedies for *too little*: milk had calcium, eggs had "complete protein," beef meant vitamins and "strength," potatoes had fiber, coffee and sugar boosted what weary consumers seemed never to have enough of—"energy."[19]

Another repositioning tactic was to gloss over questionable ingredients and emphasize what a product did not have. Thus, vegetable oil margarines and potato chips had "no cholesterol" (but often lots of equally harmful saturated fats); Super Golden Crisp had no artificial colors, flavors, or preservatives (just 100 percent natural sugar). Some harried producers also argued that their food wasn't as bad as people thought: sugar was "surprisingly

211

low in calories," pork was now "on a diet" and was therefore something you could "lean on," hot dogs had less sodium than pot pies, and butter had no more calories than margarine. All of these claims were relatively specific and had at least some truth. But some repositioning exploited the vaguest notions associated with health: e.g., beef was "real food," milk was "fitness you can drink," and the egg was just "incredibly edible." Although consumer groups challenged many claims—and even *Advertising Age* complained—the Reagan era FDA and FTC rarely policed deceptive ads.[20]

Particularly controversial was Campbell's "Soup Is Good Food" campaign in the early 1980s. Although the canned soups contained up to 1,600 milligrams of sodium per ten-ounce serving, the new pitch claimed that soup was "health insurance." The repositioning was part of president-CEO R. Gordon McGovern's larger strategy to transform Campbell from the ultrasquare sponsor of the Campbell Kids and "Lassie" into the hip "well-being company." Crediting McGovern with turning "a stodgy, production-oriented canning operation into one of the most aggressive, market-driven companies in the food industry," *Advertising Age* dubbed him "Adman of the Year" in 1982. The soup ads stretched the limits of even the Reagan era, however, in claiming, "calorie-for-calorie," more vitamin C than carrots (which don't have that much) and more protein than beef ribs (but you'd have to down quite a few cans). Although the FTC failed to act, the advertising industry's own internal watchdog induced Campbell to drop this "nutrient density" claim. Pressed by New York State's attorney general, the company also ceased its "health insurance" pitch. But the "Soup Is Good Food" theme remained. A 1986 ad depicted a seemingly endless supermarket case of the famous red and white cans with the simple title "Fitness Center." And it apparently worked, for sales increased yearly, and Campbell continued to command almost two-thirds of the soup market.[21]

Campbell did not thrive by repositioning alone. The company was also adept at acquisition, a growth strategy that was somewhat more risky, but still quite cautious. Rather than invest heavily in the sort of internal research and development that would have made their own engineers happy, food companies were increasingly prone to let other companies absorb the risks. *Business Week* estimated that only about 12.5 percent of new products reaching the test market stage eventually proved successful. Since, as one investment analyst put it, new-product ventures were "like drilling for oil," it seemed prudent to wait for the wildcatters to tap the gushers. The mid-1970s were years of great experimentation by independents, as hip entrepreneurs like those of the Bay Area Briarpatch struggled to survive in the cracks of the establishment. Although at the time these independents hoped to outlast the supposedly doomed corporate monoliths, in retrospect it seems that some were actually fulfilling the "boutique" or farm-team function of testing new concepts for the mass marketers. By the end of the decade, the majors were ready to plug the most proved innovations into their own strengths in mass production and distribution. Celestial Seasonings's sale to Kraft or General Mills's purchase of Good Earth (a "healthy foods" restaurant chain) were examples of product acquisition—an outright takeover of another brand. Examples of idea acquisition—copying proven concepts— included Kraft's "Makin' Cajun" dry dinner mixes and General Mills's Yoplait yogurt and Nature Valley granola.[22]

Like Kraft and General Mills, Campbell played both acquisition games. The company had a long history of product takeovers, having bought Franco-American in 1915, C. A. Swanson in 1955, Pepperidge Farm in 1961, and Godiva Chocolates in 1966. To exploit the ethnic boom it acquired Vlasic Foods in 1978. In the 1980s, for health-related growth it added Mrs. Paul's frozen seafood and Juice-Bowl Products, a citrus juice marketer. Each of these served as a useful base for the other sort of acquisition: copying and mass marketing those ideas proved most successful by risk-taking independents. Although Campbell was hailed as one of the 1980s' most innovative processors, virtually all of its new products were first developed and tested elsewhere: shiitake mushrooms, seafood pasta salads, croissant sandwiches, sugar-free fruit juices, Mexican salsa, and assorted frozen "gourmet," regional, and ethnic dishes.

Many newly copied products were introduced as line extensions—another risk-reducing tactic. Although they had already tested well in the farm-team phase of product development, there was still no guarantee that they would succeed in the big leagues. So new rollouts frequently made their debut as extensions of existing, veteran lines. The hope was that the veteran's proved success would rub off on the rookie. Perhaps to hedge on the $50 million start-up costs, one of Le Menu's earliest entrées was a sliced turkey breast dinner—not all that different from Swanson's staple—

213

except for the marginally more sophisticated mushroom gravy, long grain and wild rice, and "garden vegetable medley." Crossing that transitional bridge, Le Menu grossed over $200 million in 1984 with slightly more adventurous bistro-French parodies. Similarly, Campbell's lower-sodium Creamy Natural soups—cream of broccoli, asparagus, and cauliflower—appeared on the shelves next to the regular cans, distinguished mainly by a gold label and higher price. Campbell's new shiitake mushroom rollout appeared in 1986 as a spore of the six-year-old "Farm Fresh" button mushroom line. Campbell's Italian extensions suggested a colonial metaphor. It took Prego several years to establish itself as a self-sustaining colony of that aging mother country, Franco-American; then Prego itself was used as a base from which to launch an exploratory party into the freezer case: a collection of eight frozen Italian entrées, including fettuccine Alfredo and chicken piccata with rice.[23]

Of course, some imperial ventures failed. To switch metaphors, the parent stock's genes did not always insure the health of the scions and root grafts. Take the example of Pepperidge Farm's numerous line extensions. What Franco-American and Prego were to Campbell's "ethnic" nostalgia, Pepperidge Farm was to its native-born variety. Standing, in the broadest way, for old-fashioned, New England rural Americana, Pepperidge Farm did very well as the root stock for assorted homey, low-chemical "hearth breads" and fussy-but-square premium cookies. But when Pepperidge Farm reached too far beyond its WASP-dowdy image, it stumbled. Star War Cookies were just too young and faddish for a company associated with doilies, crockery, and other eternal verities. Its apple juice line fit the red barn aura but clashed with the grandma associations. (Perhaps grandmas don't drink much filtered apple juice.) Deli's—frozen puff pastries stuffed with meat or vegetables—were intended as a premium substitute for pot pies— targeted at the "Julia Child types who have neither the time nor desire to do all that cooking from scratch." But the name was a little too metropolitan, too unpastoral, although the vegetable-filled Deli's were pitched at the health-conscious. Worse, according to one Campbell marketing executive, they just "didn't taste good."[24]

Completing the spectrum of growth strategies, Campbell ventured into a few areas that, while not conceptually new, did seem uncharacteristically risky for a major processor. In particular, to capitalize on the health-related interest in salad, Campbell tested

a new Fresh Chef line of seafood, pasta, vegetable, and fr
—all prepacked for convenience (and higher price) in cl
tic trays. In an even more ambitious attempt to strad
healthy-but-tasty and quick-but-not-junk poles, Campbell also
rolled out a broad selection of cooked, refrigerated items under the
Today's Taste label. Prepared daily by local caterers, the "taste"
seemed regional Nouvelle American, with entrées like grilled
chicken with lemon and chicken with sunflower and pumpkin seed
sauce. This was a cuisine considerably less massified than Le
Menu, not to mention Swanson. But even here, risks were hedged,
partly by the narrowly focused test markets (Denver, Philadelphia), partly by the company's ability to count on the old reliables
(called "cash cows")—tomato soup, V-8, Pepperidge Farm bread
—to finance the risks. Both Fresh Chef and Today's Taste did
flop, but with so many irons in the fire, the company could afford
a few failures. Confident of his broad base, Campbell's McGovern
encouraged his executives to see themselves as entrepreneurs with
a "right to fail" as they improvised a corporate cuisine with "something for every palate." [25]

Campbell showed how, by diversifying their portfolio, large
corporations might consolidate control. It was a cautious sort of
diversification, however—not like back in the early 1970s, when
reports of food industry stagnation had scared processors into wild
acquisitions of firms making cosmetics, hardware, luggage, fashion, toys, and other nonfood products. A decade later, after numerous disappointments and disasters, a more chastened view held
that food corporations should stay in food. When processors expanded in the 1980s, they usually acquired other processors, not
doll manufacturers. The new conventional wisdom was "back to
basics"—"stick with what you know." Returning to food fundamentals, Kraft dumped Celestial Seasonings and Duracell. As the
food giants themselves became leveraged buyout targets in the late
1980s, they were valued primarily for their flagship brands—e.g.,
Nabisco for Ritz and Oreos, Kraft for Velveeta and Breyer's—
while less essential lines were auctioned off to pay the new debts. 215
Processors also thought twice about venturing into food service; as
Pillsbury struggled with Burger King, PepsiCo's success with Pizza
Hut, Taco Bell, and Kentucky Fried Chicken was considered
unique. (Likewise, the best restaurant companies—McDonald's,
Marriott—steered clear of processing.) Unloading its "theme
restaurants"—Annabelle's, H. T. McDoogals—Campbell stuck

mainly to supermarket processed foods and prospered by selling what it knew best—convenience. Virtually all of its new ventures were in some way attempts to reconcile that central benefit with consumer qualms about health, modernity, taste, and price.

As Campbell showed, the way to overcome these seemingly insurmountable contradictions was not to think in terms of a single product to cover all the needs, but rather to scatter a wide variety of processed foods, each catering to one particular need and function. Noting the "grazing" in supermarkets and at his own family dinner table, McGovern advised food marketers to accept the fact that people now ate a lot of different things, at different times, and with different—often conflicting—meanings. The appropriate corporate response, therefore, was to go grazing too. Thus, in soups alone, Campbell's McGovern practiced a peripatetic approach: "Ethnic, dried, refrigerated, frozen, microwave—you name it, we're going to try it."[26] There was no mass, no "mature market," just "niches." But there *was* an underlying theme, a method to the madness. Small *could* be beautiful. Marketers did *not* have to be confused by the apparent fragmentation and contradictions. So what if a consumer ate an Egg McMuffin with a granola bar for breakfast, a cup of yogurt with potato chips for lunch, pizza with diet soda for snack, and a Lean Cuisine with a Dove Bar for dinner? It was not such a puzzle after all. Even if all the individual components seemed hopelessly incongruous, they were linked together by the one common denominator that favored the food industry: convenience.

In this processed version of the organic paradigm, the whole was truly greater than its parts—as long as all the parts were quick and easy. Of course, the dietary model supporting this strategy was a severe reversal of holistic ideals. The countercuisine advised consumers how to get needed nutrients—both physical and spiritual—from a few simple, time-tested, inexpensive "whole foods." In the mainstream healthy foods marketplace that emerged in the early 1980s, however, shoppers were confronted with a wide array of costly products, each purporting to solve a particular negative. Such atomistic diversity fit the mainstream health paradigm, in which the body was less an organism than a mechanism whose component parts could be tinkered with individually: one-calorie soft drinks for the waistline, low-salt canned peas for the blood pressure, cholesterol-free margarine for the heart, fiber-fortified breads for the colon, ethnic frozen dinners for the soul, superpre-

216

mium ice cream for the id (or ego?), organic shampoos for the coiffure, weights for the upper body, running shoes for the lower body, a dash of high-potency vitamins to prime the engine in the morning, and a dose of herbal tea to slow it down at night. The body was thus like a corporate "portfolio matrix" requiring ceaseless analysis, rearranging, and micromanagement. Maintaining such a portfolio made personal health management an exhausting, if not almost impossible, task, but in business it made sense. Call it niche marketing, product segmentation, diversification, or just divide and conquer, in fragmentation there was strength—or at least endurance. Like the Briars, corporate survivalists could learn to live in the cracks of a confused and directionless society.

10 A HEALTHY FOODS PORTFOLIO

NUTRIFICATION

Hedging bets and juggling contradictions, the food industry did first what it did best: add value. As early as 1971, cereal manufacturers sprayed vitamins on flakes, bakers added fiber to breads, and grocers stocked dietary supplements. Alleviating worries about "too little," nutrification was convenient and undisruptive. Rather than changing basic production modes, manufacturers simply added back what they had taken out—and raised the price. By adding two cents worth of nutrients to Wheaties and renaming them Total, General Mills could charge thirty-eight cents more for a twelve-ounce box. When new micronutrients were discovered and RDAs were adjusted, taking another pill or fortified flake was easier than fighting old habits—even if costlier. In 1985 Americans bought $3 billion worth of vitamin and mineral supplements and over $4.5 billion worth of fortified cold cereals—including $650 million in the "adult bran/fiber" segment.[1]

Although a salad was probably a better source of nutrients than a pill, it would perhaps not be too reductionist to include under the nutrification umbrella at least part of the 12 percent increase in per capita consumption of fresh produce between 1975 and 1985. Indeed, for many Americans, eating a vegetable was like taking a pill: a chore performed for the sake of nutrition, not taste. Through the 1980s, the majority of Americans refused to count spinach, broccoli, and carrots as "real food." For the nonhealthy 60 percent the most popular leafy green vegetable remained iceberg lettuce, which, lacking nutrients or intrinsic taste—except crunch—served mainly as a vehicle for dressings rich in salt, fat, and calories. But members of the nutritionally concerned upper 40 percent did expand their vegetable repertoire. As demographic surveys showed, backyard vegetable gardeners, patrons of salad bars, fans of escarole, kale, and apple juice were all most likely to be those most familiar with their RDAs and "Dietary Guidelines." Almost 50 percent of higher income people polled in 1980 reported eating more fresh produce. The biggest gainer was vitamin and fiber-rich broccoli—up 214 percent between 1973–83, to 2.2 pounds per capita, though still far outweighed by lettuce, at 25 pounds per capita.[2]

Fortunately for food marketers, fresh produce's seeming solutions for "too little" were more visible than the liabilities of "too much": e.g., the high calories in many fruit products and salad dressings, the sulfites stabilizing salad bars, the many chemicals used in growing all those tomatoes, peppers, and exotic fruits imported from Third World countries with little pesticide supervision. Food engineers who were otherwise wary of healthy foods became boyishly enthusiastic when they pondered ways to keep tomatoes and strawberries "fresh" by hidden technologies such as irradiation and genetic engineering. The feudal labor relations involved in growing produce were also virtually invisible. At the very time when Campbell was niche marketing trendy vegetables in its bid to be the "well-being company," it was embroiled in a messy farm labor dispute that received little attention outside the progressive press.[3]

Like fortification, therefore, "fresh" produce offered the food industry a relatively congenial and profitable way to present a "healthy" front, gain upscale customers, and deflect attention from more troublesome concerns. Candied dried fruits, fruit-sweetened cereals, "10% real juice" sodas, and fruity wine coolers all seemed healthier, even though they were often full of additives and sugar. Restaurant chains introduced "self-involving" salad bars out front while hiding assembly-line practices out back. Supermarkets found

219

that by situating the produce counter at the entrance, they greatly enhanced their consumerist image and profits. *Advertising Age* estimated that although fresh produce averaged 7 to 8 percent of the average supermarket's total sales dollars, it might mean 25 to 30 percent of the store's gross profit. Affluent health-conscious shoppers were willing to pay more for good-looking produce—particularly of the branded variety being introduced by Campbell, Del Monte, Kraft, General Mills, Castle & Cooke, and Green Giant. For processors, the branded-produce field was an opportunity to make up for losses in canned varieties and to break into one of the last preserves of the raw commodity (along with the meat counter).

For grocers, prepackaged vegetables meant lower labor costs and much higher profit margins—as much as 60 percent more than generic produce. Moreover, since shoppers behaved impulsively at produce counters, it was possible to augment sales of packaged goods by placing them nearby. Refrigerated juices, fireplace logs, cookbooks, jams, gadgets, bird seed—all did better nestled near the potatoes and onions. Jarred salad dressings, condiments, and synthetic bacon bits sold synergistically with lettuce and tomatoes; Cool Whip complemented fresh strawberries; candied fruit bars seemed healthier when allied with plums than when placed above the pretzels. And the produce section was the logical neighborhood in which to house the high-margin, high-convenience salad line extensions of the mid-eighties: salad bars, precut and cleaned carrot and celery sticks, refrigerated pasta salads, and processed green salads, both plastic-wrapped and canned.[4]

NATURAL FOODS

While nutrification extended and elaborated existing health notions and industry practices, "natural foods" seemed a new category. Actually, the ever-compromising mass marketers split the difference between countercuisine purists, for whom nothing that was processed and plastic could be natural, and orthodox true believers, for whom everything that was processed and plastic was natural.

In the countercuisine, "natural" had three dimensions: content (more nutrients, no chemicals), time (older), and a state of mind (nonrational, romantic, improvisational). Of the three, the last component was the hardest to mainstream, for it defied standardization. To some extent, the crunchy texture and slightly irregular shapes of some "natural" cereals, breads, and snacks might convey a certain sense of resistance and vitality. Designers of "funky" theme restaurants targeted to the "hungry generation" sometimes attempted a spontaneous look by incongruously juxtaposing Victorian antiques, railway schedules, Hollywood posters, waiters in medieval costumes, pop art, and multiethnic menus. So too chains tried to "de-chain" by using obscure names: Bumbleberry, Rusty Scupper, Fuddrucker's, Flakey Jake's, T. J. Applebee's, J. J. Mugg's, Joshua Tree, Tramp's. But such adaptations could be self-defeating when mass produced, for the ultrasavvy consumer was quick to recognize a pattern. No sooner had some chains begun to replicate the "funky" theme than the *Real Paper*'s food critic was sniping at the "disco Howard Johnson" look of "corporate concept restaurants." Sensing the futility of playing this game, most mass marketers did not even try to rationalize the nonrational.[5]

Mainstreaming the time component of "natural" was easier, for it was relatively more finite; many Americans appeared to date the decline of western civilization from the arrival of the automobile, electric light bulb, and skyscraper. Conversely, a product seemed healthier, more natural, if it somehow suggested life before 1910—perhaps coincidentally, the baseline of the McGovern committee report.

Antimodernism hit the roadside especially hard, as fast-food chains faced accusations that junk foods were polluting the stomach and landscape. Although naturalizing the ultrastreamlined menu was difficult, antiquing the color scheme was relatively simple, since restaurateurs redecorated every few years anyway. From coast to coast franchised restaurants adopted a look that was part Victorian, part bungalow: light woods, shingles, hanging plants, reddish brown bricks, oak tables, mansard roofs, stained glass, earth tones everywhere. Although most of these touches had been pretested in hip/boutique restaurants, in the mass-produced version the plants, oak, and stained glass were likely to be synthetic.[6]

Earth tones dominated the packaging of supermarket natural foods too. In addition, processors used words with folksy connotations: "valley," "country," "farm," "grandma," "hearth," and, of course, "old-fashioned." Some companies already had a built-in head start in the nostalgia game. For example, in his famous 1964 *Handbook of Consumer Motivations*, Ernest Dichter noted how

221

Quaker Oats capitalized on historic associations between Quakers and "a time of sacrifice, virtue, and idealism." Moreover, oatmeal symbolized "the good old days" when people were not too "hurried" and "tense" to eat a leisurely family breakfast.[7] Thus, it was appropriate that Quaker was the first to introduce a "100% Natural" cold cereal (in 1973).

The actual content of mass-marketed natural foods could be as vague as the word itself. In the countercuisine, "natural" was both negative (no chemicals, little processing) and positive (more vitality). The negative side was tougher on processors. Sometimes, by altering production, manufacturers did cut questionable ingredients while maintaining a high value added—as, for example, when bakers substituted vinegar as a "natural" mold retardant. But few could eliminate *all* questionable ingredients, especially the salt and sweeteners added to compensate for the taste lost through processing. Thus Kraft's Cracker Barrel Natural Cheddar Cheese was low in certain additives but high in sodium.[8]

To suggest the positive side of "natural," marketers highlighted ingredients that conveyed nutrient-rich wholesomeness: honey, nut, sesame, coconut, carob, yogurt, stone ground wheat, and the like—the natural foods touchstones. In many cases, the image was repositioned while the basic nutrient content remained about the same. The sweetness in Honey Nut Cheerios—perhaps the most successful cereal line extension of the 1970s and 1980s—came from white sugar, not honey. Kellogg's old Sugar Smacks contained 43 percent grain, 57 percent refined sugars; rechristened as Honey Smacks, they had the same amount of grain, 50 percent sugar and corn syrup, plus 7 percent honey to keep it technically honest. When Kraft pitched Velveeta, the archetypal plastic food, as "a blend of natural cheeses," *Nutrition Action* concluded that "natural" had become "meaningless. It's one of those words like 'country' and 'farm' that food companies use when they want to give their products a healthful image."[9]

Although widely used, these tactics prevailed most dramatically in the breakfast cereal battles. Oligopolistic, yet fragmented into over a hundred different brands, the cereal industry was a good example of centralized decentralization, or niche marketing. The leader, Cheerios, barely sold 6 percent of the cold market. Competing for tiny shares in each subcategory, manufacturers feverishly concocted slightly different variations on the basic theme of grain, sweetener, and milk. Breakfast cereals thus typified the consumer-capitalist quest for invidious distinctions. Indeed, the morning cereal ritual introduced children into the whole convenience food environment, which encompassed not just the core processed food taste (sugar and salt) and habit (pour and eat), but also the high obsolescence consumer culture of toys and commercial kidvid. But breakfast was also a meal beset by basic contradictions. Anxious to get kids off to school efficiently (convenience), parents bribed children with something sweet (tastes good) for the sake of milk and vitamins (good for you). Yet increasingly, many parents felt guilty about serving "junk foods" to vulnerable children. Hence the challenge to develop guilt-reducing cereals that were still quick and tasty.

It took some time for manufacturers to learn how to do this. As the case of the "naturals"—or granolas—illustrated, there were perils in jumping too early into healthy foods or in attempting to accomplish too much in a single product. Hoping to overcome the bad publicity of the Choate hearings (1970), the majors quickly fortified existing brands and then, more ambitiously, introduced their own versions of granola. The original name for John Harvey Kellogg's famous flakes, granola had been reincarnated as a countercuisine staple—a portable, easily consumed all-in-one meal maximizing health, taste, and convenience. Every underground newspaper and cookbook had recipes. But co-ops and health food stores also stocked chemical-free, nutrient-rich Crunchy Granola, introduced in 1965 by Layton Gentry. Dubbed "Johnny Granola Seed" by *Time,* this fifty-year-old eccentric hoped to keep granola production small scale and decentralized. "I think if the big companies got their hands on it that it might become a bad word," Gentry told *Time* in 1972. But the first mainstreamed granolas hit the supermarkets in 1973—Quaker's 100% Natural, followed by Colgate-Palmolive's Alpen, Pet's Heartland, General Mills's Nature Valley, Kellogg's Country Morning. Boasting crunchy, wholesome-seeming nuts, grains, honey, and dried fruits, the preservative-free granolas were quite expensive—a fact emphasized in news reports of "healthy profits." [10]

223

After seizing an impressive 10 percent of the $1.3 billion ready-to-eat cereal market in 1974, the granolas dropped to a 5 percent share in 1975. In 1977 the supermarket trade journal *Chain Store Age* heralded the "return of sugar" while the naturals were "really going downhill." Although the trade press blamed high prices, the failure probably had more to do with the rather premature rollout of a radically different product at a time when healthy foods were not fully understood.[11]

Only by the end of the 1970s would the demand crystallize. First, it became clear that nutrition was mainly an adult concern. When children rejected granola's blatantly "healthy" taste and boring nostalgic aura, parents reverted to slipping in nutrients with a sugary bribe. Also, in the aftermath of the moral panic, many adults felt self-conscious about buying a "faddish" product. Moreover, if the granolas were not sweet enough for kids, they were too sweet for adults. With all the nuts, seeds, coconut, and honey, mass-marketed granolas had more calories and fewer vitamins than some fortified flakes. In the early 1980s, the cereal manufacturers learned to integrate a health pitch into conventional cereals like Nutri-Grain and, moreover, to segment the benefits: e.g., particular cereals offered a complete RDA of particular vitamins; others focused on fiber (subdivided into soluble fiber to lower serum cholesterol and insoluble fiber to prevent colon cancer); still others had less sugar (but more sodium) or less sodium (but more sugar or aspartame) or no preservatives (but more sugar and sodium); and so on.[12]

What started out as a totally new "natural" category was folded back into existing lines. But granola by no means disappeared. Reformulated into bars, granola was repositioned in a different marketing category: the "100% natural healthy *snack*." Apparently the dining context was all. Conservative at breakfast, people were more receptive when snacking. For manufacturers granola bars took up relatively little shelf space, had low ingredient costs relative to the final price, and were, as the trade press punned, "naturals" for line extensions. In 1986 over $450 million was spent on granola bars that came in a variety of tastes and forms (chewy or crunchy, nuggets, dipps, or clusters) and countless flavors (honey, chocolate, chocolate chip, yogurt, peanut butter, raisin, apple). And, inevitably, from its Nature Valley base, General Mills launched other "natural-healthy" snacks: e.g., fruit roll-ups, fruit drink sip-ups, and even a mix for "homemade" granola bars. Originally an all-purpose simple meal, granola wound up a textbook case of segmentation, proliferation, and elaboration.[13]

Natural foods also illustrated the convergence dynamic: while majors integrated "natural" features, independent sellers of natural foods adopted mainstream practices—especially the tendency to move up the food chain away from minimally processed com-

224

modities toward high-profit dietary supplements, cosmetics, snacks, and laborsaving packaged products. For one-stop convenience, some natural food chains relocated to malls and achieved supermarket size. Appraising this apparent respectability, *Nutrition Action* seemed more saddened than heartened. That natural foods sales totaled $3.3 billion in 1984 (over eighteen times the common estimate for 1970) was evidence of widened health consciousness. But much of this growth had come through the same sorts of half-truths associated with mainstream retailers. For example, "Joan's Natural Honey Bran Carob Bar" had no chemicals but as much saturated fat as a Milky Way or Three Musketeers. And the good products—like low-fat yogurt, whole wheat spaghetti, and unsweetened jam—could now be found in many regular supermarkets, often at lower prices. The contrasts were losing their sharpness. By mixing some worthwhile products with others that were at best only partially virtuous, marketers were completing on the shelves what orthodox defenders had begun in the moral panic: the destruction of the word "natural" as a meaningful distinction. While in their hearts most people still believed that only some things were natural while others were not, when it came to shopping it seemed that both everything and nothing was natural.[14]

In the mid-1980s, the "natural" category continued to refer vaguely to the absence of some chemicals, particularly preservatives. But fear of chemicals constituted a declining part of negative nutrition. For more tangible (and traditional) ingredient reduction, many healthy foods customers turned to low-calorie products.

LITE FOODS

Within the countercuisine, Gary Snyder's notion of "living lightly on the earth" capsulized the determination to live both hedonistically and ecologically, to be both effervescent and ascetic, bohemian and peasant. Living lightly meant keeping loose, open, young in spirit, yet also staying close to the earth, humble, classically conservative. To be "heavy" was to be weighed down not so much by pounds of flesh as by the burdensome attachments of middle-class culture and middle age.

Focusing primarily on the more tangible goal of reducing fat and fats, the mainstreamed "lite" had mostly to do with staying young in body size. In 1982 "lite and diet foods" constituted almost 10 percent of retail food sales, about $25 billion. But this was not quite the same old dreary dietetics of Metrecal and Melba Toast. Before the 1970s, sales of reduced-calorie products had been hindered by their association with self-denial—all "good for you," no "tastes good." In the 1970s, however, "diet" was repositioned as "lite," a hip buzzword straddling both sides: taste *and* health.[15]

This ability to overcome basic contradictions made it especially appealing in sectors beset by obvious tensions between healthy and tasty, healthy and quick: e.g., alcoholic beverages and soft drinks, TV dinners, fast food, snacks. Appropriately, two companies most worried by unhealthy images made the earliest gains with "lite" foods. Concerned about antismoking campaigns, Philip Morris (Marlboro) bought the slumping Miller Brewing Company in 1969 and turned beer sales around with its introduction of Miller Lite in 1974. As practiced in the funky inner-city saloons of Miller Lite's famous commercials, living lightly meant having it both ways: "Tastes Great, Less Filling," self-indulgence and self-discipline. Or, as one reporter put it, "Rabelaisian satisfaction and waistline retention as well." Nestlé, attacked as the world's leading promoter of costly, potentially dangerous processed foods, especially infant formulas, poured new resources into its U.S. operations, especially Stouffer's Lean Cuisine, which single-handedly transformed the downscale frozen TV dinner into a dynamic, "healthy" category. Grossing $120 million in its first year (1981), Lean Cuisine had by 1984 almost a third of the $1.4 billion "premium frozen dinner" market. Lite also brought new life to the snack industry, for it facilitated overeating. Just as "light" beer allowed heavy drinkers to guzzle a few more without guilt, buyers of sugar-free soft drinks, decaffeinated coffee, reduced-tar "light" cigarettes, and low-fat yogurt bars felt freer to consume more. Concerned about consumer criticism yet reluctant to sacrifice taste for health, fast-food executives paid close attention in the mid-1980s to the growing "semihealthy" chain, D'Lites, with its lower-calorie hamburgers and Miller-like slogan: "More of a Good Thing. And Less."[16]

One reason why lite products were able to confront so directly the tasty-healthy and quick-healthy contradictions was that lite's approach to healthy was so limited. Lite chips could be low in salt but high in fat, or low in fat but high in salt, but rarely low in everything. By not having to take all the other negatives into account—too few nutrients, too many chemicals, too modern—marketers were free to use all the modern means at their disposal to enhance the product's taste and convenience. Concerned mainly with holding down the calories and fat, D'Lites otherwise resembled a typical fast-food operation in menu and management; the founder was in fact a former Wendy's franchisee for whom McDonald's was the ultimate model of success: a burger-fry base, high-stakes franchising, and mass-production mentality. Since lite products did not have to worry about being natural, many were loaded with artificial flavorings, colors, stabilizers, and preservatives. Although there were serious questions about the safety of saccharin and aspartame, only one thing mattered—that they could substitute for sugar. As many as fifty-nine additives improved light beer's shelf life, head, and color. Virtually all frozen light dinners were loaded with monosodium glutamate, autolyzed yeast, disodium inosinate, and hydrolyzed plant proteins to "exaggerate flavors," along with mono- and diglycerides for "mouthfeel." The typical Lean Cuisine dinner had almost 1,200 mg sodium per serving. The list of ingredients in Lean Cuisine's Pork and Beef Canneloni with Mornay Sauce ran twelve lines of microscopic type; Fillet of Fish Divan had 240 calories and twenty lines of ingredients. In short, lite products let processors be processors.[17]

Although lite foods seemed to deliver a more defined and tangible benefit than "natural," they were even vaguer legally—another advantage to manufacturers. Since regulators did not consider "light" a nutritional claim, it did not have to be defined on the label. Averaging between 90 and 120 calories per can (vs. 150 for regular), light beers did not qualify as "low calorie," which the FDA defined as less than 40 calories per serving. In 1983, the CSPI asked the Bureau of Alcohol, Tobacco, and Firearms to allow no more than 100 calories in a 12-ounce light beer, but deregulatory zealots in the Office of Management and Budget prohibited BATF from hearing public comments. In January 1986, Rep. Jim Cooper (D-TN) introduced a bill requiring that light claims be spelled out on a nutritional label and that the actual reductions be significant —i.e., at least one-third fewer calories, half the fat, or three-quarters the sodium of the regular varieties. But even this mild reform got lost in committee. USDA did require that "lean" meat products be 90 percent fat-free, but lite remained in a regulatory twilight zone.[18]

Even with all the additives, many lite products conveniently

227

had lower production costs than regular lines. Light beer had more water. (Coors, one model for Miller Lite, was so watery that detractors called it Colorado Kool-Aid.) White wines—perceived as lighter than reds—used cheaper grapes. The saccharin in diet drinks was cheaper than sugar. The wood pulp used to lower calories in some breads was cheaper than whole grains, while other light breads were just sliced thinner. Similarly, Frito Lights were thinner than the regular chips, but had the same fat and calorie content per ounce. Lean Cuisine's Salisbury Steak dinner simply weighed less than the regular Stouffer's version. Indeed, serving smaller portions was the primary way to reduce calories both in the freezer case's Lean Cuisine and in the fancy restaurant's spa cuisine. Some reduced-sodium products did have higher ingredient costs, mainly because the processor had to use more vegetables, spices, even meat to make up for the loss in salted flavor. But balanced against these costs was another economic advantage of many lite products: they could be rolled out as relatively risk-free line extensions of "regular" models, as with Pepsi Lite (one calorie plus lemony tang), Diet Pepsi (one calorie, no tang), and Pepsi Free (regular calories, no caffeine).[19]

Although frequently cheaper to make, lite products could command equivalent or even premium prices. Restaurants charged the same for smaller spa cuisine portions. With half the calories and none of the costly cream and sugar of ice cream, soft-serve yogurt created a 300 percent profit for vendors. Popcorn—recommended by Weight Watchers as a healthy snack—cost under a nickel a quart to make but commanded a dollar or more in movie theaters and at franchised stands. Processors were especially enthusiastic about substituting textured vegetable protein analogs for meat; low-fat bacon look-alikes used a few cents' worth of soybeans but sold at Smithfield prices. Retailing at up to twenty-five cents more per six-pack, light beers were the main profit centers for breweries hit in the 1970s by high prices, strong competition, and heavy promotion costs. The CSPI estimated that soft-drink makers overcharged customers $300 million per year for sugar-free sodas. Supermarkets charged the same for club sodas and regular colas; Perrier, the ultimate light beverage, cost far more.[20]

According to demographic research, the typical lite customer could clearly afford the higher prices. And one way that some marketers clinched the case for spending more on less was by dressing the food in the "authentic" garb of ethnic/gourmet/regional cuisine.

228

EATING THE OTHER

While ethnographers might wince at the grouping of ethnic, gourmet, and regional foods under one heading, in practice they were hard to differentiate. Neither hip nor straight cuisines cared much for regional or national contexts. Whether in *Country Commune Cooking* or *Better Homes & Gardens*, recipes tended to blend assorted cuisines and ingredients according to whim and convenience. Just as Chez Panisse mixed obscure local materials (regional) with "country French" (gourmet) and Japanese (ethnic) techniques to produce California cuisine, so too did Safeway's freezer meld disparate styles; the distinctions could seem so marginal and fleeting that many grocers simply grouped all unusual foods in an all-purpose "Specialty," "Quality," or "Deli" category. "Gourmet" vs. "popular" differences were blurred too when a discovery was hailed as "honest" and "simple" fare even as it sold at premium prices. Uniting these diverse dishes was a common theme: a reaction against the modern. The dynamic was more therapeutic than ethnographic: a rather indirect exercise in self-definition. As in most tourism, by seeking the Other, one found the Self.

While the countercuisine interwove this therapeutic thread with survivalist and organic strands, mainstreamed ethnic/gourmet/regional foods were "healthy" in strictly personal ways. Reflecting perhaps their patent medicine heritage, Americans had long associated exotic herbs and foods with longevity, potency, and cures—as in Dr. Lin's Chinese Blood Pills, Osgood's Indian Cholagogue, and Hayne's Arabian Balsam. But the main contemporary benefit derived from negative comparisons with a beef-based diet. In line with concerns about "too much" and "too little," many exotic dishes did use less red meat, more vegetables and grains. According to the McGovern report, older cuisines based on whole grains and pastas were richer in fiber and complex carbohydrates while lower in calories and fat than the modern American beef-based diet. Cheese, chicken, and fish too seemed to be light, protein-rich substitutes for beef. Taco and pasta salads, Oriental stir-fries, Greek spinach pie, quiche, regional seafood specialties, broiled Mexican-style "pollo," grilled California-style chicken, even pizza —all were perceived as lower in contaminants than red meat. Sometimes the perception was wrong. For example, Pet's Old El

229

Paso beef burritos were significantly leaner than its cheese enchiladas; Budget Gourmet's seemingly harmless Linguini with Bay Shrimp and Clams Marinara derived 71 percent of their calories from fat, whereas Stouffer's Salisbury Steak was "only" half fat.[21]

Further addressing worries about "too much," advertisements for Dannon yogurt and Chun King guaranteed a "beautiful [i.e., thin] body." Stella D'Oro was positioned as a light, healthful alternative to Oreos and chocolate chips. Dishes at the Taco Viva chain were pitched as "easy on the waistline as well as on the wallet." Dr. Brown's Cel-Ray Tonic—a New York Jewish staple that went national in 1977—might seem good for the waistline, for it had celery; the same thinking legitimized frozen lasagna with spinach (Green Giant), zucchini (Lean Cuisine), and both spinach and zucchini (Le Menu). Pot pies wrapped in flaky filo seemed lighter than those encased in white flour dough. American sweet rolls seemed heavier than French croissants—as Sara Lee appreciated when its frozen filled croissants surpassed the dense pound cake in sales. When the theme restaurant chain, T. G. I. Friday's, decided to "lighten" its menu, it added an array of "more healthful foods like Oriental, Mexican, and northern Italian dishes with lighter sauces—everything from gourmet pizza, shrimp salad, croissant sandwiches and iced tea to red wine and fettuccine Alfredo." Clearly, such "lightening" was a matter of subtle shading, not black and white. Some nouvelle dishes *were* genuinely lighter, however, partly because creative spicing substituted for the old staples, butter and salt, and partly because servings were smaller —the same portion control principle behind Lean Cuisine and spa cuisine.[22]

Addressing concerns about "too little" taste, some nouvelle cuisine restaurants sought regional sources for savory baby vegetables, vine-ripened tomatoes, hedgehog mushrooms, free-range chicken, "wild" game, and chemical-free "designer beef." Dubbed "boutique farms" in restaurant trade papers, these organic growers survived in the cracks by supplying "quality" goods to elite customers. But even mass marketers sometimes used tastier ingredients in their upscale lines; gourmet soup had richer stock, less salt; gourmet jams had more fruit, less sugar. Frozen "Dinner Classics" had "actual cubed beef," one Armour executive boasted. "You're getting a good quality and value relationship." Like "gourmet," "classic" suggested purity and security—long the private perquisites of wealth and status. No wonder, perhaps, that sales of

230

gourmet frozen foods increased almost 20 percent annually (to about $1.4 billion in 1984) at the same time that public regulation of purity declined.[23]

Other "healthy" benefits addressed the "too modern" complaint: a touristic-nostalgic escape from encroaching McDonaldization. Whether Greek or Mexican, Cajun or epicure, the Other seemed to lead a more Authentic Life—graceful yet simple, spontaneous yet intentional, spiritual yet also close to the earth. But the archetype of otherness was spread over a spectrum, with some subtle variations in message and appeal. Characterized by costly ingredients and artful distinctions, gourmet foods offered a cool and exclusive refuge for those concerned about mass society's threat to individual "taste" and sensitivity. At the other end of the spectrum, with their messy finger foods, steamy one-pot suppers, and sweaty street fairs, ethnic foods were more warm and inclusive —communal antidotes to modern alienation.

"Regional foods" went both ways: elitist and populist. The elitist camp was fascinated by historically indigenous and currently endangered American fare—razor clams, ruffled grouse, buffalo steaks, smoked chubs, morel mushrooms, wild rice, black raspberries, and so on. The most enthusiastic publicizers of this costly, antiquarian fare were gourmet writers—James Villas, James Beard, Waverly Root—for whom authenticity mattered more than accessibility. Populists sought vernacular authenticity too, but of a more contemporary, funky variety. While elitists craved the perfect smoked wild turkey with fiddlehead ferns, populists pursued the perfect sub with fries. Celebrated by Calvin Trillin (*American Fried; Alice, Let's Eat*) and Jane and Michael Stern (*Roadfood; Good Food*), populist dishes included Louisiana oyster loaves and crawfish étouffée, Philadelphia cheese steaks, Cincinnati chili, Buffalo chicken wings, Kansas City ribs, authentic southern fried chicken, Pennsylvania scrapple, New York fries and bagels, and so on. Not always nutritionally healthy, such food offered edible resistance to the conglomerated future—which Trillin termed the One Big Kitchen. By downing a dripping brisket sandwich on plain white bread at one of Arthur Bryant's Formica tables, you beat the System, or at least the Marriott Corporation. As the Sterns put it in *Good Food*, an unassuming greasy spoon could have "character," and "you can't buy character from a restaurant design firm."[24]

While both types of regionalists disdained mass marketers, it was the populistic variety that ultimately got mass marketed. Elite

231

ingredients were just too delicate and scarce for large-scale distribution, while downscale funky "character" *could* be approximated by the One Big Kitchen. National processors, fast-food chains, restaurant suppliers, suburban mall developers, and downtown "marketplace" renovators spread all the Trillin/Stern icons—along with assorted ethnic/gourmet replicants—across the land. In an otherwise bland, highly rationalized and bureaucratic environment, such authentic foods suggested a smattering of spice, irregularity, and eccentricity, of real people and places, of old-fashioned honest labor and honest materials—in other words, an appearance of food lower down the food chain than it actually was.

Of course, to be widely distributed such foods had to be convenient to the mass marketers sitting rather high up the chain. The authentic foods best suited for mainstreaming were those that seemed "good for you" without straying very far from conventional notions of "tastes good." Dishes using strange spices, fermented or pickled delicacies, too much garlic, organ meats, or uncooked flesh rarely succeeded outside esoteric circles; for wider distribution the ingredients, flavors, and preparation techniques had to be comfortably familiar.

Thus, from the vast array of potential staples most authentic dishes drew on the familiar triad of beef, chicken, and fish fillet, with shrimp still the most popular shellfish. Outside Louisiana, Cajun popcorn meant batter-fried shrimp, not crawfish; so too food-service supplier Naturally Fresh offered an all-purpose "étouf-fée" sauce for shrimp substitutes. Despite the Third World's dependence on legumes and grains for protein, these remained largely on the side, and meat was usually added to pizza, tacos, chili, lasagna, curries, and stir-fries. Cheese, the long-time companion of ground beef, also figured largely. A popular taste combination resembled what Trillin called the "Kraft dinner": macaroni (or crispy crust), slightly overdone and encrusted melted cheese, and sometimes ground beef and tomato sauce. Into this category fell numerous Italian pasta variants, pastitsio, moussaka, taco and enchilada pies.[25]

232

Vegetable colors remained stereotyped, usually bright red or green. Sugar and salt still brightened commodities tired by extended shipping, processing, and storage. Additives also went nicely with authentic foods, since the traditionalist aura deflected concern about artificial ingredients. In line with a forty-year trend, food engineers saw good potential for tomato flavor enhancers, synthetic cheese, fabricated meats, and that promising all-purpose common denominator, textured vegetable protein—all of which were easily hidden in the shredded or stewlike textures of some exotic dishes.[26]

The crispy-fat taste was another common denominator, uniting chicken nuggets, crispy pan pizza, egg rolls, tacos, beignets, onion rings, croissants, croquettes, blintzes, biscuits, potato chips, crab cakes, and hush puppies. This was fortunate for marketers, as deep frying was what the food industry did so well, Other preparation techniques—marinating, parboiling, stewing, even baking and barbecuing—took time and skill. But fried-fat dishes froze and stored well and were easily microwaved by harried housewives at home and low-wage "thawer-outers" at chain restaurants. High-profit cocktails went nicely with crispy finger foods dipped in spicy salsa: e.g., fried mozzarella sticks, zucchini fritters, potato skins (first popularized at hippie restaurants), and Buffalo chicken wings. Mass-produced by Pierce ("Wing Zings"), Tyson ("Wings of Fire"), and Dutch Quality House ("Buffaloos"), the chicken wing moved significantly beyond what one Buffalonian told Trillin, "a blue-collar dish for a blue-collar town."[27] Indeed, in taste, reach, and manner of preparation, it was not all that different from the "Ragin' Cajun" dishes moving northward and the tempura-inspired nuggets moving eastward. All cuisines met in the deep-fat fryer.

Chicken was perhaps the core staple of ethnic/gourmet/regional food—"lite," cheap, amenable to almost any flavoring, technology, and pitch—the plastic food of the postmodern cuisine. It seemed that you could never go wrong with chicken, whatever the taste trend of the moment. To the same chicken breast could be added a stereotyped flavor that conveyed the Other but not the Weird: garlic and tomatoes made it Italian; soy sauce, Chinese; butter and cream, "gourmet"; red pepper, Cajun; chili pepper, Mexican; curry, Indian; liquid mesquite, southwestern; brown gravy, "country"; pineapple, Hawaiian . . .

Packaging and decor too sought security by incorporating well-worn motifs borrowed from 1930s Hollywood, 1950s Disneyland, and even older Cook's tour brochures. By tapping ingrained images, crude stereotypes could help a concept get started. Charlie Chan—an Oriental fast-food chain—was built on the racist Warner Oland films revived as camp in the 1960s and 1970s. The first wave of Italian-American restaurants in any area usually had red-checked 233 tablecloths, red, green, and white flags, gondolas, leaning towers, and Chianti bottles with candles, all remnants of 1890 bohemian spaghetti joints. Mexican restaurants combined Alamo and hacienda architecture, cacti, donkeys, and sombreros. Seeking a wider clientele, Tabatchnick encased its frozen matzoh ball soup in boxes decorated with *Fiddler on the Roof* scenes. Frozen croissant boxes had the familiar French tricolors. Ads for gourmet frozen dinners used silver goblets, formal dress, and classical music. Regional dishes also traded on touristic markers, popular songs, and B-movie stills. It was all so predictable—and that was the point.[28]

Stereotyped flavoring and packaging could not guarantee wider acceptance, however, particularly among the more sophisticated. In the 1950s and early 1960s big companies could get away with products that were scarcely Other—as with Chef Boy-ar-Dee, Chun King, Birds Eye Oriental Vegetables, and early Pizza Hut. But in the 1970s and 1980s the hunger for authenticity went beyond such vague, bland replicas. Mass marketers therefore looked to acquire the more genuine formulations developed by small, local companies serving subcultural markets with higher standards. Particularly ripe for acquisition were successful independents eyeing a national market but lacking the majors' strengths in production, distribution, and promotion. Many of the takeovers of the 1970s and 1980s thus served mutual needs: the small firms needed the money, the big ones needed the taste.

Pillsbury was an especially active practitioner of such "synergistic diversification." After Minneapolis's Rose Totino sold her growing frozen pizza firm—started as a takeout pizza parlor in 1952 —to Pillsbury in 1975, she achieved a nationwide market that she could never have reached on her own. Rose Totino's highly marketable ethnic aura combined with Pillsbury's expertise in making and distributing frozen baked goods to give Totino's the frozen pizza lead in the late 1970s. (Indeed, when Pillsbury started to promote Rose Totino's *mother*'s crust, Quaker responded with Mama Celeste's "abbondanza" and a whole new upscale category was born.) Similarly, in 1983 Pillsbury acquired the twenty-two-year-old, family-run superpremium ice cream manufacturer Häagen-Dazs. By plugging H-D into its strengths in fast food (Burger King) and frozen foods (especially the newly acquired Green Giant), Pillsbury looked for 35 percent annual growth rates. Further decentralized centralization came in 1985 when Pillsbury's "casual-theme" chain, Bennigan's, hired New Orleans chef Paul

234

Prudhomme to add eight new Cajun items to its eclectic s four-item menu. An indefatigable self-promoter, Prudhom almost single-handedly turned blackened redfish into a national fad, but to make it a trend he needed the clout of a conglomerate, which in turn, needed his authenticity.[29]

Conglomerate clout by no means guaranteed success, however. Indeed, Pillsbury stumbled badly in the late 1980s as it struggled to absorb too many acquisitions while trying to keep mainstay Burger King competitive with McDonald's. Some tastes also seemed to defy corporate replication. In 1985 Pillsbury bought the nine-unit Quik Wok chain, which the company hoped to turn into the Burger King of Oriental fast foods. Although there were as yet no major Chinese food franchises, Pillsbury's move was not that speculative, for Quik Wok's menu had already been mainstreamed during its formative years in San Antonio and Fort Lauderdale. Even so, the concept failed as did Charlie Chan's; Oriental food remained popular only in Oriental hands. Even more problematic were recent arrivals like Cajun. Even at the height of the craze, some upscale consumers were already complaining about being "Cajuned-out." As jokes spread about the blackening fad, redfish supplies diminished and the more discriminating wondered about the authenticity of anything outside of Louisiana. The apparent willingness of Cajun-Creole chefs to sell their name to almost anybody may have reflected a desire to cash in before the inevitable crash; they could always go back to their home restaurants anyway.[30]

Abhorring roller coaster rides, corporate planners constantly sought to smooth out the bumps in the taste obsolescence cycle. In the 1970s, some dinner house chains adopted a "casual theme" or variety show approach: an assortment of unrelated and interchangeable acts. By weaving several themes together, managers could replace fading individual threads without unraveling the whole fabric. The net effect was rather unsettling. In the 1980s designers pushed a more low-key or "laid-back" approach to bet hedging. At McDonald's and Denny's, Pizza Hut and Del Taco, Houlihan's and T. G. I. Friday's, executives favored "relaxed decor packages": hanging plants, skylights, natural woodwork, and light walls hung with inexpensive prints suggesting the theme of the moment. Since only the wall hangings had to be changed periodically, "recycling" costs were significantly lower. Sometimes called "the California look," this ambiguously contemporary decor

235

nicely complemented the all-purpose international-style glass boxes so popular with corporate cost accountants.[31]

Along with the California decor might go a panethnic menu that roughly approximated the kaleidoscopic California cuisine—with some differences. A Bennigan's menu grouped Oriental, Cajun, and Italian entries separately: at a marketplace food court you actually had to walk a few steps from Buffalo to Hunan, Philadelphia, or Athens. But recalling the countercuisine's improvisational one-worldism, haute-California crossed boundaries not just within the same room or menu, but on the same plate—as in crispy potato latkes (pancakes) with crème fraîche and three caviars, mu shu fajitas, and pasta squares with Japanese herbs and shredded chicken in ginger broth. Whether served by Alice Waters, Pillsbury, or the Rouse Corporation, however, the advantages of panethnicity were unmistakable: easy convertibility and a something-for-everyone appeal that reflected and reinforced the contemporary dietary confusion.[32]

Still, confusion was not a particularly secure long-term base. It was not a marketing concept but rather a lack of one, and its very instability led to a "back to basics" reaction. In 1985 *Los Angeles Times* food critic Colman Andrews dismissed the California cuisine as the "Kitchen Sink School of Cuisine." Offered a "sea bass moistened with a pineapple beurre blanc," Andrews blasted such "bad baroque art" and mused that the next trend might get back to the "reassuring folk authenticity of a Big Mac," or to his personal favorite, "red-boothed steakhouses." Addressing restaurant executives that same year, Calvin Trillin ridiculed California's "one perfect raspberry" style and wondered what happened to the old standards like chicken a la king and beef stroganoff. As healthy/hip food menus moved to ever-more-finicky heights of picturesque eclecticism, a primitivist nostalgia for decidedly "plain" cooking seemed inevitable. In 1986, the cofounder of D'Lites left that "healthy" fast-food chain and bought L-K Restaurants, with the idea of converting its sixty-one coffee shops into "back-to-basics" diners: deco trim, soda fountains, jukeboxes, and "daily blue plate specials."[33] The move signified yet another authenticity niche: neosquare.

236

NEOSQUARE:
ANTIHEALTH FOODS

On the surface, the antihealth trend of the mid-eighties seemed to confirm what many believed or hoped: that history was basically cyclical, that sooner or later just about everything would "come back." This frame was particularly popular in ironic journalistic commentary on the ever-revising health news, as in Meg Greenfield's mid-1984 reaction to the latest advice from the They Institute of America: "By now [the public] suspects that what is banned today is likely to be administered intravenously in all the best clinics tomorrow. . . . Nixon is back, Everything is back. Twinkies will be back. They will be telling us to put more salt on them."[34]

To an extent, the Cajun craze proved Greenfield's point, for the food was clearly reactionary: rich in calories, fat, salt and, if blackened, carcinogens. It also embodied regressive, Reagan era values: enjoy today and damn the consequences. The Louisiana of the 1980s had much to teach the rest of the country about partying well in the midst of economic stagnation, environmental decay, and political scandal. To the doomsaying ants worrying about the approaching winter, the Cajun grasshoppers responded with a fiddle and a two-step. But Louisiana was rather extreme—both in spicing and culture—a subregional oddity. For a young professional from Minneapolis, San Diego, or New Haven, Cajun was still very Other, requiring yet another act of touristic self-consciousness. It could not represent the effortless, guilt-free "basics" to which the overly stimulated dietary tourist might want to return. Tired of performing in the nonstop improvisational theater of theme dining, some wanted to read their own script, to play with their own props. Seeking their own roots, some turned inward and autobiographical—to the sort of foods suggested on the front cover of Jane and Michael Stern's *Square Meals*—"Mom's best pot roast and tuna noodle casserole."[35] For the ultimate in home cooking, why go out when you could just as easily stay in and tear open an envelope of dry onion soup mix?

Here the Sterns probably one-upped Calvin Trillin in the populist-authenticity game. Ever in search of grass roots resistance to mass culture, Trillin's later discoveries seemed more obscure and forced than in the days of *American Fried*, 1970–74, when almost anything off the interstate seemed fresh. After a decade of backroading, however, the Sterns knew enough to get off the road altogether, for sooner or later every offbeat discovery was bound to wind up in a mall food court. Heading back up the suburban driveway, they looked to mass culture itself as perhaps the last preserve of what they called "forthright food"—meat loaf and instant mashed potatoes, Jell-O mold, S'mores, Rice Krispies cookies, English muffin pizzas. Perhaps, as the camp/pop artists of the early 1960s had known, the best way to resist kitsch was to embrace it wholeheartedly. Like Andy Warhol, the Sterns idolized Campbell's soup.

But the spirit of *Square Meals* was more 1980s than 1960s, more fundamentalist than mod. If Cajun food fit the official policy of *laissez les bon temps rouler* (live today/pay tomorrow), square food touched another Reagan era theme: the leap of faith, the suspension of disbelief, the suppression of judgment. Just as most voters seemed willing to give Ronald Reagan the benefit of the doubt when he espoused homely platitudes and B-movie anecdotes, *Square Meals* enthusiasts seemed ready to stop worrying about bacon grease, white sugar, maraschino cherries, artificial coloring, processed American cheese, and other junk food clichés of the time when Reagan's "General Electric Theater" was a prime-time favorite (1953–62). Maybe Campbell's mushroom soup did make "the perfect tuna casserole," oven-fried corn flake chicken was "wholesome," and Jell-O was the "chef's magic powder." For those worn out by the latest theories, trends, and analyses, the Sterns had this message: "Our book really says that hey, it's O.K. to be retarded once in a while." For peace of mind, forget the quarrelsome doomsayers and head for the "heartland," where simple patriotism and Cool Whip cookery still thrived. Like Reagan, the Sterns lived among sophisticates but envied "corn."[36]

The nostalgia was selective, of course, more reverie than social history. Just as some critics questioned the accuracy of Reagan's corny memories, the Sterns admitted to wishful thinking. "It's meals like mom made—or like we wish she had." If, as poet Gil Scott-Heron quipped, Reagan evoked a mythic time "when movies were in black and white and so was everything else," *Square Meals* too conjured up the mass cultural heritage of Golden Age reruns. As an edible dynamic, square food brought diners together in front of the tube as couch potatoes. The hallowed Oreo was the equivalent of Proust's madeleine—a medium for reflection, only here the remembrances were of "Lassie" and "Leave It to Beaver." [37]

This fantasy was as two-dimensional as the touristic projections of ethnic/gourmet/regional, but at least it honestly acknowledged the hegemony of middle-class culture. Most young urban professionals had roots in middle-class apartments and suburban split-levels, not farmhouses or chateaus; their home cooking had more to do with Fannie Farmer and Betty Crocker than Grandma Walton or Wolfgang Puck. There was a ring of truth to the labels applied by food writers extolling this trend: "home fare," "plain fare," "homespun," "America's populist culinary legacy," "soothing," "nurturing," "comfort food," and "Momma food." "Nursery food" was the label preferred by Carol Flinders, of *Laurel's Kitchen*, who devoted a 1986 syndicated column to neo-Proustian rhapsodizing over shepherd's pie, macaroni and cheese, creamed eggs over toast—"food you'd eat after you'd played your little heart out in the open. It is food you'd eat while your parents are at supper with the other grown-ups. No special effects, no surprises—predictable, almost to a fault." [38]

Eyeing the infantile regression, *New Product News* observed that many processed rollouts of 1986 were "designed to remind yuppies of all those things they didn't get enough of as children." Coca Cola's cherry coke revival was labeled one of the year's "blockbusters." Swiss Miss's hot cocoa and marshmallow mix experienced unexpected growth. Recalling those fruity cocktails served to your parents (while you played your little heart out in the rec room), Bacardi's Tropical Fruit Mixes were a major hit. (Analysts were more skeptical of Ragu's jarred pasta meals, however, which seemed too inexact a makeover of Spaghetti-Os.) Dunkin Donuts, Mrs. Fields, and Procter and Gamble's Duncan Hines were all reported ready to capitalize on the muffin trend, which *Advertising Age* termed part of the "mom cuisine" revival—and a heavy rebuff to the croissant. [39]

Still, the retro version was not quite the same thing that Mom served in the 1950s (or that many Moms in the downscale 60 percent continued to serve in the 1980s). Reviewing this "culinary craze" for "American food," Laura Shapiro observed, "What's really American about American cooking is change: we don't cook the way our mothers did, and neither did our mothers." Some of the Sterns' "homespun" recipes actually originated as Progressive

239

era reforms: e.g., Waldorf salad, baked spaghetti, and Perfection Salad—the title of Shapiro's book on scientific cookery. Also, many retro versions bowed to contemporary concerns. Swiss Miss's cocoa and marshmallows were sugar-free. Flinders's vegetarian version of shepherd's pie, Kid Stuff Spinach Patties, used fresh spinach, real mashed potatoes, and, of course, no meat. At New York's renovated diner Moondance, a cheeseburger had bleu cheese and cost $6.25. At G. D. Ritzy's, a Columbus-based "1940s shake shop" concept, the "signature" peanut butter and jelly sandwiches came with fresh sliced strawberries and crushed peanuts—probably dry roasted to cut fat. Advertising "plain burgers," Sonic Drive-In's James Dean look-alike was healthier, less threatening than the original—more Fonz than greaser.[40]

The upper middle class went slumming in Squaresville, but they wore hip sunglasses. No one *really* wanted the Velveeta, the Skippy, the grease. Despite the "cheap-looking" wood paneling, the aqua iridescent leather booths, the "authentic-looking plastic-bound menus," and the gum-smacking waitresses, patrons never forgot that Ed Debevic's Short-Order Deluxe was a "hip place doing meat loaf," "a greasy looking place without the grease." With start-up costs of $1.2 million per unit—far more than the diner/greasy spoon model on which it was based—the chili dog with cheese cost $2.75, the milk shakes $2.25. Although the decor "was purposely keyed to 1952 because it was 'a dull time,'" the sales volume was strictly up to date, averaging over $4 million a year per unit. But with check averages of $5.00–$6.00 per person, Ed Debevic's was considerably cheaper than other "reverse chic" restaurants described in *Nation's Restaurant News*. For a devil's food cupcake "made to look and taste 'just like Hostess'—right down to the white squiggle of icing on top"—patrons at Los Angeles's City Restaurant paid $3.00, the price of a full meal at a preconversion L-K coffee shop. At Max's Diner of San Francisco the requisite "blue plate" lunch of meat loaf and mashed potatoes "with little lumps" ran close to $10.00. Also in San Francisco, a chili dog at the Fog City Diner cost $5.40.[41]

240

Despite the cult of plainness, neosquare consumers did not *really* want to be stuck in Lake Wobegon, where Dorothy's Chatterbox Café had just one daily special. Although neosquare spoke to a longing for simple choices, for underextension, in practice there was no going back to a lower key. Like many retro diners the Fog City sparkled with more neon, tile, chrome, and Formica than the real thing; the menu offered both hot roast beef sandwiches *and* "nouvelle chow" such as garlic custard and stuffed fresh pasilla pepper. JJ's American Diner of Miami had blue plates *and* mesquite-grilled swordfish. The Broadway Diner offered both grilled American cheese *and* grilled chicken with avocado mayonnaise. In addition to maximizing options, marketers also hedged their bets, for what if the antihealth trend proved a passing fad? Ed Debevic's was just one niche in Richard Melman's portfolio, whose company, Lettuce Entertain You Enterprises, was involved in just about every culinary fashion. Coke, of course, would continue to offer both diet and cherry versions. Neosquare suggested retraction, but it fit well into the corporate strategy of extension.[42]

There was indeed something excessive about many retro dishes. Flown in at considerable expense from New York, Max's pastrami was served in "grotesque" proportions with special mustard from Baltimore; the Broadway Diner's burgers weighed ½ pound; Ed Debevic's chicken-tuna-egg salad sandwich was served between 9- by 6-inch slices of bread. Muffins and cinnamon rolls returned much bigger and heavier than ever; countering the lite soft drink trend, "Jolt" cola boasted of 100 percent cane sugar and *twice* the caffeine of Coke. It seemed that, to offset the healthy trend, some square dishes had to go overboard the other way. Or perhaps, in line with the childhood regression, the portions had to be magnified to approximate the perspective of a nine-year-old in 1956, when a muffin or tuna sandwich *did* appear big. But would the optical illusion work? Was it possible to go back and erase the troubling years in between? "Thomas Wolfe did say you can't go home again," one square food enthusiast noted, "but he never said you couldn't try to eat yourself there." Visiting a new Ed Debevic's near Los Angeles, local columnist John Bogert was more skeptical. True, the look of the place did seem to negate recent history. Debevic's was "exactly the style of restaurant that was bumped off during the last 15 years by places featuring hanging plants and salad bars." But one wonders if the "wisecracking, gum-smacking" waitress kept cracking and smacking when Bogert's lunch companion asked her, "Is this place fun, or is it just pretending to be?"[43]

Observing how difficult it was for hip communards to sustain their guise of childlike innocence amidst the troubles of the late 1960s, Ray Mungo wrote, "It is awfully difficult to be nine once you'll never see nineteen again."[44] Sooner or later, the political and biological realities had to catch up. The war, the environment, the economy—these all had a way of making their demands felt, even in Vermont. Similar problems faced the chic meat loafers of the mid-1980s, except now the apocalypse was fifteen years closer. The cracks were too wide to be patched by extralarge portions of meat and potatoes. Of course, for those who thought in cycles rather than ends, there was this thought: if Nixon and mashed potatoes could come back, so too could Gary Snyder and brown rice.

EPILOGUE

As a historian, I don't believe in apocalyptic ends, which deny our ability to influence the future. Nor do I believe in cycles, which blur historical awareness and thereby allow instant mashed potatoes to be paraded as traditional home cooking. Worse, cycles imply that since everything eventually returns, we might as well stop worrying and enjoy the spin. Rather, I do worry, especially about the food I eat. We are living with the aftermath of the food wars. One way to assess that impact is to ask what might have happened had those battles gone differently.

What if the word "natural" actually meant something nowadays? Would biotechnologists be able to defend gene splicing as no different from natural breeding? Would NutraSweet Co. be able to claim that Simplesse is a natural fat substitute derived from milk and egg proteins and thus exempt from testing requirements?[1] Can it really be possible that we don't know what's natural and what isn't?

What if organic agriculture had not been so thoroughly libeled in the early 1970s? Would so many small farmers have gone under when the costs of high-tech overproduction became obvious during the farm crisis of the mid-1980s? Would the Environmental Protection Agency now be ranking pesticides in food and drinking water as one of the nation's most serious health and environmental problems?[2]

What if living lightly meant watching resources, not waistlines? Would we now be worrying about acid rain, toxic dumps, or the greenhouse effect—that slow, but not-so-distant apocalypse?

What if voters pushed for more, not less, federal regulation of food advertising? Would we now be hearing that beef is "real food" from James Garner, a recent coronary bypass patient? Would we now have *Ghostbusters*—the movie, soundtrack album, toy collection, cold cereal, kidvid cartoon?

What if we were more open to holistic healing? Would we still be hearing silly gags about nuts and twigs? Would health care costs be so high? Would we be expecting so much—too much—of doctors? Would so many of us be popping pills and counting calories —and still getting fatter and sicker?

Some of these questions lead us back to the late 1960s, when food consciousness sprouted in a thousand directions, and then into the 1970s, when the moral panic pruned back all but a few spare stalks. What if the food industry had spent more on research and less on ideological propaganda? What if politicians had appropriated more for exploring alternatives to agrochemicals? What if reporters had spent more time understanding rather than ridiculing those alternatives? And what if the countercuisine hadn't been quite so open to ridicule, so easily stereotyped, so weakly grounded? What if those communards had studied the old utopian mistakes?

Of course this line of thinking makes us confront many hard realities. What if businessmen didn't pursue short-term interests? What if politicians didn't worry about elections? What if reporters didn't face deadlines, word limits, and impatient editors? What if consumers had more time to read, shop, and cook? What if hippies weren't so young, so middle class? And, ultimately, we back into that catalyzing event: Vietnam. If there had been no war, there might not have been the polarization, the hyperbole and paranoia, the destructive moral panic. But then again, without a crazy war making young people desperate for fresh alternatives, there might not have been an ecology movement in the first place.

Dizzied by the second-guessing, I grope for present facts.

244

Where are we now? Having inherited this chronology, are we any better off? Is there any hope?

There are some encouraging signs. We certainly enjoy more opportunities for healthful eating—e.g., more vegetarian dishes at restaurants, more low-fat, low-salt choices in groceries. In 1970 who would have thought that yogurt, tofu, 2-percent milk, herbal tea, and bulk grains would now be supermarket norms, or that salad bars would offer alfalfa sprouts and sunflower seeds—or that fast-food chains would even *have* salad bars? With cholesterol a household word, heart disease is down. As fresh produce sales boom, people seem to be reawakening to chemical threats. An impressive 76 percent of those surveyed by the Food Marketing Institute now rate pesticide residues on fruits and vegetables a "serious hazard." In response more supermarket chains are eyeing organic supplies and even the Reagan/Bush administration has stepped up chemical testing.[3]

The interest in nonchemical, decentralized agriculture is indeed greater than ever—although we'll never know the full costs of the delay. In Pennsylvania the Rodale Research Center thrives as an experimental station for "regenerative agriculture." Rodale's pragmatic monthly *New Farm* shows farmers how to get off chemicals gradually. The universities of Vermont, Minnesota, and California at Santa Cruz and Iowa State University all offer programs in "sustainable agriculture"—a significant breach in the old university-agribusiness alliance. Fired in 1982 as the USDA's only organic specialist, Greenbelt, Maryland's Garth Youngberg now gets more attention working under a prestigious MacArthur Foundation "genius award." Rescuing regional agriculture, the state of Massachusetts preserves endangered pasture land, subsidizes composting equipment, links local growers with urban retailers, and makes loans to in-state processors. Texas Agriculture Commissioner Jim Hightower promotes low-chemical pest management in the state's huge cotton fields, sponsors research in water-saving irrigation systems, and helps small farmers to diversify crops and form marketing and processing cooperatives; still a populist critic of corporate farming, Hightower is often mentioned as a possible candidate for governor, senator, or, most ironic, USDA secretary. The USDA confirms what Hightower argued fifteen years ago: big farms are far less efficient than small ones—especially metropolitan area truck farmers who, on just half the acreage of traditional rural farms, earn twice as much per acre and gross 3 percent more

245

overall. Those community gardeners were right after all; cities—
or rather, suburbs—*can* grow their own food! [4]

Stunned by the farm crisis, the diehards are mellowing. Having only recently pronounced organic farming a dead end, conservatives at USDA now have an Office of Small-Scale Agriculture, fund "low-input" research, and have cosponsored a workshop with, of all people, the Rodale Research Center. Perhaps more telling are changes at the Council for Agricultural Science and Technology. Consisting of staunch agribusiness allies, CAST was formed in 1972 specifically to argue the orthodox case in the moral panic. It was CAST who, in 1977, mounted the fiercest attacks on the initial McGovern committee report. Now, however, a CAST panel studying the long-term viability of American agriculture includes Robert Rodale and Iowa organic farmer Dick Thompson; one final recommendation: reduce agrichemical use. Captioning such developments, *Newsweek* concludes, "The Time Is Ripe for Organic Agriculture." Even the puns have changed! [5]

Living in the cracks has benefited other radical veterans too. Building from her *Diet for a Small Planet* base, Frances Moore Lappé has expanded the Institute for Food and Development into a full-fledged radical think tank probing worldwide hunger and poverty. In addition to exposing marketing shams and offering sensible alternatives in *Nutrition Action Health Letter*, Michael Jacobson's Center for Science in the Public Interest lobbies loudly and relentlessly for stronger federal regulations. While Lappé and Jacobson pursue global and national strategies, countless grass roots groups work to change consciousness while feeding the hungry: i.e., food as medium. Echoing—and often outperforming—Digger improvisational theater, the ascetic life actors at Washington, D.C.'s Community for Creative Non-Violence (CCNV) win media attention and federal funds without succumbing to fame or burnout. And spreading the news are the scrappy independent media. *Newsweek* has only just rediscovered pesticides and organic farming, but in the *Progressive* they've never been forgotten.

246   There are many discouraging signs too. The long-awaited surgeon general's report on nutrition and health merely confirms the consensus achieved eight years earlier in the "Dietary Guidelines" and counsels the same privatistic, negative advice: cut fat, sodium, calories. Even this advice has limited impact. Sprouts and seeds aside, fast-food burgers keep red meat consumption above 1965 levels; with all the litening up, we seem to weigh more too. De-

spite healthy inroads in supermarkets, food industry executives remain skeptical about significant changes; indeed, announcing a consumer shift to a "life is short" attitude, *Advertising Age* finds more sumptuous treats and fewer healthy rollouts than ever at the 1988 Food Marketing Institute convention. The majority of adults remain indifferent, while, lacking any comprehensive model, the healthy minority practice the portfolio management which can lead in the silly, if not also futile, directions suggested in the last chapter. Still focusing on single dangers, we overlook or even increase others. Cutting cholesterol, we buy more poultry contaminated by salmonella wrought by overcrowding in chicken factories. Adding fiber to cut colon cancer, we munch strawberries bathed in carcinogenic pesticides. Is it really, as one *Washington Post* food writer shrugs, "doomed if we do, doomed if we don't"? Or are there more radical cures for chemical addiction? Organic respectability notwithstanding, mainstream reporters generally remain oblivious to such possibilities. No wonder that even the most health-conscious go on nihilistic binges.[6]

Compounding the confusion are the career and family pressures favoring the convenience cop-out—the food industry's trump card. Fast food, frozen "gourmet" meals, supermarket takeout counters—all show steady gains. A Pillsbury study classifies a quarter of adult consumers as "chase and grabbits" who "have effectively said good-bye to their kitchens," while "Happy Cookers" who provide three meals a day, with many dishes "from scratch," make up just 15 percent—down 35 percent in fifteen years.[7] Like most parents nowadays, both my wife and I work full-time. Although we've found quick vegetarian recipes for ourselves, we still don't know what to serve our seven-year-old, who hates beans and bulgur, barely tolerates tofu, but loves fish sticks, McNuggets, and fries; once he gets molars, our toddler no doubt will side with her.

A strong alternative food network might ease these private dilemmas with a supportive social context and a cohesive ideology, but the countercuisine's infrastructure seems weaker now than in the early 1970s. Readers of *New Farm* should feel heartened by the proved viability of low-input methods, but there's a *déjà vu* quality to articles deploring distribution gaps, persistent fraud, high prices, and the lack of national standards. In 1972 we could at least unite around the metaphorical "organic," but now there are at least a dozen alternatives to that much-bruised name.[8] While the food industry consolidates, organic force fragments into piecemeal prag-

247

matism. The progressive press reports the scandals, but where are the recipes, shopping tips, and restaurant reviews of the long-defunct underground papers? Where are the bohemian ghettos where one can try living well on less? Where are the communal farms, hip cafés, food conspiracies? While supermarkets grow larger and fewer, co-ops disappear or barely hang on.

With its whole grains, overalled volunteers, and reggae tapes, our local co-op has survived the shakeout, but visits there compound my uncertainty. On hopeful days I see people of all classes and races buying good food and browsing the latest macrobiotic cookbooks and self-health manuals. Having spun off a vegetarian restaurant and now seeking funds to build a larger building, the co-op seems a vital movement center. At other times, however, I feel I'm entering a time warp, a countercultural museum—or simply selecting one minor option from the multicourse postmodern menu.

I do not know which perception is right, but since the odds against us were always steep, I suppose there's no reason to lose heart now.

ACKNOWLEDGMENTS

I t is customary for authors to attribute all credit to others while personally accepting all the blame. With this book, however, I am not quite sure who should get fingered for what, but I will certainly allow that there's plenty of responsibility to go around.

First, there are all the friends, colleagues, and acquaintances who, in the course of conversation or correspondence, encouraged my research, added essential details, suggested new directions, posed hard questions, forced me to go back to the library, or otherwise refused to let me compost in peace: Pat Aufderheide, Charles Camp, Mark Foster, Todd Gitlin, Joan Gussow, Howie Harris, Steven Kaplan, Phil Langdon, Jackson Lears, Tom Lifson, Barbara Melosh, Rich Miller, Kay Mussell, Terry Sharrer, Robert Spekman, Brett Williams, and, last but definitely not least, Wilbur Zelinsky.

I am, of course, much indebted to all the authors, critics, officials, and businesspeople cited—and hopefully not too abused —in the text. I especially want to credit Frances Moore Lappé, Ross Hume Hall, Jim Hightower, and the folks at the Center for

Science in the Public Interest for permanently changing my way of thinking about food. And, while reading these writers makes it impossible for me to eat the way I used to, Calvin Trillin still makes me ache for brisket and packaged macaroni and cheese.

Then there are my American Studies mates at the University of Maryland Baltimore County who, now that the book is done, probably hope that I will stop nitpicking the menu at our departmental feasts: Carolyn Ferrigno, Joan Korenman, Carole McCann, Ed Orser, Leslie Prosterman, Pat Secrist, and Linda Shopes. Thanks also to recent members of my department who, before moving on to hopefully less contentious luncheon venues, supported me in many ways: Jim Arnquist, Kathy Peiss, and David Whisnant.

Three institutions deserve special credit: A full-year fellowship from the National Endowment for the Humanities and a summer grant and sabbatical from UMBC were invaluable. The extraordinary staff at the Library of Congress offered me a quiet office (with a view!), stack privileges, and, of course, free access to an amazing collection of cookbooks, trade periodicals, underground newspapers, and so on. I remember fondly all my steadfast companions in the LC's thriving cafeteria society, and I also appreciate those considerate U.S. Capitol groundskeepers who mowed around me as I catnapped before returning to the stacks.

I could write a full chapter about my world-class editor, Wendy Wolf, but since she would hack it to pieces, a brief paragraph will have to do. After years of supplying me with what has to be the world's largest collection of food-related postcards, Wendy seized my sprawling "paean to sprouts" (her words) and single-handedly shaped it into something sensible. I am fortunate indeed to have such a demanding and perceptive reader.

Since, as the preface notes, this book recalls and revives the old dinner table battles, I want to identify the principals. My fellow coconspirator for over twenty years, Amy Fried Belasco, has eaten more tofu with me than anyone else, and this is as much her story as mine. Our wonderfully contentious sisters and brothers will also see themselves in these pages: Clare and Dave Heidtke, Hal, Leni, and Marty Fried, Betty Daniel, and Mike Augspurger. Shirley Belasco and Joyce and Ed Fried moderated the debates with all the grace and aplomb one would expect of wise parents. In opening a new front at home, our children, Sonia and Nathaniel, have shown us how hard it is to eat right—and how important it is that we try.

NOTES

PREFACE

1. Julie Liesse Erickson, "Kellogg Adds to Nutri-Grain," *Advertising Age*, May 2, 1988, p. 4.

2. Judann Dagnoli, "Riding Oat Craze," *Advertising Age*, January 2, 1989, p. 2.

CHAPTER 1. AN EDIBLE DYNAMIC

1. James C. Whorton, *Crusaders for Fitness: The History of American Health Reformers* (Princeton: Princeton University Press, 1982); Harvey Green, *Fit for America: Health, Fitness, Sport, and American Society* (New York: Pantheon Books, 1986); Ronald G. Walters, *American Reformers, 1815–1860* (New York: Hill & Wang, 1978), pp. 145–72.

2. "Eat and Enjoy," *San Francisco Express Times*, September 25, 1968, p. 12.

3. "Delving the Diggers," *Berkeley Barb*, October 21, 1966, p. 3; Emmett Grogan, *Ringolevio: A Life Played for Keeps* (Boston: Little, Brown, 1972), pp. 238–50, passim.

4. Helen Swick Perry, *The Human Be-In* (New York: Basic Books, 1970), pp. 53–54; Ruth Benedict, *Patterns of Culture* (New York: Mentor, 1946), p. 19; "Evaluation of a Fast," *New Left Notes*, February 18, 1966, p. 1; "Grape Strike Report Number," *New Left Notes*, March 18, 1966, p. 2.

5. "Trip Without a Ticket," *Communication Company*, Spring 1967, in Jesse Kornbluth, ed., *Notes from a New Underground: An Anthology* (New York: Viking Press, 1968), p. 105; Charles Perry, *The Haight-Ashbury: A History* (New York: Random House, 1984), pp. 142, 137–38, 273.

6. Perry, *Haight*, pp. 261, 148–149, 205, 239; Garrett De Bell, ed., *The Environmental Handbook* (New York: Ballantine Books, 1970), pp. 234–52.

7. Perry, *Haight*, pp. 99, 183–84. For SDS hostility, see Todd Gitlin, *The Sixties: Years of Hope, Days of Rage* (New York: Bantam Books, 1987), pp. 222–38.

8. "Grab Land," *Good Times*, April 23, 1969, p. 7.

9. "Trip Without a Ticket," in Kornbluth, *Notes*, pp. 101–6. For the theory of living theater: John Irwin, *Scenes* (Beverly Hills, Calif.: Sage Publications, 1977), pp. 163–224; Perry, *Haight*, pp. 250–55.

10. *Berkeley Barb*, April 13, 1969, quoted in David Armstrong, *A Trumpet to Arms: Alternative Media in America* (Boston: South End Press, 1981), pp. 46–47; Kornbluth, *Notes*, p. 102; "Vietnam Tactics in Berkeley," *San Francisco Chronicle*, May 22, 1969, p. 40.

11. Keith Lampe, "Earth Read-Out," *Fifth Estate*, June 12, 1969, p. 10; Snyder quoted in Todd Gitlin's review of *Earth House Hold*, *Fifth Estate*, August 7, 1979, p. 8.

12. Pantagruel, "Earth Revolts: Man Victim—the Necessity of Ecology," *Rat*, July 9, 1969, pp. 14–15; Keith Lampe, "Earth Read-Out," *Rat*, July 1969, p. 11; Pocahontas, "Ecology Action East," *Rat*, November 19, 1969, p. 10. The 500+ statistic is for 1969 and is from Abe Peck, *Uncovering the Sixties: The Life and Times of the Underground Press* (New York: Pantheon Books, 1985), p. xv.

252

13. Todd Gitlin, "All Fences Down," *Good Times*, May 28, 1969, p. 5; "People's Pods," *Good Times*, July 24, 1969, p. 14.

14. Ehrlich quoted by Leo Marx, "American Institutions and Ecological Ideals," in Carroll Pursell, ed., *From Conservation to Ecology: The Development of Environmental Concern* (New York: Thomas Y. Crowell, 1973), p. 93; and reviewed by Keith Lampe, "Earth Read-Out," *Fifth Estate*, August 21, 1969, p. 6; John G. Mitchell, "On the Spoor of the Slide Rule," in Mitchell, ed., *Ecotactics: The Sierra Club Handbook for Environment Activists* (New York: Pocket Books, 1970), p. 24. According to Gallup, pollution passed race, crime, and teenage problems as the most worrisome public concern in late 1969, early 1970. Gallup Poll, August 29, 1970. *Time* rated the environment "Issue of the Year" for 1970. January 4, 1971, pp. 21–22.

15. Peck, *Uncovering the Sixties*, p. 161. On the late sixties left impasse: Gitlin, *The Sixties*, pp. 377–419, and *The Whole World Is Watching: Mass Media in the Making and Unmaking of the New Left* (Berkeley: University of California Press, 1980), pp. 180–204.

16. Gitlin's review of *Earth House Hold: Fifth Estate*, August 7, 1970, p. 8; Lampe, "Earth Read-Out," *Fifth Estate*, September 4, 1969, p. 20.

17. "The Young Eco-Activists," *Time*, August 22, 1969, p. 43; "Ecology: The New Jeremiahs," *Time*, August 15, 1969, p. 38; "The Campus Whole Earth Co-op," *Organic Gardening and Farming*, September 1970, p. 73; Marion Edey, "Eco-Politics and the League of Conservation Voters," *Environmental Handbook*, p. 315.

18. Peter R. Janssen, "Where the Action Is," *Ecotactics*, p. 55.

19. *The Last Whole Earth Catalog* (Menlo Park, Calif.: Portola Institute, 1971), p. 43; Paul Shepard and Daniel McKinley, eds., *The Subversive Science—Essays Toward an Ecology of Man* (Burlington, Mass.: Houghton Mifflin Co., 1969).

20. Keith Lampe, "Beat Poet Returns," *Rat*, January 24, 1969, p. 20.

21. Peck, *Uncovering the Sixties*, pp. 177–80.

22. Judie Davis, "Eat It!" *Fifth Estate*, March 15, 1968, p. 5.

23. *Food for Us All: The Yearbook of Agriculture 1969* (Washington, D.C.: U.S. Department of Agriculture, 1969), pp. 5, 53.

CHAPTER 2. RADICAL CONSUMERISM

1. Judie Davis, "Eat It!" *Fifth Estate*, December 15, 1967, p. 18; Barbara Garson, "Eat and Enjoy," *San Francisco Express Times*, September 25, 1968, p. 12; Rosenberg reviewed in *Kaleidoscope*, December 22, 1966, p. 14.

2. Diane DiPrima, "Poems for the Summer Solstice 1968," *San Francisco Express Times*, June 19, 1968, pp. 10–11; *The Last Whole Earth Catalog* (Menlo Park, Calif.: Portola Institute, 1971), p. 198; Kerry Thornley, "What to Do Until the World Ends," *Fifth Estate*, September 19, 1968, p. 3. On the apocalyptic, street-fighting, revolutionary talk of 1968–70: Todd Gitlin, *The Sixties: Years of Hope, Days of Rage* (New York: Bantam Books, 1987), pp. 285–304, 341–61; Abe Peck, *Uncovering the Sixties: The Life and Times of the Underground Press* (New York: Pantheon Books, 1985), pp. 121–62, 223–40; David Armstrong, *A Trumpet to Arms: Alternative Media in America* (Boston: South End Press, 1981), pp. 116–59.

3. "Medical Cadre," *Quicksilver Times*, March 13, 1970, p. 16; Judy Swann, "Food Fun," *Quicksilver Times*, March 24, 1970, p. 20. For an excellent evocation of the "Amerika" spelling, see Geoffrey O'Brien, *Dream Time: Chapters from the Sixties* (New York: Viking Press, 1988), pp. 122–39.

4. David Baise, letter to editor, *Rat*, July 1969, p. 2; "State of the Nation," *Good Times*, February 12, 1971, pp. 12–13.

5. Jerry Berman and Jim Hightower, "Lettuce Boycott in Its Fourth Month," *Liberation News Service* #317, February 10, 1971, p. 8; "War Pollution," *Northwest Passage*, March 29, 1971, p. 16; Windcatcher, "There's No Good Reason Why We Can't Exchange Our Goods and Smoke Our Money," *Good Times*, July 17, 1969, p. 6; Marcia, "Cosmic Clinic," *Good Earth*, November 12, 1971, p. 14.

6. "Food Fun," *Quicksilver Times*, July 28, 1970, p. 16; "Medical Cadre," *Quicksilver Times*, March 13, 1970, p. 16; Ita Jones, *The Grubbag: An Underground Cookbook* (New York: Random House, 1971), p. 3; "Eat and Enjoy," *Good Times*, February 3, 1971, pp. 13–14; Ita Jones, "Kugel and Rhubarb," *Liberation News Service* #148, March 15, 1969, p. 8.

7. Susan Glick, "Bod Squad," *Good Times*, March 12, 1971, p. 10; Swann, "Food Fun," *Quicksilver Times*, March 24, 1970, p. 20; "Food Conspiracy," *Good Times*, April 2, 1970, p. 3; "Supermarket Survival," *Liberation News Service* #337, April 24, 1971, p. 8; Marcia, "Cosmic

Clinic," *Good Earth*, November 12, 1971, p. 14; Stuart Wilson, "Getting in Shape for the Revolution," *Northwest Passage*, March 1, 1971, p. 11.

8. "Beans Are a Gas," *Good Times*, September 17, 1971, p. 28.

9. On the feminist revolt against sexism in the New Left and underground media: Robin Morgan, "Free All Sisters," *Rat*, August 12, 1969, p. 10; Gitlin, *The Sixties*, pp. 362–76; Peck, *Uncovering the Sixties*, pp. 207–21; Armstrong, *Trumpet to Arms*, pp. 225–53.

10. Book Jones quoted in Annette Kolodny, *The Lay of the Land: Metaphor as Experience and History in American Life and Letters* (Chapel Hill: University of North Carolina Press, 1975), p. 146; Robin Morgan, "Goodbye to All That," reprinted in *Observer* (Bard), March 11, 1970, pp. 6–7; "Women and Ecology," *off our backs*, March 19, 1970, p. 2; Gina, "Nature: Our Sister in the Struggle," *It Ain't Me Babe*, May 31, 1970, p. 5.

11. Armstrong, *Trumpet to Arms*, pp. 226–29; Roberta Weintraub, "Women: The Fat of the Land," *Liberation News Service* #255, May 13, 1970, pp. 16–19; "Food Fetish," *off our backs*, Summer 1971, p. 19; Anne Kent Rush, *Getting Clear: Body Work for Women* (New York: Random House, 1973), pp. 76–89; Susie Orbach, *Fat Is a Feminist Issue: The Anti-Diet Guide to Permanent Weight Loss* (New York: Paddington Press: 1978).

12. *Our Bodies, Ourselves* sold 250,000 copies in 1970 alone. Armstrong, *Trumpet to Arms*, p. 236. "The Male-feasance of Health," *Rat*, March 3, 1970, p. 9; "Women and Health," *off our backs*, Summer 1971, p. 8; Robin Morgan, "Taking Back Our Bodies," in Susan Rennie and Kirsten Grimstad, eds., *The New Woman's Survival Sourcebook* (New York: Alfred A. Knopf, 1975), p. 33. This was an extension of Grimstad and Rennie, eds., *The New Woman's Survival Catalog* (New York: Coward, McCann & Geoghegan, 1973), pp. 71–91.

13. Norma Allen Lesser, "Nothin' Says Lovin' Like Somethin' from the Oven," *off our backs*, May 30, 1970, p. 10; "The Rape of Edible Food," *Great Speckled Bird*, March 1, 1969, p. 3; cartoon, *off our backs*, October 25, 1970, p. 16; Mary Ann Cronin, "Let's Keep the Crap out of the Kitchen," *off our backs*, May 16, 1970, p. 16.

255

14. Ross Hume Hall, *Food for Nought: The Decline of Nutrition* (New York: Harper & Row, 1974), p. 39.

15. The "damp-cloth utopian" hopes for plastic are explored by Jeffrey L. Meikle, "Plastic, Material of a Thousand Uses," in Joseph J.

Corn, ed., *Imagining Tomorrow: History, Technology, and the American Future* (Cambridge, Mass.: MIT Press, 1986), pp. 77–96.

16. True Light Beavers, *Eat, Fast, Feast* (New York: Doubleday, 1972), p. 259; Panurge, "The Politics of Ecology: View from the Street," *Rat,* August 12, 1969, p. 12; "Organic Revolution," *Northwest Passage,* March 29, 1971, p. 3; R. Chill, "America, the brutiful," *Northwest Passage,* July 9, 1973, p. 16.

17. Susan Sontag, *Illness as Metaphor* (New York: Vintage Books, 1979); Raymond Williams, *Keywords* (New York: Oxford University Press, 1976), pp. 181–89.

18. R. B. Read, *The San Francisco Underground Gourmet,* 3rd ed. (New York: Simon & Schuster, 1975), p. 81; Raymond Mungo, *Famous Long Ago: My Life and Hard Times with Liberation News Service* (Boston: Beacon Press, 1970), pp. 114–15.

19. Windcatcher, "Our Hands Labor Out of Love," *Good Times,* August 28, 1969, p. 10; Robert Houriet, *Getting Back Together* (New York: Coward, McCann & Geoghegan, 1971), p. xiii.

CHAPTER 3. RADICAL THERAPY

1. On the countercultural defiance of contradictions: Todd Gitlin, *The Sixties: Years of Hope, Days of Rage* (New York: Bantam Books, 1987), pp. 196–220; Theodore Roszak, *The Making of a Counter Culture: Reflections on the Technocratic Society and Its Youthful Opposition* (Garden City, N.Y.: Anchor Books, 1969).

2. My definition of cuisine is drawn from: Elizabeth Rozin, "The Structure of Cuisine," in Lewis M. Barker, ed., *The Psychobiology of Human Food Selection* (Westport, Conn.: AVI Publishing, 1982), pp. 189–203; Roland Barthes, "Toward a Psychosociology of Contemporary Food Consumption," in Robert Forster and Orest Ranum, eds., *Food and Drink in History* (Baltimore: Johns Hopkins University Press, 1979), pp. 166–73; Peter Farb and George Armelagos, *Consuming Passions: The Anthropology of Eating* (Boston: Houghton Mifflin Co., 1980), pp. 190–98.

256

3. On the "semantics of selection" underlying deviant subcultural styles: John Clarke, "Style," in Stuart Hall and Tony Jefferson, eds., *Resistance Through Rituals: Youth Subcultures in Post-War Britain* (London: Hutchinson, 1976), pp. 175–91; Dick Hedbidge, *Subculture: The Meaning of Style* (London: Methuen, 1979).

4. On deprofessionalization: Roszak, *Counter Culture*, pp. 1–41, 124–77; Peter Clecak, *America's Quest for the Ideal Self: Dissent and Fulfillment in the 60s and 70s* (New York: Oxford University Press, 1983), p. 151; John Case and Rosemary C. R. Taylor, eds., *Co-ops, Communes, and Collectives: Experiments in Social Change in the 1960s and 1970s* (New York: Pantheon Books, 1979). For the original Progressive era campaign *against* food improvisation: Laura Shapiro, *Perfection Salad: Women and Cooking at the Turn of the Century* (New York: Farrar, Straus & Giroux, 1986), pp. 71–105.

5. Ita Jones, "The Grub Bag," *First Issue* #10 (Ithaca), February 1969, p. 49; "Eat and Enjoy," *Good Times*, July 17, 1969, p. 12; Charles Perry, *The Haight-Ashbury: A History* (New York: Random House, 1984), p. 254; Mark Zanger, *Robert Nadeau's Guide to Boston Restaurants* (Boston: World Food Press, 1978), pp. 292–93.

6. Judie Davis, "Eat It!" *Fifth Estate*, March 15, 1968, p. 5; sarah, "Eat and Enjoy," *Good Times*, April 23, 1969, p. 15; Lucy Horton, *Country Commune Cooking* (New York: Coward, McCann & Geoghegan, 1972), p. 15.

7. Edward Espe Brown, *Tassajara Cooking* (Berkeley, Calif.: Shambhala, 1973), p. 1.

8. Frances Moore Lappé, *Diet for a Small Planet* (New York: Ballantine Books, 1971), pp. xiv, 5–7; ibid. 10th anniversary edition (New York: Ballantine Books, 1982), pp. 18, 16–26.

9. True Light Beavers, *Eat, Fast, Feast* (New York: Doubleday, 1972); mother bird, "Bread Bakin': A Garden of Kneadin'," *Northwest Passage*, January 10, 1972, p. 4.

10. Ross Hume Hall, *Food for Nought: The Decline of Nutrition* (New York: Vintage Books, 1976), pp. 190–214.

11. mother bird, "Bread Bakin'," p. 4; "Food," *Quicksilver Times*, July 14, 1970, p. 18; Ita Jones, "Grub Bag," *Kaleidoscope*, January 3, 1969, p. 7.

12. Windcatcher, "Our Hands Labor Out of Love," *Good Times*, August 28, 1969, p. 10; Helen Swick Perry, *The Human Be-In* (New York: Basic Books, 1970), p. 65; Diane DiPrima, "Revolutionary Letters," *Great Speckled Bird*, March 1969, p. 3; *The Last Whole Earth Catalog* (Menlo Park, Calif.: Portola Institute, 1971), p. 200.

13. "Food," *Quicksilver Times*, July 14, 1970, p. 18.

257

14. On the importance of white sauces in Progressive era "scientific" cookery: Shapiro, *Perfection Salad*, pp. 91–95.

15. Roszak, *Counter Culture*, p. 13; "Beware!! Dangerous Drugs," *Good Times*, May 28, 1971, p. 15. For a much-read critique of the way bread manufacturers had mechanized the "organic," see: Siegfried Giedion, *Mechanization Takes Command* (New York: Norton, 1969), pp. 169–208; also Hall, *Food for Nought*, pp. 9–34.

16. Brown quoted in *Last Whole Earth Catalog*, p. 191; Laurel Robertson, Carol Flinders, and Bronwen Godfrey, *Laurel's Kitchen* (New York: Bantam Books, 1978), p. 20. Sales statistics in David Armstrong, *Trumpet to Arms: Alternative Media in America* (Boston: South End Press, 1981), p. 291. *Laurel's Kitchen* sold 80,000 in its Nilgiri Press edition before Bantam mass-produced it.

17. Ita Jones, "Grub Bag," *Liberation News Service* #135, January 30, 1969, p. 4.

18. "Beans Are a Gas," *Good Times*, September 17, 1971, p. 28; Jeanie Darlington, "Soul Food," *Good Times*, June 11, 1971, p. 15; Windcatcher, "Our Hands," p. 10; Alicia Bay Laurel and Ramon Sender, *Being of the Sun* (New York: Harper & Row, 1973), n.p. On Horace Fletcher: Harvey Green, *Fit for America: Health, Fitness, Sport, and American Society* (New York: Pantheon Books, 1986), pp. 295–302; James C. Whorton, *Crusaders for Fitness: The History of American Health Reformers* (Princeton: Princeton University Press, 1982), pp. 174ff.

19. Gaskin quoted in alicia bay laurel, *Living on the Earth* (New York: Vintage Books, 1971), p. 108; Jeanie Darlington, "Grow Your Own," *Good Times*, April 23, 1969, p. 14.

20. Robertson et al., *Laurel's Kitchen*, p. 46. On the 1950s drive-in: Philip Langdon, *Orange Roofs, Golden Arches: The Architecture of American Chain Restaurants* (New York: Alfred A. Knopf, 1986), pp. 57–77.

21. Pierre Bourdieu, *Distinction: A Social Critique of the Judgment of Taste* (Cambridge: Harvard University Press, 1984), pp. 56–74. On the bohemian's mediating/pioneering role: Richard Miller, *Bohemia: The Protoculture Then and Now* (Chicago: Nelson-Hall, 1977).

22. Susan Strasser, *Never Done: A History of American Housework* (New York: Pantheon Books, 1982), pp. 23–24, 36–49; Daniel J. Boorstin, *The Americans: The Democratic Experience* (New York: Vintage Books, 1973), pp. 109–12; Langdon, *Orange Roofs*, pp. 74–77; Ruth Schwartz Cowan, *More Work for Mother* (New York: Basic Books, 1983), p. 150.

23. On the convenience dilemmas: Strasser, *Never Done*, and Cowan, *More Work*. On the love of convenience and wizardry: Boorstin, *Democratic Experience*, pp. 307–31; Harvey Levenstein, *Revolution at the Table: The Transformation of the American Diet* (New York: Oxford University Press, 1988), pp. 16–172. On marketers' guilt-reducing techniques: Ernest Dichter, *Handbook of Consumer Motivations* (New York: McGraw-Hill, 1964), pp. 16, 45, 51, 58.

24. Robertson et al., *Laurel's Kitchen*, pp. 38–50. For the Victorian equivalent: Harvey Green, *The Light of the Home: An Intimate View of the Lives of Women in Victorian America* (New York: Pantheon Books, 1983), pp. 59–92; Shapiro, *Perfection Salad*, pp. 11–33.

25. Letitia Brewster and Michael Jacobson, *The Changing American Diet* (Washington, D.C.: Center for Science in the Public Interest, 1983), pp. 34–36; Norge W. Jerome, "The U.S. Dietary Pattern from an Anthropological Perspective," *Food Technology*, February 1981, p. 39.

26. There were, to be sure, scattered articles about arsenic in chicken feed, mercury in fish, DDT in animal fat, and the use of hormones and antibiotics to promote animal growth. But these same contaminants were also in the dairy products that were acceptable to most vegetarians. "Arsenic and Old Chickens," *Dallas News*, January 27, 1971, n.p.; "The State of the Nation," *Good Times*, February 12, 1971, pp. 12–13; "Food for Thought," *Liberation News Service* #336, April 21, 1971, p. 6.

27. On later respect: *Health Foods and Natural Vitamins Market* (New York: Frost & Sullivan, 1979), pp. 111–12.

28. On earlier therapeutic fascination with Japan: T. J. Jackson Lears, *No Place of Grace: Antimodernism and the Transformation of American Culture, 1880–1920* (New York: Pantheon Books, 1981), pp. 225–37.

29. For one hip interpretation: Mary Schoener, "Dining," *Good Times*, January 22, 1970, p. 14; "Eat and Enjoy," *Good Times*, January 30, 1970, n.p., and "Digging You," *Good Times*, December 4, 1970, p. 17. On soy's versatility: Farb and Armelagos, *Consuming Passions*, p. 193.

30. For underground criticism of macrobiotics: Eugene Schoenfeld, "HIPprocrates," *Berkeley Barb*, April 4, 1967, p. 9; "Eat Chomp Chomp Eat," *Good Times*, November 13, 1969, p. 12; "Food," *Quicksilver Times*, July 14, 1970, p. 18.

31. Sales statistics in Lappé, *Diet* (1982), p. 7. Protein statistics in Lappé, *Diet* (1971), pp. 7–9.

259

32. Lappé, *Diet* (1971), pp. xi–xiv, 28–30; Lappé, *Diet* (1982), pp. 3–57; Lappé and Joseph Collins, *Food First: Beyond the Myth of Scarcity* (New York: Ballantine Books, 1979).

33. Lappé, *Diet* (1971), pp. 33–55.

34. Ibid., p. 13.

35. Horton, *Country Commune Cooking*, pp. 14–15: "Adventures of a Hungry Girl Freak," *Florida Free Press*, November 21, 1968, p. 6; Adam Raskin, "Eat But Beware of Food Fads and Phonies," *University Review*, April 1973, pp. 16–17.

36. Ita Jones, "Grub Bag," *First Issue*, February 1969, p. 49; Jones, "On Not Eating Meat and on Eating Meat," *Liberation News Service* #188, August 23, 1969, p. 10.

37. *Last Whole Earth Catalog*, p. 198; *January Thaw* (New York: Times Change Press, 1974), p. 125.

38. For recent continuation of the debate: "We Eat the Meat We Love, We Love the Meat We Eat," *Womanspirit* 6 (September 1979): 24–27; Mark Mathew Braunstein, *Radical Vegetarianism: A Dialectic of Diet and Ethic* (Los Angeles: Panjandrum, 1981).

39. Ann Pietschman, ed., *Food for Thought* (Los Angeles: Institute of Mentalphysis, 1954).

40. Anna Thomas, *The Vegetarian Epicure* (New York: Vintage Books, 1972).

41. Robert Alter, "A Fever of Ethnicity," in David R. Colburn and George E. Pozzetta, eds., *America and the New Ethnicity* (Port Washington, N.Y.: Kennikat, 1979), pp. 189–90; Michael Novak, *The Rise of the Unmeltable Ethnics* (New York: Macmillan, 1971); Sallie Te Selle, ed., *The Rediscovery of Ethnicity* (New York: Harper Colophon Books, 1973). My definition of "core ethnic" draws on Wsevolod W. Isajiw, "Definitions of Ethnicity," *Ethnicity* 1 (July 1974): 111–24, and James H. Dorman, "Ethnic Groups and Ethnicity: Some Theoretical Considerations," *Journal of Ethnic Studies* 7 (Winter 1980): 23–26.

42. On hip panethnicity, especially the fascination with nonwestern mystical or "revolutionary" models: Roszak, *Counter Culture*, pp. 124–54; Gitlin, *Sixties*, pp. 261–82.

43. John L. Hess and Karen Hess, *The Taste of America* (New York: Penguin Books, 1977), pp. 173–96; Alice Waters, *The Chez Panisse Menu Cookbook* (New York: Random House, 1982), p. 165.

44. Boorstin, *Democratic Experience*, p. 323; Waverly Root and Richard de Rochemont, *Eating in America: A History* (New York: William Morrow, 1976), p. 114; Hess and Hess, *Taste*, pp. 152–72; James Villas, *American Taste: A Celebration of Gastronomy Coast-to-Coast* (New York: Arbor House, 1982); Perla Meyers, *The Peasant Kitchen: A Return to Simple Good Food* (New York: Harper & Row, 1975). On the vernacular vs. cultivated traditions: John A. Kouwenhoven, *The Arts in Modern American Civilization* (New York: Norton, 1967), pp. 13–74.

45. *Last Whole Earth Catalog*, pp. 80–81. Callenbach quoted in *The Briarpatch Book* (San Francisco: New Glide, 1978), p. 16. Angier quoted in *Last Whole Earth Catalog*, p. 192. *Dairy Goat Guide* quoted in ibid., p. 64. For the "new provincialism" in 1970s alternative media: Armstrong, *Trumpet to Arms*, pp. 201–24.

46. Hess and Hess, *Taste of America*, p. 153.

47. Ralph Larkin and Daniel Foss, "Lexicon of Folk-Etymology," in Sohnya Sayres et al., *The 60s Without Apology* (Minneapolis: University of Minnesota Press, 1984), pp. 373–74.

48. E.g., "Too Many Vitamins, Not Enough Milk," *Northwest Passage*, January 4, 1971, p. 24; "Food," *Quicksilver Times*, July 14, 1970, p. 18; "The Belly of the Beast," *off our backs*, February 26, 1971, p. 15; "Power to the Lifestyle," *Good Times*, May 28, 1971, p. 12.

49. Snyder reprinted in *Mother Earth News*, January 1970, p. 4.

50. David E. Shi, *The Simple Life: Plain Living and High Thinking in American Culture* (New York: Oxford University Press, 1985), p. 49.

CHAPTER 4. ORGANIC FORCE

1. Elsa Gidlow, "Notes on Organic Gardening," *Oracle* #3 (Spring 1967), n.p.

2. Raymond Williams, *Keywords* (New York: Oxford University Press, 1976), pp. 189–92. On turn-of-the-nineteenth-century neomedievalism: T. J. Jackson Lears, *No Place of Grace: Antimodernism and the Transformation of American Culture, 1880–1920* (New York: Pantheon Books, 1981), pp. 141–81.

3. *The Last Whole Earth Catalog* (Menlo Park, Calif.: Portola Institute, 1971), p. 46. Gandhi quoted in Lane De Moll and Gigi Coe, eds., *Stepping Stones: Appropriate Technology and Beyond* (New York: Schocken

Books, 1978), p. 68. Indore method described in Robert Rodale, ed., *The Basic Book of Organic Gardening* (New York: Ballantine Books, 1971), pp. 59–61.

4. Wade Greene, "Guru of the Organic Food Cult," *New York Times Magazine*, June 6, 1971, pp. 30ff; *Encyclopedia of Organic Gardening* (Emmaus, Pa.: Rodale Books, 1978), pp. 956–58. According to Greene, farm chemical use actually increased sevenfold between 1940 and 1971.

5. Robert Rodale, "The New 'Back to the Land' Movement," *Organic Gardening and Farming*, September 1969, pp. 21–24; *Last Whole Earth Catalog*, p. 50; Greene, "Guru," p. 31.

6. Jerome Goldstein, "Organic Force," in Richard Merrill, ed., *Radical Agriculture* (New York: New York University Press, 1976), pp. 212, 214. The following summary is also based on: Murray Bookchin, "Radical Agriculture," in Merrill, pp. 3–13; Wendell Berry, "Where Cities and Farms Come Together," in Merrill, pp. 14–25; William H. Hylton, ed., *Organically Grown Foods: What They Are and Why You Need Them* (Emmaus, Pa.: Rodale Press, 1973).

7. Barry Commoner, "The Uses of Power," in Joan Dye Gussow, ed., *The Feeding Web: Issues in Nutritional Ecology* (Palo Alto, Calif.: Bull Publishing, 1978), pp. 300–306; David Pimental et al., "Food Production and the Energy Crisis," in ibid., pp. 294–99. On nature's adaptation to pesticides: Rachel Carson, *Silent Spring* (New York: Fawcett Crest, 1962), pp. 217–31; Rodale, *Basic Book of Organic Gardening*, p. 228.

8. Due largely to economic trends and government policies that favored the most heavily capitalized operations, between 1945 and 1970 25 million Americans had left agricultural areas, most of them poor and black. Marty Jezer, "Future Farmers," in *Working Papers for a New Society* 4 (Summer 1976): 67. Over 900,000 family farms were lost between 1954 and 1960 alone. Gilbert C. Fite, *American Farmers: The New Minority* (Bloomington: Indiana University Press, 1981), p. 133.

9. Wendell Berry, "Think Little," in *A Continuous Harmony: Essays Cultural and Agricultural* (New York: Harcourt Brace Jovanovich, 1970), p. 84. E. F. Schumacher, *Small Is Beautiful: Economics as if People Mattered* (New York: Harper & Row, 1973).

10. Frank Kathman, "Heap Good Garbage . . . The Story of Compost," *Northwest Passage*, March 29, 1971, pp. 9–10.

11. Statistics in David Moberg, "Experimenting with the Future: Alternative Institutions and American Socialism," in John Case and Rose-

mary C. R. Taylor, eds., *Co-ops, Communes, and Collectives: Experiments in Social Change in the 1960s and 1970s* (New York: Pantheon Books, 1979), pp. 285–87. Judson Jerome thought there might be 5,000–10,000 rural communes, involving 300,000 people. *Families of Eden: Communes and the New Anarchism* (New York: Seabury, 1974), p. 41. Other secondary sources on communes: William Hedgepath and Dennis Stock, *The Alternative: Communal Life in New America* (New York: Macmillan, 1970); Keith Melville, *Communes in the Counterculture: Origins, Theories, Styles of Life* (New York: William Morrow, 1972); Dolores Hayden, *Seven American Utopias: The Architecture of Communitarian Socialism, 1790–1975* (Cambridge, Mass.: MIT Press, 1976); Theodore Roszak, ed., *Sources* (New York: Harper Colophon Books, 1972); Laurence Veysey, *The Communal Experience: Anarchist and Mystical Communities in 20th Century America* (Chicago: University of Chicago Press, 1978); Rosabeth Moss Kanter, *Commitment and Community: Communes and Utopias in Sociological Perspective* (Cambridge: Harvard University Press, 1972); Robert Houriet, *Getting Back Together* (New York: Coward, McCann & Geoghegan, 1971).

12. Mark Kramer, *Mother Pig and the Pig Tragedy* (New York: Alfred A. Knopf, 1972), p. 7; Berry, "Discipline and Hope," in *Continuous Harmony*, p. 168.

13. *Last Whole Earth Catalog*, p. 177.

14. Hayden quoted in Richard Fairfield, ed., *Utopia U.S.A.* (San Francisco: Alternatives Foundation, 1972), p. 102. Also: Houriet, *Getting Back Together*, p. 403; Richard Lovin, "The Concrete Commune," in Fairfield, *Utopia*, pp. 132–133.

15. Mason Dixon, "Country Communes Escapist?" in Fairfield, *Utopia*, pp. 102–5; editorial, "Organic Revolution," *Northwest Passage*, March 29, 1971, p. 3.

16. Lucy Horton, *Country Commune Cooking* (New York: Coward, McCann & Geoghegan, 1972), p. 17; Jerome, *Families of Eden*, p. 41.

17. elaine sundancer, *celery wine: story of a country commune* (Yellow Springs, Ohio: Community Publications Cooperative, 1973), p. 134.

18. Ibid.

19. Ibid., p. 135.

20. *January Thaw: People at Blue Mountain Ranch Write About Living Together in the Mountains* (New York: Times Change Press, 1974), p. 35.

263

21. *Last Whole Earth Catalog,* p. 181.

22. Patsy Richardson, "No More Freefolk," (1970) in Roszak, *Sources,* pp. 308–10; Paul Williams, *Apple Bay, or Life on the Planet* (New York: Warner Books, 1976), p. 2; Raymond Mungo, *Total Loss Farm: A Year in the Life* (New York: E. P. Dutton, 1970), p. 136.

23. "Cops Commune," in Fairfield, *Utopia,* pp. 174–75; Robin Morgan, "Free All Sisters," *Rat,* August 12, 1969, p. 10; editorial, *Good Times,* May 14, 1970, p. 5.

24. Robin Morgan, "Goodbye to All That," *Observer,* March 11, 1970, pp. 6–7; Vivian Estellachild, "Two Hip Communes: A Personal Experience," in Fairfield, *Utopia,* p. 191.

25. David E. Shi, *The Simple Life: Plain Living and High Thinking in American Culture* (New York: Oxford University Press, 1985), pp. 137–38.

26. Estellachild, "Two Hip Communes," p. 190; Kit Leder, "Women in Communes," in *Last Whole Earth Catalog,* p. 222; Sally Hacker, "Farming Out the Home: Women and Agribusiness," in Jane Rachel Kaplan, ed., *A Woman's Conflict: The Special Relationship Between Women and Food* (Englewood Cliffs, N.J.: Prentice-Hall, 1980), p. 235; Jeanne Tetrault and Sherry Thomas, eds., *Country Women: A Handbook for the New Farmer* (Garden City, N.Y.: Anchor Books, 1976).

27. According to David Moberg, about 1,000 rural communes remained by 1978. Moberg, "Experimenting with the Future," pp. 285–86. Rodale quoted in Jezer, "Future Farmers," p. 72.

28. Nancy Jack Todd, ed., *The Book of the New Alchemists* (New York: E. P. Dutton, 1977); Gil Friend, "Nurturing a Responsible Agriculture," in Lane De Moll and Gigi Coe, eds., *Stepping Stones: Appropriate Technology and Beyond* (New York: Schocken Books, 1978), pp. 146–57; Merrill, ed., *Radical Agriculture*; Daniel Zwerdling, "Curbing the Chemical Fix: Organic Farming: The Secret Is It Works!" *Progressive,* December 1978, pp. 16–25; "Rodale Reaches for the Mainstream," *Business Week,* October 27, 1980, pp. 85–86. For the Rodale overview of the entire U.S. food system: *Empty Breadbasket? The Coming Challenge to America's Food Supply and What We Can Do About It* (Emmaus, Pa.: Rodale Press, 1981).

29. Kramer, *Mother Pig,* p. 188; *Three Farms: Making Milk, Meat, and Money from the American Soil* (Boston: Little, Brown, 1980); Jim Hightower, *Eat Your Heart Out: Food Profiteering in America* (New York: Crown

Publishers, 1975). Other book-length extensions of underground press themes included: Wendell Berry, *The Unsettling of America: Culture and Agriculture* (San Francisco: Sierra Club Books, 1977); Catharine Lerza and Michael Jacobson, eds., *Food for People, Not for Profit* (New York: Ballantine Books, 1975).

30. sundancer, *celery wine*, p. 156.

31. alicia bay laurel, *Living on the Earth* (New York: Vintage Books, 1971). Publication details are from David Gates, "Author Alicia Bay Laurel," *Boston Phoenix*, June 15, 1971, p. 12.

32. Moonwoman, review, *Good Times*, March 26, 1971, p. 18; Elizabeth Schiff Glassman, review, *off our backs*, May 6, 1971, p. 9; "Her Hymn to Nature Is a Guidebook for the Simplest of Lives," *New York Times*, March 26, 1971, p. 34; Christopher Lehmann-Haupt, review, *New York Times*, March 25, 1971, p. 37; Gates, "Author Alicia Bay Laurel," p. 12.

33. Gates, p. 12; Alicia Bay Laurel and Ramon Sender, *Being of the Sun* (New York: Harper & Row, 1973).

34. Jeanie Darlington, review, *Good Times*, May 28, 1971, p. 22; Nika Hazelton, *New York Times Book Review*, December 12, 1971, p. 31. Lappé recounts her recent experiences in *Diet for a Small Planet: 10th Anniversary Edition* (New York: Ballantine Books, 1982), pp. 23–24. For other food activist outgrowths of the late 1960s: Bill Valentine and Frances Moore Lappé, *What Can We Do? Food and Hunger: How You Can Make a Difference* (San Francisco: Institute for Food and Development Policy, 1980).

35. Books not previously cited: Gene Marine and Judith Van Allen, *Food Pollution: The Violation of Our Inner Ecology* (New York: Holt, Rinehart & Winston, 1972); Ross Hume Hall, *Food for Nought: The Decline in Nutrition* (New York: Vintage Books, 1976); Jacqueline Verrett and Jean Carper, *Eating May Be Hazardous to Your Health* (New York: Simon & Schuster, 1974); Ernest Callenbach, *Ecotopia: The Novel of Your Future* (New York: Bantam Books, 1975).

265

36. Richard J. Margolis, "Coming Together the Cooperative Way: Its Origins, Development, and Prospects," *New Leader*, April 17, 1972, pp. 6, 19. The following also draws heavily on William Ronco, *Food Co-ops* (Boston: Beacon Press, 1974); Daniel Zwerdling, "The Uncertain Revival of Food Cooperatives," in Case and Taylor, *Co-ops, Communes, and Collectives*, pp. 89–111.

37. "The Age of Acquireous," *Good Times*, December 11, 1970, p. 10; Windcatcher, "There's No Reason Why We Can't Exchange Our Goods and Smoke Our Money," *Good Times*, July 17, 1969, p. 7.

38. "Big Boycott Battle Shapes Up in Berkeley," *Berkeley Barb*, May 13, 1966, p. 1; "Boycott Safeway," *Good Times*, April 16, 1969, p. 5; Gordon Inkeles, "Free Your Food," *Good Times*, March 5, 1970, p. 21; Jerry Walker, "Cheap Eats," *Good Times*, April 2, 1970, p. 10; "Crack Down on Food," *Good Times*, September 3, 1971, p. 18.

39. Ronco, *Food Co-ops*, pp. 103–4; Marine and Van Allen, *Food Pollution*, p. 336; Roger Lovin, "Concrete Commune," in Fairfield, *Utopia*, pp. 132–33.

40. Zwerdling, "Uncertain Revival," p. 98.

41. "The Campus Whole Earth Co-op," *Organic Gardening and Farming*, September 1970, p. 73; Garrett De Bell, ed., *The Environmental Handbook* (New York: Ballantine Books, 1970), p. 306.

42. Laurel Robertson, Carol Flinders, and Bronwen Godfrey, *Laurel's Kitchen* (New York: Bantam Books, 1978), pp. 14–16.

43. Zwerdling, "Uncertain Revival," pp. 90–92.

44. Garrison Keillor, *Lake Wobegon Days* (New York: Penguin Books, 1986), pp. 118–19; Daniel Zwerdling, "Shopping Around: Nonprofit Food," *Working Papers for a New Society* 4 (Summer 1975): 25.

45. "Food," *Good Times*, April 9, 1970, p. 13; "Food Co-ops," in Fairfield, *Utopia*, p. 136; Jerry Walker, "Eat," *Good Times*, April 23, 1970, p. 9; Zwerdling, "Shopping Around," pp. 25, 24.

46. "Food Co-ops," in Fairfield, *Utopia*, p. 136.

47. Zwerdling, "Shopping Around," pp. 24–27; Ronco, *Food Co-ops*, p. 93.

48. Zwerdling, "Shopping Around," p. 22; Zwerdling, "Uncertain Revival," pp. 100–110; Moberg, "Experimenting with the Future," pp. 283–84; John Magney, "New Wave Co-ops Prosper," *In These Times*, November 5–11, 1980, p. 24; Sam Zuckerman, "Food Co-ops Face Tough Times," *Nutrition Action*, March 1984, pp. 6–9.

49. On the commercial "middle underground": Jock Young, "The Hippie Solution," in Ian Taylor and Laurie Taylor, eds., *Politics and*

Deviance (Harmondsworth, England: Penguin Books, 1973), pp. 182–208.

50. Alice Waters, *The Chez Panisse Menu Cookbook* (New York: Random House, 1982), pp. 3–8; Barbara Kafka, "Très Fresh!" *Vogue*, November 1982, pp. 368–71ff; Alice May Brock, *My Life as a Restaurant* (Woodstock, N.Y.: Overlook Press, 1975), pp. 139–42.

51. "Mother Courage Restaurant," in Kirsten Grimstad and Susan Rennie, eds., *The New Woman's Survival Catalog* (New York: Coward, McCann & Geoghegan, 1973).

52. Raymond Mungo, *Cosmic Profit* (Boston: Little, Brown, 1980), pp. 117–20; recent Dragonwagon information from book jacket of *I Hate My Brother Harry* (New York: Harper & Row, 1983).

53. Mollie Katzen, ed., *The Moosewood Cookbook* (Berkeley, Calif.: Ten Speed Press, 1977), pp. vii–viii.

54. Mungo, *Cosmic Profit*, p. 124; Michael Phillips, "The Restaurant That Does Everything Wrong," in *The Briarpatch Book* (San Francisco: New Glide, 1978), pp. 48–51.

55. Charles Perry, *The Haight-Ashbury: A History* (New York: Random House, 1984), pp. 77, 295; John O'Rourke, " 'Hip' to Health Foods," *Organic Gardening and Farming*, October 1969, pp. 60–62.

56. O'Rourke, " 'Hip,' " pp. 60–62; "Age of Acquireous," p. 10; "Organic Merchants," *Good Times*, October 16, 1969, p. 10.

57. "The 'Nowhere' Store That's Going Places," *Organic Gardening and Farming*, August 1970, p. 59; Phyllis Glazer, "Shopping and Eating Nature's Way," *Real Paper*, August 11, 1976, p. 19; Jack Cook, "Erewhon: Purveyor of Natural Foods," *Blair and Ketchum's Country Journal*, March 1978, p. 35.

58. Cook, "Erewhon," pp. 34–40; David Armstrong, *A Trumpet to Arms: Alternative Media in America* (Boston: South End Press, 1981), pp. 277–82, 303; Mungo, *Cosmic Profit*, p. 130; Peter Barry Chowka, "Natural Foods: Commodity in Crisis," *New Age*, p. 34.

267

59. Mungo, *Cosmic Profit*, pp. 95–102.

60. Ibid., p. 101.

61. On little vs. small business: Joseph Dexter Phillips, *Little Business in the American Economy* (Urbana: University of Illinois Press, 1958),

pp. 8–20; Rowland Berthoff, "Independence and Enterprise: Small Business in the American Dream," in Stuart Bruchey, ed., *Small Business in American Life* (New York: Columbia University Press, 1980), pp. 28–48. On Siegel: Steven Haines, "Celestial Reasonings," *Whole Food Natural Foods Guide* (Berkeley, Calif.: Whole Foods Publishing Co., 1979), pp. 287–94; Janet Neiman and Jennifer Pendleton, "Celestial Fits Kraft to a Tea," *Advertising Age*, March 26, 1984, p. 73; "Celestial Low Life," *In These Times*, November 1, 1987, p. 5. When, in 1988, tea rival R. C. Bigelow filed an antitrust suit to block Lipton's acquisition of Celestial Seasonings, Kraft decided to sell to Vestar Capital Partners instead. Judann Dagnoli, "Bigelow Tea Suit Keeps Boiling," *Advertising Age*, September 26, 1988, p. 67.

62. Moberg, "Experimenting with the Future," p. 281; Armstrong, *Trumpet to Arms*, p. 292; *Briarpatch Book*, pp. vii–xiii.

63. Andy Alpine, "Creating a Briarpatch Society," *Briarpatch Book*, p. 22.

64. "Management in the Briarpatch," *Briarpatch Book*, p. 32.

65. Ibid., p. 28.

66. *Briarpatch Book*, p. viii; "The 'Nowhere' Store," p. 59; Mungo, *Cosmic Profit*, p. 105.

67. Chowka, "Natural Foods," p. 34.

68. Nina Martin, "Steve's Entangled in Cold War Over Ice Cream," *Washington Post*, January 14, 1985, p. 1; Chowka, "Natural Foods," p. 34. As of early 1989, however, Herrell's was beginning to expand. "I Scream, You Scream," *Newsweek*, January 2, 1989, p. 50. For another ongoing hip ice cream saga—Ben & Jerry's: Erik Larson, "Forever Young," *Inc.*, July 1988, pp. 50–62.

69. On the "product life cycle": Philip Kotler, *Marketing Management*, 4th ed. (Englewood Cliffs, N.J.: Prentice-Hall, 1980, pp. 289–309.

70. Michael Phillips, "The Joy of Business," in *Briarpatch Book*, p. 106.

71. Zwerdling, "Uncertain Revival," p. 110; Paul Starr, "The Phantom Community," in Case and Taylor, *Co-ops, Communes and Collectives*, p. 268.

72. For postmortems: Todd Gitlin, *The Sixties: Years of Hope, Days of Rage* (New York: Bantam Books, 1987), pp. 408–38; Abe Peck, *Uncov-*

ering the Sixties: The Life and Times of the Underground Press (New York: Pantheon Books, 1985), pp. 287–325. For televised "creative coping" in the postliberal 1980s: Gitlin, *Inside Prime Time* (New York: Pantheon Books, 1983), pp. 312–13.

73. Armstrong, *Trumpet to Arms*, pp. 255–72; Langdon Winner, "Building the Better Mousetrap: Appropriate Technology as a Social Movement," in Franklin A. Long and Alexandra Oleson, eds., *Appropriate Technology and Social Values: A Critical Appraisal* (Cambridge, Mass,: Ballinger Publishing Co., 1980), p. 43; "The Red Chef," "Eating It: A Gluttonous Guide to Bean City," *Real Paper*, September 19, 1973, p. 18; Mark Zanger, *Robert Nadeau's Guide to Boston Restaurants* (Boston: World Food Press, 1978), p. 5.

74. E.g.: George Will, "Sandbox 'Revolutions,' " *Washington Post*, June 1, 1978, p. A15; Fred Block, "The New Left Grows Up," *Working Papers*, September 1978, pp. 41–49; Robert Goldstein, "Woodstock: The Way We Were," *Washington Post*, August 15, 1979, p. B1. Recent examples: "The Graying of Aquarius," *Newsweek*, March 30, 1987, pp. 56–58; Daniel Goleman, "Profiting from Experience," *New Age Journal*, April 1986, pp. 32–37ff.

75. The "settling down" thesis was popularized by Laurence Kasdan's 1983 hit film, *The Big Chill*; but there was a less well-known alternative: the "older, wiser, and still committed" portrait in John Sayles's *Return of the Secaucus Seven* (1981).

CHAPTER 5. THE ORTHODOX DEFENSE

1. Jim Hightower, *Eat Your Heart Out* (New York: Vintage Books, 1976), p. 110; Stan Cohen, *Folk Devils and Moral Panics* (London: MacGibbon & Kee, 1972), p. 160.

2. John Clarke et al., "Subcultures, Cultures, and Class," in Stuart Hall and Tony Jefferson, eds., *Resistance Through Rituals: Youth Subcultures in Post-War Britain* (London: Hutchinson, 1976), p. 40.

3. Jim Mintz, "Boston's Agri-Biz Academics: Go Ahead and Eat It!" *Real Paper*, December 4, 1976, p. 19; Benjamin Rosenthal, Michael Jacobson, and Marcy Bohm, "Professors on the Take," *Progressive*, November 1976, pp. 42–47; Judith Van Allen, "Eating It! From Here to 2001," *Ramparts*, May 1972, pp. 27–30; Hightower, *Eat Your Heart Out*, pp. 108–12; Frederick J. Stare and Elizabeth M. Whalen, *Panic in the*

Pantry (New York: Atheneum, 1975) quoted in *Health Foods and Natural Vitamins Market* (New York: Frost & Sullivan, 1979), p. 33. For the historical roots of these alliances: Harvey Levenstein, *Revolution at the Table* (New York: Oxford University Press, 1988).

4. James Trager, "Health Food: Why and Why Not," *Vogue*, January 1, 1971, p. 134. On the rationale for setting up committees of proindustry experts, see *Food Technology*, June 1972, pp. 11–13, and the monthly column on the Institute of Food Technologists' "Public Information Program," 1972–82. On the "special press seminars" of the Grocery Manufacturers of America: William O. Beers, "Openly Confronting Public Anxieties over Food Safety," *Food Product Development*, July–August 1976, p. 33.

5. "Organic Foods," *Food Technology*, January 1974, pp. 71–74. Another much-quoted compendium of expert opinion was "Nutrition Misinformation and Food Faddism," the July 1974 issue of *Nutrition Reviews* —funded by the pro-industry Nutrition Foundation.

6. For a taste of the case against nature, see the previous two articles and James J. Albrecht, "What About Chemicals in Foods?" *Fast Food*, March 1972, p. 14; Hilda S. White, "The Organic Food Movement: What It Is and What the Food Industry Should Do About It," *Food Technology*, April 1972, pp. 29–33; "Nutritional Claims for 'Natural Foods' Questioned in IFT Annual Report," *Food Product Development*, December 1972, p. 62; William J. Darby, "Fulfilling the Scientific Community's Responsibilities for Nutrition and Safety," *Food Technology*, August 1972, pp. 35–37; Vernal S. Packard, *Processed Foods and the Consumer: Additives, Labeling, Standards, and Nutrition* (Minneapolis: University of Minnesota Press, 1976); and the essays and advertisements collected in Joan Dye Gussow, ed., *The Feeding Web: Issues in Nutritional Ecology* (Palo Alto, Calif.: Bull Publishing, 1978), pp. 119–204.

7. Beers, "Openly Confronting," p. 33.

8. Natalie Gittelson, "The $2 Billion Health Food . . . Fraud?" *Harpers Bazaar*, November 1972, p. 33; T. J. White, "Pesticides, Pollution, Politics, and Public Relations," in Phillip O. Foss, ed., *Politics and Ecology* (Belmont, Calif.: Wadsworth, 1972), p. 152.

9. Michael F. Jacobson, *Eater's Digest: The Consumer's Factbook of Food Additives* (Garden City, N.Y.: Doubleday, 1971), pp. 15–16.

10. White, "Pesticides, Pollution, Politics," p. 151; Jamie Whitten, *That We May Live* (New York: Litton, 1966). On the persistence of pest

losses despite the chemical escalation: Rachel Carson, *Silent Spring* (New York: Fawcett Crest, 1962), pp. 217–31; John L. Hess and Karen Hess, *The Taste of America* (New York: Penguin Books, 1977), pp. 318–22. About a fifth of the nation's crops were lost to pests in 1986—about the same percentage as in 1945, before widespread chemical usage. "Silent Spring Revisited?" *Newsweek*, July 14, 1986, p. 73.

11. Arthur J. Snider, "Beware Back-to-Nature Fads," *Science Digest*, September 1972, p. 48.

12. Hightower, *Eat Your Heart Out*, pp. 71–72.

13. Earl Butz quoted in Hess and Hess, *Taste of America*, p. 316. Pennwalt ad in Tom Turner, "The New, Improved Ecopornography," in Garrett De Bell, ed., *The Environmental Handbook*, 2nd edition (New York: Ballantine Books, 1980), p. 229.

14. Stare quoted in *Food Additives Market* (New York: Frost & Sullivan, 1978), p. 13; Dena Cederquist, "Questions and Answers," in Gussow, *Feeding Web*, p. 127.

15. Cederquist, p. 127; "Natural Poisons in Food," *FDA Consumer*, October 1975, p. 6.

16. Firmenich ad, "The way to a woman's heart is through their stomachs," in Gussow, *Feeding Web*, p. 178.

17. U.S. Congress, Senate Select Committee on Nutrition and Human Needs, Panel on Nutrition and Availability, *Report and Recommendations* (Washington, D.C.: GPO, June 1974), pp. 2–3.

18. Roy Teraniski and Robert A. Flath, eds., *Flavor Research: Recent Advances* (New York: Marcel Dekker, 1981), frontispiece; Kelvin Wall quoted in Charles M. Apt, ed., *Flavor: Its Chemical, Behavioral, and Commercial Aspects* (Boulder, Colo.: Westview, 1978), p. 195; "Nutrition Claims for 'Natural Foods' Questioned in IFT Annual Report," *Food Product Development*, December 1972, p. 62.

19. Durkee ads, *Food Product Development*, January 1974, February 1974; Joan Gussow, "Who's Going to Eat the Breakfast of Champions?" *Feeding Web*, p. 203; Gussow, "Whatever Happened to Food?" *Feeding Web*, pp. 200–204; "Nabisco: Diversifying Again," *Business Week*, October 20, 1980, p. 74.

20. E.g., Roland Marchand, *Advertising the American Dream: Making Way for Modernity, 1920–1940* (Berkeley: University of California Press,

271

1985); Stuart Ewen, *Captains of Consciousness: Advertising and the Social Roots of the Consumer Culture* (New York: McGraw-Hill, 1976); T. J. Jackson Lears, "From Salvation to Self-Realization: Advertising and the Therapeutic Roots of the Consumer Culture, 1880–1930," in Richard Wrightman Fox and T. J. Jackson Lears, eds., *The Culture of Consumption* (New York: Pantheon Books, 1983), pp. 1–38.

21. On cars: James J. Flink, *America Adopts the Automobile, 1895–1910* (Cambridge, Mass.: MIT Press, 1970). On cigarettes: Michael Schudson, *Advertising, the Uneasy Persuasion* (New York: Basic Books, 1984), pp. 178–208. Entertainment: Todd Gitlin, *Inside Prime Time* (New York: Pantheon Books, 1983), p. 28. Early food processing: Daniel Boorstin, *The Americans: The Democratic Experience* (New York: Vintage Books, 1974), pp. 307, 322. Frozen beans: Susan Strasser, *Never Done: A History of American Housework* (New York: Pantheon Books: 1982), pp. 272–76. Irradiated pork: Patricia Picone Mitchell, "Treating Food with Irradiation," *Washington Post*, January 22, 1984, p. L1.

22. Clarke et al., "Subcultures"; Jock Young, "The Hippie Solution: An Essay in the Politics of Leisure," in Ian Taylor and Lauri Taylor, eds., *Politics and Deviance* (Harmondsworth, England: Penguin Books, 1973), pp. 182–208.

23. Laura Shapiro, *Perfection Salad: Women and Cooking at the Turn of the Century* (New York: Farrar, Straus & Giroux, 1986), pp. 228–29; Leon P. Ullensvang, "Food Consumption Patterns in the Seventies," *Vital Speeches of the Day*, November 1969, pp. 240–46; Jean Mayer, foreword to Jacobson, *Eater's Digest*, p. xvi.

24. Ruth Schwartz Cowan, "Why I Love/Hate My Clothes Washer," *Washington Post*, February 15, 1987, p. C3. On women's convenience dilemmas: Cowan, *More Work for Mother* (New York: Basic Books, 1983); Strasser, *Never Done*; Shapiro, *Perfection Salad*; Jane Rachel Kaplan, "Introduction: Beauty and the Feast," in Kaplan, ed., *A Woman's Conflict: The Special Relationship Between Women and Food* (Englewood Cliffs, N.J.: Prentice-Hall, 1980), pp. 7–8. For establishment awareness of consumer concerns about convenience foods: "Food Shoppers' Beliefs: Myths and Realities," *FDA Consumer*, October 1974, pp. 13–15; "Nutrition Beliefs: More Fashion Than Fact," *FDA Consumer*, June 1976, pp. 25–27; "What the Industry Can Do About Growing Public Distrust," *Food Engineering*, August 1975, pp. 35–38.

25. Marylin Chou, "Welcome to the 1980s," *Food Engineering*, December 1979, p. 53; Packard, *Processed Foods and the Consumer*, p. 178; also John C. Whitaker, *Striking a Balance: Environment and Natural Re-*

272

sources in the Nixon-Ford Years (Washington, D.C.: American Enterprise Institute, 1976), pp. 24–25.

26. Lawrence D. Gibson, "The Psychology of Food," *Food Technology*, February 1981, p. 55; Charles F. Niven, "Where Should We Go From Here in Improving the U.S. Diet?" *Food Technology*, September 1978, pp. 91–93; Cederquist, "Questions and Answers," p. 127. On heart disease as an ideological emblem of affluence: Barbara Ehrenreich, *The Hearts of Men* (Garden City, N.Y.: Anchor Books, 1984), pp. 69–87.

27. On nutritionists' cultural lag: Ross Hume Hall, *Food for Nought: The Decline of Nutrition* (New York: Vintage Books, 1976), pp. 46–55, 190–258. On changing nutrient consumption: Letitia Brewster and Michael Jacobson, *The Changing American Diet* (Washington, D.C.: Center for Science in the Public Interest, 1983). On the roots of vitamin consciousness: Richard Osborn Cummings, *The American and His Food* (Chicago: University of Chicago Press, 1941), pp. 144ff; Levenstein, *Revolution at the Table*, pp. 147–72.

28. White, "Pesticides, Pollution, and Politics," p. 174. The pro-industry "moderate" position is nicely summarized by Bernard L. Oser, "Benefit/Risk: Whose? What? How Much?" *Food Technology*, August 1978, pp. 55–58. For a good sample of the vocabulary, see *Nutrition Reviews'* July 1974 attack, "Nutrition Misinformation and Food Faddism."

29. E. F. Schumacher, *Small Is Beautiful* (New York: Harper & Row, 1973), p. 58.

30. Beatrice Trum Hunter, *Consumer Beware! Your Food and What's Been Done to It* (New York: Simon & Schuster, 1971); Mrak quoted in "Organic Myths," *Newsweek*, March 11, 1974, p. 52; Maureen Meyers and Joan Gussow, "Whatever Happened to Food?" in Gussow, *Feeding Web*, p. 123.

31. "Manufacturers Spend Little on Nutrition," *Chain Store Age—Supermarkets*, March 1978, p. 88; Sheila Harty, *Hucksters in the Classroom* (Washington, D.C.: Center for the Study of Responsive Law, 1979), pp. 18–39; Danielle K. Mooney, *Mass-Merchandised Healthy Foods* (Stamford, Conn.: Business Communications Co., 1982), pp. 28–32. On earlier links between "nutrition education" and the food industry: Strasser, *Never Done*; Shapiro, *Perfection Salad*; Levenstein, *Revolution at the Table*.

32. On the politics of "variety": "In the Media's Eye," *Fast Service*, October 1976, pp. 30–33; "Food Leaders, FTC Discuss Nutrition

Drives," *Advertising Age*, June 30, 1980, p. 1; Mooney, *Mass-Merchandised Healthy Foods*, p. 30.

33. Paul Starr, *The Social Transformation of American Medicine* (New York: Basic Books, 1982), pp. 9–10, 408–11.

CHAPTER 6. THE MESS IN WASHINGTON

1. See USDA, *Food for Us All, The Yearbook of Agriculture 1969* (Washington, D.C.: GPO, 1969), pp. 66–92; *USDA, Contours of Change: The Yearbook of Agriculture 1970* (Washington, D.C.: GPO, 1970), pp. 244–357. For an overview of government's "helping hand": Jim Hightower, *Eat Your Heart Out* (New York: Vintage Books, 1976), especially pp. 231–38 on the "great grain robbery"—the Russian wheat deal. For an update: Fred Powledge, *Fat of the Land* (New York: Simon & Schuster, 1984), pp. 152–72.

2. Daniel Zwerdling, "Down on the Farm: The Seeds of Bad Policy Yield a Crop of Failure," *Progressive*, September 1983, pp. 18–23; Ward Sinclair, "Growing Broke," *Washington Post*, March 26, 1985, p. A8; Ward Sinclair, "No Chemicals? Officials Give Organic Farmer Unusual Hearing," *Washington Post*, March 4, 1986, p. A5; Daniel Zwerdling, "Curbing the Chemical Fix: Organic Farming: The Secret Is It Works!" *Progressive*, December 1978, p. 18.

3. John L. Hess and Karen Hess, *The Taste of America* (New York: Penguin Books, 1977), pp. 316, 311, 284–93; Hightower, *Eat Your Heart Out*, pp. 43–47.

4. "Backing Down on Benefits," *Time*, October 12, 1982, pp. 32–44; Robert M. Hadsell, "Food Processing: Search for Growth," in Joan Dye Gussow, ed., *The Feeding Web: Issues in Nutritional Ecology* (Palo Alto, Calif.: Bull Publishing, 1978), pp. 138–40.

5. Hightower, *Eat Your Heart Out*, pp. 222–25.

6. Jacobson and White quoted in Hightower, *Eat Your Heart Out*, p. 271; Ross Hume Hall, *Food for Nought: The Decline in Nutrition* (New York: Vintage Books, 1976), pp. 80–81; Jacqueline Verrett and Jean Carper, *Eating May Be Hazardous to Your Health* (New York: Simon & Schuster, 1974), p. 36. In private, however, industry lobbied for a relaxation of the Delany Clause, especially as new testing equipment made it easier to detect toxins at lower levels. In this they were supported by Secretary Butz and FDA Commissioner C. C. Edwards, who argued for a "safe"

level of carcinogens—an argument heard again during the Reagan administration. "Delany Amendment Under Attack Again!" *Organic Gardening
and Farming,* January 1973, pp. 128–29.

7. "A Peck of Dirt," *Newsweek,* April 10, 1972, p. 94.

8. "Nutritional Labeling: Do You Have the Answers?" *Chain Store
Age—Supermarkets,* October 1974, pp. 43–51; *Health Foods and Natural
Vitamins Market* (New York: Frost & Sullivan, 1979), pp. 184–85; "Prox-
mire Liberates Vitamins," *Business Week,* March 29, 1976, p. 36; "The
Food Fad Boom," *FDA Consumer,* December 1973, pp. 5–12; "Natural
Poisons in Food," *FDA Consumer,* October 1975, pp. 5–7.

9. John C. Whitaker: *Striking a Balance: Environment and Natural
Resources in the Nixon-Ford Years* (Washington, D.C.: American Enterprise
Institute, 1976), pp. 27–42, 125–45; Robert L. Sansom, *The New Ameri-
can Dream Machine* (Garden City, N.Y.: Anchor Books, 1976), pp. 23–62.
On the parallel "conservative assimilation of reform" of health care in the
early 1970s: Paul Starr, *The Social Transformation of American Medicine*
(New York: Basic Books, 1982), pp. 393–405.

10. For a critique of USDA pesticide policies: Harrison Wellford,
Sowing the Wind (New York: Grossman, 1972).

11. Sansom, *Dream Machine,* p. 30; Hall, *Food for Nought,* pp. 120–
31; "Silent Spring Revisited?" *Newsweek,* July 14, 1986, p. 73; David
Pimental estimated a 33-percent annual crop loss to pests despite a tenfold increase in chemical use since 1940. Ward Sinclair, "America's Pesticide Use Raises New Safety Fears," *Washington Post,* January 30, 1983,
p. A8.

12. Verrett and Carper, *Eating May Be Hazardous,* p. 216.

13. For a brief history of the FDA bans: *Health Foods and Vitamins
Market,* pp. 91–96; Molly Sinclair, "Debate over Food Safety Launched
by Cranberry Scare of '59," *Washington Post,* November 26, 1980, p. C1.
On the DES controversy and delays: Orville Schell, *Modern Meat: Anti-
biotics, Hormones, and the Pharmaceutical Farm* (New York: Random
House, 1984), pp. 181–254.

275

14. Clifford Grobstein, "Saccharin: A Scientist's View," in Robert
W. Crandall and Lester B. Lave, eds., *The Scientific Basis of Health and
Safety Regulation* (Washington, D.C.: Brookings Institution, 1981),
pp. 117–30; Oliver E. Williamson, "An Economist's View," ibid.,
pp. 131–52; Richard A. Merrill, "A Regulator's View," ibid., pp. 153–70;
"Diet Lines Getting Fatter on Shelves," *Chain Store Age—Supermarkets,*

July 1978, p. 150. On Reagan era regressions: Michael F. Jacobson, "Undoing Delany," *Nutrition Action Healthletter*, September–October 1985, p. 7; Patricia Picone Mitchell, "Battling Over Food Dye," *Washington Post*, March 31, 1985, p. H1.

15. Michael F. Jacobson, *Eater's Digest* (Garden City, N.Y.: Anchor Books, 1976), pp. 200–206; "The U.S.'s Toughest Customer," *Time*, December 12, 1969, reprinted in William T. Kelley, ed., *New Consumerism* (Columbus, Ohio: Grid, 1973), p. 57. For the activist position: Hall, *Food for Nought*, pp. 58–59, 81–82; Beatrice Trum Hunter, *The Great Nutrition Robbery* (New York: Scribner's, 1978), pp. 161–69; Maureen Meyers and Joan Gussow, "Whatever Happened to Food?" in Gussow, *Feeding Web*, pp. 122–25.

16. Jacobson, *Eater's Digest*, pp. 213–15; "Nutrient Labeling," *Chain Store Age—Supermarkets*, October 1974, pp. 43–51.

17. George E. Inglett, *Fabricated Foods* (Westport, Conn.: AVI Publishing, 1975), p. 3; Danielle K. Mooney, *Mass-Merchandised Healthy Foods* (Stamford, Conn.: Business Communications Co., 1982), pp. 28, 41; "Industry Hits FDA's Nutritional Guidelines," *Food Technology*, June 1972, pp. 24–26; Vernal S. Packard, Jr., *Processed Foods and the Consumer* (Minneapolis: University of Minnesota Press, 1976), p. 178.

18. William O. Beers, "Openly Confronting Public Anxieties over Food Safety," *Food Product Development*, July–August 1976, pp. 33–34. For consumer response to labels, e.g.: Johanna Dwyer, "Nutrition in Family Life," *Food Product Development*, November 1976, pp. 44–50; "Shoppers Good, Not Great, says FDA," *Chain Store Age—Supermarkets*, July 1977, p. 13; "Food Labels Get High Readership," *FDA Consumer*, July 1979, pp. 10–11; "Nutrition Information—Consumer's Views," *National Food Review*, Spring 1981, pp. 18–20.

19. "Mandatory Labeling Advocates Losing Ground in Washington," *Nation's Restaurant News*, October 6, 1986, p. F54; Mooney, *Healthy Foods*, pp. 152–53.

20. Lisa Belkin, "Food Labels: How Much They Do, and Don't Say," *New York Times*, September 18, 1985, p. C8; Powledge, *Fat of the Land*, pp. 195–203.

21. Albert J. Zanger, "What Was the Impact of the Choate Study on the Cereal Market?" in Kelley, *New Consumerism*, pp. 285–300; Hightower, *Eat Your Heart Out*, pp. 135–40.

22. "FTC vs. the Food Industry," *Food Engineering,* November 1980, p. 91.

23. Robert M. Liebert et al., *The Early Window: Effects of Television on Children and Youth,* 2nd ed. (New York: Pergamon, 1982), pp. 149–55.

24. Liebert, *Early Window,* p. 155; Arnold Deutsch, "Are We All Children?" *Restaurant Business,* November 1, 1978, p. 200; "New FTC Law Clarifies Mandate," *Food Engineering,* August 1980, pp. 40–42; "FTC vs. the Food Industry," p. 61. For the chairman's view, see the chapter, "Stoning the National Nanny," in Michael Pertschuk, *Revolt Against Regulation: The Rise and Pause of the Consumer Movement* (Berkeley: University of California Press, 1982), pp. 69–117.

25. "Nutrition Information—Consumers' Views," *National Food Review,* Spring 1981, p. 20. In 1973, 97 percent of those polled by the FDA wanted *more* government regulation of food advertising. H. Neal Dunning, "What Do Consumers Know About Nutrition?" *FDA Consumer,* June 1974, p. 15.

26. "The FTC as National Nanny," *Washington Post,* March 1, 1978, in Pertschuk, *Revolt,* pp. 69–70. For television-as-baby-sitter, see Marie Winn, *The Plug-In Drug: Television, Children, and the Family* (New York: Viking Penguin, 1977).

27. Merrill Brown, "Candidates Hit FTC Cereal Action," *Washington Post,* November 4, 1980, p. D7. Campaign worries also forced the FTC to drop a controversial proposal to subject restaurant menus to "truth in advertising" regulations. "FTC Backs Off," *Fast Service,* June 1980, pp. 18A–18B.

28. "FTC vs. the Food Industry," p. 61; "What Food People Want in the Next Four Years," *Food Engineering,* December 1980, pp. 22–24; Sam Zuckerman, "Food Ad Anarchy: The FTC Opts Out," *Nutrition Action,* May 1984, p. 6; Patricia Picone Mitchell, "Marketing Nutrition," *Nutrition Action,* April 24, 1983, p. L1.

29. This account is drawn from Frost & Sullivan's *Health Foods and Natural Vitamins Market,* pp. 57–79.

30. For the USDA data used in the McGovern report, see Letitia Brewster and Michael Jacobson, *The Changing American Diet* (Washington, D.C.: Center for Science in the Public Interest, 1983).

31. Mary T. O'Brien, "Senate Group Hearkens to Comments, Criticism, Revises Dietary Goals," *Food Product Development,* February 1978,

pp. 11–12; O'Brien, "Semantic Changes in the Diet Don't Alter Mc-Govern's Goals," *Food Product Development*, March 1978, pp. 76–79.

32. John Connor, "Food Product Proliferation," *National Food Review*, Summer 1980, pp. 10–12; Mel Seligsohn, "Could 50 Firms Own Food Industry in Year 2000?" *Food Engineering*, May 1980, pp. 50–55; Mooney, *Healthy Foods*, p. 38.

33. U.S. Departments of Agriculture and Health, Education, and Welfare, *Nutrition and Your Health: Dietary Guidelines for Americans* (Washington, D.C.: GPO, February 1980); Victor Cohn, "U.S. Urges Public to Eat Less of Popular Foods," *Washington Post*, February 5, 1980, p. A5.

34. Mimi Sheraton, "Conflicting Nutrition Advice Bewilders U.S. Consumers," *New York Times*, June 11, 1980, p. C14.

35. "The 'Dietary Guidelines': New Opportunities for Food Firms?" *Food Engineering*, June 1980, pp. 18–20; G. R. Jansen, "The Food and Nutrition Mosaic," *Food Technology*, p. 55; Mooney, *Healthy Foods*, pp. 31–33.

36. Cohn, "U.S. Urges"; Sarah Fritschner, "Who Gets the Pieces When They Cut Up the USDA Pie?" *Washington Post*, October 27, 1982, p. E1; John Shepard, " 'People Are Surely as Smart as Hogs . . . ' " *Environmental Action*, October 1984, pp. 26–27; "Dietary Guidelines Revised—Sort of," *Nutrition Action*, November 1985, p. 3. As the last three articles show, the "Guidelines" *were* under threat for a while. Hence, the surprise expressed in "Dietary Guidelines Escape Unscathed," *Nutrition Action*, June 1985, p. 2. For an overview of food policies in Ronald Reagan's first term: "Reagan's Banquet," *Nutrition Action*, October 1984, pp. 8–9.

37. Compare the 1973 and 1984 responses to this question: Who is most responsible for protecting one's health? In 1973, 26 percent put government first; in 1984, 18 percent. In 1973, 27 percent gave processors primary responsibility; in 1984, 11 percent. In 1973, 24 percent thought individual consumers most responsible; in 1984, 48 percent. *Food and Nutrition: Knowledge, Beliefs* (Princeton, N.J.: Response Analysis, 1974), pp. 37–38; "Harris Poll Finds Public Faith in Food Safety," *Nation's Restaurant News*, May 7, 1984, p. 100.

38. Examples of orthodox press bashing: Jansen, "Food and Nutrition Mosaic," p. 55; Victor Herbert and Stephen Barrett, *Vitamins and 'Health' Foods: The Great American Hustle* (Philadelphia: George F. Stickley, 1981), pp. 139–47; Bruce R. Stillings, "The Food Industry's Re-

sponsibilities in Food and Nutrition Education," *Food Technology*, December 1980, p. 64; Arthur T. Schramm, "State of the Institute," *Food Technology*, August 1982, pp. 8–20; Charles F. Niven, "Where Should We Go from Here in Improving the U.S. Diet?" *Food Technology*, September 1978, p. 92.

CHAPTER 7. THE PRESS

1. On earlier media campaigns against folk wisdom: Stuart Ewen, *Captains of Consciousness: Advertising and the Social Root of Consumer Culture* (New York: McGraw-Hill, 1976); Roland Marchand, *Advertising the American Dream: Making Way for Modernity, 1920–1940* (Berkeley: University of California Press, 1985); Harvey A. Levenstein, *Revolution at the Table: The Transformation of the American Diet* (New York: Oxford University Press, 1988); Paul Starr, *The Social Transformation of American Medicine: The Rise of a Sovereign Profession and the Making of a Vast Industry* (New York: Basic Books, 1982). Recent surveys: "H. Neal Dunning, "What Do Consumers Know About Nutrition?" *FDA Consumer*, June 1974, p. 15; *Health Foods and Natural Vitamins Market* (New York: Frost & Sullivan, 1979), p. 97; *Nutrition: A Study of Consumers' Attitudes and Behavior Towards Eating at Home and Out of Home* (New York: Yankelovich, Skelly & White, 1978); "Nutrition Information—Consumers' Views," *National Food Review*, Spring 1981, pp. 18–19.

2. A good parallel was how mainstream media treated Vietnam. As the furor over the war threatened to destroy American society, some influential editors began to promote an end to the bombing of North Vietnam, which they viewed as a "pragmatic" compromise between immediate withdrawal (the left "extreme") and further escalation (the right "extreme.") Illustrating hegemony's "moving equilibrium," opinion leaders adjusted for the sake of long-term interests. For further treatment of hegemony theory: Todd Gitlin, *The Whole World Is Watching: Mass Media in the Making and Unmaking of the New Left* (Berkeley: University of California Press, 1980), pp. 9–11, 249–92.

3. Michael Parenti, *Inventing Reality: The Politics of the Mass Media* (New York: St. Martin's Press, 1986), p. 62; Judith Van Allen, "Eating It! From Here to 2001," *Ramparts*, May 1972, pp. 27–30; Choate quoted in John L. Hess and Karen Hess, *The Taste of America* (New York: Penguin Books, 1977), p. 319; U.S. Congress, Senate Select Committee on Nutrition and Human Needs, *Dietary Goals for the United States*, 2nd ed. (Washington, D.C.: GPO, 1977), pp. 59–64; Jim Hightower, *Eat Your Heart Out* (New York: Vintage Books, 1976), pp. 135–53. Citing previous

FTC studies, Hightower suggested that as the number of firms within an industry *declined,* advertising expenditures *increased*—and so did prices and profits (p. 137). A 1979 USDA study estimated that food industry concentration cost consumers between $10 billion and $15 billion a year —5.7 percent of the overall food bill. Fred Powledge, *Fat of the Land* (New York: Simon & Schuster, 1984), p. 68.

4. Herbert J. Gans, *Deciding What's News* (New York: Vintage Books, 1980), p. 256.

5. Kathryn Weibel, *Mirror Mirror: Images of Women Reflected in Popular Culture* (Garden City, N.Y.: Anchor Books, 1977), p. 152; Laura Shapiro, *Perfection Salad: Women and Cooking at the Turn of the Century* (New York: Farrar, Straus & Giroux, 1986), pp. 226, 228.

6. Two classic documentary exposés of extremes: CBS's 1960 "Harvest of Shame," and the 1973 ABC, "Food: Green Grow the Profits." On Soviet failures: Parenti, *Inventing Reality*, pp. 130–47.

7. James Trager, "Health Food: Why and Why Not," *Vogue,* January 1, 1971, p. 122. Gans ties this faith in experts to Progressive alliances between muckrakers and rising professionals: *Deciding What's News,* pp. 204–11.

8. On expert lag: Ross Hume Hall, *Food for Nought: The Decline in Nutrition* (New York: Vintage Books, 1976), pp. 179–218; R. F. Kandel and G. H. Pelto, "The Health Food Movement: Social Revitalization or Alternative Health Maintenance System?" in Norge W. Jerome, Kandel, and Pelto, eds., *Nutritional Anthropology* (Pleasantville, N.Y.: Redgrave Publishing Co., 1980), pp. 327–63; Patrick Conover, *The Alternate Culture and Contemporary Communes: A Partly Annotated Bibliography* (Monticello, Ill.: Council of Planning Librarians Exchange Bibliography #952, January 1976); Daniel Zwerdling, "Curbing the Chemical Fix: Organic Farming: The Secret Is It Works!" *Progressive,* December 1978, pp. 16–25.

9. On frames: Gitlin, *Whole World,* pp. 7–8; Parenti, *Inventing Reality,* pp. 220–22.

10. Elizabeth Lansing, "The Move to Eat Natural," *Life,* December 11, 1970, p. 48; "The Stuff of Life," *Newsweek,* May 25, 1970, p. 100; Sara Davidson, "Open Land: Getting Back to the Communal Garden," *Harper's,* June 1970, pp. 91–102.

11. "Organic Foods: Not So Pure," *Business Week,* February 12, 1972, p. 21; "Rotton Apples," *Newsweek,* p. 72; "Stuff of Life," p. 100.

12. "Organic Foods: Not So Pure," p. 21; "The Attorney General vs. Phony Health-Food Claims," *Changing Times*, May 1973, pp. 24–27.

13. Reported in *Health Foods and Natural Vitamins Market*, pp. 231–33.

14. Wade Greene, "Guru of the Organic Food Cult," *New York Times Magazine*, June 6, 1971, p. 30; "The High Priestess of Nutrition," *Time*, December 18, 1972, p. 72; Natalie Gittelson, "The $2 Billion Health Food . . . Fraud?" *Harpers Bazaar*, November 1972, p. 33.

15. "Eating May Not Be Good for You," *Time*, December 18, 1972, p. 69; Daniel Zwerdling, "The Uncertain Revival of Food Cooperatives," in John Case and Rosemary C. R. Taylor, eds., *Co-ops, Communes, and Collectives* (New York: Pantheon Books, 1979), p. 89.

16. William H. Hylton, ed., *Organically Grown Foods: What They Are and Why You Need Them* (Emmaus, Pa.: Rodale Press, 1973), pp. 27–35; Jerome Goldstein, "Are We Burying the Organic Food Industry?" *Organic Gardening and Farming*, September 1972, pp. 40–45; "Organic Foods: Not So Pure," p. 21.

17. Trager, "Health Food," p. 122.

18. E.g., Gerald Carson, *Cornflake Crusade* (New York: Rinehart, 1957); Ronald Deutsch, *The Nuts Among the Berries* (New York: Ballantine Books, 1961); Alice Felt Tyler, *Freedom's Ferment* (Minneapolis: University of Minnesota Press, 1944); Richard Hofstadter, *The Age of Reform: From Bryan to F.D.R.* (New York: Vintage Books, 1955); Christopher Lasch, *The New Radicalism in America, 1889–1963: The Intellectual as a Social Type* (New York: Vintage Books, 1965).

19. Trager, "Health Foods," p. 122.

20. Corinne H. Robinson, *Fundamentals of Normal Nutrition* (New York: Macmillan, 1968), p. 40; Frederick J. Stare and Margaret McWilliams, *Living Nutrition* (New York: John Wiley & Sons, 1973), p. 122; Gifft and Washbon quoted in Gail Chapman Hongladarom, "Health Seeking Within the Health Food Movement," (Ph.D dissertation, University of Washington, 1976), p. 91.

21. R. Schafer and E. A. Yetley, "Social Psychology of Food Faddism, Speculations on Health Food Behavior" (1975), quoted in Diva Sanjur, ed., *Social and Cultural Perspectives in Nutrition* (Englewood Cliffs, N.J.: Prentice-Hall, 1982), p. 129; Trager, "Health Foods," p. 136; Tom Wolfe, "The Me Decade and the Third Great Awakening," in *Mauve*

Gloves & Madmen, Clutter & Vine (New York: Bantam Books, 1977), pp. 111–47.

22. *Journal of the American Medical Association* (1971), quoted in Robinson, *Fundamentals*, p. 400.

23. "Kosher of the Counterculture," *Time*, November 16, 1970, pp. 59–63; Joseph Bell, "Those Mushrooming Food Fads," *Seventeen*, July 1971, p. 111.

24. Lansing, "Move to Eat Natural," p. 52; "What's So Great About Health Foods?" *Life*, September 29, 1972, pp. 45–47.

25. "Kosher," p. 63; Joseph Morgenstern, "Radicalization of an Eater," *Newsweek*, January 18, 1971, p. 11; "What Tastes Terrible and Doubles in Sales Every 60 Days?" *Wall Street Journal*, February 16, 1972, p. 1; "Oh No, Not Yogurt!" *Wall Street Journal*, February 28, 1972, p. 1.

26. John Irwin, *Scenes* (Beverly Hills, Calif.: Sage, 1977), pp. 54–61, 127–31.

27. E.g., Harvey Green, *Fit for America* (New York: Pantheon Books, 1986); James C. Whorton, *Crusaders for Fitness* (Princeton: Princeton University Press, 1982); Steven Nissenbaum, *Sex, Diet, and Debility in Jacksonsian America: Sylvester Graham and Health Reform* (Westport, Conn.: Greenwood, 1980); Hongladarom, "Health Seeking"; Kandel and Pelto, "The Health Food Movement"; Frederick Stare quoted in Frost and Sullivan, *Health Foods*, pp. 111–12.

28. USDA Study Team on Organic Farming, *Report and Recommendations on Organic Farming* (Washington, D.C.: GPO, July 1980), pp. xii–xiv; Luther J. Carter, "Organic Farming Becomes 'Legitimate,' " *Science*, July 11, 1980, pp. 254–56; Jack Cook, "The Agricultural Establishment Goes Natural," *Blair and Ketchum's Country Journal*, September 1980, p. 55.

29. S. K. Levin, "USDA Threatened by Organic Farming Alternatives," *In These Times*, September 5–11, 1984, p. 5; Ward Sinclair, "More Farmers Taking the Organic Route," *Washington Post*, April 3, 1983, p. H1; Ward Sinclair, "Farm Achieves Natural Balance," *Washington Post*, March 1, 1987. p. A3; Jim Hightower, "Noose Tightens on the Family Farm," *In These Times*, October 31, 1984, p. 17; David Moberg, "Disappearing Dreams," *In These Times*, February 13, 1985, p. 8. In 1988 Ward Sinclair left the *Post* to work full-time at his Pennsylvania truck farm, the Flickerville Mountain Farm and Groundhog Ranch. On Sundays I buy his fine organic produce at the Takoma Park farmers' market.

30. Gans, *Deciding What's News*, pp. 46, 204–206.

31. E.g., "Edible Violence," *Time*, July 25, 1969, pp. 22–23; "Food Additives: Blessing or Bane?" *Time*, December 19, 1969, pp. 41–42; "The Perils of Eating, American Style," *Time*, December 18, 1972, pp. 68–76; "A Peck of Dirt,"*Newsweek*, April 10, 1972, p. 94; Tim Alexander, "The Hysteria About Additives," *Fortune*, March 1972, pp. 63ff; "Food: Green Grown the Profits," (ABC News Documentary, 1973); Albert J. Zanger, "What Was the Impact of the Choate Study on the Cereal Market?" in William Kelley, ed., *The New Consumerism* (Columbus, Ohio: Grid, 1973), pp. 285–300. For the FTC, see Chapter 6.

32. Flora Davis, "How 85,000 Women Feel About Food and Cooking," *Redbook*, January 1975, pp. 10–16; "Flap Over Food," *Life*, August 21, 1970, p. 45; "Perils of Eating," p. 76; "Are You a Consumer of Natural, Organic, Health Foods?" *Consumer Bulletin*, May 1972, p. 2; William Rice, "Food Day: You Are What You Eat," *Washington Post*, April 17, 1975, p. G1.

33. "Edible Violence," pp. 22–23; "The U.S.'s Toughest Customer," *Time*, December 12, 1969, reprinted in Kelley, *New Consumerism* (Columbus, Ohio: Grid, 1973), p. 62. On earlier consumerism: ibid., pp. 13–45.

34. "Toughest Customer," p. 52.

35. Ibid., p. 54; Marilyn Bender, "Capitalism Lives—Even in Naderland," *New York Times*, January 7, 1973, reprinted in Kelley, *New Consumerism*, pp. 65ff.

36. On hip commerce as a "safe" alternative: Armstrong, *Trumpet to Arms*, pp. 161–80; Irwin, *Scenes*, pp. 156–58; Aristides, "Boutique America," *American Scholar* 44 (Autumn 1975): 533–39.

37. Patricia Morrisroe, "Restaurant Madness," *New York*, November 26, 1984, p. 49; Daniel Pedersen, "Hold the Yeast, Pass the Quince," *Newsweek*, December 12, 1983, p. 96; Gerald Lubenow, "Palate Power in the New Berkeley," *Newsweek*, August 22, 1983, pp. 42–43; Stuart J. Elliott, "Rodale Press Getting in Shape for the '80s," *Advertising Age*, December 24, 1984, p. 4.

38. Gans, *Deciding What's News*, p. 48.

39. For end-of-the-decade recaps: Marian Burros, "The '70s: A Decade of Concern," *Washington Post*, December 30, 1979, p. B1.; Molly Sinclair, "Debate Over Food Safety Launched by Cranberry Scare of

'59," *Washington Post*, November 26, 1980, p. C1. For the same pattern in the 1980s: Don Colburn, "Pursuing the Disease of the Moment: How the Press Helps Create Health News," *Washington Post Health*, February 10, 1987, p. 7.

40. On "Social Order and National Leadership": Gans, *Deciding What's News*, pp. 52–69.

41. Rice, "Food Day," p. G1; Marian Burros, "The 1970s: A Decade of Fads . . . ," *Washington Post*, January 3, 1980, p. E1; Mimi Sheraton, "Conflicting Nutrition Advice Bewilders U.S. Consumers," *New York Times*, June 11, 1980, p. 1; "The Confusing Pursuit of Good Nutrition," *Washington Post*, July 17, 1983, p. D1; Meg Greenfield, "Give Me That Old-Time Cholesterol," *Washington Post*, June 20, 1984, p. A21; Paul Starr, *The Social Transformation of American Medicine* (New York: Basic Books, 1982), pp. 9–17.

42. "Eating May Not Be Good for You," *Time*, December 18, 1972, cover; Bob Garfield, "Eat at Your Own Risk," *Washington Post Magazine*, February 1, 1987, p. 17.

43, Jean Mayer, "Why People Don't Eat Meat," *Washington Post*, April 17, 1975, p. G5; Marian Burros, "Fiber—Fad or Necessity?" *Washington Post*, April 17, 1975, p. G1.

44. Marian Burros, "All Fiber Is Not Created Equal," *Washington Post*, January 29, 1981, p. E1; Patricia Picone Mitchell, "Varying Yardsticks Confuse the Issue," *Washington Post*, January 15, 1986, p. E1.

45. "America's Nutrition Revolution," *Newsweek*, November 19, 1984, pp. 111–18. A good summary of the early 1980s moderate consensus (identifying obvious negatives while downplaying the chemical threat) was the best-selling *Jane Brody's Nutrition Book* (1984), by the *New York Times*'s much-quoted personal health columnist.

46. For general figure trends: Lois Banner, *American Beauty* (Chicago: University of Chicago Press, 1983), pp. 283–91; William Bennett and Joel Gurin, *The Dieter's Dilemma: Eating Less and Weighing More* (New York: Basic Books, 1982), pp. 107–41, 168–209. Statistics in Paul Garfinkel and David Garner, *Anorexia Nervosa: A Multidimensional Perspective* (New York: Brunner-Mazel, 1982), reported in Harriet Edleson, "Fear of Fat: Does Obsession with Weight Reflect a Distorted Self-Image?" *Washington Post Health*, April 30, 1986, pp. 14–16. For the heavier realities: Hillel Schwartz, *Never Satisfied: A Cultural History of Diets, Fantasies, and Fat* (New York: Free Press, 1986), p. 337. According to government

data, there were just as many overweight people in 1985 as in 1965. Carole Sugarman, "Weighing the Axioms of Dieting—Then and Now," *Washington Post*, January 30, 1985, p. E1. In 1965, Americans ate 1,381 pounds of food per capita a year; in 1985, 1,431 pounds. "Consumers Not Cutting Back," *Advertising Age*, September 19, 1985, p. 16.

47. "Fashion Rises on Sunset Strip," *Men's Wear*, August 9, 1968, p. 64; "Trans-Sexual Fashion," *Men's Wear*, August 23, 1968, pp. 103–9; "Hip Hip Hooray!" *Men's Wear*, November 2, 1967, p. 74; "The Big Costume Put-On," *Saturday Evening Post*, July 27, 1968, pp. 24–29. Tads ads in *Men's Wear*, October 9, 1970, p. 130; October 23, 1970, p. 22.

48. *The Youth Culture* (Chicago: Playboy Press, 1971); "The Big Costume Put-On," *Saturday Evening Post*, July 27, 1968, pp. 24–29. On the sexualization of revolutionary gestures: David Kunzle, "Scratching Our Revolutionary Itch—How Advertising Absorbs the Imagery and Slogans of Radicalism," in Joseph Boskin, ed., *Issues in American Society* (Encino, Calif.: Glencoe Publishing Co., 1978), pp. 295–313; Valerie Carnes, "Icons of Popular Fashion," in Ray Browne and Marshall Fishwick, eds., *Icons of America* (Bowling Green, Ohio: Popular Press, 1978), pp. 228–40.

49. Frances Moore Lappé, *Diet for a Small Planet*, 3rd ed. (New York: Ballantine Books, 1982), p. 23; "Beauty Sense and Nonsense," *Harpers Bazaar*, December 1971, p. 124; Joseph Bell, "Those Mushrooming Food Fads," *Seventeen*, July 1971, p. 110; "Nature's Table," *Seventeen*, September 1971, p. 166; "Health Is Busting Out All Over," *Vogue*, February 1, 1971, p. 57.

50. For soft-core dietetic advice, see such self-oriented magazines as *Vogue, Seventeen, Cosmopolitan*, and, of course, *Self*.

51. J. D. Reed, "America Shapes Up," *Time*, November 2, 1981, p. 97.

52. Ibid., pp. 95, 97. Reed's statistics were dubious. In 1987 it still seemed that only 25 percent of the adults exercised as much as twice a week. Adam Paul Weisman, "Look Who's Walking," *Washington Post*, March 24, 1987, p. 13. See Chapter 8 for more on this disparity. 285

53. E. M. Foster, "Is There a Food Safety Crisis?" *Food Technology*, August 1982, p. 92.

54. "It's Natural! It's Organic! Or Is It?" *Consumer Reports*, July 1980, pp. 410–15.

CHAPTER 8.
"OPPORTUNISM IN THE MARKETPLACE"

1. Hilda S. White, "The Organic Food Movement," *Food Technology*, April 1972, pp. 29–33; William E. Marshall, "Health Foods, Organic Foods, Natural Foods," *Food Technology*, February 1974, p. 56; George F. Stewart and Howard Mattson, "Food Advertising and Promotion—A Plea for Change," *Food Technology*, November 1978, pp. 30–33.

2. Bruce R. Stillings, "The Food Industry's Responsibilities in Food and Nutrition Education," *Food Technology*, December 1980, p. 65; "It's Natural! It's Organic! Or Is It?" *Consumer Reports*, July 1980, pp. 410–15; E. M. Foster, "Is There a Food Safety Crisis?" *Food Technology*, August 1982, p. 92.

3. Philip Kotler, *Marketing Management*, 4th ed. (Englewood Cliffs, N.J.: Prentice-Hall, 1980), p. 594. For the related resistance of engineers to "industrial design" in the 1920s and 1930s: Jeffrey L. Meikle, *Twentieth Century Limited: Industrial Design in America, 1925–1939* (Philadelphia: Temple University Press, 1979), pp. 69–84.

4. Milton Moskowitz, Michael Katz, and Robert Levering, *Everybody's Business: An Almanac* (New York: Harper & Row, 1980), pp. 10–11.

5. "Why Food Processors Are Starving for Profits," *Business Week*, December 1, 1973, p. 89; Robert M. Hadsell, "Food Processing: Search for Growth," (1971) reprinted in Joan Dye Gussow, ed., *The Feeding Web: Issues in Nutritional Ecology* (Palo Alto, Calif.: Bull Publishing, 1978), pp. 131–40; Walter Kiechel, "The Food Giants Struggle to Stay in Step with Consumers," *Fortune*, September 11, 1978, pp. 50–56; Fred Powledge, *Fat of the Land* (New York: Simon & Schuster, 1984), pp. 49–70.

6. John Connor, "Food Product Proliferation: Part II," *National Food Review*, Summer 1980, pp. 10–12; Mel Seligsohn, "Could 50 Firms Own Food Industry in Year 2000?" *Food Engineering*, May 1980, pp. 50–55.

7. S. J. Kazeniac, "Flavor Trends in Natural Foods," *Food Technology*, January 1977, pp. 26–33; Radcliffe F. Robinson, "The Future of Textured Protein Products," *Food Technology*, May 1972, pp. 59–63; W. J. Wolf, "What Is Soy Protein?" *Food Technology*, May 1972, pp. 44–54; Ruth Rosenbaum, "Today the Strawberry, Tomorrow . . ." (1976) in Gussow, *Feeding Web*, pp. 169–77.

8. Mel Seligsohn, "Food Regulations: What's Coming Down the Road?" *Food Engineering*, September 1979, pp. 50–55; Marilyn Chou, "Welcome to the 1980s," *Food Engineering*, December 1979, pp. 51–55; Michael Pertschuk, *Revolt Against Regulation: The Rise and Pause of the Consumer Movement* (Berkeley: University of California Press, 1982), pp. 47–68.

9. James J. Albrecht, "Technology's Role in Product Development," *Food Technology*, September 1982, p. 75; Trish Hall, "Changing Menu: U.S. Food Firms Face More Imports and Rise in Foreign Plants Here," *Wall Street Journal*, November 18, 1986, p. 1.

10. Alexander Schmidt quoted in *FDA Consumer*, July–August 1975, p. 3; S. R. Rothschild, "Responding to Consumer Needs in New Product Development," *Food Product Development*, February 1978, p. 17; Arnold Deutsch, "The New Food Consciousness," *Restaurant Business*, December 1, 1978, p. 162.

11. "It's Natural! It's Organic!" p. 411; Judy Brown, "Health Foods —Finding Their Way onto Supermarket Shelves," *National Food Review*, Summer 1981, pp. 18–19.

12. "Taste cultures" is from Herbert J. Gans, *Popular Culture and High Culture* (New York: Basic Books, 1974). For an overview of market segmentation: Kotler, *Marketing Management*, pp. 194–212.

13. Family wage system: Barbara Ehrenreich, *The Hearts of Men: American Dreams and the Flight from Commitment* (Garden City, N.Y.: Anchor Books, 1984), pp. 3–13.

14. "Working in the USA: New Age, Low Age," *Dollars & Sense*, April 1987, pp. 12–13; David Moberg, "Middle Class May Be Losing the Economic War of Attrition," *In These Times*, November 12–18, 1986; David Nylen, *Advertising: Planning, Implementation, and Control*, 2nd ed. (Cincinnati, Ohio: South-Western Publishing Co., 1980), p. 180; Ehrenreich, *Hearts*, p. 174; Ehrenreich, "Is the Middle Class Doomed?" *New York Times Magazine* (1986), reprinted in *Seeds*, December 1986, p. 17. The *Wall Street Journal* capsulized the trend in an article aptly titled: "Growing Gap: U.S. Rich and Poor Increase in Numbers; Middle Loses Ground," September 22, 1986, p. 1.

15. "Wienerschnitzel: Hot Dogs Again," *Nation's Restaurant News (NRN)*, January 3, 1983, p. 2; "New Vendor Strategy: Small Is Better," *NRN*, January 3, 1983, p. 48.

16. *Food and Nutrition: Knowledge, Beliefs* (Princeton, N.J.: Response Analysis, 1974), p. 61; Diane Schrayer, "Consumer Response to Nutri-

287

tion Labeling," *Food Technology*, December 1978, pp. 42–45; *Health Foods and Natural Vitamins Market* (New York: Frost & Sullivan, 1979), p. 97; "Nutrition Beliefs: More Fashion than Fact," *FDA Consumer*, June 1976, pp. 15–17; Judy Lea Jones and I. J. Abrams, "Relating Diet-Health Concerns to Food Choices," *National Food Review*, Fall 1979, p. 27.

17. "What Mr. Mainstream Eats," *NRN*, June 16, 1986, p. 10; Adam Paul Weisman, "Look Who's Walking," *Washington Post Health*, March 24, 1987, p. 13; "Untapped Market Seen in 'Self-Care' Life Style," *Advertising Age*, April 4, 1983, p. 39; Judy Jones and Jon Weimer, "A Survey of Health-Related Food Choices," *National Food Review*, Fall 1980, p. 19; Bonnie Liebman, "The All-American Junk Food Diet," *Nutrition Action Newsletter*, May 1968, p. 8; "USDA Study Indicated Vegetable Consumption Is Up," *NRN*, January 27, 1986, p. 40.

18. "Gallup Survey: Nutrition Plays Strong Role in Dining Decisions," *NRN*, July 14, 1986, p. 37; "Steak, Prime Rib Still Most Popular Dinner Entrées," *NRN*, May 19, 1986, p. 184; "Poll: Burger Is Prime Takeout Choice," *NRN*, June 2, 1986, p. 3; Trish Hall, "Steady Diet: What Americans Eat Hasn't Changed Much Despite Healthy Image," *Wall Street Journal*, September 12, 1985, p. 1; "Teen-Age Vegetarians," *Washington Post*, May 22, 1985, p. E1; Rhonda L. Rundle, "New Efforts to Fight Heart Disease Are Aimed at Blue-Collar Workers," *Wall Street Journal*, March 16, 1987, p. 25.

19. D. M. Levine, "Values and Life Styles Give Madison Avenue New Target," *NRN*, May 20, 1985, p. 25; Brad Edmondson, "You Are What You Buy," *Washington Post*, October 16, 1986, p. B3; "Inside the Consumer's Mind," *Newsweek*, December 20, 1985, p. 30.

20. J. D. Reed, "America Shapes Up," *Time*, November 2, 1981, p. 97; "America's Nutrition Revolution," *Newsweek*, November 19, 1984, p. 112; Herbert Gans, *Deciding What's News* (New York: Vintage Books, 1980), p. 127.

21. Judith Packer, "Study: Diners Are More Nutritionally Aware," *NRN*, October 22, 1984, p. 26: "Gallup Survey: Nutrition Plays Strong Role in Dining Decisions," *NRN*, July 14, 1986, p. 37; Judann Dagnoli, "Health Hot, But Calories Still Count," *Advertising Age*, April 14, 1986, p. 32; Rick Telberg, "Patrons Seek Healthier Foods," *NRN*, June 9, 1986, p. 21. Other examples in footnotes 17 and 18 above.

22. David Zuckerman, "Gallup Eating-Out Survey Offers Special Psychographic Analysis," *NRN*, May 12, 1986, p. 80; Ernest Dichter,

Motivating Human Behavior (New York: McGraw-Hill, 1971), p. 161; Steve Barnett, "Today's Teens Reject '60s Values," *Advertising Age*, April 21, 1986, p. 56.

23. Norge W. Jerome, "The U.S. Dietary Pattern from an Anthropological Pattern," *Food Technology*, February 1981, pp. 37–42. Ross Hume Hall argues that the split between "palatability" and "nutrition" was fostered by nineteenth-century analytical chemists, for whom the chemical elements (nutrients) were all, while taste was of no scientific concern and had no relevance to determining nutritional value. *Food for Nought: The Decline in Nutrition* (New York: Vintage Books, 1976), p. 45. But Sidney Mintz notes the same phenomenon throughout the world. Whenever asked about their cuisine, people speak about its taste, not its health benefits. *Sweetness and Power: The Place of Sugar in Modern History* (New York: Viking Press, 1985), p. 11.

24. Feminization: Laura Shapiro, *Perfection Salad* (New York: Simon & Schuster, 1986). Class variables: Johanna Dwyer and Elizabeth Alston, "Nutrition in Family Life," *Food Product Development*, November 1976, p. 50; Lee Rainwater, Richard Coleman, and Gerald Handel, *Workingman's Wife* (New York: MacFadden Books, 1959), p. 184; Brett Williams, "Why Migrant Women Feed Their Husbands Tamales: Foodways as a Basis for a Revisionist View of Tejano Family Life," in Linda Kellor Brown and Kay Mussell, eds., *Ethnic and Regional Foodways in the United States* (Knoxville: University of Tennessee Press, 1984), pp. 113–26.

25. Pierre Bourdieu, *Distinction: A Social Critique of the Judgement of Taste* (Cambridge: Harvard University Press, 1984), p. 180; Brown and Mussell, eds., *Ethnic and Regional Foodways*, passim.

26. E.g., "Nutrition Beliefs More Fashion than Fact," *FDA Consumer*, June 1976, pp. 25–27; "What the Industry Can Do About Growing Public Mistrust," *Food Engineering*, August 1975, p. 35; "Harris Poll Finds . . ." *NRN*, July 4, 1983, p. 55; Dagnoli, "Health Hot," p. 32.

27. Michael Schudson, *Advertising: The Uneasy Persuasion* (New York: Basic Books, 1986), pp. 53–66.

CHAPTER 9.
STRADDLING THE CONTRADICTIONS

1. "The 1981 Challenge: Give Them the 'Warm Fuzzies,' " *Health Food Business*, January 1981, p. 42; Danielle K. Mooney, *Mass-Merchan-*

dised Healthy Foods: Markets, Trends (Stamford, Conn.: Business Communications Co., 1982), p. 4.

2. William Robbins, "Food Industry Focusing More on Nutrition," *New York Times*, June 12, 1980, p. 1.

3. Chemical fears predominate: e.g., 1975 data in I. J. Abrams, "Determining Consumer Demand and Marketing Opportunities for Nutritional Products," *Food Technology*, September 1978, pp. 79–85; "Nutrition Update Newsletter Directed to Health Professionals," *Food Product Development*, December 1976, p. 58. Shift from chemicals to calories: "Food Labels Get High Readership," *FDA Consumer*, July 1979, pp. 10–11; G. Burton Brown et al., "Additives and Processing: What the U.S. Consumer Knows, Thinks, and Practices When It Comes to Nutrition," *Food Product Development*, May 1978, p. 35; Mimi Sheraton, "Conflicting Nutrition Advice Bewilders U.S. Consumer," *New York Times*, June 11, 1980, p. 1.

4. Mooney, *Healthy Foods*, pp. 4, 12, 30–32, 70–93; John L. Hess and Karen Hess, *The Taste of America* (New York: Penguin Books, 1977), pp. 34–55, 265–78; Brown, "Additives and Processing," p. 35; *Health Foods and Natural Vitamins Market* (New York: Frost & Sullivan, 1979), p. 53; Sheraton, "Conflicting Nutrition Advice," p. 1; "Produce: A Source of Profits," *Advertising Age (AA)*, April 27, 1981, p. S42.

5. S. R. Rothschild, "Responding to Consumer Needs in New Product Development," *Food Product Development*, February 1978, p. 18; "It's Natural! It's Organic! Or Is It?" *Consumer Reports*, July 1980, p. 44; Leonard L. Berry and Ian H. Wilson, "Retailing: The Next 10 Years," *Journal of Retailing* 53 (Fall 1977): 20–21. For persistence of this trend: Leonore Skenazy, "Welcome Home! Trend Experts Point to 'Neo-Traditional,' " *AA*, May 16, 1988, p. 38.

6. Peter Clecak, *America's Quest for the Ideal Self: Dissent and Self-Fulfillment in the 60s and 70s* (New York: Oxford University Press, 1983), p. 6; Tom Wolfe, "The Me Decade and the Third Great Awakening," in *Mauve Gloves & Madmen, Clutter & Vine* (New York: Bantam Books, 1977), p. 146; Christopher Lasch, *The Culture of Narcissism: American Life in an Age of Diminishing Expectations* (New York: Norton, 1979).

7. James L. Ferguson, "General Foods' Formula for Facing Changing Times," *Progressive Grocer*, September 1982, pp. 34–35.

8. "Predicts 25-to-34-Year-Olds Will Rule '70s Market," *Nation's Restaurant News (NRN)*, April 12, 1971, p. 2; "The Care and Feeding of

the Hungry Generation," *NRN*, October 11, 1971, pp. 10–22; "Jerrico's Nellie Kelly's First Funk Scene Entry," *NRN*, September 30, 1974, p. 2.

9. "Hungry Generation Grows Up," *NRN*, January 5, 1976, p. 18; Paul Kahn, "One- and Two-Member Household Feeding Patterns," *Food Product Development*, October 1976, pp. 22–30; Norge W. Jerome, "Changing Nutritional Styles Within the Context of the Modern Family," in Debra P. Hymovich and Martha Underwood Barnard, eds., *Family Health Care*, 2nd ed. (New York: McGraw-Hill, 1979), pp. 194–203.

10. Leo J. Shapiro and Dwight Bohmbach, "Heavy Grazers Pace Consumers," *AA*, November 12, 1984, p. 82.

11. Mortimer Feinberg, "The Fickle Consumer," *Restaurant Business*, October 1, 1978, p. 152; "Lazer Ties Restaurateurs' Failures to Low Priority Given to Marketing," *NRN*, June 18, 1984, p. 34; "Consultant Tells Industry: Let's Stop Confusing Efficiency with Excellence," *NRN*, June 21, 1971, p. 3; "Baum: Baby Boomers Wary of Broad-Based Marketing," *NRN*, December 10, 1984, p. 81; "Industry Reeling from '82 Results," *NRN*, January 3, 1983, p. 104.

12. Jan Hoffman, "The Feeding Habits of Yuppies," *Village Voice*, April 16, 1985, pp. 11–15; George F. Will, "Yippety Yumpies," *Washington Post*, March 25, 1984, p. A19; Robert J. Samuelson, "Selfishness and Sobriety," *Newsweek*, April 9, 1985, p. 63.

13. " 'Yuppies' Willing to Pay: Study," *AA*, June 25, 1984, p. 14; "Yuppie Impact Measured in Restaurant Growth," *NRN*, June 10, 1985, p. 10; "The Next Trend," *AA*, July 11, 1985, p. 18; "Yockin' with Yuppies," *AA*, July 8, 1985, p. 18.

14. Hoffman, "Feeding Habits," p. 11; " 'Yuppies' Willing to Pay," p. 14.

15. "The Year of the Yuppie," *Newsweek*, December 31, 1984, pp. 16–17; "What Baby Boomers Make," *Newsweek*, November 25, 1985, p. 5; "Boomers Gone Bust," *NRN*, October 28, 1985, p. 12; "Yuppies vs. Poppies," *AA*, July 8, 1985, p. 18.

16. "Tough News—You Didn't Have to Buy that BMW to Make the Grade," *AA*, May 30, 1985, p. 10; Jay Ogilvy, Eric Utne, and Brad Edmondson, "Boom with a View," *Utne Reader*, May–June 1987, pp. 119–28; Stewart Alter, "Yuppie Pursuit: It's Too Trivial for Marketers," *AA*, July 14, 1985, p. 3.

291

17. Walter Kiechel III, "The Food Giants Struggle to Stay in Step with Consumers," *Fortune*, September 11, 1978, p. 50; Kiechel, "Two-Income Families Will Reshape the Consumer Markets," *Fortune*, March 10, 1980, pp. 110–20.

18. E. B. Weiss, "Thirty-Three Ways Marketers Are Coping with the New Era of Restrictions and Regulations," *AA*, November 8, 1971, pp. 119–21; Mooney, *Healthy Foods*, pp. 22–37; "Junk Food a Star Attraction at USDA's Food and Fitness Extravaganza," *Nutrition Action (NA)*, October 1984, p. 4; "12 O'Clock High from Campbell," *NA*, March 1986, p. 16.

19. E.g., "Positioning Old Products in New Niches," *AA*, May 3, 1984, p. M50; Carole Sugarman, "Storm Brewing Over Coffee," *Washington Post*, December 21, 1983, p. E1; "Consumer Group Targets Food Commodity Boards," *AA*, October 25, 1984, p. 52.

20. "Sugar Smacked," *NA*, July 1985, p. 10; "Sugar Ads Fight Sour Image," *AA*, September 27, 1984, p. 18; "Pigging Out—the 'Lean' Way," *NA*, September 1984, p. 5; "Hard (Sell) Butter Drive Due," *AA*, November 4, 1985, p. 92; Sam Zuckerman, "The FTC Opts Out: Food Ad Anarchy," *NA*, May 1984, pp. 5–8.

21. Nancy Giges, "Campbell Cooks Up Menu for Consumers," *AA*, February 27, 1984, p. 66; Gay Jervey and Nancy Giges, "Campbell's McGovern Top Adman," *AA*, January 3, 1983, p. 1; editorial, "Nutrition Claim *Déjà Vu*," *AA*, December 12, 1983, p. 20; "Campbell Soup Agrees to Discontinue Health Insurance Ad Claims," *NA*, December 1984, p. 4; "Segmentation Heats Up," *AA*, October 13, 1984, p. S34. In early 1989, the FTC did complain about Campbell's claim that its low-cholesterol (but high-sodium) soup reduced the risk of heart disease.

22. "The New Food Giants," *Business Week*, September 24, 1984, p. 138; Nancy Giges, "Food Giants Dish Up New Marketing Moves," *AA*, February 25, 1985, p. 6; Nancy Giges and Janet Neiman, "Acquisition Aggressiveness Crucial to Food Companies," *AA*, February 27, 1984, p. 3.

23. "Campbell's McGovern," p. 38; "New Food Giants," p. 136; Gay Jervey, "Campbell Dipping into Lipton's Soup Market," *AA*, July 15, 1985, p. 2; Julie Franz and Brian Lowry, "Produce Marketers Take Fresh Approach," *AA*, October 13, 1986, p. 3; Nancy Giges, "Prego Adds Frozen Entrées to Menu," *AA*, August 25, 1986, p. 12.

24. "Campbell's McGovern," p. 38; Nancy Giges, "Pepperidge Farm's Fallow," *AA*, February 21, 1985, p. 2.

25. Nancy Giges, "Campbell to Toss Salad into Test," *AA*, October 15, 1984, p. 14; Giges, "Line of Fresh Entrées to Get Campbell Test," *AA*, August 27, 1984, p. 2; Giges, "Pepperidge Farm's Fallow," p. 2; Christopher Eklund, "Campbell Soup's Recipe for Growth: Offering Something for Every Palate," *Business Week*, December 24, 1984, pp. 66–67; Judann Dagnoli, "Campbell's Fresh Chef Wilts," *AA*, April 6, 1987, p. 1.

26. Eklund, "Campbell Soup's Recipe," p. 66

CHAPTER 10.
A HEALTHY FOODS PORTFOLIO

1. Danielle K. Mooney, *Mass-Merchandised Healthy Foods: Markets, Trends* (Stamford, Conn.: Business Communications Co., 1982), pp. 47–48; Jim Hightower, *Eat Your Heart Out* (New York: Vintage Books, 1976), pp. 98–102; Kathleen Reidy, "Adding Nutrients to Foods: Pluses and Minuses," *National Food Review*, Winter 1981, pp. 29–30. Statistics in Susan Katz, "Getting Sick on Vitamins," *Newsweek*, May 19, 1986, p. 80; Julie Franz, "Kellogg Bran-Ching Out with New Cereal," *Advertising Age (AA)*, July 7, 1986, p. 40.

2. Robert Johnson, "Suppliers Strained, Buyers Cautious in Midst of Fresh-Produce Boom," *Wall Street Journal*, January 27, 1986, p. 27; "USDA Study Indicates Vegetable Consumption Is Up," *Nation's Restaurant News (NRN)*, January 27, 1986, p. 40; Peter Francese, "Eating Habits Changing with Life Styles," *AA*, December 6, 1984, p. 38.

3. Fueled mainly by the produce boom, food imports rose 40 percent between 1982 and 1986; in 1986 Mexico supplied more than half of the vegetables eaten by Americans between December and March. Barry Meier, "Poison Produce: As Food Imports Rise, Consumers Face Peril From Use of Pesticides," *Wall Street Journal*, March 26, 1987, p. 1. Elaine Blume and Michael F. Jacobson, "Food Irradiation: Is the Time Ripe?" *Nutrition Action (NA)*, November 1986, pp. 1–7. Bebe Raupe, "Farmers' Union Still Fighting Campbell for Fair Contract," *In These Times*, August 21, 1985, p. 8.

4. Mooney, *Healthy Foods*, pp. 28–33, 98; "Fresh Produce: A Source of Profits," *AA*, April 27, 1981, p. S42; Mary McCabe English, "Catering

293

to Different Segments," *AA*, September 19, 1985, p. 18; Christopher Eklund, "Will a Tomato by Any Other Name Taste Better?" *Business Week*, September 30, 1985, p. 105; Julie Franz and Brian Lowry, "Produce Marketers Take Fresh Approach," *AA*, October 13, 1986, p. 13.

5. "Bumbleberry Prexy Sees Chain of Funky Restaurants in Future," *NRN*, September 30, 1974, p. 37; Robert Nadeau, "Out to Lunch," *Real Paper*, August 4, 1976, p. 12.

6. Philip Langdon, *Orange Roofs, Golden Arches: The Architecture of American Chain Restaurants* (New York: Alfred A. Knopf, 1986), pp. 133–65.

7. Ernest Dichter, *Handbook of Consumer Motivations* (New York: McGraw-Hill, 1964), pp. 65, 29.

8. Kenneth Wylie, "Bread Returns to Humble Beginnings," *AA*, May 3, 1984, p. M62; "It's Natural, It's Organic, Or Is It?" *Consumer Reports*, July 1980, p. 411; *Health Foods and Natural Vitamins Market* (New York: Frost & Sullivan, 1979), p. 162.

9. Mooney, *Healthy Foods*, pp. 24–25; "Smacks Redux," *NA*, May 1984, p. 12; " 'Natural'—From Our Laboratory," *NA*, September 1984, p. 6.

10. "Johnny Granola Seed," *Time*, March 6, 1972, pp. 65–66; *Healthy Foods*, pp. 162–64.

11. "GF's Fortified Natural Enters Cereal Market," *Food Engineering*, November 1975, p. 47; "Breakfast Foods Mark the Return of Sugar," July 1977, pp. 113–16.

12. "Licensed Characters Can Get Soggy Sales Fast," *AA*, September 27, 1984, p. 34; "Cereal Picture Stays Sweet," *AA*, May 3, 1984, p. M58; Bonnie Liebman, "Fiber Follies," *NA*, April 1986, pp. 10–11.

13. Larry Edwards, "Granola Again Hot—Now as Solid Snacks Breakfast Bars," *AA*, June 14, 1977, p. 1; Mooney, *Healthy Foods*, pp. 26, 155–56; Jule Franz, "Survivors Fight for Granola-Bar Market," *AA*, February 17, 1986, p. 4.

14. Peter Barry Chowka, "Natural Foods: The Quest for Standards," *New Age*, August 1982, pp. 47–51; Sam Zuckerman, "The Natural Facts: How the Natural Foods Industry Rates on Nutrition," *NA*, November 1984, pp. 5–11; Trish Hall, "Steady Diet: What Americans

Eat Hasn't Changed Much Despite Healthy Image," *Wall Street Journal*, September 12, 1985, p. 1.

15. Bonnie Liebman, "Light Foods You Can *Lean* On," *NA*, September 1986, p. 10. For a fuller discussion: Warren J. Belasco, " 'Lite' Economics: Less Food, More Profits," *Radical History Review* 28–30 (1984): 254–78.

16. "Make Way for Miller," *Forbes*, May 15, 1976, pp. 45–47; "The Frothy Profits in Light Beers," *New York Times*, August 7, 1977, sect. III, p. 12; "Nestlé: Centralizing to Win Bigger Payoff in the U.S.," *Business Week*, February 2, 1981, pp. 56–58; "Gourmet Frozen Foods Flavored with Time," *AA*, September 19, 1985, p. 44; "New Desserts Try to Tap Health Concerns," *AA*, February 28, 1983, p. 32; Mooney, *Healthy Foods*, pp. 150–62; Jim Auchmutey, "A D'Lite-ful Response to the Lean and Mean," *AA*, November 21, 1983, p. M20.

17. *Wall Street Journal*, October 22, 1981, p. 29; Auchmutey, "D'Liteful Response," p. M20; "For a Success Story, Here's to Beer! " *New York Times*, August 9, 1978, p. C1; "Food Preservative Scare Threatening to Flare Up," *NRN*, January 31, 1983, p. 2; Carole Sugarman, "Frozen Assets: The New 'Light' Dinners," *Washington Post*, April 19, 1983, p. G1.

18. Carole Sugarman, "Difficult Questions Come to 'Lite,' " *Washington Post*, October 14, 1984, p. K1; "Exasperated Congressman Wants 'Lites' Out," *NA*, April 1986, p. 3; "The Facts of Light," *NA*, September 1986, p. 11.

19. "The Frothy Profits in Light Beers," *New York Times*, August 7, 1977, sect. III, p. 11; Sugarman, "Difficult Questions," p. K5; "Operators Leaning Toward Low-Fat Nutritional Cooking," *NRN*, March 18, 1985, p. 13; Carole Sugarman, "When Less Is More: Paying the Premium for Eating 'Lite,' " *Washington Post*, February 3, 1988, p. E12; "Time— and Theme—Is Now for Pepsi," *AA*, March 7, 1983, p. 2.

20. "Operators Leaning," p. 13; "Soft-Serve Yogurt: New Kid on the Block," *Fast Service*, December 1976, p. 20; "Flavored Popcorn Finds a Burgeoning Market," *NRN*, May 25, 1983, p. 13; "The Light Beer Game," *Forbes*, January 15, 1976, pp. 30–31; "Brewers Tap Light to Spark Sales," *Wall Street Journal*, September 3, 1980, p. 29; "Vegetarian Meats," *Consumer Reports*, June 1980, pp. 361–65; CSPI statistics quoted in Frances Moore Lappé, *Diet for a Small Planet*, 3rd ed. (New York: Ballantine Books, 1982), pp. 149–50.

21. On patent medicines: Michael Schudson, *Advertising: The Uneasy Persuasion* (New York: Basic Books, 1984), p. 162. On wrong perceptions: Bonnie Liebman, "Cold Comfort," *NA*, November 1985, pp. 8–10. On the ethnic-health-business connection: Warren J. Belasco, "Ethnic Fast Foods: The Corporate Melting Pot," *Food and Foodways* 2 (1987): 1–30. Given the blurring of categories, statistics vary. According to one account, sales of ethnic processed foods increased 10 percent annually between 1974 and 1984 to over $4.5 billion. Sewell Whitney, "Ethnic Products Satisfy Craving for Something New," *AA*, September 19, 1985, p. 46. But a Frost & Sullivan study estimated sales of "ethnic prepared foods" at $21 billion in 1984 and predicted an 8.9-percent annual increase to $31 billion by 1989. "Ethnic Food Sales Soar," *NRN*, March 17, 1986, p. 9.

22. "The Americanization of Stella," *Snack Food*, June 1973, pp. 40–41; "The Celery Sell," *Washington Post*, December 28, 1977, p. 81; "Nutrition, Low Cost Emphasized in Taco Viva's New Ad Strategy," *NRN*, March 14, 1983, p. 1; "T.G.I. Friday's Lightening Menu," *NRN*, August 24, 1983, p. 3; Paul Frumkin, "Mossiman Sees 'Cuisine Naturelle' as Healthier," *NRN*, September 23, 1985, p. 11; Florence Fabricant, "Operators Leaning Toward Low-Fat Nutritional Cooking," *NRN*, March 18, 1985, p. 13.

23. Jeff Cox, "New Haute Cuisine," *Organic Gardening*, May 1986, pp. 68–75; " 'New Consumer Puts New Rules in the Vegetable Till," *NRN*, May 9, 1983, p. M10; Sugarman, "Frozen Assets," p. G2; Len Strazewski, "Gourmet Frozen Foods Flavored with Time," *AA*, September 19, 1985, p. 45.

24. For elitist-populist trends: Seymour Britchky, "All-American," *New York*, January 16, 1984, pp. 44–56. Populists: Calvin Trillin, *American Fried: Adventures of a Happy Eater* (New York: Vintage Books, 1979), p. 174; Jane Stern and Michael Stern, *Good Food: The Adventurous Eater's Guide to Restaurants Serving America's Best Regional Specialties* (New York: Alfred A. Knopf, 1983), p. ix.

25. Cajun Étouffée ad, *NRN*, October 20, 1986, p. 59. "Kraft Dinner": Trillin, *American Fried*, p. 143.

26. Belasco, "Ethnic Fast Foods," pp. 15–20.

27. Calvin Trillin, *Third Helpings* (New Haven, Conn.: Ticknor & Fields, 1983), p. 21.

28. Belasco, "Ethnic Fast Foods," pp. 20–24.

29. "A Revolution in the Frozen Pizza Business," *Quick Frozen Foods*, August 1979, p. 47; "Pillsbury Gets into Ice Cream," *AA*, June 13, 1983, p. 3; "Bennigan's Adds Cajun Dishes to Menu." *NRN*, June 3, 1985, p. 2. On "synergistic diversification," Joseph Guiltinan and Gordon Paul, *Marketing Management: Strategies and Programs* (New York: McGraw-Hill, 1982), p. 26.

30. "McDonaldizing Chinese Cuisine," *NRN*, August 5, 1985, p. 3; "Pillsbury Trims But Doesn't Amputate," *NRN*, January 25, 1988, p. 4; "Independents in '86," *NRN*, January 1, 1986, p. F3.

31. Belasco, "Ethnic Fast Foods," pp. 22–24.

32. On panethnicity: Peter Romeo, "Chains Go Grazing for Increased Traffic Counts," *NRN*, March 16, 1987, p. 1; Florence Fabricant, "East Meets West by Mixing Ingredients, Styles of Both Worlds," *NRN*, September 7, 1987, p. 11; "New York Rides California Wave," *NRN*, January 6, 1986, p. 1; Gael Greene, "Sampling the Seaport," *New York*, July 2, 1984, p. 42.

33. Richard Martin, "West Coast Report," *NRN*, October 7, 1985, p. 12; "Calvin Trillin on Food Industry," *NRN*, June 3, 1985, p. 20; "L-K Opens First Diner Conversion," *NRN*, July 14, 1986, p. 1.

34. Meg Greenfield, "Give Me that Old-Time Cholesterol," *Washington Post*, June 20, 1984, p. A21.

35. Jane Stern and Michael Stern, *Square Meals* (New York: Alfred A. Knopf, 1984).

36. Ibid., pp. 270, 296, 313, xiii; Bryan Miller, "Basic American Food Comes Back to the Table," *New York Times*, p. C1, C8.

37. Jane and Michael Stern, "Did Mom Know Best?" *Washington Post*, September 26, 1984, p. E5; Gil Scott-Heron, "B-Movie," *Reflections* (New York: Arista Records, 1981); Stern and Stern, *Square Meals*, p. xv.

38. Carol Flinders, "Laurel's Kitchen," *Washington Post*, January 22, 1986, p. E19.

39. Betsy Morris, "Nerds and Shiver: Selecting the Best and Worst Food Products of 1986," *Wall Street Journal*, December 19, 1986, p. 25; Julie Franz, "Food Sellers Bracing for Muffin Mania," *AA*, January 13, 1986, p. 3.

40. Laura Shapiro, "All Hail the Mashed Potato," *Newsweek*, December 17, 1984, p. 94; "Hey, Dottie—Diners Are Back," *Newsweek*,

March 3, 1986, pp. 54–55; Rurick Telberg, "Shake-Shop Styled G. D. Ritzy's Charts Explosive Expansion," *NRN*, November 21, 1983, p. 3; Howard Riell, "Trend Toward Convenience May Signal Boom for Sonic," *NRN*, February 3, 1986, p. 3.

41. Patricia Stoll, "Second Ed Debevic's Is Launched in Chicago," *NRN*, November 26, 1984, p. 4; Marilyn Alva, "Old-Style Diners Sweeping Nation," *NRN*, January 27, 1986, p. 1; "Independents in '86," *NRN*, January 1, 1986, p. F3; Rick Van Warner, "San Francisco's Max's Diner Teeming with Activity," *NRN*, September 1, 1986, p. 18; Marilyn Alva, "Sales Perk at Ex-Coffee Shop," *NRN*, August 4, 1986, p. 3.

42. "Hey, Dottie," p. 54; Alva, "Sales Perk," p. 3; Jo Ellen Daily, "Rich Melman: The Hot Dog of the Restaurant Business," *Business Week*, February 11, 1985, pp. 73–76.

43. Susan Spedalle, "Down-Home Cooking," *NRN*, January 21, 1985, p. 14; Bogert quoted in Richard Martin, "Ed Debevic's Time Is Now," *NRN*, August 18, 1986, p. 27.

44. Raymond Mungo, *Total Loss Farm: A Year in the Life* (New York: E. P. Dutton, 1970), p. 136.

EPILOGUE

1. On genetic engineering: Jack Doyle, *Altered Harvest: Agriculture, Genetics, and the Fate of the World's Food Supply* (New York: Penguin Books, 1985). On Simplesse: Julie Liesse Erickson, "Not so Simplesse: FDA Sours NutraSweet," *Advertising Age*, February 1, 1988, p. 2.

2. Lawrie Mott and Karen Schneider, "Pesticide Alert," *Organic Gardening*, June 1988, pp. 70–78.

3. Carole Sugarman, "Facing the Issue of Pesticide Residues," *Washington Post*, June 3, 1987, p. E1.

298

4. David Ehrenfeld, "Sustainable Agriculture Takes Root in America's Countryside," *Utne Reader*, November–December 1987, pp. 54–57; Ward Sinclair, "Garth Youngberg's Fertile Vision," *Washington Post*, August 1, 1988, p. B1; Ward Sinclair, "Northeast States Cultivate Rebirth of Small Farms," *Washington Post*, November 15, 1987, p. A1; Mike Brusko, "Farming Where the Money Is," *New Farm*, July–August 1988, pp. 10–11ff.

5. "USDA Creates New Small-Scale Ag Office," *New Farm*, February 1987, p. 28; Ken McNamara, "USDA, Rodale Host RegenAg Workshop," *New Farm*, January 1988, p. 37; George DeVault, "CAST Picks Rodale, Thompson for Task Force," *New Farm*, February 1987, p. 8; letter to editor, *New Farm*, July–August 1988, p. 2; Laura Shapiro, "The Time Is Ripe for Organic Agriculture," *Newsweek*, October 5, 1987, p. 88.

6. Carole Sugarman, "Scared Skinny," *Washington Post*, August 3, 1988, p. E1; "The Changing American Diet," *Washington Post*, April 6, 1988, p. A23; Carole Sugarman, "For the 'Life Is Short' Crowd," *Washington Post*, May 18, 1988, p. E1; "Fed Up with Filthy Chickens?" *Safe-Food Gazette* (CSPI), p. 1; Sugarman, "To Eat or Not to Eat," *Washington Post*, June 8, 1988, p. E1.

7. Patricia Picone Mitchell, "The Late Great Art of Cooking," *Washington Post*, June 8, 1988, p. E1.

8. E.g., George DeVault, " 'Fake' Organic Carrots Rock Market," *New Farm*, July–August 1988, pp. 22–25.

INDEX

300

301

303

ABOUT THE AUTHOR

W arren J. Belasco is an associate professor of American studies
at the University of Maryland Baltimore County. His previous
book, *Americans on the Road,* was published by MIT Press. He lives
in Washington, D.C.